Julius II

1 Cardinal Giuliano della Rovere, aged about thirty: detail of the fresco by Melozzo da Forlì commemorating the foundation of the Vatican Library (see plate 3), now in the Pinacoteca Vaticana. (© Musei Vaticani)

Julius II

The Warrior Pope

——— · ———

CHRISTINE SHAW

First published 1993
Reprinted 1994
First published in paperback 1996

Blackwell Publishers Ltd
108 Cowley Road
Oxford OX4 1JF, UK

Blackwell Publishers Inc.
238 Main Street
Cambridge, Massachusetts 02142, USA

British Library Cataloguing in Publication Data
A CIP catalogue record for this book is available from the British Library

Library of Congress Cataloging in Publication Data
Shaw, Christine
Julius II: the warrior pope / Christine Shaw
p. cm.
Includes bibliographical references and index.
ISBN 0–631–16738–2 — ISBN 0–631–20282–X (pbk)
1. Julius II, Pope, 1443–1513. 2. Popes—Biography. I. Title.
BX1314.5.S45 1993
282'.092—dc20 92–36845
[B] CIP

This book is printed on acid-free paper

Contents

———— • ————

List of Plates

———— · ————

Acknowledgements

——— • ———

Although I have been working on this book for about ten years – and I first had the idea of writing a biography of Julius II about fifteen years ago – my interest in him has never flagged, and I have not needed any encouragement to go on with it. But I do wish to thank those who have taken an interest in this project, and have encouraged me to believe that others might find Julius as fascinating a character as I do; some of them have also helped with references to enable me to obtain grants to finance some of the archival research that I have undertaken in Italy. Particular thanks are due to: Brenda Bolton, Professor Henry Loyn, Professor Michael Mallett, Dr Robert Oresko, Marco Pellegrini, Susan Reynolds, Professor Nicolai Rubinstein and Simon Shaw. Professor Sir John Hale kindly provided photographs of two of the fortresses of which Julius was especially fond. I am also grateful to the British School at Rome, Lady Margaret Hall, Oxford, and Westfield College for grants towards the cost of research. That research has been greatly facilitated by the helpfulness of archivists and librarians in Italy and England; I wish to record my gratitude to the staff of the Archivi di Stato of Bologna, Florence, Mantua, Milan, Modena, Rome, Siena and Venice, of the Archivio Segreto Vaticano, of the British Library and of Cambridge University Library.

If I have failed to do justice to the subject that has given me such pleasure, the fault is entirely mine.

Abbreviations

——— • ———

AGonzaga – Archivio di Stato, Mantua, Archivio Gonzaga, Serie E, XXV.

AOrsini – Archivio Capitolino, Rome, Archivio Orsini, Serie I.

AS Florence, Otto – Archivio di Stato, Florence, Archivio della Repubblica: Otto di Pratica, Carteggi, Responsive.

AS Florence, X – Archivio di Stato, Florence, Archivio della Repubblica: Dieci di Balìa, Carteggi, Responsive.

AS Modena, Roma – Archivio di Stato, Modena, Cancelleria Ducale, Carteggio, Ambasciatori, Roma.

ASforzesco – Archivio di Stato, Milan, Archivio Sforzesco, Potenze Esteri.

ASV – Archivio Segreto Vaticano.

AS Venice, X, Roma – Archivio di Stato, Venice, Consiglio dei X, Dispacci degli Ambasciatori da Roma.

Bibl. Marc. 3622 – Venice, Biblioteca Marciana, Cod. Marc., Latino X, 175 (mss. 3622).

BL – British Library, London.

CUL – University Library, Cambridge.

Note – Unless otherwise specified, despatches from ambassadors and other letters quoted from archival and printed sources should be taken as addressed to the ruler or governing councils of the state to which the letter was addressed, and as coming from Rome.

Short-titles are used for published works of which full details appear in the lists of primary and secondary printed sources.

Introduction

———— • ————

The Renaissance Papacy

For the papacy as an institution, the Renaissance was not a golden age. As patrons of the visual arts, the Renaissance popes, their cardinals and courtiers left behind them works of such beauty that the modern visitor to Rome is inclined to think of them with indulgence. Visitors to Rome during the period from the mid-fifteenth to the mid-sixteenth century that is known as the Roman Renaissance generally looked upon the popes of the day and their court with a less benevolent eye, particularly if they had come to transact business with the papal bureaucracy, the curia. Even for those with the right connections at court, dealing with the officials of the curia could be an expensive, time-consuming and frustrating business – secular governments usually retained 'procurators', experts in the ways of the papal administration, to steer their business through the obstacle course. Few looked to the papacy for spiritual leadership. There were reform movements in the Church of the fifteenth century, but secular governments played a greater role in sponsoring them than did the papacy. It was only in the later sixteenth century that the popes began to rise effectively to the challenge of Protestantism. Most of the energies of the Renaissance popes were absorbed by the politics of Italy, by diplomacy and warfare, by the desire to maintain and extend their temporal rule over the provinces of central Italy, stretching from the borders of the kingdom of Naples to the borders of Tuscany and Lombardy, and known as the Papal States. In this, as well as in his role as an outstanding patron of the visual arts, Julius II was the epitome of a Renaissance pope.

For all the failings of the Renaissance popes, the second half of the fifteenth century in fact was a period of revival in the fortunes of the papacy. During the fourteenth century the popes had been based at Avignon in southern France, largely because the disorder in their Italian dominions was so bad that they could not feel safe in Rome. When, after seventy years of 'exile', the seat of the papacy was moved back to Rome, a worse crisis soon followed, a schism in the Church that lasted for about forty years. It had begun in 1378 when a group of cardinals had seceded from the pope whom they had just helped to elect, Urban VI, because he had proved to be violent and overbearing, and had elected another, Clement VII. The powers of Europe divided their allegiance between the rival popes largely along the lines of the political divide between England and France, with the French and their allies backing Clement, who based himself at Avignon, and the English and their allies backing Urban, who stayed in Rome. The refusal of these popes, and of their respective successors, to give way to their rivals ultimately so troubled the cardinals of both obediences that many of them seceded, held a council at Pisa in 1409, declared both popes deposed and elected another. Unfortunately, since the popes refused to accept their deposition, the cardinals initially succeeded only in endowing Western Christendom with three popes at once. Still, their initiative had pointed the way to a possible resolution of the problem, and in 1414 a great general council of the Church meeting at Constance effectively solved it, by securing the resignation of two popes and depriving the third of most of his obedience, thereby clearing the way for the cardinals to elect a new pope, Martin V. The Avignonese pope stubbornly persisted in regarding himself as the true one until his death in 1423, but there was then a schism among the four cardinals whom he had left; the 'pope' whom three of them elected, Clement VIII, managed to hang on to some recognition in Aragon until 1429, when, for political reasons, the King of Aragon needed an agreement with Martin V, and Clement abdicated.

Then another problem arose. The Council of Constance had decreed that, in future, general councils should be held at regular intervals to review the state of the Church and take steps to promote necessary reforms. This idea did not appeal to Martin V and his successors. Martin summoned the councils at the pre-scribed intervals, though without great enthusiasm, and dissolved them as soon as he could. The proponents of the theory that a general council should share with the pope the governance of the Church, and that, indeed, it constituted the supreme authority in the Church, superior even to the pope in certain circumstances, did eventually overplay their hand. The council that met at Basle and began to do battle with Martin's successor, Eugenius IV, eventually even declared him deposed. The solitary cardinal who remained with it elected a former Duke of Savoy, Amadeus, who had retired from the world to a luxuriously equipped retreat to lead a contemplative life in the company of a few chosen companions. Amadeus was tempted from his seclusion by his 'election' as pope, and took the title Felix V, but he made little headway in gaining recognition from the European powers, while the action of the council in thus threatening to drag the Church into another schism discredited the conciliar movement.

By the time Francesco della Rovere, Pope Sixtus IV, uncle of Giuliano della Rovere, the future Pope Julius II, was elected to the papal throne in 1471, the conciliar movement within the Church had been defeated, though some proponents of its ideas remained. But the idea of summoning a general council to criticize, discipline, even depose the pope had become established as one option open to the secular powers in their dealings with the papacy. Dissident cardinals could play a significant role in making such threats real – as Julius himself found when he was faced by a council summoned by cardinals supporting the King of France in 1511. Nothing worried the popes of the second half of the fifteenth century more than talk of summoning a council to sit in judgement on them. This anxiety, and the damage to their authority wrought by the prolonged crisis that the papacy had undergone, made them alert to threats to their power and keen to assert their supremacy in the Church. The cardinals, however, were not inclined to yield without a contest the ground they had won during the years of the schism. They tried to keep their number at or below a fixed level; they did not want their influence and privileges, nor the communal income of the College, to be divided among too many.

Another problem confronting the Renaissance popes that was partly a legacy of the troubles of the fourteenth and early fifteenth century was their uncertain control over much of the Papal States. The temporal government of the papacy had never been notably strong or efficient in maintaining order, but several decades of absence of the papacy from Rome, followed by several more during which the authority of the Roman pope was challenged first by rival popes and then by the conciliar movement, had not improved matters. Establishing a firmer grip on the Papal States was more important to the pope now than before, because the crisis that the papacy had passed through, and notably the agreements reached with individual rulers and governments to help persuade them to support the pope rather than the conciliarists, had resulted in losses of revenue from taxes and other charges payable to the pope in his capacity as head of the Church. An increasing proportion of the pope's income was being derived from revenues from his temporal dominions. For the popes, the Papal States had come to seem an essential bastion of an independent papacy. This was how Julius regarded them, and much of his pontificate was devoted to the recovery of lost territory, and the attempt to acquire more.

The temporal government of the papacy aroused little loyalty or enthusiasm among the pope's subjects. Their primary allegiance was often to other men, either the leaders of political factions or local lords, *signori* whose families had come to dominate one or more towns and their districts in the northern and eastern provinces of the Papal States, the Romagna and the Marche.

Political factions linked town to town in a complex pattern of alliances that extended beyond the boundaries of the Papal States. While, at a local level, the factions usually took the name of a leading family, they could also be identified by the names of the parties that connected the factions of many of the towns into recognized groups. Thus members of the Chiaravallesi faction of Todi, for example, were also identified as Ghibellines and as the 'parte Colonna' of the town, while their rivals the Catalaneschi were Guelfs, and members of the Orsini party. Within the context of the politics of the Papal States, the ancient party labels of Guelf and Ghibelline had lost their significance in denoting supporters of the papacy or the Holy Roman Emperor, but this does not mean that they can be dismissed as meaningless relics of a bygone age. The Guelf and Ghibelline parties were living forces in the life of large areas of the Papal States, generating passions and loyalties that the papal government could never hope to arouse. They linked urban factions to baronial families, including those of Rome – hence the acknowledged leadership of the major Roman baronial clans, the Orsini and the Colonna, of the factions of Umbria, where they had virtually no lands, as well as of the regions encircling Rome, the Patrimony, Sabina, and the Campagna and Marittima, where they had far more influence than the papal officials. Partisans of the parties were to be found in the curia, the papal court and the pope's own household, and among the cardinals. The popes themselves and their families were rarely entirely neutral, and sometimes openly partisan. Much trouble between factions was caused by the pope or his officials supporting one side against the other, in a way that can be difficult to interpret as the implementation of a policy of 'divide and rule'. Julius himself, as cardinal and as pope, had strong links with the Colonna family.

Life for the signorial families of the Papal States was becoming increasingly difficult in the later fifteenth century. Often their ambitions had exceeded their resources, and their rule became increasingly corrupt and burdensome to the citizens of the towns they dominated. Some of them had formal concessions of 'vicariates' from the papacy, so that they were ruling, in theory, as agents of the popes, but this did not stop them from regarding the towns as their property. Other families had never succeeded in obtaining such a grant, or had never bothered to try, but the fact that the Bentivoglio of Bologna, for example, were officially merely citizens like any others did not stop them from being regarded as the effective rulers of their city, despite the fact that Bologna was the second most important centre, after Rome, of the pope's temporal government. The Renaissance popes were occasionally hostile to these signorial families, and ready to exploit opportunities to drive them out of the towns – sometimes to instal members of their own families as *signori* in their stead.

This was never a straightforward matter, for other Italian powers considered that they too had interests in the Romagna and the Marche. Centuries of weak rule by the popes had opened up the cities of the northern Papal States to the political and economic influence of Florence, Milan and Venice. Even in treaties involving the pope, these cities and the signorial families were frequently named as the *adherenti* or *raccomandati* of these other Italian powers. Such political alliances, based as they were on important mutual interests, proved very durable: they would provide Julius II with some of his greatest challenges.

If other Italian states were not very respectful of the temporal sovereignty of the pope, and were used to thinking of him and dealing with him as one of them, as a potential ally or an enemy or a rival, this did not mean they forgot about his role as head of the Church. The endless disputes that arose between the papacy and Italian states over appointments to benefices, jurisdiction and taxation of the clergy reminded them of that all too often. They were also aware of the spiritual role of the pope, though Italians, who knew the popes best, may have found it harder than other people to bear that role in mind when dealing with him. Princes and nobles outside Italy could still feel it was their duty to come to the defence of Holy Church, and not be entirely at their ease if they were attacking the pope with military force; to the Italians, being on the opposite side to the pope in a war was a routine affair, and one that aroused no qualms of conscience. They were well accustomed to separating out the pope as a man from the pope as a fellow temporal ruler, or as the head of a competing jurisdiction, or as the head of the Church.

Spiritual sanctions at the pope's disposal, such as excommunication and interdict, could still have some impact, even on Italians. For Italian bankers and merchants in particular, to incur the censure of the Church meant being vulnerable to the confiscation of their property wherever it was to be found, and disruption to business could be considerable. Most people, however cynical they might be about the hierarchy of the Church, were not comfortable at being deprived of the sacraments for any length of time. Nevertheless, if temporal rulers were in dispute with the pope, they were prepared to make war on him, to challenge his jurisdiction and even to threaten him with a general council of the Church or calls for ecclesiastical reform.

The most notable attempts by the popes of the later fifteenth century to assert their spiritual leadership were their appeals to Christian powers to join under the banners of the papacy in a crusade against the Turks. Pope Pius II had died in Ancona in 1464 on his way, he hoped, to lead a crusade in person. His successor, the Venetian Paul II, had also been notable for his zeal for the crusade. An awareness of the threat from the Ottomans was part of his Venetian heritage, for Venice, with her trading ports and settlements and colonies in the eastern Mediterranean, was in the front line of Western Christendom's attempts to hold back the expansion of the dynamic Muslim empire. Julius's uncle, Sixtus IV, made some attempt to equip a fleet to send against the Turks in the early years of his pontificate, and he tried to rally the Christian powers behind him by sending legates exhorting them to join his crusade. But the shockwaves spread through Europe by the fall of Constantinople to the Ottomans in 1453 had soon died away, leaving the crusade as a common aspiration of Christian princes, but one that always seemed to be of less pressing concern than other problems. Only states such as Hungary and Venice, for whom the Turks were a direct threat, felt any urgency in the matter. They knew all too well that there was little point in relying on help from others in their perennial struggles (though some help was occasionally forthcoming) and could see little advantage in accepting the papacy's lead in confronting a situation that they understood better than anyone. Sixtus's attempts to assert the moral and political leadership of the papacy in the crusade were met with the same response as similar attempts by his predecessors had been, varying from polite indifference to half-hearted offers of help that were probably never meant to be realized, and offers strictly dependent on other powers doing their share as well.

Sixtus's interest in the crusade, if largely ineffectual, was genuine, and should be borne in mind. It is a reminder that he was a pious and learned man, sincere in his concern for the Christian faith. In one sense, it helps to put into perspective the preoccupation with the interests of his family that was so prominent a feature of his pontificate, but in another, it throws that preoccupation into still harsher relief. That such a man should have been prepared to go to war to further the ambitions of a nephew, as he did, is a more striking testimony to how deeply the practice of nepotism had become rooted in the institution of the papacy than the more notorious example of the cynical and worldly Borgia pope, Alexander VI.

Historians have sometimes tried to rationalize the nepotism of the Renaissance popes as being in the best interests of the papacy. The placing of papal *nipoti* – nephews, great-nephews, cousins of various degrees, even sometimes sons – in the College of Cardinals by Sixtus and the other Renaissance popes has been excused by those anxious to vindicate the honour of the papacy, or by those convinced that there had to be some explanation other than mere family affection and dynastic ambition, as a necessary step if the popes were going to re-establish the authority of the papacy over the cardinals. Their relatives were the only men, it is argued, whom they could really trust to have a care for their interests, if they were to manage the cardinals effectively. Exactly how the appointment to the College of one or two, or even more, papal relations, usually inexperienced and under-qualified, and sometimes under-aged, was supposed to help the pope control rebellious cardinals has not been explained. Papal *nipoti* in the College of Cardinals evidently could be useful in persuading their colleagues to agree to the pope's wishes, either by the force of their arguments or the attraction of their influence over papal patronage.

But they were also responsible for much of the dissension between the Renaissance popes and the College; indeed, papal nepotism was arguably the greatest single cause of trouble between popes and cardinals after the tensions stemming from the conflicting secular loyalties of the cardinals themselves. Was the appointment of *nipoti* to the College really the only expedient the popes could devise to assert their authority over the cardinals?

Just as it has been argued that the popes needed to promote relatives to the College of Cardinals to help support papal supremacy, so it has been argued that the endowment of lay *nipoti* with estates and lordships was a useful strategy to suppress disorder, provide secure and reliable government for key areas, and dislodge the families of *signori* from cities in the Papal States, thus in the end strengthening the rule of the popes over their temporal dominions. This is not what Sixtus ever claimed to be doing, nor what contemporaries thought he was about.

It soon became clear to the other Italian powers that the way to win an alliance with Sixtus was to offer benefices to his ecclesiastical *nipoti*, and lands and richly dowered brides to the laymen of his family. The main contenders were the Duke of Milan, Galeazzo Maria Sforza, and the King of Naples, Ferrante d'Aragona. Both had reason to feel insecure in their rule. Both were keen to secure an alliance with the pope, could find lands with which to endow papal *nipoti*, and had girls in their family who could be offered as brides.

It was nepotism that launched Giuliano della Rovere on the career as a cardinal that would lead him to the papal throne. Being a papal nephew was unquestionably a good start on the road to the papacy, but the progression was not an inevitable one. It took him thirty years to achieve that goal – thirty years in which he established himself as one of the most formidable members of the College of Cardinals. He was a major figure in the politics of Italy long before he became Pope Julius II.

1

·

The Papal Nephew

On 15 December 1471, just four months after he had become pope, Sixtus IV wrung from the reluctant cardinals the election of two of his nephews to their College. One of these new cardinals was Giuliano della Rovere, the future Julius II, the other his cousin and rival, Pietro Riario. Their election was still supposed to be kept secret for a while, though it was a secret known to many. It was considered a rather shocking breach of the conventions of the court when they appeared a week later, in a public procession, wearing their red hats before their election had been formally published outside consistory.

This was only the first sign that the young cardinals were determined to make the most of their new rank. Giuliano della Rovere was destined to become a formidable member of the College – one whose influence, even when he spent years in exile, was felt and sometimes feared in Rome – before he became one of the most remarkable popes in the history of the papacy. Pietro Riario would keep the gossips and censors of Rome fully occupied in the few years he had to live before his dissipations killed him.

The two men had had little claim to the status of cardinal other than their relationship to the pope, but the cardinals' resistance to their election had stemmed less from opposition to them as individuals than to the increase in their own number that it would mean. Before he had become pope, Sixtus had promised not to put up any new candidates to the College until the number of cardinals had fallen below twenty-four. Experience should have already taught the cardinals that, once elected, the popes were inclined not to consider themselves bound by the promises they had made in conclave. When Sixtus wanted to give red hats to his nephews, both sides could consider that they had compromised: the cardinals had not refused to increase their number, and the pope had not insisted on the election of any other candidates.

Sixtus's own election as pope, on 10 August 1471, had itself been a compromise. Since none of the powerful cardinals who aspired to the papacy had been able to win sufficient votes to secure it for himself, they had agreed to choose Francesco della Rovere, a learned theologian. He had risen from obscurity to become head of the Franciscan order, and had only been a cardinal since 1467. He was held to be a good and religious man, though some observers considered him lacking in spirit. Nothing in his behaviour before he was elected seems to have warned that he would supply his own want of courage and resolution by putting himself and the direction of the papacy almost without reserve into the hands of his *nipoti*, who flocked to Rome after his election.

Even before they were made cardinals, Giuliano della Rovere and Pietro Riario stood out among the gathering throng of papal relatives. Like his uncle Francesco, Giuliano della Rovere was born in Albissola, a village near Savona on the Ligurian coast. The della Rovere of Savona were neither rich nor powerful; the della Rovere of Savoy, who may have been distant relatives of the Savonese family, ranked among the Savoyard nobility, but did not claim cousinhood until Francesco's intelligence and learning had brought him to the heights of the ecclesiastical hierarchy. It is not known how Giuliano's father, Raffaele, made his living, nor is anything known of the family of his mother, Theodora Manerola, who was said to have been of Greek origin. Even the year of Giuliano's birth is not known for sure, though the balance of evidence points to 1445; what is certain is that he was born on 15 December.

He probably owed his education at the Franciscan friary in Perugia to his uncle's patronage. While he was there, he acquired a manuscript of Justinian's *Institutes*, so he would seem to have been studying civil, or Roman, law. Since he was probably destined from the first for an ecclesiastical career, it is likely that he studied canon law, the law of the Church, as well. A knowledge of 'both laws' had been the basis of many a clerical career since the twelfth-century collection, codification and classification of the texts of the civil and canon law had made them one of the foundations of university education. In later years Giuliano was no great scholar, though he had wide and cultivated tastes, and there is no evidence he was being trained to follow in his uncle's footsteps as a theologian and university teacher.

His destination for a career in the Church, however, was underlined by his taking holy orders at Perugia. This was by no means an essential preliminary to appointments to even the highest ecclesiastical offices – it was quite possible to become a cardinal, even pope, without having been ordained a priest. He himself, as the senior cardinal, would ordain the newly elected Pope Pius III in 1503. That Giuliano should have taken orders at this early stage in his career, when he could easily have hoped to acquire benefices through his uncle's patronage without ordination, is worthy of note. Whether it was an expression of personal commitment or a response to pressure from his uncle is not known.

The pope's other particular protégé, Pietro Riario, was if anything still closer to him. His father, Paolo, was married to Francesco's sister Bianca. Paolo died when the boy was twelve years old, and his uncle brought Pietro to Siena, where he was teaching. Studying at Pavia, Padua, Venice, Bologna, Siena and Ferrara, he joined the Franciscans and, like Giuliano, took orders.[1] In the light of his character and later behaviour, it is hard to believe that Pietro did this of his own volition – even more than in the case of Giuliano, the suspicion arises that he was ordained at their uncle's insistence.

Aged twenty-five at Sixtus's accession, Pietro had been his servant in the conclave and, it was said, had played some part as a go-between and negotiator in securing his election. From the first, it was clear that he enjoyed the pope's confidence and would be a powerful figure in the new papal court. Soon he was joined by his younger brother Girolamo, then aged about twenty-four, who, after Pietro's early death, would succeed to his position near the pope.

Still the Riario brothers did not monopolize the pope's affection, and Giuliano della Rovere had his share of the papal bounty. When they were made cardinals in December 1471, it was Giuliano who was given his uncle's titular church of San Pietro in Vincoli. It was as 'San Pietro ad Vincula' or 'in Vincoli' ('Saint Peter in Chains'), that he would be known throughout his long career as a cardinal, and he passed the title on to first one, and then another, of his own nephews, thus keeping it in the della Rovere family for half a century. Pietro was given the title of 'San Sisto', by which he was generally known.

The argument that Renaissance popes appointed relations to the College because they were the only men on whose support they could rely rests on the assumption that papal *nipoti* would always act together to support the pope. Giuliano della Rovere and Pietro Riario are prime examples of how papal *nipoti* could be bitter rivals, more intent on the promotion of their own interests than on working together. When this contest began is not clear. There is no account in the reports from Rome of any sudden quarrel, or any gradual breakdown of a friendship between them; their antipathy to each other was more or less taken as read. Historians have seen this antipathy as based on incompatibility of character and purpose. Giuliano has been portrayed as a serious and responsible young man, holding aloof from the extravagant excesses of Pietro, and as a sober and disinterested counsellor of his uncle, but one whose advice was all too often rejected in favour of his more persuasive rival.

This picture of Giuliano seems to derive from the writings of nineteenth-century German historians, whose works were used by the most famous historian of the papacy, Ludwig Pastor, author of the monumental *History of the Popes from the Close of the Middle Ages*. For a man of such decided views, Pastor surprisingly frequently contented himself with quoting other authors' opinions on the subjects with which he was dealing, and many of the comments and judgements on the *nipoti* of the Renaissance popes, including those of Sixtus IV, in his work are simply quotations from the works of other scholars. Thus it is the view of Giuliano della Rovere and of his influence with Sixtus put forward by the nineteenth-century German school of historians, as disseminated by Pastor, that, in the absence of any other authoritative account of Giuliano della Rovere's early years as a cardinal, has become the standard one.

'The grave and resolute character of this nephew justly inspired him [Sixtus] with confidence. Like himself he had been trained in the strict discipline and privations of the monastic life, and there had been an almost constant interchange of thought between them'. . .

[Giuliano] 'was not distinguished by brilliant intellect or fine literary culture, but he was a man of serious disposition and great prudence, though frequently rough in his manner and proceedings. He did not surround himself with an extravagant number of attendants, and indulged in no needless expense in apparel or in living, yet his taste was good in his house and furniture, and he loved excellent workmanship. On suitable occasions, he knew how to give free play to the largeness of his nature'.[2]

'Even at an early age he gave evidence of those qualities which rendered his long and brilliant career so distinguished alike in the political history of Italy and in the annals of intellectual culture. If, like others, he profited by the abuse which had now become a system, and allowed numerous bishoprics and abbeys to be conferred upon a single individual, with the sole object of enriching him ... Giuliano manifested in the expenditure of his income, and in his whole manner of living, a prudence and seriousness which contrasted favourably with the conduct of many other prelates. If his moral character was not unblemished, his outward demeanour was always becoming, and, immediately after his elevation to the purple, he began to devote that attention to the fine arts, and especially to architecture, which won for him lasting renown. The serious character of his other studies, although they were mostly directed to secular subjects, contributed to develop those exceptional abilities of which his labours in later life gave such signal proof, and which had begun to manifest themselves even during the pontificate of Sixtus IV.'[3]

Such is the traditional account of Giuliano della Rovere – not uncritical, but on the whole favourable, praising him for 'prudence' and 'seriousness', for his devotion to the arts, his excellent taste. Contrast this with the picture of the character of Pietro Riario built up by Pastor, primarily from the denunciations of those who observed his career at first hand.

He was intelligent and cultivated, courteous, witty, cheerful, and generous, but his good qualities were counterbalanced by a lust of [*sic*] power, a boundless ambition and pride, and a love of luxury which rendered him utterly unworthy of the purple ... His yearly revenues before long exceeded 60,000 golden florins; but even this sum was far from satisfying his requirements, for Riario, 'transformed in one night from a mendicant monk into a Croesus, plunged into the maddest excesses'.[4] The Cardinal, says Platina, set himself to collect together unheard of quantities of gold and silver plate, costly raiment, hangings and carpets, splendid horses and a multitude of servants in scarlet and silk. He patronised young poets and painters, and delighted in contriving and carrying out pageants and tournaments on the most magnificent scale. . . . He was very generous to scholars, and to the poor. Moreover, he began a palace in the vicinity of the Church of the Holy Apostles,

the extensive foundations of which bespoke a colossal superstruc-
ture. He seemed to vie with the ancients in pomp and grandeur –
and, it may be added, in vices. Instead of the habit of Francis, he
went about in garments laden with gold, and adorned his mistress
from head to foot with costly pearls.
The ostentation of Cardinal Riario, says Ammanati, surpassed
anything that our children will be able to credit, or that our fathers
can remember.[5]

Even allowing for the rhetorical exaggeration of the sources that
Pastor used to compile this character-sketch, it is clear that Riario
made an extraordinary impression on those who watched his
progress, and, apart from his patronage of scholars and poets, not
a favourable one.

   Quite where the view of Giuliano as a serious, studious,
sober young man came from is something of a mystery. No
contemporary evidence to support it is ever cited, as it is for the
descriptions of Pietro Riario. Certainly, by contrast with Pietro,
almost anyone would seem sober and frugal, but prudence is
about the last quality with which those who would report and
comment on the unfolding career of San Pietro ad Vincula would
seem inclined to credit him. Perhaps the stature of Pope Julius II
and the extraordinary impact he would make on the history of
Italy in the early sixteenth century made historians project back
on to the young cardinal the qualities they felt must have foreshadowed such an imposing career – though even as pope,
audacity, even rashness, rather than prudence, was the hallmark
of his actions. Perhaps, too, they were seduced into taking a
sympathetic view of him by his patronage of the arts, by the sheer
quality and number of the works that he commissioned. But the
character of Giuliano della Rovere as it has traditionally been
depicted bears little resemblance to the figure who emerges from
the letters of sharp-eyed diplomatic agents and other observers
who reported on the court of Sixtus IV to their masters or their
friends, while their comments on Pietro Riario are in accord with
the image of his character that has come down to us.

   From such contemporary reports, there is no evidence that
Giuliano disapproved of the influence of Pietro Riario on Sixtus
IV because he disapproved of his way of life, his ostentation and
extravagance, his open flaunting of his mistress. Giuliano loved a
show, too, and was no celibate. As pope, he openly acknowledged
his daughter Felice and brought her to Rome, and he may have

had other children, though he was apparently more discreet than San Sisto or some other cardinals. Nor is there any evidence that he felt the affairs of the papacy should not be dominated by a young relative of the pope with no experience in ecclesiastical or secular government. He would just have preferred that that young relative should be himself.

As the Riario brothers became closely identified with Milanese interests in Rome, and favoured the alliance of the papacy with Milan, so Giuliano deliberately set out to form a similar association with the Duke of Milan's main rival among the princes of Italy, the King of Naples, and acted as a spokesman for Neapolitan interests. The diplomatic records of the Aragonese Kings of Naples have largely disappeared, and the surviving archive that yields most information about Giuliano della Rovere is that of the Sforza Dukes of Milan. Precisely because he was perceived as an enemy by the Sforza, their ambassadors in Rome watched him closely, but this means that the best sources of information about him during his years as a cardinal are a series of hostile witnesses. Perhaps it was not merely personal jealousies and ambition that made him an advocate of better relations between the pope and the King of Naples; perhaps he genuinely believed this to be in the best interests of the papacy. It has to be said, however, that this would not accord with his behaviour during the early years of the next pontificate, when he was the prime mover behind Innocent VIII's espousal of the cause of the Neapolitan barons rebelling against King Ferrante.

But the issues that dominated relations between the pope and the King of Naples in the early 1470s, indeed the issues that dominated Sixtus's diplomacy, were the personal interests of his family and not, by and large, the interests of the papacy.

On more than one occasion, Sixtus told the Milanese ambassadors in Rome that, as a native of Savona (which had been under Milanese rule since 1464), he considered himself to be Milanese. Before he had been elected, he had assured them that if he became pope, the duke would have the papacy at his disposal as though it were his own state, because he was the duke's subject and servant, and had no ties to any other prince or government than him. After his election, Sixtus, now a sovereign prince in his own right, no longer called himself anyone's subject, but he did say that he did not want his *nipoti* to be obliged to anyone other than their 'natural lord', the Duke of Milan. At first, he seemed keen that Giuliano should forge close links with Milan, telling the duke that he had 'dedicated' Giuliano to him, and that he had decided that Giuliano 'should be all yours, and to give him benefices in your lands'.[6]

Initially, Giuliano appeared to fall in with his uncle's wishes. He offered his services to Galeazzo Maria, and said he would like to arrange a Sforza marriage for his young brother Giovanni. The duke responded that he was pleased by the cardinal's proffered devotion. But the negotiations for Giovanni's marriage did not go smoothly, and Vincula withdrew the boy from Pavia in the duchy of Milan, where he had been studying, summoning him to Rome at the end of March 1472. Various explanations were given to the Milanese ambassador in Rome for this departure from Pavia. Sixtus, ever the affectionate uncle, said the boy had wanted to come to see him; San Sisto said Vincula had not liked the terms offered and had decided against a Milanese match for his brother; Vincula said San Sisto had been trying to marry the boy off without his knowledge and sow discord between him and Giovanni.[7] This marked the effective end of negotiations about the match. In truth, Vincula did not like the terms on offer. Neither did Sixtus, and though he was willing for negotiations to continue, he did not overrule his nephew. In late April, Vincula said he was ready to send the boy back to Pavia, and would come himself to the Milanese if the duke wanted him to, showing that he was the duke's loyal servant. By then, however, the hostility between the two cardinal nephews was open and explicit and it was clear to the Milanese ambassadors that they could work either with San Sisto or with San Pietro ad Vincula, but not with both. They had no hesitation in recommending that the choice be San Sisto, and the duke was in complete agreement with their opinion.

This was an important turning-point for Giuliano della Rovere, and not only in his relations with Milan. Mutual distrust between him and the Sforza would help determine other major decisions that he was to make at crucial moments in his later career. For the historian, the fortunate side-effect was the close attention paid by the Sforza to his actions and friendships, resulting in many reports by their ambassadors about him, and in a fair number of intercepted letters by and to him finding their way into their diplomatic archives.

Not only did Giuliano break off negotiations for a Milanese match for his brother, he was, according to San Sisto, largely responsible for encouraging the pope to arrange a Neapolitan marriage for another della Rovere, Leonardo. The leading lay *nipote* in the early years of Sixtus's pontificate, Leonardo was given command of some papal troops, and the title of Prefect of Rome, but he never cut a convincing figure as a soldier, nor did he show any signs of intelligence or political skill. In himself, he could not be considered much of a catch for a Neapolitan princess, but Ferrante did well out of the marriage. The king had been quick off the mark in suggesting to Sixtus a match in Naples for one of his *nipoti*, proposing that some territories in dispute between Naples and the papacy, Pontecorvo and the duchy of Sora, could be used to endow the bridegroom. Sixtus had initially rejected the idea, saying if the lands did indeed belong to the Church, it would be presumptuous of him to give them to his *nipote*, but Ferrante persisted, and soon Sixtus agreed to the scheme. He was somewhat ashamed of the transaction, blushing when Girolamo Riario said how much the king would stand in his debt for handing over territory that was of such importance to the Papal States.[8] Vincula was said to be encouraging the match, to spite San Sisto.[9] Both he and Leonardo were also believed to have tried to persuade Ferrante to visit the Papal States in the summer of 1472, again with the primary intention of trying to undermine San Sisto's hold over the pope.

About the time that Vincula put an end to negotiations for a Milanese marriage for his brother, Ferrante floated a scheme to marry Giovanni to a Neapolitan heiress, but nothing came of it. A few months later, yet another match for Giovanni was under discussion, this time one that would eventually bear fruit. The proposed bride was a daughter of the Count of Urbino, Federico da Montefeltro. So close were the ties of Urbino to Ferrante that this marriage could be seen as being Neapolitan at one remove. (In fact, the king did not approve, but did not want openly to oppose the count's plans.) To Urbino, it was an opportunity to bring further territory in the Marche of the Papal States around his own lands under his influence. He initially suggested that Giovanni should be given the town of Cesena; Sixtus said he wouldn't give him any territory of the Church.[10] Vincula was evidently keen for his brother to have a Montefeltro bride, and his persistence at length overcame Sixtus's reluctance to agree to Giovanni being endowed with some papal territory. By agreeing to Girolamo Riario becoming lord of the Romagnol town of Imola in December 1473, as part of the terms on which he married an illegitimate daughter of Galeazzo Maria Sforza, Sixtus made it harder for himself to resist Vincula's pressure.

The Neapolitan dimension to the Urbino match was emphasized by Ferrante's part in the complicated settlement needed to free the town of Senigallia in the Marche from other claims on it so that it could be given to Giovanni. Antonio Piccolomini, the *nipote* of Pope Pius II, had received this territory as part of the settlement of his own marriage to an illegitimate daughter of Ferrante a decade before. The cardinals had been unwilling to approve the grant to Piccolomini, and were no keener that it should go to the reigning pope's nephew. Intensive lobbying by Vincula and Montefeltro was needed before the cardinals would consent to the arrangements and the match could finally be concluded, in October 1474. Vincula did well for his brother's family by this alliance with the Montefeltro. Giovanni's son, Francesco Maria, would be adopted as heir by Federico da Montefeltro's childless son, and thus the della Rovere would succeed the Montefeltro as Dukes of Urbino.[11]

Vincula might have had even more trouble in gaining the consent of the pope and the College had San Sisto still been alive in the autumn of 1474, but he had died in January. Rumour had it that he had tried to remove his rival from the scene as well. It was reported that he had appeared to him in a dream, calling to him and saying that he must follow. Giuliano, ill himself, was terrified by this apparition, began to obey his doctors, which he usually refused to do, and recovered.[12] He was always a doctor's nightmare as a patient, consistently ignoring their injunctions. On the other hand, given the treatments visited on hapless patients in those days, his obstinacy may have been as much responsible for his long and vigorous life as was his iron constitution.

San Sisto might well have succeeded in thwarting the settlement of the Urbino match: he had been more adept than Vincula at managing their fellow-cardinals, as well as the pope. He had, however, exhibited a boundless appetite for benefices and offices, accumulating an enormous income (in spite of which he left all his benefices in debt for two or three years' revenue on his death), and he had not hesitated to cross senior members of the College in his search for yet more money and power. Even Sixtus may have begun to find him somewhat overbearing. Grief-stricken as he was by the loss of his nephew, he bore up under the blow better than had been anticipated – some said because he had been afraid of him and felt a sense of relief from subjection at his death.[13]

Another source of consolation for Sixtus was Pietro Riario's brother, Girolamo. Within days of the cardinal's death, it was evident that Girolamo would be the heir to his influence, as well as to his property. Yet there was one important sphere of action that Girolamo could not take over. As a layman, he could not play the same role as advocate for the policies of the pope among the cardinals. This role should naturally have devolved upon Vincula, but he failed to fill it. He lacked the political skills of persuasion, of ability to manipulate men and their opinions. Affection for him did not blind Sixtus into thinking him fitted for the task.

The pope did, however, want him to take on another function from Pietro Riario, that of special ally and advocate of Milan within the curia and consistory. Vincula showed willing to do this, offering himself to Milan as a replacement. He repeated his offers of service, and the Milanese ambassador believed he might be sincere, as his friendship with Naples had not yielded as much in the way of benefices as he might have hoped. Milanese distrust of him was not to be dispelled so easily though. Nor did the duke have a very high opinion of his ability and usefulness: only three months before, he had compared his mental abilities and reputation very unfavourably with those of San Sisto. Sforza's ambassador, assessing his potential just after his rival's death, did not think him capable of doing much on his own initiative, but rather to be a man who would be controlled by others.[14] Girolamo Riario's offers of service and protestations of devotion received a more generous response. While Vincula might be the only *nipote* other than Girolamo Riario to handle much business with the pope, and like Girolamo had men among the pope's servants who reported to him on all that went on, he was not able to exploit the opportunity opened up for him by the death of his rival.

Frustration at his failure to fill San Sisto's place, and to prevent Girolamo Riario from filling it in his stead, was perhaps at the root of the enthusiasm with which he undertook the first major commission with which he was entrusted, in the summer of 1474. This was to settle the faction-fighting that had broken out in the Umbrian towns of Todi and Spoleto, and to curb the growing dominance of Niccolò Vitelli over Città di Castello. The expedition of 1474 provides the first real opportunity to study Vincula in action, and foreshadows one of the policies for which, as pope, he is particularly remembered. His reputation as restorer of the Papal States rests in part on his efforts to master the factions that, above all in Umbria and the Romagna, shaped the political life of the region.

Todi, where prolonged street-fighting had resulted in over forty deaths, according to one report, and the destruction of many houses, was the first goal of the expedition. Piergiovanni da Canale, a leader of the Ghibelline Chiaravallesi party of Todi, had been seized on suspicion of being responsible for the murder in Rome of Gabriele degli Atti, a head of the rival Guelf Catalaneschi. The Chiaravallesi rose in Todi, and Piergiovanni's brother, Matteo, brought exiles from the city and other allies of their faction to join in the attack on the Catalaneschi. Allies of the Guelfs, too, flocked to Todi, including members of the Orsini, the Roman baronial family, who were leaders of the Umbrian Guelfs. Matteo da Canale was driven from the city, leaving the Catalaneschi dominant once more. As the troubles in Todi reached their climax in early June 1474 with the Orsini intervention and Matteo's expulsion, Vincula was appointed to lead the forces sent to pacify the city.

His was not regarded as an impartial intervention – at least not by the Orsini, for they were friends of Girolamo Riario, and Cardinal Orsini was sure he would favour the Canale. Most of the other cardinals also opposed his appointment. A few days after he left Rome on 4 June, the Milanese ambassador was already expressing fears that he was anxious to make a reputation for himself and would move on from Todi to other trouble spots, such as Spoleto and Città di Castello. Others shared these suspicions, and some thought he might use force to induce Senigallia and other places resisting the proposal that they should be given to Giovanni della Rovere to drop their opposition.

Before he arrived at Todi, Vincula sent ahead a confidential agent, Lorenzo Zane. On 10 June the cardinal himself entered the town with 3,500 infantry and some men at arms. The next day, he wrote to the pope to report that, although the faction leaders had fled, he had arrested others who had taken part in the fighting.[15] He also sent to all the villages in the city's territory to demand that they forswear further obedience to the priors of Todi, and issued a decree that everyone, except for Matteo da Canale and his brothers and sons and a couple of other individuals, should return within six days, on pain of a sentence of rebellion and the confiscation of all their goods.[16] The castellan, who was believed to have facilitated the entry of the Orsini into the city, was replaced by Obietto Fieschi.

Up to this point, the show of force had been fairly successful, and Vincula had taken the usual measures to try to bring the factions back under control. His choice of agents was more questionable. Lorenzo Zane, incumbent of one of the titular sees in Moslem lands, *in partibus infidelium*, the Patriarchate of Antioch, had a reputation as a troublemaker, and a few years later Vincula would have cause to regret his patronage of this man. Obietto Fieschi, holder of a prestigious ecclesiastical dignity, that of apostolic protonotary, that did not seem to entail any spiritual duties, was a Genoese faction leader with conspiracy in his blood, and a thorn in the flesh of the Sforza. When the expedition moved on to Spoleto, there would be other indications of poor judgement on Vincula's part.

Spoleto was the major stronghold of the Umbrian Guelfs. The year before, the Ghibellines had been expelled from the city, and efforts by Sixtus to have them readmitted met with no response. Partisans from both factions of Spoleto had joined in the fighting in Todi, and the Orsini and their men had withdrawn there as the papal troops drew near.

Once again, Vincula sent Lorenzo Zane ahead to negotiate. With him this time was Braccio Baglioni of Perugia. Braccio was a friend of the Spoletan Guelfs, but his presence did little to reassure them, for the leading *condottiere* in the papal camp was Giulio Varano, the lord of Camerino. Between his subjects and the Spoletans there was 'natural and ancient hatred',[17] and many men from Camerino were with him. Exiles from Spoleto were also in the camp, and the restoration of the exiles was one of the main points that Zane and Braccio Baglioni were sent to discuss. Nothing had been settled when the legate and his troops approached the city, and as they drew near to one gate, the leading Guelfs left by another. A procession including many clergy went to meet the legate, but this only resulted in the crosses and reliquaries that they were carrying being among the first objects looted in the sack of the city that followed.

This sack was not Vincula's intention – he just could not control the exiles and partisans who were with him. The news of the devastation of this important papal city was badly received in Rome, and Cardinal Orsini and his allies in the College did their best to blacken the picture, though Sixtus tried to hide his vexation out of his love for his nephew. No one seriously blamed the legate, because it was generally acknowledged that the factions cared little for the authority of the papal government; even the papal fortress in Spoleto barely served to keep them in check in normal times. But the episode can have done little to enhance his standing with the troops, and problems were in store for him when military operations began in earnest at Città di Castello.

Some observers considered from the first that this city was the real object of the campaign. Action against Città di Castello had been clearly on the cards for some time, for the pope and the cardinals were not willing to accept the dominance of Niccolò Vitelli over it, a dominance he had exercised since expelling his rivals, the Giustini, in April 1468. Although claiming to be merely a private citizen, Niccolò in fact had such authority that he was lord of the city in all but name, despite the presence of a papal governor. He enjoyed an extensive network of political alliances among his neighbours both within the Papal States, for example with the Count of Urbino, and outside them, notably with Florence. What might appear to be a simple matter of the internal policing of the Papal States became, through Niccolò Vitelli's connections, a major diplomatic crisis. Here was the best opportunity that San Pietro ad Vincula had yet had to show what he could do.

Niccolò Vitelli had many friends within the city. He was a charismatic man, always laughing, never angry, according to the papal governor Gianantonio Campano, and regarded by the citizens with awe, credited by them with anything that happened to the benefit of the city. Campano tried to intercede with Sixtus but all he achieved was his own disgrace.[18]

Vitelli's friends outside the city also came to his defence. Florence forbade her subjects in Borgo San Sepolcro, near the border of the Papal States, to send supplies to the papal camp, and brought troops up to the border. Galeazzo Maria Sforza, who had in the past made general offers of Milanese military assistance to Sixtus, ordered his *condottieri* not to join the camp at Città di Castello if they were requested to do so by the legate. Yet Sforza hesitated to come openly into conflict with Sixtus, especially when the pope turned to Milan's rival, Naples, for support; instead, he offered his services as mediator. As Milan held back, so Florence too did not make good her threats of military support for Niccolò Vitelli. Lorenzo de' Medici lost the *depositeria*, the office of papal banker (although, with a pope as spendthrift as Sixtus, this was something of a relief to the Medici bank), and other Florentine bankers and merchants feared that they would also suffer reprisals against their extensive interests in Rome. Ferrante, on the other hand, seized the opportunity to win Sixtus's good graces by sending Neapolitan troops to strengthen the papal camp, and joined Sixtus in giving a *condotta* to the Count of Urbino, who was elevated to the rank of duke by the pope in a ceremony in Rome on 21 August.

Diplomatic developments, then, appeared to be favouring the pope and his legate, and Vincula was to be joined by the foremost soldier in Italy, the prospective father-in-law of his brother. But he did not want to share the glory he longed to win from this enterprise. He did not want the conflict to be resolved by diplomatic negotiations, and he probably did not want Urbino coming to the camp and taking over command of the military operations.

As the papal camp settled down to besiege Città di Castello in the last days of June, Vincula was confident the city could be taken without bombardment, and he was confident he had the backing of the pope. A week later, Sixtus's resolution was already faltering under the diplomatic pressure from Milan and Florence, and he was ready to agree to the suggestion that the legate should enter the city with his household and a token force of infantry to receive Niccolò Vitelli's token subjection. Letters from Vincula saying that if he had to withdraw now he wouldn't be able to bear to show his face in Rome again,[19] and the persuasion of Lorenzo Giustini, Vitelli's greatest enemy, who had been sent to Rome to argue against such an agreement and to ask for bombards and more infantry, changed Sixtus's mind. The pope gave orders for the despatch of the bombards and sent Giustini back to the camp on 10 July with a commission to raise more infantry.

Unfortunately, those troops that were already at Città di Castello were not being put to good use. Vincula had no military experience and was not providing effective leadership. The camp was in disorder. The soldiers engaged in skirmishes more or less as the fancy took them, and usually came off worse to the defenders of the city. When the bombards arrived, they were not brought into use at once; instead, at the end of July, ineffectual attempts were made to divert the water out of the ditches around the city walls. News of further proposals for a negotiated peace seemed to galvanize Vincula into more vigorous efforts, and the bombards began to fire, but without making much impression.

With negotiations continuing, and with Urbino at last setting off from Rome to join the camp on 21 August, Vincula made a final effort to win some military glory before Urbino arrived to eclipse him. But an assault on the walls was repulsed after bitter fighting, with losses of about 30 dead and over 150 wounded among the papal troops.

Even before Urbino reached the camp, it was known that he favoured settling the business by agreement rather than force. It was also known that Vincula would be a bigger obstacle to this than would Niccolò Vitelli. Within a few days of reaching the camp, Urbino managed to negotiate an agreement that saved the legate's face. Vincula was able to report to Sixtus on 31 August that envoys had come to him from the city 'with all humility, seeking pardon and mercy', and that the city had been surrendered to him without conditions. The citizens were assured their persons and property would be safe, and Niccolò Vitelli and some other citizens were to accompany Vincula back to Rome, without seeking to have their safety guaranteed by Florence or Milan or Naples.[20] On arriving in Rome, Vitelli himself claimed he had come under the security of Ferrante, given to him by the duke, because he wouldn't have trusted himself to the word of priests. In fact, he had been promised by Urbino that, if he came to Rome and could not get acceptable conditions from the pope, he would nonetheless be restored to Città di Castello. Vitelli certainly did not behave like a beaten man when he had an audience with Sixtus. When the pope reproached him, he refused to admit that he had erred, spurning the humble speech Urbino had prepared for him. Despite his obduracy, Sixtus spoke to him kindly (which did not please Vincula at all), and it was agreed that, though he would be exiled from Città di Castello, he would receive full compensation within a year for all his property, with 5,000 ducats to be paid on account.[21]

Although Giuliano della Rovere returned to Rome 'under full sail'[22] and, when he reached the city on 9 September, was met at Santa Maria del Popolo by all the cardinals, on Sixtus's orders, his legation had hardly been a triumphant success. He had been outmanoeuvred in the settlement for Niccolò Vitelli. He had showed no particular aptitude for military leadership, losing control of his troops at Spoleto and failing to use them effectively at Città di Castello. He had failed to keep in check the political exiles who saw this expedition as a chance to pursue their private vendettas, though it has to be said that he was not unusual in allowing exiles to join in military operations against their own city. He had also been clumsy in his handling of the chronic local territorial disputes that were as potent a cause of disorder and bloodshed as factional rivalries. Using his powers as legate to deprive Spoleto of its subject territories, arguing that the settlement of Spoletan affairs was the key to peace in the whole region, and the confiscation of her territories the most exemplary punishment that could be inflicted, was one thing; giving the *castello* of San Giovanni to Trevi, a neighbouring city that had long been disputing its possession with Spoleto, was quite another.[23]

The campaign had not improved Vincula's standing with his fellow cardinals, still less his popularity, and had earned him the hatred of the powerful Cardinal Orsini. Indeed, the whole Orsini family considered themselves to be offended by his treatment of their partisans at Todi and Spoleto. They had been friends with the Riario, rather than with Vincula, before; but now there was an element of active hostility in their attitude to him, and in later years he would come to be regarded as one of the bitterest enemies of the Orsini.

In sum, the legation had done little to enhance Vincula's reputation as a politician or to bring him renown as a military leader, and it made no evident difference to his standing or role at the papal court. Nor did the more cordial relations between Sixtus and Ferrante, which Ferrante's support for the pope during the Città di Castello campaign (ambiguous though it may have been) had helped to confirm, yield the dividends for San Pietro ad Vincula that his role as an advocate of better relations with Naples during the first two years of the pontificate might have earned for him.

Ferrante visited Rome twice during these years, and his second son, Federico, spent several days there when he left Naples to seek his fortune, in the guise of a bride with a lavish dowry, outside Italy. Vincula was called on to help honour and entertain them. In April 1474 he gave a banquet for the king at his palace by the church of Santi Apostoli. It did not rival the magnificent entertainments San Sisto had given there in his day, when he had far outshone his rival in sumptuous display and liberality. Vincula had been rebuked by the pope for his repeated refusals to entertain ambassadors and other foreign guests in Rome[24], but with San Sisto gone, he was now expected to fulfil this important function in the diplomacy and ceremonial of the papal court. Just before the banquet for Ferrante, the pope had instructed him to invite the King of Dacia, who was being fêted in Rome, to dine at Santi Apostoli: San Sisto would not have had to be asked.

When Federico came to Rome in November 1474, Vincula, on the pope's orders, was the only cardinal to be sent to greet him at the gate of the city. Two months later, Ferrante was back again, taking advantage of the jubilee year to earn spiritual grace and to emphasize his alliance with the pope. This time another cardinal, Rodrigo Borgia, was sent with Vincula to greet the king. Ferrante came to Rome only for a few days. When he left, the two cardinals accompanied him to Marino, and stayed with him as he lingered in the Alban Hills; he dined with Vincula at Grotta-ferrata, the great abbey he held *in commendam*.[25]

Whatever warmth and trust such personal contacts might have brought about, there were conflicting aims and interests that served to undo the good work. For one thing, Ferrante strove against the Urbino match for Giovanni della.Rovere, trying to promote one with a daughter of Antonio Piccolomini, the *nipote* of Pius II who had claims to Senigallia, which was the intended endowment for Giovanni. Efforts by Ferrante's shrewd ambassador in Rome, Anello Arcamone, to scupper the Urbino match by fostering opposition among the cardinals to the grant of Senigallia came to Vincula's knowledge in October 1474. For his part, Vincula gave Anello and other Aragonese in Rome grounds for complaint in August 1475, when he was sent by Sixtus to investigate an attack near Rome by some Genoese on two galleys in the service of Ferrante's uncle, the King of Aragon. He plainly favoured the Genoese, and stayed all night being entertained on one of their galleys while he was supposed to be investigating the whereabouts of some captives from the Aragonese ships, making Anello and the Aragonese ambassadors wait for him on the shore.

These difficulties did not prevent Vincula from taking advantage of another opportunity for the promotion of Giovanni's interests, created by the death of Leonardo della Rovere in 1475. He wanted Leonardo's estates in Naples and his position as Prefect of Rome for the boy. At first, Sixtus was inclined to make Antonio Basso, a son of his sister, Leonardo's successor as Prefect and as husband of Ferrante's daughter, but Ferrante baulked at the idea of such an obscure son-in-law with so many landless relatives who would no doubt expect the king to make provision for them. Soon the cardinal got his way, and Leonardo's Neapolitan duchies of Arci and Sora, and the Prefecture, were given to his brother. Giovanni was to be 'the only one from whom the della Rovere family would be descended'.[26] Another prize he coveted for Giovanni, the prestigious office of Great Constable of Naples, eluded his grasp. When Vincula, having ostensibly set out with his brother to take possession of the duchies of Arci and Sora, apparently changed his mind and went no further than Grottaferrata, there was speculation that the refusal of the Great Constableship had caused a breach between him and the king.

Sixtus continued to show his cardinal–nephew favour, while not giving him any special power. Vincula was made a member of some groups of cardinals deputed to consider matters of particular importance, but he had served on such commissions before without making any notable impression. When Sixtus appointed a commission of cardinals to study proposals for a general league of the Italian powers in late January 1475, Vincula was not even among those initially chosen, though he was out of Rome at the time, accompanying Ferrante. Only when Sixtus dropped some members of the commission two weeks later, was he added, together with, at his insistence, Rodrigo Borgia. Towards the end of the year, he was one of three cardinals asked to consider raising a tax for the crusade, and one of nine appointed in February 1476 to consider further crusading plans, but shortly afterwards he was sent off on another legation, one that marked an important stage in his career.

This legation, to Avignon and France, was an even more significant milestone than the Umbrian one had been. It introduced Vincula to the political scene with which much of his subsequent career as a cardinal, especially during the last decade before he became pope, was connected and that would have great influence on his pontificate. This was the beginning of his personal contacts with the King of France, and with the politics of the area between France and the Holy Roman Empire to which, in a way, his home town of Savona belonged.

The crisis at Avignon that drew him into this world was only one aspect of the complex drama of the duel between Louis XI of France and Duke Charles the Bold of Burgundy. The Valois dukes of Burgundy, a cadet line of the Valois kings of France, had added to the duchy of Burgundy, by marriage and inheritance and conquest, a powerful and prosperous group of dominions stretching from Flanders in the north to Burgundy on the Rhône. Charles the Bold dreamed of turning these dominions into an independent kingdom, a revival of the kingdom of Burgundy, which had been the middle section of the tripartite division of Charlemagne's vast empire among his sons.

This middle portion had included the kingdom of Italy, but the interest of the Italian powers in Charles the Bold's fortunes did not stem from fears that he intended to continue his expansion southward into the peninsula. It was the claims of the French princely houses of Anjou to the kingdom of Naples and of Orléans to the duchy of Milan that were the focus of their concern.[27]

Together with the important trade and banking interests of Italian merchants in France, and Louis XI's personal fascination with Italian politics, these had brought the French into the Italian systems of alliances.

Relations between Sixtus and Louis were a mixture of confrontation and cooperation. Louis manipulated the Gallican tradition of the French Church – that determination to keep French benefices for Frenchmen, and to limit both the intervention of the pope in the ecclesiastical affairs of the kingdom and the amount of money flowing from France to Rome – to suit his own purposes. Generally, king and pope worked together fairly comfortably, recognizing one another's interests in appointments to benefices and taxation of the clergy. But Louis could always fall back on the 'Gallican liberties' if he wished to dig his heels in or bring pressure on the pope, and was also ready to make use of the threat most feared by late-fifteenth-century popes, that of calling a general council for the reform of the Church. Sixtus, like other popes, was willing to pay the price of some concessions to the king in order to maintain access to the rich benefices and revenues of the French Church.

The pope's position as temporal ruler added a further dimension to his relations with the French king. As an Italian prince, he was involved in the alliances that linked and divided the powers of the peninsula, among whom, in a sense, France could be numbered. As the lord of the city of Avignon and the neighbouring Comtat Venaissin, bought for the papacy after the popes had settled there in the fourteenth century, his lands bordered on French territory, with all the potential for disputes over boundaries and tolls and trade and fugitives that this entailed.

At the time the crisis at Avignon arose, relations among the Italian powers, France and Burgundy were remarkably confused. No two powers clearly had the same interests in each of the several concurrent diplomatic issues. Of particular concern to the curia were proposals for an ecclesiastical council backed by one or more of the ultramontane powers, and proposals for a crusade against the Turks, who were on the move again. Rome pressed the proposals for a crusade in order to ward off those for a council, still perceived by the papal court, as the secular princes well knew, as a threat. The other question that concerned the papacy directly was that of the fate of the dominions of the aged and childless René d'Anjou, which bordered on Avignon and the

Comtat Venaissin. As the prospect of the King of France acquiring these lands seemed the least inviting possibility, as Louis had just declared that a council should be held, and as Charles of Burgundy seemed the ruler most likely to succumb to the glamour of the prospect of holding a crusade, the papacy was, on the whole, on rather better terms with the duke than with the king. Many of the difficulties San Pietro ad Vincula would encounter on his legation sprang from Louis's perception of the pope as an ally of Burgundy.

The crisis at Avignon that arose in early 1476 was partly a consequence of Vincula's appointment as Bishop of Avignon in May 1474. There had been dissension between the pope and the legate of Avignon before that, for Sixtus had not really wished to appoint Charles de Bourbon, Archbishop of Lyons and a member of one of the most powerful princely houses of France, to this important legation in 1472. He had refused to make Charles a cardinal, restricted his spiritual powers as legate, interfered with appointments within the city of Avignon usually left to the decision of the legate or his governor, and, in 1473, appointed a separate governor for the Comtat. Charles won the support of the people of Avignon, who petitioned Sixtus to give back to Charles the rights and powers that his predecessor had enjoyed, but Sixtus only diminished them further. Following Vincula's appointment as Bishop of Avignon, relations between the Avignonese and their legate became less harmonious. Gradually, they turned to Vincula for help with business at Rome, appointing his chancellor, Gabriele Sclafenati, as their proctor there. The pope took the opportunity of the death of the Archbishop of Arles, in early November 1475, to withdraw the see of Avignon from subordination to Arles, thus ending the ecclesiastical subordination of the papal state to a see outside it, and made Avignon an archbishopric, putting the bishoprics of Carpentras, Cavaillon and Vaison under its jurisdiction. The papal bulls and letters announcing the promotion of their see to the Avignonese mention that Vincula had had a part in bringing it about.

Louis XI was not pleased by these developments. In so far as he trusted any of the French princes, he was on good terms with the Bourbons; he married his daughter Anne to Charles's brother Pierre, while Louis, the half-brother of Charles and Pierre, was the Admiral of France, and the Duke of Bourbon himself was the King's lieutenant in Languedoc. In early February 1476 he ordered the seneschal of Beaucaire, Antoine de Chateauneuf, to go to Avignon to exact reparations for the insults he accused the Avignonese of inflicting on Charles de Bourbon and on the king himself by asking the pope to diminish the legate's power. Though the seneschal seems to have behaved with restraint when he came to Avignon, it was the intervention of the king that brought about the revocation of Bourbon's powers as legate, and his replacement by Giuliano della Rovere on 21 February. Two days earlier, the cardinal had left Rome for Avignon.

After being delayed at Ostia for some days by storms, he set sail on some Milanese galleys that had been commandeered by Sixtus, reaching Genoa on 29 February. His arrival there was unexpected, and there were hurried consultations between the Genoese and the Milanese officials about what honours should be paid to him. He plainly enjoyed being accorded the honours due to a papal legate on his home ground. When visited by two Milanese officials, who were to accompany him throughout his stay, he received them graciously but, it was noted, kept them standing with their hats in their hands, while he remained seated.[28] After a few days, the cardinal went to Savona, from where he wrote to thank Galeazzo Maria for his reception in Genoa. Although he could not deny, he said (perhaps a little tactlessly), that he was previously popular there anyway, he would be ungrateful not to recognize the benevolence shown to him through the public celebrations ordered by Milan.[29] Leaving Savona on the morning of 5 March, he travelled on the same galleys to Arles, where he disembarked.

When Louis heard of the cardinal's arrival, at first he wanted to prevent him from coming ashore, but then was persuaded to let him travel to Avignon. On 17 March he entered the city in great state, accompanied by the citizens first to his cathedral and then to the bishop's palace. The next day he had a long discussion with the consuls of Avignon and some of the leading gentlemen, and his first confrontation with the men of Charles de Bourbon. They accused the Avignonese of writing complaints to Rome about their legate. The Avignonese had never complained of Charles de Bourbon, Vincula replied, only of his officials, and to whom else should they turn for help against oppression but their lord the pope?[30]

Meanwhile, the cardinal had sent Andrea de' Spiriti, protonotary of Viterbo, to the king. Andrea had served as a papal envoy in France for a lengthy period, and Louis liked him so much that he had protested when he was recalled to Rome, and had refused to accept his replacement. The king agreed to receive his favourite, but sent his own ambassadors to the cardinal to warn him not to try to expel Charles de Bourbon from his legation. He should come to court, where he would be honoured, especially as he was the nephew of the pope. He would also be allowed to exercise his powers as legate to France, provided they did not prejudice the rights of the crown. The cardinal replied he had come to visit his diocese, and to settle the disputes between his flock and the legate's officials. He would come to Louis after Easter. But first it would be a good idea to appoint a new lieutenant in Avignon, one of the prelates in his train, for instance.[31] Louis did not think this a good idea; he wanted one of his own subjects as lieutenant.

The cardinal had yet to announce formally his own appointment as legate of Avignon in place of Charles de Bourbon, but Bourbon's men were barricaded in the papal palace there, which was built like a fortress. Vincula had not been allowed in. Urged on by the Bourbons, who played on the king's suspicions of the cardinal's intentions, Louis ordered a strong force of men-at-arms to move to the neighbourhood of Avignon to lend support to Charles de Bourbon's men. There were reports that supplies to the palace from the town had been cut off. Bourbon later claimed, in a letter of self-justification to the pope, that it was for this reason that the French troops had been sent, but from other sources it is by no means clear at what stage supplies were cut.[32]

The crisis was precipitated by an incident on 18 April. This was the arrival in the city of about ten men, claiming to be members of the king's household on their way to Provence, who wanted to come into Avignon for a meal. They were admitted, but immediately made for the palace, which they entered. A large barge full of victuals for the palace came by river; this the cardinal had confiscated. The next day, infantry from the palace came out and seized some eggs and capons from one of Vincula's household officials. This marked the opening of overt hostilities. Siege engines were prepared; a wooden outwork by one of the palace gates was burned; officials and partisans of Charles de Bourbon were arrested, and some were tortured. Vincula finally made public the deposition of Bourbon from the legation of Avignon and his own appointment as legate.

If he had hoped to be master of the palace before the arrival of the French troops, he had miscalculated. On 20 April an envoy of the Admiral of France, Louis de Bourbon, arrived in Avignon;

the next day there were talks outside the city between envoys of the cardinal and the Admiral. As the French troops commanded by the Admiral and by Pierre de Bourbon and his brother Charles occupied the Comtat Venaissin and made rapidly for Avignon itself, Vincula left the city on 25 April to go to the king. He did not want to go, but felt that it was the best course of action in the circumstances.[33] The Bourbons and their troops entered Avignon five days later, peacefully enough. The following day a letter arrived from the cardinal, advising the Avignonese to submit to Charles de Bourbon as their legate.[34]

Vincula may have finally decided to go to court, as Louis had suggested, but the king was not now prepared to see him. He made his way to Vienne, waiting for the king's summons. Louis, however, wanted him to revoke Charles de Bourbon's dismissal from the legation of Avignon. He ordered the cardinal to wait near Lyons. Vincula was now in a very difficult position. He was surrounded by Louis's troops, so he could not return to Avignon; nor could he go to see the king before he received permission. Meanwhile, prelates were gathering in Lyons for the council Louis had summoned, and it seemed that the convocation of a general council of the Church would follow. An eyewitness account of the king's reception of an envoy of the cardinal shows just how hostile to him Louis was. A merchant arriving in Genoa from the fair at Lyons said that while he had been there he had seen a 'Florentine bishop' (Antonio de' Pazzi, Bishop of Sarno), sent by Vincula, in the king's apartments. When the king approached, the bishop kneeled and began to speak, but before he had got very far, the king interrupted him furiously. He insulted the bishop and his master, saying that the cardinal was in league with Burgundy, that he knew he had come to Avignon to fortify it and help the Duke of Burgundy gain Provence, and that that 'confessed Jew' ('iudeo confesso'), King Juan of Aragon, and 'that bastard' King Ferrante, had had a hand in these schemes, as had the Duke of Milan and the Duchess of Savoy; they were all in it together, but Louis had foiled them by securing Avignon and Provence.[35] There was, indeed, another report that one of the reasons why Vincula was kept waiting for an audience with Louis so long was to give the king an excuse to keep his troops in the papal territories, so that they could move into Provence quickly if necessary.[36] The king arrested Antonio Pazzi and another envoy the cardinal had sent, together with Andrea de' Spiriti, who had been with Louis all the time.

This proved to be the turning point. It came to light that Andrea de' Spiriti had been playing a double game. Trying to make himself indispensable, with his ambition fixed on the legation of France and a cardinal's hat, he had been encouraging both the king and the cardinal to stand firm. He had told the king Vincula was his enemy; he had urged the cardinal not to leave Avignon. Once his duplicity had been revealed, Louis became willing for Vincula to come to Lyons, though not before Vincula had put his seal to letters patent, dated 27 May, ordering the inhabitants of Avignon and the Venaissin to obey Bourbon, and freeing them from their oaths of fidelity to him as legate.[37] On 31 May the cardinal was finally allowed to enter Lyons, and he had an audience with the king the next day.

The outcome of this meeting was extraordinary. Suddenly Louis's hostility was turned to marked favour. One by one, all the causes of dispute were resolved in favour of the cardinal and the papacy. Louis dropped the proposal for a general council of the Church. He agreed to Vincula replacing Bourbon as legate of Avignon. He agreed to his exercising his powers as legate of France, and ordered all French subjects having business in Rome to transact it through his agency. In order, he declared, to show his love for the cardinal, to thank him for the services he had rendered, and in the hope he would continue to render such services and have the affairs of the king and his subjects in special recommendation, he would permit him to possess all the benefices with which he was canonically provided in France, although he was not a French subject.[38] So friendly had the king been to Giuliano ever since that first meeting, the cardinal's uncle Filippo della Rovere, master of his household, wrote to his mother, Theodora, in Savona, you would think they had grown up together.[39]

Charles de Bourbon also showed himself friendly to his rival, agreeing to surrender his legation (in return for a promise of favour in obtaining a cardinal's hat), and lodging him in his own episcopal palace. All the disputes that the Avignonese had had with the king's officials were settled in their favour, specifically to please the cardinal, and he also negotiated further privileges for them, although in return they had to swear not to receive any troops of enemies of the king. Vincula left Lyons on 24 June to return to Avignon, which he reached five days later. He stayed in the area until early September, when French galleys were put at his disposal for his journey home.

Had he accomplished what he had come to do? The answer obviously depends on what the aim of the legation is thought to have been.

Louis maintained that Vincula was plotting with the Duke of Burgundy to help him to take over Provence and was willing to put Avignon at his disposal for this purpose. When Vincula had first arrived in Avignon, he had sent an envoy to Charles. Arguing that Louis was planning to introduce his own troops into the city as a step towards taking over Provence himself, the duke had tried to convince him that Avignon should be put under Burgundian guard. There is no evidence that this scheme held any appeal for the cardinal. What advantage would the papacy gain by entrusting Avignon to Duke Charles, one of the most warlike and acquisitive rulers of his day, and assisting him to take over Provence? What could justify the risk of letting such a man bring his troops to the papal territories?

The cardinal said he had come to try to pacify and protect the people of his diocese, and all his actions were consistent with that aim. As soon as Vincula had heard from his vicar in Avignon that the city was in danger of being taken over by the French with the help of Charles de Bourbon, he had been keen to go there in person. If the cardinals would not agree to his going as legate, he said, he would go as a private individual in his capacity as Archbishop of Avignon, to succour his diocese, and he was ready to die for that Church and its territory.[40] The astonishing change in the king's behaviour towards the cardinal is more readily explicable if he had first believed Vincula to be intriguing against him with his arch-enemy, was prompted to begin to revise his opinion by the revelation of Andrea de' Spiriti's duplicity, and then was further reassured by the cardinal when they actually met. As diplomatic skill was never Vincula's strong point, but he did acquire a reputation for honesty and forthrightness in his speech, perhaps these qualities were the decisive ones. If Louis was suspicious to the point of paranoia in his later years, he was also a clever politician and a shrewd judge of character. To such a man, someone like Giuliano della Rovere would have been an open book. The warmth of the king's welcome, the lavishness of his favour, may have been partly due to relief, but was probably largely an effort to repair the damage to relations with the papacy caused by his threat of a council and his humiliation of the pope's legate and nephew. Would Louis have been so generous had he known that the Duke of Burgundy was about to be heavily defeated by the Swiss at the Battle of Morat on 26 June?

Nevertheless, the legation had resulted in the settlement of the disputes between the Avignonese and the royal officials, the acceptance by the king that Vincula should replace Charles de Bourbon as legate of Avignon and the dropping of the proposal to summon a general council. The only concession of substance made in return was a promise to help Charles de Bourbon to acquire a cardinal's hat. Some measure of credit for this success must go to Giuliano della Rovere for keeping his nerve during the long wait before Louis would see him, for not trying to buy himself out of a very awkward position.

What did this legation do for his standing in Rome?

While it was believed that most of the cardinals could not wait to see the back of him, they had been divided about whether or not he should go. Predictions that he would run into trouble were widespread, though for some this was not an unwelcome prospect. Sixtus also had his doubts, and only let his nephew go because he was so eager to do so. Once the pope had yielded to his persuasion, he gave him all the powers as legate that he could. He was said to believe that some of the cardinals were perhaps encouraging the threat of a council for their own ends, and to have sent his nephew because he was the only cardinal he trusted.[41]

When reports about Vincula's difficult situation in May reached Rome, Sixtus became very anxious about him. Lamenting that he had only sent his nephew because he had been so importunate, he hinted that he was not impressed by his performance; yet, because he was his nephew and a cardinal, the first priority was to get him safely out of Louis's hands.[42] The curia was anxious as well, though not for the legate's personal safety. 'If he were the only one to suffer the consequences, as he deserves, there isn't a man in this court who wouldn't laugh and hope he did, but seeing the adversity it might bring on Italy and the affairs of the Church, everyone here is displeased.'[43]

As the news improved and letters arrived from Vincula reporting how well Louis had received him, even Sixtus was not convinced. There were suspicions that the legate must have struck some secret bargain with Louis to win his favour, for example by promising him help in taking Genoa and Savona, and rumours that he had agreed to René resigning his claim to the kingdom of Naples to Louis. It was widely believed that he had promised the king that Charles de Bourbon would be made a cardinal and given the legation of France for life. These rumours were reported back to Vincula, who wrote vigorously denying them. Even though some of his enemies, such as the Milanese ambassador who had been gloomily predicting what his 'lack of sense' might lead to, became reassured that 'the cardinal isn't so stupid that he hasn't realized what the king is like', his men were still having to contradict the rumours in September.[44]

All in all, the cardinal won little credit for the success of the legation, because few people, even the pope, really believed that he was fitted for the task. The problems and dangers he had faced he was accused of bringing on himself; there was widespread reluctance to believe the good news when it finally came, and by the time that it had sunk in and he had arrived back at the papal court in October, opposition was already building up to giving a cardinal's hat to Bourbon, the one matter on which Vincula had made a promise to the king.

Indeed, Vincula's overall lack of success in the politicking surrounding the promotion of cardinals during the next two years indicates clearly that the legation to France had done little to enhance his prestige in the curia. He would have, if anything, less, rather than more, influence with Sixtus as the pontificate went on, and Girolamo Riario became ever more dominant over the pope and tightened his grip on all aspects of papal patronage. He would even be eclipsed as cardinal–nephew by Riario's own nephew, brought into the College in 1477.

The first battle to be won when Vincula rejoined the papal court in early October was for the fulfilment of his promise to procure Bourbon's election to the College of Cardinals. He insisted that if this was not done, Louis would once again threaten the independence of Avignon, and he himself would be humiliated. The cardinals were not too averse to making Bourbon a member of the College, because there was small chance of his coming to join them in Rome, but they were worried that if that promotion were made, others would have to be made too. There were standing promises of hats to protégés of the Holy Roman Emperor, Ferrante and the King of Portugal. The Duke of Milan, King of Hungary, Duke of Burgundy and Florence all had candidates of their own in mind, and there were old associates of Sixtus that he was keen to promote. Vincula had another man in mind himself, Lorenzo Zane, the Patriarch of Antioch, who had served him on the Umbrian legation and had acted as his agent in Rome while he had been away in France. This was not a popular choice, for Zane had many enemies in Rome and was not generally considered to be worthy of a place in the College. On the other hand, Vincula was opposed – on the grounds that he was a Breton and would therefore be displeasing to Louis – to an old friend of his uncle, the protonotary Pierre de Foix, whom Sixtus was much inclined to make a cardinal.[45]

In the event, Sixtus not only had de Foix made a cardinal, he also obtained the promotion of another of his old friends, Pedro Ferrici. Charles de Bourbon got his promotion, but Zane did not, though Vincula fought hard for him to the last moment. He made a scene in the final consistory at which the promotion was decided on 18 December 1476, protesting, even weeping, according to the account reported by the Milanese ambassador, and threatening that if Sixtus was willing for him to suffer such damage to his reputation by the refusal of his candidate, he would go away and never appear before him again.[46] So angry and humiliated was he by his loss of face, that he would not attend the public consistory at which two of the new cardinals were to be formally admitted. He left Rome to nurse his grievance, and it was the middle of January 1477 before Sixtus could coax him back. It might have been some consolation to him if he had known that he had in fact gained far more at this promotion than he could have done had his own candidate been successful. One of the new cardinals, Jorge da Costa, Archbishop of Lisbon, was to become perhaps his closest friend in the College after coming to Rome in 1480. An upright man, who won the esteem and respect of his colleagues, he would be a friend worth having, one who remained loyal to Vincula for the rest of his life.

Vincula returned to Rome still determined that Zane should be a cardinal, and it was said he had been promised he would have his wish. If a cardinal was to be created, there would have to be others, so the question of who those others should be was opened again before the newly created cardinals had settled into their scarlet robes. Again Sixtus had his own candidates in mind, this time two *nipoti*, Cristoforo della Rovere, Archbishop of Tarantais (one of the recently discovered 'cousins' from Piedmont)[47] and Girolamo Basso della Rovere, Bishop of Recanati, son of Sixtus's sister. Again Vincula opposed the pope's wishes. Why he should have opposed them is not clear, unless he simply feared to share what power his position as sole cardinal-nephew gave him, though his desperation at the realization that Zane's candidature would again be unsuccessful was said to have played a part. In any case, it was not a wise move. He managed to rally enough support in consistory to force the pope to drop the idea for the moment, but at the cost of quarrelling with Sixtus more acrimoniously than before.[48]

Nor was this the only cause of dispute between them. They also had conflicting attitudes to the Milanese domination of Genoa. While Vincula supported the Fieschi and Campofregoso, who stimulated a rebellion against Milanese rule in March 1477, Sixtus backed the Sforza. The Genoese rebels needed a leader and turned to Obietto Fieschi. Sixtus tried to keep him in Rome, but Obietto managed to escape by boat, with the connivance of some cardinals. Given Vincula's earlier connection with Obietto, and his support for the rebellion, it is likely that he had a hand in his flight. Another cardinal who openly supported the rebels was the Genoese Gianbattista Cibò, known as Cardinal Malfetta, the future Pope Innocent VIII. He and Vincula put to the pope the suggestion of the Genoese that Sixtus should take Genoa under his protection, even take it directly under his rule, but Sixtus would have none of it, and continued to support the Milanese. While the pope excommunicated Obietto, Vincula sent him money.[49] There is not enough evidence to form a clear picture of Vincula's stance in Genoese politics, except to indicate a partiality for the exiles. He had been a patron for some years of Obietto Fieschi and his brother Urbano, whom he had wished to have a cardinal's hat in December 1476. Several other Genoese exiles had accompanied him to Rome on his return from Avignon. Whatever his motives were, Sixtus did not appreciate them. He told his nephew on several occasions, even in full consistory, that he was displeased by his behaviour, but to no avail.

By the end of April the rebellion at Genoa was over, but very soon there was yet another reason for Sixtus to be angry with his nephew. He was accused of plotting to kill Girolamo Riario. Two of his protégés, the Genoese Domenico Doria, and Matteo da Canale from Todi, were imprisoned in the Castel Sant' Angelo. The rooms he had occupied in the papal palace were taken from him, a sign that Sixtus was prepared to believe that there was something in the accusations. Indeed, since his return from France, the rivalry between Vincula and his cousin had been more bitter than before. Riario's determination that his efforts to have Lorenzo Zane made a cardinal should come to nothing had brought about open hostility between them, even in the presence of Sixtus. Now Zane had shown his loyalty to his patron by going to Riario and speaking of a conspiracy against him by Vincula and Obietto Fieschi.

Under interrogation, Domenico Doria and Matteo da Canale had a different tale to tell. According to them, there had been some talk of killing Riario, at the time when it was clear that Zane would not be made a cardinal, but Zane himself had been the principal instigator of the plot. While he had asked them several times to kill Riario, claiming to be speaking on behalf of the cardinal, Vincula himself had never spoken to them about the matter. Soon it became apparent that Vincula was guilty, at worst, of not revealing the threat to Riario, which may have come to his ears. He pressed for Zane to be tried, but Riario, despite the revelation that Zane was the principal culprit, defended him and said that he had promised that he would not be persecuted for his disclosures.[50]

Though the greater evil of one papal nephew conspiring to kill another had proved to be a fabrication, the fact that relations between them were such that the pope himself could believe it might be true was scandal enough, and Sixtus was concerned that the two should be reconciled. By early June it seemed that they had settled their differences, and the storm had blown over.

Nevertheless, Vincula did not recover the ground that he had lost in the contest with Girolamo Riario. In December 1477 he also lost his position as the sole *nipote* in the College of Cardinals, since no less than three of the seven new cardinals promoted in that month were relatives of Sixtus: Cristoforo della Rovere, Girolamo Basso della Rovere and Riario's own nephew, Raffaele Sansoni Riario. Cristoforo della Rovere, who had been the castellan of Castel Sant' Angelo, died less than two months after his promotion. Sixtus was distraught, thinking that the stresses of the castellanship must have been the cause of his death; to console him, the cardinals suggested that the pope should give Cristoforo's hat to another relative, and Sixtus gladly gave it to Cristoforo's brother, Domenico. Neither Girolamo Basso nor Domenico became powerful figures in the College, though Sixtus entrusted Domenico with a number of commissions. Raffaele Riario, however, though only aged sixteen when he was promoted, with his uncle's backing was to become a serious rival to Vincula.

Girolamo Riario was consolidating his dominance in other ways too. In November 1478, after angling for over a year, he got one of his former grooms, now a bishop, appointed castellan of Castel Sant' Angelo; he already had his men as castellans of several other major papal fortresses. His supremacy was increasingly recognized by the other Italian powers. If Sixtus sent Vincula, again with Cardinal Borgia, to greet the Duke of Calabria when he visited Rome in June 1478, it was Girolamo Riario that Calabria's father Ferrante really wanted as an ally at the court. Riario was invited to Naples and offered the office of Great Constable that Vincula had wanted for his brother; the following year, he did in fact become Great Constable.

The strongest evidence of Girolamo Riario's hold over Sixtus was the way in which he persuaded the pope to agree to backing the conspiracy of the Pazzi against Lorenzo de' Medici in April 1478, precipitating a war with Florence and her allies that lasted for two years. In this war, while Ferrante backed the pope, the Sforza stood by Florence. Inevitably, this meant that relations between Riario and Milan grew considerably cooler, giving scope for Vincula to turn the tables on Riario for supplanting him as Naples' favoured *nipote*.

A rapprochement with Milan had been one of the conditions of Vincula's 'reconciliation' with Riario in 1477. He had shown himself willing to observe this by, for example, giving Milan a guarantee that a prominent Genoese exile, Paolo Campofregoso, the Archbishop of Genoa, would abide by the conditions imposed by Milan on his exile in Rome. When he heard of another plot against Milan in Genoa, in May 1478, this time instigated by Ferrante, he passed on what he had learned to the Sforza's ambassador – and took the opportunity to assure them that his influence over the Genoese exiles could be used to their advantage. A couple of months later, he even told the Milanese ambassador how Sixtus had asked the Archbishop of Genoa, who was lodged in his palace at Santi Apostoli, to go to Genoa (presumably to stir up trouble for Milan), and how the archbishop had refused.

This time, there were no reports that Sixtus was angered by his nephew taking a different line to that of the pope in Genoese affairs, but then there are very few reports about Vincula at all during the years of the Pazzi War. How far he sought to counter the policies Riario was urging on Sixtus is impossible to say. It is known that he was one of the cardinals deputed to conduct negotiations with a French embassy that came to Rome in early 1479 to try to bring about peace in Italy, and Lorenzo de' Medici advised the ambassadors to pay particular court to him.[51] Riario's response to the confidence placed in Vincula by the French ambassadors was to press offers of his own services on Louis.

It was France that gave Vincula a chance to move back into

the limelight. Louis had asked for a papal legate to be sent, as a move in his diplomatic battle with Duke Maximilian, the Habsburg husband of Marie of Burgundy, daughter and heiress of Charles the Bold. The French ambassadors in Rome themselves suggested that Vincula should be appointed. He was eager to go, and in late April 1480 bulls were issued giving him powers as legate in France, Brittany, Provence, Savoy and the Low Countries, together with accreditation, though not such full powers, for Scotland and England. His main task was to be the promotion of peace between Louis and Marie and Maximilian, so that the Christian powers could unite against the Turks. A secondary mission was to get custody of two ecclesiastics arrested by Louis in 1469, one a cardinal and former royal favourite, Jean Balue, and the other the Bishop of Verdun, Guillaume de Harancourt, who had both been intriguing with Charles the Bold. The legate was to hold an enquiry into the matter, independent of royal officials, and to report his findings to Rome, where the judicial decision would be made. After delaying to attend the marriage of his sister Luchina to Gianfrancesco Franciotti of Lucca, he left Rome on 9 June.

In marked contrast to the hostile reception that Louis had given him on his previous legation, this time he was fêted and allowed the free exercise of his powers, though when the king's delegates met him outside Lyons on 2 August, he had to make a formal declaration this would not in any way infringe the rights of the French crown. His report to Sixtus on the messages the king had sent rings with pleasure and optimism, especially as he had heard that a six months' truce had been arranged between Louis and Maximilian.[52] Three weeks later he met the king at Vendôme, and reported that same evening the warmth of Louis's greeting, his words of concern about the threat from the Turks, and his generous offers of help against them – offers that were conditional, however, on other Christian princes doing their share. There was going to be a meeting on 15 October between envoys of the king and of the duke, at which the legate was to be present. If he should find Maximilian as well disposed as Louis had shown himself to be, the prospects for success in his legation were good.[53]

But Maximilian was not so accommodating. Indeed, he refused to see Vincula at all, or even to admit him into Burgundian territory. Vincula left Paris for Picardy on 15 September, and lingered on the borders of Maximilian's lands for about three months. Double-dealing by Luca de' Tollenti, papal nuncio to the court of Burgundy, and by Marco de Ponte, the Archbishop of Rhodes, the envoy sent by Vincula to try to open negotiations, wrecked any chances he might have had to overcome Maximilian's distrust.

Louis warned him that he was being betrayed – he had been betrayed ever since he had left Rome by de' Tollenti, who did not want to lose his own legation – and advised him to try to exploit the dislike of Maximilian's councillors felt by the people of Ghent. If he could win them over, the king said, they had the power to admit him as legate despite Maximilian and his council.[54] Vincula replied that he had been aware of the treachery and had written to Ghent and other towns in Flanders, telling them how the duke had refused him entry and asking them to send men to him. De Ponte, he wrote, was a Greek (evidently he did not regard this as a compliment), and had done what he had through greed and ambition. He could not be left to cause trouble in Flanders and England, but Vincula wanted to be careful not to dishonour the status of archbishop that he held. Could the king order some men to remove him discreetly from the scene, without allowing him to write or speak to anyone, and take him to Châteauneuf-du-Pape near Avignon, where Vincula would investigate what he had been up to in Flanders? As for de' Tollenti, Sixtus had ordered Vincula to look into what he had been about; before he left Picardy, de' Tollenti would not know where to turn.[55]

While he was waiting in vain to be admitted to Flanders, Vincula heard the news of the Turks' capture of the city of Otranto in the kingdom of Naples, which gave the subject of the crusade a little more topicality and urgency than usual. Sixtus, terrified, ordered him to prepare the palace at Avignon as a refuge for the papal court. In late December Vincula, perhaps spurred by the news, turned back to rejoin the king, whose release of Cardinal Balue was the first tangible fruit of the legation. Louis was still professing interest in the idea of undertaking the crusade. When Vincula wrote to Sixtus on 10 February 1481 from Tours, he said that if only the quarrel between Louis and Maximilian could be settled, he was sure much of the French army would take the cross; many of the nobles to whom he had spoken had declared themselves willing to do so. If Sixtus would take upon himself the adjudication of their dispute, as Vincula had urged him to do before, this would surely help to bring peace.[56] Sixtus duly ordered a three-year truce between all Christian princes;

when Louis received this bull in late April, he declared himself ready to agree, provided he had guarantees that his enemies would do the same.

The king was soon to become less friendly, however, as the question of the fate of Provence came to the fore again. Louis had accepted René d'Anjou's designation of Charles du Maine as his heir, but Sixtus would not recognize either Charles or the other claimant, the Duke of Lorraine, as Duke of Anjou, still less invest one of them with the papal fief of the kingdom of Naples. As Vincula made his way back to Avignon, which he reached on 27 May, he had to negotiate with Jean de Dinteville, the captain of one of the armed bands that were already taking advantage of the inheritance dispute to indulge in a little profitable campaigning in Provence, more or less on behalf of one or the other claimant, and spilling over into the neighbouring papal territories. Theoretically neutral, Vincula may have been favouring the Duke of Lorraine; certainly Charles du Maine accused him of doing so, and became increasingly hostile. Jean de Dinteville, who had been fighting on behalf of Lorraine, plotted to capture the legate; Charles du Maine wrote on 10 August denying he had anything to do with this,[57] but the mere fact he should feel obliged to deny responsibility for the activities of his rival's captain, indicates there were suspicions that Dinteville had shifted allegiance. Louis was furious at the arrest of Dinteville and his accomplices when the plot was discovered. If he ever laid hands on the legate, he wrote, 'never would I listen to him, nor would I let him go, cardinal and Bishop of Avignon though he be.'[58] Dinteville was his vassal and subject and servant, Louis told the people of Avignon; if he had committed any fault, the king would see to it that he was duly punished.[59]

As on his first legation, therefore, Vincula was marooned in Avignon, unable to leave for Rome because of hostile troops along his route. Appeased by the release of Dinteville, after he had asked for pardon, Louis wrote to say that the legate had nothing to fear from him. But there was still Charles du Maine, demanding that Lorraine's supporters be expelled from Avignon. Vincula's response was to arrange for one of Lorraine's captains, the Basque Menaud d'Aguerre, to be taken into service by the Avignonese. He evidently took to Menaud, giving him revenues in Avignon and having him made a citizen. But Louis did not approve, and threatened the Avignonese that he would back Charles du Maine against them if they did not dismiss Menaud; they insisted that he leave, but he did not finally go until after the departure of the legate. He had escorted Vincula – who also had an escort of troops paid for by the citizens of Carpentras – when he at last left Avignon in mid-November. The legate was not being over-cautious: just before he left, another plot by Charles du Maine's men to capture him had been discovered. He avoided Provençal territory, and returned by way of Orange and Dauphiné. Less than a month after the legate's far from triumphant departure from Avignon, the fate of Provence was finally settled, as Charles du Maine died and Louis himself was his successor. At least Vincula benefited from this personally, for the estates he held in Provence, which Charles du Maine had confiscated, were restored to him by the king.

Paradoxically, this second legation to France does seem to have enhanced Vincula's standing in Rome. When he ran into trouble on his return to Avignon, there were no reports this time of malicious pleasure among the cardinals and members of the curia. Supporters of Burgundy in Rome, led by Cardinal Mâcon, did claim that he was administering the legation of Avignon badly, and was furnishing Louis with a pretext to annex the Comtat Venaissin, but in general he seems to have met with more sympathy for his dilemma than during the first legation. Many cardinals were said to be looking forward to his return.[60] Sixtus stood by his nephew, and when difficulties arose, he did not begin dropping querulous hints that he doubted his capacity to deal with the situation. Instead, he wrote to Louis reminding him of the privileges of legates and emphasizing his confidence in his nephew. He threatened Provence with ecclesiastical censures, appointing a commission of cardinals to report to consistory on the affair. At the height of the trouble in Avignon, Sixtus had the notion of appointing a council of four to oversee the temporal and spiritual affairs of the Church, to increase his personal control and diminish that of the cardinals – San Pietro ad Vincula was to be one of the four, Girolamo Riario another, and the remaining two were to be Cardinal Domenico della Rovere and the *depositario*, Gianfrancesco Franciotti, Vincula's brother-in-law – but the leading cardinals soon put paid to this idea.

When Vincula set out to return to Rome, he intended to travel by sea again; Sixtus asked him to travel by land, giving him commissions to carry out in Milan. It was predicted that on his return to Rome Sixtus would give him responsibility for much business and would rely on him to a great extent.[61]

His reception when he finally arrived at Rome on 3 February 1482 with Cardinal Balue was a triumph. Eight cardinals and many prelates, as well as the ambassadors accredited to the Roman court, went several miles out of the city to greet him. A little further on, he was met by Girolamo Riario together with the Venetian ambassador and a large crowd of Roman barons and gentlemen. The two rival *nipoti* gave a great demonstration of mutual affection, embracing each other, laughing. A mile from the city, the Governor of Rome, the Senator, Conservators and other Roman officials and citizens were waiting for him. Just outside the Porto del Popolo were all the rest of the cardinals, who also greeted him affectionately, and the papal guard. That night he and Balue rested at the monastery of Santa Maria del Popolo, just inside the gate, and the following morning they were escorted from there by all the cardinals and the members of the curia to the Vatican to be received formally by Sixtus in a public consistory. These ceremonial greetings on the return of a legate were customary, but the honour of the reception was calculated by how many cardinals, *curiali* and citizens turned up, and how far from Rome the advance welcoming parties went. Vincula's reception on this occasion was judged quite exceptional.

Naturally, there were limits to the welcome extended to him. Girolamo Riario was not about to allow him an equal share in influence over the pope. The cardinals who had the privilege of chambers in the papal palace, Raffaele Riario and Ferriaco de Cluny, had tried to prevent Sixtus from preparing rooms for Vincula there. Nor was Raffaele Riario the only other nephew among the cardinals whom Sixtus kept with him frequently – Domenico della Rovere and Girolamo Basso della Rovere were also high in his favour.

Nevertheless, Vincula was the senior *nipote* in the College, holder of major offices in the Church and fresh from an important legation. He may not have had much success in promoting peace between Louis and Maximilian, and he had had his problems at Avignon, but he had secured the release of Cardinal Balue and of Guillaume de Harancourt, and the maintenance of the prestige of the clergy and their immunity from lay jurisdiction ranked high among the priorities of the court of Rome. The cardinals had decided even before Vincula left Avignon that there should be no judicial proceedings instituted in Rome against Balue, as Louis was insisting there should be, and as the cardinals themselves had agreed only days before changing their minds. Balue must not be tried, they decided, 'for the honour of the Apostolic See and of all the College of Cardinals'.[62] His considerable political skills made him an influential figure in the College. In securing his liberation, Vincula gained a friend and a useful ally.

It was not only in Rome that there were expectations that Vincula would have a greater say in the making of papal policy. The league of Florence, Milan and Naples was looking to him to counterbalance Girolamo Riario, no longer regarded even by Milan as a trustworthy ally since he and Sixtus had cultivated friendship with Venice after the end of the Pazzi War in 1480. Vincula had been sounded out in Milan and Florence on his journey south, and was eager to seize the opportunity offered to him. Sixtus was ready to use him as a link with the league, and happy for him to play an important role in diplomacy.

The role he was called upon to play, as advocate of a league whose major concern was the containment of Venice, was to assist Ercole d'Este, the Duke of Ferrara, in trying to settle a dispute that had blown up between Ferrara and Venice. This dispute centred on the exercise of special privileges that Venice had enjoyed in Ferrara since the early fourteenth century, which included the maintenance of a Venetian official, the *visdomino*, in the city, with jurisdiction over the Venetian merchants who came there. Ferrara was a papal fief, and Sixtus might have been expected to back the duke against the overbearing Venetians and try to free this papal dominion from the encroaching authority of a powerful neighbour. Girolamo Riario, however, was looking to Venice for support in furthering his personal ambitions, and the pope was in fact backing the Venetians.

A list of the undertakings Sixtus wanted the duke to promise to observe towards Venice was drawn up, with Cardinal Raffaele Riario acting as secretary and the pope looking over his shoulder through his spectacles as he dictated the text himself. Vincula and several other cardinals were present, and though Sixtus suggested that Vincula should keep a copy, he explicitly said that he did not want this to be seen as something arranged by Vincula without the participation of Girolamo Riario.[63] Vincula thought that if the duke would agree to these undertakings, as in fact he did, war could be avoided. Sixtus himself said that he did not want war. But Girolamo Riario did, and once again his will prevailed.

Only days after the document had been drawn up, Vincula was being excluded from important discussions on the dispute between Ferrara and Venice, and Sixtus had spoken to him in such a manner that he had determined to stay at home and not go to the palace, although Cardinal Cibò persuaded him to change his mind. Cibò told the Milanese ambassador that Vincula was the only cardinal who dared to speak to Sixtus about the danger of war; the other cardinals had talked about doing so, but none could summon up the nerve to broach the subject.[64] Girolamo Riario prevailed with the pope, despite the fact that victory for Venice was bound to be to the prejudice of the papacy's rights in that area of the Romagna. Even before the outbreak of the War of Ferrara at the beginning of May, Vincula's role as the accepted spokesman for the league in the pope's circle was plainly over.

Up to the end of the pontificate, Riario's position as the dictator of papal policy seemed stronger than ever. He managed to prevent Vincula from taking any effective part in the negotiations that brought the pope over from the side of Venice to that of the league in December 1482 and in the prolonged and various peace negotiations that at length brought the war to an end in August 1484. Whenever contacts and proposals initiated by Vincula looked as if they might bear fruit, Riario made it clear that any peace negotiations conducted through those channels would not be acceptable to him. Yet there are signs that he recognized he could not exclude his cousins Giuliano and Giovanni from the pope's circle completely, and that some sort of accommodation was reached between the rivals that prevented overt demonstrations of ill-will, such as had led to the scandal of 1477.

This explains the support that Riario gave to a proposal that the Prefect, Giovanni della Rovere, should become captain of the Sienese troops. He and the pope pressed Siena on this matter throughout the spring of 1482, at first, apparently, without telling Vincula. The motive behind this sudden concern of Riario for the furtherance of Giovanni's career was primarily an attempt to remove him from the sphere of influence of Urbino and Naples. The Duke of Urbino had sent the Prefect to Rome in January 1482 to try to counteract Riario's influence; Riario welcomed him with open arms and a marriage alliance was agreed between their infant children. The pressure began on Siena to give the Prefect a *condotta*. Opposition by the Prefect to the prospect of war caused Riario to lose interest in the idea for a while and the pope to become rather ambivalent, but Vincula had taken up the scheme with enthusiasm. Once the pope had switched sides and become an ally of Naples, Riario's rationale for promoting the *condotta* disappeared, and the plan was dropped, to the relief of Siena.

A *condotta* for the Prefect with Milan and Naples instead was arranged in July 1483. Whatever the tactical reasons behind Riario's efforts to get the Sienese captaincy for the Prefect, it is interesting that he felt that the effort had to be made, and that he could not simply try to neutralize the Prefect by blackening him in the pope's eyes as tainted by his association with Urbino and Naples. Similarly, it is interesting that Vincula should so readily have taken up a proposal concerning his brother's career apparently hatched by Riario, and that the scheme was not automatically suspect to him by the very fact of Riario's involvement.

The ambiguities of relations between the cousins are illustrated by the position Riario adopted in a dispute that Vincula had with the Duke of Ferrara over a benefice. It was Sixtus who first advised Ercole d'Este's ambassadors to consult Riario about how to induce Vincula to renounce the benefice, but Riario, describing the cardinal as 'inexorable', told them that he was not the man to do this. When Vincula asked him to write to the duke on his behalf, he did so, but told Ercole's ambassadors the letter should be ignored, and advised that the cardinal should not be given possession of the benefice before the pope had recovered from a bout of illness and Riario could speak to him about the matter. The Ferrarese ambassador warned that Vincula did not like Riario being consulted on the matter; this was not, the ambassador explained, simply because they were rivals, but because they also had some mutual understanding, and would keep one another informed and at times help one another.[65]

Two major benefices, far more important than the one in dispute with the Este, had already come the cardinal's way in these final years of Sixtus's pontificate. One, which he was given in February 1483, was the bishopric of Ostia, the most important bishopric of the region around Rome because of the fortress there guarding the mouth of the Tiber. This became one of his favourite residences, and he would make major alterations to the fortress and commission the enlargement and decoration of the episcopal church. He loved to relax at Ostia, fishing and hunting. It also became a refuge, and somewhere he could brood when out of sorts. The other major benefice was the bishopric of Bologna, which was given to him, together with the important legation of Bologna, in October 1483. He did not spend much time at Bologna as a cardinal, but this, the most important city in the Papal States after Rome, was a focus of the most decisive campaigns of his pontificate. His interests as bishop, even more than his experience as legate, shaped his attitude to the real rulers of the city, the Bentivoglio family and their allies, and embroiled him in a number of disputes with the Este of Ferrara – that in which Riario had become involved was the first. As pope, he would drive the Bentivoglio from Bologna and do his best to drive the Este from Ferrara. His relations with these families as a cardinal were not the direct cause of his hostility to them as pope, but undoubtedly contributed to it.

Ostia fell to Vincula's lot when it was vacated by the death of a senior cardinal, Guillaume d'Estouteville. He had been the *camerlengo*, the head of the Apostolic Chamber, the main accounting office of the Church and the body responsible for the administration of the Papal States. His successor in this role was to be the youngest cardinal, Raffaele Riario. Possession of the office would be enough in itself to make him a major figure in the College, even after Sixtus's death. Appointment to it was for life, or until the holder became pope. Possibly for this reason, there was no report of Vincula trying to get it for himself; he already held such an office, that of Grand Penitentiary. His was less powerful, and, indeed, his position as Penitentiary was scarcely ever alluded to by diplomats,[66] but it may have prevented him from aspiring to be *camerlengo*. Cardinal Riario's acquisition of such a plum did not prevent Girolamo from trying to get the bishopric and legation of Bologna for him as well, suggesting the archbishopric of Pisa as a consolation prize for Vincula. Although that attempt failed, he was successful in pushing Cardinal Riario into greater prominence at the papal court. When Girolamo left Rome in the early summer of 1483 for the campaign around Ferrara, he made his nephew responsible for the conduct of business in his absence, and it was to him that Sixtus duly referred ambassadors.

In public at least, Vincula did not protest about this. Perhaps in itself this is an indication of increasing political maturity. He no longer indulged in extravagant public sulking when things did not go his way, and gave his enemies less opportunity to ridicule him and laugh at his discomfiture. In fact, he was quietly strengthening his own position in the College, building up the number of his friends. Jorge da Costa was now a recognized friend. Gianbattista Cibò had been a protégé before and after he became a cardinal. Gabriele Rangone acknowledged him as the sponsor of his own promotion. Paolo da Campofregoso, the

Archbishop of Genoa whom Vincula had protected and sheltered in his palace, had been made a cardinal in 1480. Balue still saw him as his liberator and a friend of France. Two of the Roman baronial cardinals, Savelli and Colonna, had become his allies. Between Vincula and the other two della Rovere cardinals there was no hint of enmity; perhaps they too could be counted as friends, though neither was a strong enough personality to be a really useful ally. This could not be said of Cardinal Borgia, the vice-chancellor, who was friendly enough and could be an ally if his interests ran the same way. By the end of his uncle's pontificate, Giuliano della Rovere was no longer, as he had seemed at times in the 1470s, an isolated figure of fun.

2

·

The Power Beside the Throne

If Giuliano della Rovere could look forward to a long career as a pivotal figure in the College of Cardinals after his uncle's death, and could indeed always see a prospect of becoming pope himself one day, Girolamo Riario knew all too well that, once Sixtus was gone, his own days of power were numbered. The turmoil that he created during what proved to be the last months of Sixtus's pontificate in 1484 arose out of the acts of a man desperate to eliminate his potential enemies while he still had the means to do so. The foes that he was trying to rid himself of were the Colonna, the baronial clan that had for centuries vied with the Orsini for predominance in and around Rome. The most lasting result of Girolamo's assault on the Colonna was to strengthen an association between them and Vincula that persisted in some form for the rest of his life.

The Colonna di Paliano and di Marino, the main branches of the family and the leaders of the Colonna party, had been in eclipse for much of the 1470s, not least because the death of Antonio Colonna in 1471 had removed the last senior male member of that line. Not until the end of the decade did the younger generation grow to maturity. By the early 1480s Prospero Colonna and his cousin Fabrizio had embarked on their careers as *condottieri*, which would lead to them becoming two of the foremost commanders in Italy. Prospero's brother Giovanni became a cardinal in May 1480, and Fabrizio's brother Lorenzo Oddone was an apostolic protonotary. At this point, Oddone seems to have been the dominant figure in the family; like other apostolic protonotaries, such as Obietto Fieschi, he often behaved more like a soldier than a cleric.

Vincula became related to the Colonna through his brother Giovanni's marriage to Giovanna da Montefeltro, as Fabrizio Colonna was betrothed to Giovanna's sister Agnese, whom he married in 1488. Among the leading Roman families who were adherents of the Colonna, Vincula was said to be related to the Margani and Porcari,[1] and he was friendly with the Savelli, the other major Roman baronial family of the faction. The promotion of Giovanni Colonna and Gianbattista Savelli to the College of Cardinals in May 1480 added to his growing band of allies there.

Girolamo Riario's increasingly close association with the Orsini, an association encouraged by Sixtus, had led to the Colonna becoming alienated from the pope. When Sixtus was at war with Ferrante of Naples in 1482, they accepted *condotte* from Ferrante. When Sixtus and Riario threatened reprisals against Cardinal Colonna and the protonotary Oddone if they did not prevail upon their brothers to renounce these *condotte*, Vincula became involved in the efforts being made to reconcile the Colonna to the pope. But distrust on both sides ran too deep for any reconciliation to be possible. In June 1482 Sixtus arrested Cardinals Savelli and Colonna; Savelli was lodged in Vincula's apartments at the Vatican before they were both transferred to the Castel Sant' Angelo. The Colonna put their estates and strongholds south of Rome at the disposal of the Neapolitan troops, and the pressure these forces brought to bear on Rome did much to convince Sixtus and Riario that they would do better to desert their Venetian allies and join the league defending Ferrara against Venice, in December 1482.

One of the terms of the peace agreement between Sixtus and Ferrante was that the Neapolitan counties of Tagliacozzo and Albi, which the king had granted to the Colonna, should be returned to the Orsini, who had held them until 1480. These counties were situated over the border with the Papal States from the one area where Colonna lands met those of the Orsini. Neither family could willingly resign these lands to their rivals, and the Colonna refused to surrender them. Virginio Orsini, who stood to gain the estates, got Girolamo Riario to insist that the question of their return stayed high on the diplomatic agenda.

By the time Cardinals Colonna and Savelli were released, in November 1483, the question of Tagliacozzo and Albi was becoming a major diplomatic problem. Riario's exasperation at the refusal of the Colonna to surrender the counties was given an edge of desperation by his fear that unless Virginio Orsini was satisfied, he would go over to the Venetians, taking the other Orsini *condottieri* with him. In his more hysterical moments, Riario said that he feared for his life after Sixtus's death, if he had neither the Colonna nor the Orsini to support him.[2]

By mid-March 1484 the Colonna were gathering men together at their castles – for self-defence, they said. Riario claimed that they were threatening to burn his house down around him. Another attempt at a negotiated agreement, by which Vincula would have been one of those cardinals to take custody of the cash and lands involved in the proposed settlement, failed in April. The following month the situation took a more dangerous turn; there were raids in the Campagna, while in Rome the factions took up arms. Oddone Colonna barricaded himself in Cardinal Colonna's house, and the Orsini too began to collect arms and men in their area of the city. When Oddone agreed to go to the papal palace, his own men forced him back. At last, on 30 May, a full-scale assault on Cardinal Colonna's palace was launched by the papal guard, led by Girolamo Riario, and by Orsini troops. The palace was taken and sacked, and Oddone arrested.

Riario wanted to hang him then and there, but he was stopped by Virginio Orsini, who also protected Oddone when Riario tried to knife him on the way to the Vatican. But Virginio could not protect Oddone from insult by Sixtus, nor from harsh imprisonment and torture in the Castel Sant' Angelo. Meanwhile, other houses of the Colonna party were sacked and some burned. Vincula gave refuge in his palace to many of their supporters, but neither he nor the other cardinals who tried to pacify Sixtus and Riario could stop them now. Vincula's abbey of Grottaferrata was used as a base by the papal troops sent to take the Colonna lands, although he did not approve of what was happening. He had a furious row with Riario before Sixtus, when Riario reproached him for harbouring 'rebels' against the pope in his house. The cardinal replied that they were not rebels but very faithful to the Church, yet Riario wanted to drive them out of Rome and bring the Church to destruction – he was the one who would bring the pope and all the cardinals to ruin. Riario retorted he'd like to drive Giuliano out of Rome, he'd like to sack and burn his palace, as he had that of Cardinal Colonna.[3]

Now Sixtus and Riario would not hear of any compromise. Riario was set on taking all the Colonna lands for himself, and Sixtus was set on destroying the family. Barely able to stand after the tortures he had suffered, Oddone was executed on 30 June.

The situation of the Colonna was becoming desperate, but still they knew that the pope was mortal and that, when he died, Riario would fall from power, and they would be able to recover their lands.

The pope's death came sooner than expected, on 12 August 1484. When the news reached the papal camp at Paliano, preparations began immediately to raise the siege. The College of Cardinals ordered Riario to bring the troops nearer to Rome, which he did. Within a few days, the Colonna had recovered all their lost lands and fortresses.

Confident in his command of the papal troops, in the possession of the Castel Sant' Angelo garrisoned by his men, in the backing of the Orsini family and their faction, and in the support of some cardinals, including, it was said, the vice-chancellor, Borgia, Riario began intriguing for the election of a pope to his liking. With the pope dead, however, he did not have as many friends as he thought he had, and his position was not as strong as it looked. Giuliano della Rovere's position, on the other hand, was now a very strong one. He was a natural focus for those who wanted to see an end to Riario's power. With this group, he was able, like a wrestler, to use Riario's own strengths to bring him down. Declaring that they felt unsafe while the papal palace and fortress were in the hands of Riario and his supporters, Vincula and three other cardinals, Savelli, Colonna and Cibò, refused to attend the obsequies for Sixtus (which would last for nine days) and said they would not be able to come to the palace for the conclave. No papal election could be held without them, without the risk of a schism, or, at the least, accusations that the election would be invalid.

Nor were these four the only cardinals to feel insecure. All the cardinals' palaces were fortified and guarded day and night. The Roman factions were in arms, and were reinforced by Orsini and Colonna partisans from outside the city. By 18 August, it was estimated, the Colonna, Savelli and Vincula had about 3,000 armed men at their disposal; Fabrizio Colonna was staying with Vincula at Santi Apostoli.

The violence and robbery in the streets did not turn into full-scale faction-fighting, however. The Colonna had brought their supporters into Rome primarily as insurance, for protection; the Orsini were not prepared to use their troops to support Riario by force; neither faction contemplated using violence to try to influence the outcome of the papal election. On 22 August the

Orsini and Colonna agreed to establish a truce until one month after the election of the new pope and to send their troops out of the city.

It was also agreed that Riario, who, on the orders of the College, had been staying at Isola, an Orsini estate north of Rome, should leave for his lands in the Romagna. The next day, Vincula, with Cardinals Savelli and Cibò, attended the service for Sixtus's obsequies. On their way to the Vatican they avoided passing the Castel Sant' Angelo, but took the direct route past the fortress on their return. Riario's wife, Caterina Sforza, was still in it, however, and 150 of Riario's troops were reported to have joined her there. None of the 'Colonna' cardinals, including Vincula, attended the last day of the ceremonies for Sixtus. The College showed its united determination to resist the threat from the Riario by sending a deputation of eight of its number to the Castel Sant' Angelo, which forced Caterina and all Riario's men to leave. At last, the cardinals could devote themselves to the business of electing a new pope.

After the drama and tension of the previous weeks, the conclave that resulted in the election of Cardinal Cibò, who took the title Innocent VIII, proceeded fairly smoothly. So smoothly, in fact, that little information about the play of forces in it seems to have leaked out. The two fullest accounts of what happened in the conclave are, unfortunately, very different, although both allot a crucial role to Vincula. One is to be found in the diaries of Stefano Infessura, an official of the Roman municipal administration, the other is a report by the Florentine ambassador, Guidantonio Vespucci.

Much gossip and rumour found its way into Infessura's diary, which consequently needs to be used with caution. Still, his circumstantial account does have a ring of truth. As the twenty-five cardinals were holding the first ballot or 'scrutiny', he wrote, Vincula approached Barbo, who had just had eleven votes in his favour, and said that if he would promise to give his palace to Cardinal d'Aragona, Ferrante's son, he could procure him three further votes, which would give him a majority. Barbo replied that not only would buying votes in this way render any election uncanonical, but his Palazzo Venezia (still today one of the largest and most imposing palaces in Rome) was stronger than Castel Sant' Angelo and would offer Ferrante a base from which to dominate the city and disrupt the entire Papal States. Thus rebuffed, Vincula took himself off to Cardinal Borgia, who hated

Barbo and needed little encouragement to agree to the proposal that he should join with Vincula in electing a pope of their choice. When night fell, and the cardinals retired to sleep, they visited them one by one in their cells, making generous promises in return for an undertaking to vote for Cibò. Several of the senior cardinals were left undisturbed; while they slept, the others gathered together and elected Cibò. When the senior cardinals awoke in the morning and were told that Cibò had been chosen, they too gave their consent, because they saw there was nothing else they could do.[4]

Vespucci's report to Florence was of a much more complex process of accretion of support for Cibò. First Vincula brought about an agreement between the Colonna and the Orsini and Cardinal Riario to support him; then Ascanio Sforza, seeing which way the wind was blowing, came over to the idea. Borgia hastened to join in, reckoning that if he did not support him, the chances were that the pontificate would fall to one of his own enemies; and then d'Aragona came too. As the group approached the number needed for a majority, its members told those who still remained opposed that they had actually garnered enough votes to elect Cibò, so that the others, anxious not to be seen to oppose the new pope, all voted for him at the next scrutiny. Other reports reaching Florence contradicted this apparently knowledgeable account. One reaching Lorenzo de' Medici said that it had been Ascanio and d'Aragona who had reconciled Vincula with Cardinals Riario and Orsini. The Florentine government gave credence to a report that he had joined forces with d'Aragona and Ascanio to block Barbo's candidacy. Years later, Vincula himself would claim that he had wanted Barbo to be pope, but that the other cardinals had refused to support him.[5]

Much Church property was said to have been pledged in return for votes. Not all of the promises that Infessura and others reported were kept, however, if they were indeed made. Vincula, for one, was supposed to have been promised that Fano would be given to his brother the Prefect, but this did not happen. One rumour had it that Giovanni was to lose the office of Prefect, which was to be returned to the Colonna, from whom Sixtus had taken it, but that he would be made Captain of the Church instead. This position was, in fact, given to Giovanni, but he did not have to surrender the Prefecture. Some property and offices certainly were disposed of to cardinals as rewards for support – or payment for votes. Gianbattista Orsini was given the legation of the Marche, for example, Gianbattista Savelli that of Bologna. Some of the property and offices that were distributed were surrendered by Vincula, lending substance to the reports that he had had a leading role in winning over votes to Cibò. Savelli's prize, the legation of Bologna, had been his. His legation of Avignon was given to Cardinal Nardini, but this did not turn out to be too great a sacrifice, for Nardini died on 22 October and Vincula was given it back. Cardinal Borgia's cooperation had its price too, it seems, for the day after the election the clerks of the Apostolic Chamber recorded that Vincula had surrendered to Borgia a pension, which had been given to him by Sixtus, of 600 gold florins on an abbey.[6] Other such transactions may have gone unrecorded. Vespucci reckoned that his sacrifices had done much to make Cibò pope.[7] Cibò himself had been a comparatively poor cardinal – he had received the monthly allowance given to cardinals whose income from benefices fell below a certain level – and had little to offer of his own as inducement for support. His house went to d'Aragona, his treasure (what there was of it) to Colonna.

There is no way to reconcile all these conflicting versions in detail, and no sure ground for choosing one version rather than another. Normally, reports by ambassadors could be considered as more authoritative than a source such as Infessura, but here they contradict one another. Infessura writes as though he has received a detailed account from someone on the inside, but it is perhaps significant that he starts from the position that there were two factions in the conclave, led by Vincula and Borgia. It was reported before the conclave that there were such factions, but other accounts generally say that they were of no significance during it. And why did Borgia get so little reward if he was one of the two major figures helping Cibò to the pontificate? If he had done so much for so little, he was not the man to let such ingratitude go unremarked and unresented. All that can be said with any degree of confidence is that Barbo received the majority of votes in the first scrutiny but that he was not acceptable to some of the leading cardinals, probably because he was a Venetian; that sufficient support then rallied behind Cibò to make him pope; and that Giuliano della Rovere had an important, perhaps the crucial, role in winning over vital votes. And it was immediately obvious that Giuliano was to be the single most influential figure in the new court – 'for all practical purposes pope', or even 'more than pope'.[8]

It should not be assumed, however, that Innocent was completely under his thumb. Even within the first year of the pontificate, he showed in his handling of an outbreak of fighting between the Colonna and Orsini that he could take a different line from Vincula. After two years, it became evident that the cardinal no longer dominated the pope, though relations between them, after some initial coolness, remained cordial enough to the end of the pontificate. There was no successor to the position that he had enjoyed, from among the cardinals or from the pope's own family. Sixtus, usually reputed a much stronger pope than Innocent, had never managed to free himself from the tutelage of the Riario.

Cardinal Cibò had not been a prominent figure in Sixtine Rome. He had been brought up in Naples, where his father was a city official, but he was very much a Genoese. He was Bishop of Savona before being transferred to the Neapolitan see of Molfetta in 1472. When elevated to the College, in 1473, he had been datary (in charge of the pope's personal finances), and was well thought of in the court and by the pope. At that time he was said to be close to Vincula (who was later reputed to have been behind his promotion to cardinal), and he remained his friend and associate throughout Sixtus's pontificate. When Vincula left Rome in a sulk in January 1477, it was Cibò whom Sixtus sent to coax him back. When he was indignant at being kept in the dark about the pope's negotiations with Venice concerning Ferrara in March 1482, and decided to stay away from the Vatican, it was Cibò who persuaded him to change his mind. These are indications that Cibò's relationship with him when they were both cardinals may have been that of older friend and counsellor, rather than protégé. In the later years of the pontificate, Cibò was sent on a couple of legations, to Germany and Hungary in 1480, and to Siena in 1483, and handled them creditably. Although he was not one of the leading figures in the College, he was considered 'papabile'. There was no great surprise or indignation when he was mentioned as a candidate, nor when he was elected.

At the time of his elevation to the papacy he was in his early fifties. A good-humoured, easy-going, amiable man, not much of a scholar or artistic patron, but a friend of scholars, he was known to have at least one son, Franceschetto, and had married daughters in Rome. He was fond of his family, and many of them came to Rome. Some were given offices and other pickings, but they never had anything like as high a profile in the papal court as the family of Sixtus had had, or the family of Innocent's successor,

Alexander VI, was to have. Innocent made a good impression in the opening months of his pontificate. The Romans liked him, and the diplomats thought him peaceable, not likely to visit upon Italy the trials that had sprung from Sixtus's ambitions.

There is no indication that Vincula tried to monopolize the pope's favour. Among the cardinals, Ascanio Sforza was thought to be a favourite, but his influence in Rome derived rather from his position as a leading member of the ruling family of Milan and his keen interest in politics. Barbo was frequently consulted, particularly as Innocent began to seek an alliance with Venice; da Costa was another valued advisor. The laymen who had influence at court, apart from members of the pope's own family, were largely Genoese, and among the most prominent were associates of Vincula. Domenico Doria was made captain of the papal guard, a post he held throughout the pontificate, and Obietto Fieschi, who first had to be released from a Milanese prison, was also specially invited to Rome. The Prefect made great efforts to obtain a share of papal bounty for his brother-in-law, Agostino Campofregoso, who was given a papal *condotta* in March 1485. The pope's son Franceschetto, who was aged about thirty, came to Rome in October, but was kept out of the limelight; it was even said that the pope did not want him to stay in the Papal States. Of mediocre intelligence and limited personal charm, with no political or military experience, Franceschetto identified Cardinal ad Vincula as the main obstacle to his ambitions, complaining 'I don't count as much as I would like to, because of Cardinal San Pietro ad Vincula.'[9]

Although there were many comments on the extent of Vincula's power during the first year of Innocent's pontificate, and although, as more than one observer noted, he had far more influence over Innocent than he had had over Sixtus,[10] describing the effects of his influence on papal policy is quite difficult. Innocent had a mind of his own, and it would be wrong to attribute all his actions and utterances to the promptings of San Pietro ad Vincula. References to conversations of the cardinal with ambassadors were surprisingly infrequent. Though this is partly due to the patterns of survival of the diplomatic archives, Innocent spoke for himself far more than Sixtus had been wont to do in his later years. In any case, the enormous debts that Sixtus had left for his successor to deal with – Innocent himself reckoned they might amount to two years' revenue – left the pope and Vincula little scope for taking any initiative for the first year or so.

Traces of loans that Vincula made to help tide the pope over can be found in the accounts of the Apostolic Chamber.[11]

Revisions of the papal *condotte* that were soon under way were partly due to the need for economy, but also to the need to get rid of some of Girolamo Riario's closest associates and replace them with men whom the pope and Vincula felt better able to trust. Riario had made an attempt to force the new pope to pay him the considerable sum of money – 45,000 ducats, he had claimed in August – that he said he was owed by the Apostolic Chamber, before he would surrender the fortresses of Todi and Spoleto, which were held by his men; but he had been forced to yield them after about a month. He had also asked Innocent for the continuation of his appointment as captain of the papal troops, for lands in the Marche, and for a pension. These demands, Vincula said, would have been exorbitant ('disonesto') even in Sixtus's day;[12] they were all refused. Those of Riario's men who showed their faces in Rome were shunned in the streets. He and his chief lieutenant lost their papal *condotte*, and he was fortunate to retain the vicariates of Forlì and Imola. It was reported that Vincula and Innocent wanted him to lose even these,[13] but no direct attempt was made to bring this about. He was already making himself so unpopular with his subjects that it had been predicted there would be a revolt against him. When the revolt came, in April 1488, and Riario was assassinated, there was little surprise, and no one mourned his passing.

Shortage of money had been the ostensible reason for the reductions in papal *condotte*, but new *condottieri* had been recruited immediately. Here Vincula can be seen at work, for the negotiations of the new contracts were clearly in his hands. Technically, Cardinal Riario, as Chamberlain, should have been the one responsible for making the contracts, and there may be a hint of disapproval among the clerks at their chief being pushed aside, in the phrasing of some of their records of the contracts negotiated by Vincula. Thus they noted that the *condotta* with Niccolò Caetani da Sermoneta was concluded and signed on behalf of the pope by him, on Innocent's express verbal instructions – 'so he says'.[14] On the same day, he also made contracts with Prospero Colonna and Giacomo Conti, and in April 1485 he concluded one with Giovanni Bentivoglio of Bologna. He negotiated others too, but not all. He is not mentioned in the note of Agostino da Campofregoso's contract in March, nor in that for Vicino Orsini in December 1485: as matters stood between him and the Orsini at that moment, it was probably easier for someone else to handle the negotiations that brought Vicino into papal service when the rest of his family were fighting against the pope.[15] The last *condotte* that he is recorded as negotiating were agreed in February 1486. Soon after, Vincula left Rome; and when he returned, his position at court had changed. At first, Niccolò Cibò, the Archbishop of Cosenza, handled most of the *condotte*, but gradually Cardinal Riario asserted his rights, and in the later years of Innocent's pontificate it was generally he who dealt with them.[16]

One feature of the first year of Innocent's pontificate that probably can be attributed to Vincula's influence, and was so at the time, was the suspicion the Orsini displayed towards the new regime. At the time of his election, Innocent was reported to be a Guelf, and therefore friendly to the Orsini. Vincula, however, was regarded as their enemy. When a promise to Paolo Orsini that he would be made captain of the papal guard was not fulfilled, it was put down to his intervention. When the Orsini stayed away from Rome, it was, a Roman diarist said, because he was their 'deadly enemy'.[17] Efforts were made to tempt Virginio Orsini to Rome, with Obietto Fieschi writing to assure him that all would be well and that Obietto and Innocent himself would effect a reconciliation between Virginio and Vincula.[18] But Virginio did not heed these assurances, and, in any case, did not want to accept any renewal of his contract that entailed being under the command of the Prefect. By contrast, the Colonna, impoverished though they were by the devastation that their lands had suffered from Riario's attack, were resurgent; but there was some disquiet that, under Vincula's protection, they were abusing their good fortune, harbouring thieves and compensating for lost income by robbing travellers. In March 1485, while Innocent was suffering a bout of illness so severe that it gave rise to reports of his death, the Orsini seized several bridges across the Tiber. Vincula took the precaution of removing some of his valuables to the Castel Sant' Angelo. Innocent soon recovered, and the Orsini abandoned the bridges, but the threat of trouble between the baronial clans persisted.

The threat was realized in June, when Prospero Colonna kidnapped Girolamo d'Estouteville. He was the son of Cardinal d'Estouteville and brother-in-law of Virginio Orsini, whose sister Ippolita he had married in 1483, the year of his father's death. Two years previously, Cardinal d'Estouteville had given three territories to the south of Rome, Civita Lavinia, Nemi and Genzano, which he had bought from Oddone Colonna, to

Girolamo and his brother Agostino. The Colonna wanted them back, particularly Civita Lavinia, which was an important stronghold. Having kidnapped Girolamo, Prospero made an unsuccessful attempt on Civita Lavinia and then took Nemi, where Girolamo's wife and son were captured, and Genzano. The Colonna laid siege to Civita Lavinia, but their camp was broken up by the Orsini at the end of June. Both sides rallied their forces, summoned their allies from the Guelf and Ghibelline factions, and began raiding each other's lands and livestock. Innocent had attempted to intervene and impose a judicial settlement, but no one, least of all the Orsini, believed that the matter would receive an impartial hearing while the Colonna had such a powerful friend at Innocent's side. There were reports that Innocent was being urged to attack the Orsini and that only his good nature and reluctance to spend any money prevented him from doing so.[19] The Prefect was said to have lent the Colonna some troops, and Prospero himself held a papal *condotta* concluded with him by Vincula, as did Niccolò Caetani da Sermoneta, who took a prominent part in the fighting on the side of the Colonna. Cardinals Colonna and Savelli were frequently in the Vatican, holding discussions with the pope and Vincula, and Vincula was wholly on their side.[20]

But the Colonna presumed too far. On the night of 20 July they took several hundred horse and foot through Rome itself in order to reach the Orsini estates on the north bank of the Tiber. Innocent was furious. He sent Giovanni Conti to Ostia to prevent the Colonna from bringing their plunder back that way, and ordered them to surrender it to the captain of the guard. He sent supplies to Paolo Orsini and offered to let him bring his troops to Rome. The Colonna themselves were summoned to the palace, and when they went (going first to see Vincula to consult him), they were held for a few days to signal Innocent's displeasure at what had occurred. Girolamo d'Estouteville was released, and Innocent enforced a truce. According to the Florentine ambassador, Vincula showed indignation at Innocent's actions; according to the Mantuan ambassador, his indignation, like that of Innocent, was directed at the Colonna.[21] Since there is no report of his taking umbrage and withdrawing to his own palace, and since he was present, without protest, at the conclusion of *condotte* for Virginio, Giulio and Paolo Orsini on 30 July and also welcomed Virginio on a visit to Rome in early September, it looks as though he did approve of Innocent's vigorous response to the affront by the Colonna to the papal authority.

The most notorious instance of Vincula's influence over Innocent is the papal intervention in the Neapolitan Barons' War in 1485, when Innocent backed the barons who were rebelling against King Ferrante. At the time, it was generally believed that he was responsible for the pope's championing of the barons' cause, and there is no evidence to refute that belief. The argument that, at least in part, Innocent was spurred into action by notions of feudal rights of the papacy over Naples,[22] squares less well with what he said, and with what happened, than an interpretation of the events that portrays Innocent as dragged in the wake of Vincula, who was himself impelled by personal motives.

The simplest explanation that has been offered for Vincula's support of the barons is that he hated Ferrante – but the strongest evidence for such personal dislike is the very entry of the papacy into the Barons' War. For much of Sixtus's pontificate, he had been regarded as one of the king's men in the curia, though less so in later years, as he had developed contacts and interests in Liguria and across the Alps, some of them with enemies of the Aragonese dynasty. During the war, Vincula sought to utilize Genoese antagonism to the Aragonese and the Duke of Lorraine's claims to the throne of Naples. But he did not provoke Innocent to war with Ferrante in order to make the Duke of Lorraine King of Naples.

The real key to understanding his zeal in the cause of the Neapolitan barons is his protection of the interests of his brother Giovanni. At the core of the group of rebel barons were Antonello da Sanseverino, Prince of Salerno, and his relatives. These included Giovanni della Rovere, who was Antonello's brother-in-law, for Antonello was married to a daughter of Federico da Montefeltro. Other husbands, or promised husbands, of the Montefeltro sisters were involved too – Fabrizio Colonna and Agostino da Campofregoso (who was killed during the war). Roberto da Sanseverino, the leading (if perhaps over-rated) *condottiere* of the day, though he bore the same name as Antonello, was the son of an illegitimate son of the prolific Sanseverino family, and was not in fact very closely related to him. The Prince of Salerno was one of the most powerful barons in the kingdom, and the one who stood to lose the most if Ferrante's son, Alfonso, Duke of Calabria, had his way. Calabria had made clear his contempt for the barons and his desire to humble them. One of his proposals was that all lands within a thirty-mile radius of the city of Naples should be brought directly under the crown, and much of Salerno's land lay in that area. This was but one of the reasons why the barons had become increasingly restive under the rule of Ferrante, and regarded the prospect of Alfonso's succession to his father with still less favour, though the story of Ferrante's dealings with his barons is very complicated and by no means clear. What was clear, was that if Salerno lost most of his estates, and with that much of his power and status, Giovanni della Rovere lost his most powerful relative in the kingdom of Naples – not a prospect that Vincula, in his role as guardian of the future of his family, could take lightly, for the della Rovere needed all the classy relatives they could get, if they were to become firmly established as a signorial dynasty.

Reports of contacts between Vincula and the barons in the months before the rebellion was launched, and the barons' own accounts of the preliminaries to the war, show that he encouraged them to appeal to Innocent for help, and persuaded Innocent to come to their aid. As late as September, Salerno was saying that Innocent did not want to support the barons, but that Vincula was confident he could bring him round.[23] Innocent's constant refrain when discussing the situation with the ambassadors who were trying to defuse the growing tension between pope and king in the summer of 1485 was the need to ensure the barons' security. Rarely did he speak in terms of the papacy's feudal rights over the kingdom – by his account the barons appealed to him as pope, as the universal father, as the final court of appeal for those suffering injustice, not as the overlord of the king. Quite possibly, if Vincula had not been there, the barons would still have appealed to Innocent and he would have taken their part, but it is unlikely that he would have championed their cause to the extent of going to war for them. This was felt to be a crazy thing to do, and once again caustic comments were made about Vincula's lack of political sense.[24]

Unfortunately for Vincula and the Sanseverino, once fighting began events did not turn out as they had planned. One crucial reason for this was that the Orsini fought for Ferrante. The apparent reconciliation between Vincula, Innocent and the Orsini had not gone far enough for the Orsini to choose the pope when they had to choose between him and the king. Like the Colonna lands in 1482, the Orsini estates provided a chain of bases in papal territory for the Neapolitan forces, providing shelter, strongholds and supplies. Instead of the papal troops being able to reinforce the barons in the kingdom, most of them were pinned down in papal territory, facing the Neapolitan forces surrounding

Rome and then troops sent by Ferrante's allies, Florence and Milan, which gathered to the north of the Papal States at Pitigliano, a territory belonging to Niccolò Orsini.

One of the first proofs that Innocent intended to match his words on behalf of the barons with deeds was the despatch of the Prefect to his Neapolitan estates centred on Sora with fourteen squadrons, in September. Some troops had already been sent there at the end of August, but for the Prefect himself, the Captain of the Church, to go there, was a different matter. Agents of the Prince of Salerno and his cousin Girolamo da Sanseverino, Prince of Bisignano, had been lodging with him and with Vincula in Rome for some weeks. Soon after he left Rome, Vincula was also away for several days, inspecting fortresses and, it was reported, holding secret talks with Salerno, though some did not believe this. In early October the barons were already complaining that they were not getting the help from the papacy they had been promised, but when the Orsini agreed *condotte* with Milan and Florence at the end of the month, the prospects of substantial reinforcements being sent from Rome to the kingdom receded further. By the time Roberto da Sanseverino arrived on 10 November to take command of the papal troops, it was clear that his first task would have to be the defence of Rome.

Once in Rome, Roberto joined Vincula in directing the war. Although there was a commission of four cardinals, including Vincula, nominally responsible for advising Innocent, its other members, Balue, Barbo and da Costa, were not admitted to all discussions nor given all the relevant information. The briefs that Innocent wrote in reply to reports or enquiries about the conduct of the war were usually limited to encouragement and exhortation and the comment that San Pietro ad Vincula would be replying in greater detail.[25] In and around Rome both sides played for time, with Virginio Orsini pretending to negotiate an agreement that the Orsini estates would not be employed in fighting, as he waited for the Duke of Calabria to arrive. Innocent and Vincula busied themselves with raising money as they waited for Roberto's troops, who were making their way to Rome.

The waiting game was over when news of Calabria's arrival at Virginio's territory of Vicovaro, to the north of Rome beyond Tivoli, was brought to the city on 29 November. On hearing that Calabria was near, Virginio had already written to the Conservators of Rome, saying Innocent had not believed his offers not to involve his estates in the war, and that now he had no choice but to put his lands at the disposal of his employers. Fearing for their livestock and lands outside Rome, and for the loss of income that disruption of the normal business of the papal court would bring, the Romans decided on 30 November to go to Innocent and ask him to make peace. Innocent was nervous and sent a placatory message to Bracciano, asking Virginio not to commit his estates, but Vincula's response was to banish any prospect of compromise.

Innocent had ordered soldiers to be placed in Montegiordano, the Orsini area of Rome, to prevent Orsini troops from taking up position there. Situated inside a ring of high-walled houses with few openings from the outside world into the warren of narrow streets within, on some old maps of Rome the area has the aspect of a small fortified town within the city, and this was a sensible precaution. On 30 November, Vincula, Roberto da Sanseverino, the captain of the papal guard, and Cardinals Balue, Colonna and Savelli had accordingly led their troops within the walls. But many of those troops were Colonna partisans, who began to sack and burn the houses of the Orsini and their supporters, while the cardinals stood aside and watched from the Ponte Sant' Angelo. There can be no doubt of Vincula's responsibility for this. When Innocent heard of the fires, he ordered them to be extinguished, but nothing now could extinguish the fury of Virginio Orsini. Leaflets were found scattered in Rome in which Virginio exhorted the Romans to rebel against Innocent, who, he claimed, was no true pope. Vincula he accused of sodomy, vowing that if God gave him victory, he would carry the cardinal's head through Rome on the point of a lance.[26] That the Colonna had been used in the assault on Montegiordano added insult to injury, and the partisan edge given to the war around Rome was sharpened by arrests of Orsini supporters and the appointment of Cardinals Colonna and Savelli to supervise the guarding of the walls and gates of Rome. Vincula joined them in their armed patrols.

In late December, Roberto's troops at last reached Rome. Within days of their arrival, on 28 December, he brought them into action, taking a vital bridge over the Tiber, the Ponte Lamentano, which the Orsini had been holding. A week later, he led them over the bridge to attack Lamentana, Paolo Orsini's main stronghold, took the town, and then, on 11 January, the fortress. On that day, Cardinal Orsini came to see him and made terms on behalf of his branch of the family, the Orsini da Monterotondo. After being received by Innocent in Rome, Cardinal Orsini left with Roberto to put the fortresses of

Monterotondo and of his strategically important abbey of Farfa into the custody of the papal troops. Calabria, fearing that he would be cut off from the kingdom of Naples, panicked, abandoned his men to their fate, and fled north, to Pitigliano. The only defence for his action was the suspicion that Virginio and Paolo Orsini would follow the cardinal's example, but, greatly to the relief of the league, they held firm. Paolo collected together Calabria's troops and took them to safety on Virginio's lands. The indecision of the commanders of the Florentine and Milanese troops assembling at Pitigliano was aggravated by Calabria's exaggeration of the size of Roberto's army, as he tried to justify his shameful retreat, and the Orsini who had remained loyal to the league feared that they would be unable to resist the papal troops unless reinforcements arrived soon. But Roberto failed to press home his attack on the Orsini while they were vulnerable.

By the middle of March, Innocent was losing heart. A letter he wrote to Venice saying that he had no money, that Roberto had contacts with the league and was not doing all he could against the Orsini, and that unless he received help from Venice he would be forced to make peace, fell into Virginio's hands.[27] Such reports about the state of affairs in Rome made some say, when they heard that Vincula had left for Ostia on 23 March, that he too was discouraged and feared he would be attacked. Others said that he was retreating to Ostia just as he often did when things were not going his way and he was out of humour. Others guessed, correctly, that he was going to Genoa.

At first sight, with Innocent's resolve faltering, it seems odd that Vincula should have left him to be a prey to his own doubts and to the persuasions of those who wanted an end to the war. Running away from difficulties was not characteristic of Giuliano della Rovere, however. Impetuosity, a desire for action, dislike of being cooped up in Rome for long periods, were. The notion of changing the whole pattern of the war by going to Genoa to urge on the Duke of Lorraine to come to claim the throne of Naples, would be much more appealing than sitting in Rome with little influence on the military action. Clearly, Innocent had been persuaded that Vincula's journey to Genoa could be decisive. If he could see that troops were raised and a fleet prepared, and if the fleet could impede supplies reaching Naples, Innocent wrote to him a week after his departure, victory would be certain.[28] On what Vincula had to report, wrote the Mantuan ambassador, would hang the choice for peace or war.

Vincula got down to work quickly when he reached Genoa, and soon there was good news to encourage Innocent. By 18 April it was said that he had arranged a loan of 100,000 Genoese pounds and secured some ships. Another report said he had raised 20,000 ducats without interest, and could raise as much as he wanted with security and at interest. By the end of May a large cash sum (variously reported as 25,000 or 35,000 ducats) was nearing Rome. He also raised some infantry,[29] probably for the fleet. His Genoese contacts, and, in particular, the fact that the Doge of Genoa was his friend Cardinal Campofregoso, were yielding dividends. Negotiations had already been under way with the Duke of Lorraine before he had left Rome, and he lost no time once he reached Genoa in sending a courier to the duke. By late April an envoy of Lorraine was with him in Genoa, and Lorraine himself was expected there soon. A month later, Vincula reported that the negotiations were going well. Lorraine himself wrote to many people saying that he was coming. Envoys from Lorraine and France reached Rome on 30 May and there were reports his troops were mustering.

Much had been accomplished, and much more promised, and Innocent wrote in mid-May to thank the Genoese and to praise the cardinal's diligence. But his letter to Vincula, written on 11 May, had a ring of anxiety too. There had been much talk of Lorraine's coming, he wrote, but nothing had actually happened yet. Money and ships were urgently required.[30] By the time Lorraine's envoy reached Rome, Roberto da Sanseverino was talking of peace, saying that it would be difficult for Innocent to find money to carry on the war, and that he could have peace if he wished. The Bishop of Alessandria, Gianantonio di Sangiorgio, a confidant of the pope, had already been trying to get peace talks started at the beginning of May, and there were negotiations between the commanders of the armies. Innocent wrote to the Prefect, who had got wind of these latter talks, that he had rejected the proposed terms as dishonourable. He was going on with the war, and he urged the Prefect and the barons to do so too. But on the very day he wrote to the Prefect, 11 June, the Ferrarese ambassador in Naples was being told that the negotiations begun by Sangiorgio had been continued, at first by Cardinal Michiel, then by Cardinal Ascanio Sforza.[31] Infessura had picked up gossip about a stormy consistory, in the first week of June, when some cardinals, including Piccolomini, Savelli and Borgia, had called on Innocent to make peace, while Balue opposed them, saying all France was backing Lorraine. Tempers had run high, with Borgia accusing Balue of being drunk and Balue calling Borgia the son of a whore.[32] At a more decorous consistory a few days later, the appointment of Cardinal Michiel to be legate to the papal camp was announced. If the report from Naples was correct, he had already been trying to pave the way to peace; as legate he would have a good opportunity to continue his efforts. He did, indeed, have a prominent part in the negotiations that resulted in the conclusion of a peace on 11 August. Innocent may not have been as keen as some of the cardinals on making peace – in early July an agent of Ascanio complained the pope was playing for time. But money was short, and in Naples the resistance of the barons was faltering. When the Genoese ships Vincula had raised arrived in July, all that Innocent could ask them to do was to go to Salerno to try to pick up the prince. The Duke of Lorraine was still preparing to come south, but it was now too late. Peace was concluded. Innocent ordered Vincula to return home and the Prefect to withdraw to the papal territory of Benevento, and prepared to dismiss Roberto da Sanseverino.

Barely two days after the peace had been signed in Rome, Ferrante arrested some of the leading barons. Those who remained at liberty, at least for the moment, and their allies the citizens of Aquila, hoped that Vincula would be able to stimulate Innocent to take up their defence with vigour, perhaps with force. On his return to Rome in mid-September, he did try to get Innocent to repudiate the peace treaty, but to no avail. The pope was concerned about the fate of those against whom Ferrante was now taking vengeance. His protests about the king's treatment of the barons, and about his failure to pay the census in recognition of the rights the papacy claimed over the kingdom, rumbled on, threatening the peace of Italy on more than one occasion, until the final year of his pontificate. But he was not prepared to go to war with Ferrante again.

When Vincula returned to Rome, he went straight to the Vatican, where he lodged in his usual apartments. Next morning, crowds of people came to pay their respects to him. Innocent had been eagerly awaiting his return. But if outward appearances suggested that, despite the fact that the peace had been concluded without his participation, his influence and prestige were undiminished, they were deceptive. Within a month, he had retreated to Ostia, annoyed that he could not bring Innocent to renounce the peace. It was noted that Vincula had lost much ground at court, though he was still esteemed by the pope and no other cardinal had been singled out in his place. Those closest to the pope were two Cibò archbishops, Lorenzo, Archbishop of Benevento, and Niccolò, Archbishop of Cosenza, and the datary, the Genoese Antoniotto Pallavicino, but Innocent was determined to be his own master.[33] He was heard speaking critically of Vincula in public. Some thought that this was a smokescreen, that Innocent was still working closely with him, but wanted to be able to disown what he did if things went wrong.[34] Many in the Vatican took their cue from the pope, and began to voice hostility to the man whom they had once courted, now that his star was declining.

Vincula had not given up, notably in his efforts to undo the peace with Ferrante. Before he returned to Rome, Innocent planned to send him as legate to Naples. Hearing this, Ferrante sent an envoy to him, with instructions to tell him how much the king looked forward to his coming. Ferrante was sure that he would help him to recover the good graces of the pope. During Sixtus's pontificate, he had wanted to commend his affairs in Rome to the cardinal's care; he was not sure why this had not come about, but he would like it to happen now. He thanked him for calling off the Duke of Lorraine, and promised to follow his guidance in seeking reconciliation with the barons, Ferrante's dearest wish.[35] But Vincula was not sent to Naples, and was not to be won over by the king. Nor had he abandoned hope that Lorraine would come. When the Prince of Salerno sent an envoy to him, he sent him on to Lorraine. Innocent's dismissal of Lorraine's envoy in January 1487 sent him into another bout of sulking.[36] He was also displeased when the Princes of Salerno and Bisignano came to terms with Ferrante. Salerno came to Rome in January, claiming that he wanted to reconcile Vincula with the king. Assuming he really intended to do so, he was instead himself won over to fresh intransigence. Needless to say, proposals for a marriage between Innocent's son and one of Ferrante's brood of natural daughters were opposed by the cardinal.

The fact that these proposals came to nothing is not necessarily an indication of Vincula's continued influence over the pope. Innocent had not much liked the terms that Ferrante offered anyway. A surer indication that Innocent still listened to his advice was a league with Venice agreed in December 1486. Vincula was very pleased with this; one of the terms was that Venice and the pope promised protection to the Prefect. The

league was not announced until January, and Innocent may not
have wanted it to be published then: its publication was said to be
Vincula's doing, intended to keep the pope steady on the course
that he was trying to set for him.

Another sign of Innocent's continued confidence was
Vincula's appointment as legate of the Marche on 2 March 1487,
to deal with a rebellion at Osimo. The leader of the rebellion,
Boccolino di Guzzone, whose family had been prominent in
the town since the thirteenth century, was a proud, aggressive,
self-willed man. He had won some repute as a soldier, and
the patronage of the Duke of Calabria. He nursed ambitions to
become lord of Osimo, and in March 1486 signed a pact with
Calabria, agreeing to bring about a rising there against the
Church. A few days later, Boccolino answered a summons from
the priors of the city by appearing with his troops and friends;
several councillors were killed and others fled. The papal governor
of the Marche prepared to restore order, but hesitated when he
saw the scale of the rising. Osimo was well fortified and on a site
that made attack difficult. Attempts by Innocent to win over
Boccolino and his supporters by offers of pardon were unsuccessful, and in October 1486 he ordered the governor to besiege the
city. Harsh winter weather sent most of the papal troops back to
their quarters, but Boccolino was apprehensive about what would
befall in the spring. He sent envoys to Sultan Bajazet II at
Constantinople, offering to give him possession of Osimo in return
for help. The Sultan was interested in the offer and took up the
negotiations. Boccolino's nephew was captured by Ferrante's men
in early February on his way to Constantinople, and the young
man and the letters he was carrying were sent to Rome. It was
the threat of a Turkish invasion that brought about Vincula's
appointment as legate.

Over two dozen letters from him, mainly to Innocent, written
during this legation have survived, far more than for any other
stage of his career as a cardinal, and they provide the opportunity
to see how he approached the problems that faced him, including
the deterioration of his relations with the pope.[37]

His first letter, dated 16 March, simply reported that he had
reached Serravalle, and how he hoped to settle affairs at Osimo
and return to Innocent soon. By 23 March he was beginning to
realize that the task might be more difficult than he had thought.
He had sent several envoys to Boccolino, who had ostensibly
welcomed the legate's arrival, but had refused to submit, largely

because he had summoned the Turks. Now he had agreed to leave if he received compensation for his property, and an honourable *condotta*. Three days later, Vincula reported he had broken off the negotiations because he had become convinced Boccolino was only playing for time. Now he was concentrating on raising troops, but this required money, and there was none to be had from the province, so Innocent must send it. Osimo was very strong, but there were few troops inside, and he hoped it could be captured quickly, if reinforcements did not reach it. He had written to Venice asking for help. There was some progress to report on 30 March, when the small town of Montefano, which was being held for Boccolino, was taken; the fortress would surrender the next day, he said, if no help arrived. Again, he stressed the need for money.

A long letter of 3 April reveals that Vincula had been given another commission by Innocent, to settle a dispute between Ascoli and Fermo. He had summoned envoys from both towns. Those from Fermo had come provided with a full mandate, those from Ascoli had not, for which he had rebuked them. Both sides had also been rebuked for their slowness in paying their taxes. Other matters that Innocent had asked him to sort out with Fermo he thought had better be left a while, so as not to have too much business on hand at once. Montefano, he found, was more important than he had thought; he was seeing to a garrison for it. If the Recanatesi asked Innocent for it, he should put them off. As for Osimo, Boccolino was evidently optimistic about receiving outside help, but Vincula was hopeful that the citizens might rebel against him at the approach of the papal camp. More troops were needed though. The following day, he reported on another problem, the need to guard the coasts from the threat of a Turkish fleet. The people of the province could not do it alone, and he had sent some of the horsemen who had accompanied him from Rome to help them.

The source of trouble the day after was Ascoli. After their envoys had left the legate, the Ascolani had attacked Aquaviva, which was held by Fermo. Vincula immediately sent the Bishop of Cervia to order both sides to lay down their arms, and prepared to leave himself, to deal with the matter personally and prevent the disorder from spreading. But a postscript said that he did not need to go, for Fermo had driven off the attack. He had ordered the Bishop of Cervia to report on the situation.

By 10 April, Vincula was becoming a little edgy about

Innocent's lack of response to his appeals for money and reinforcements. The capture of another envoy sent by Boccolino to the Turks, Pietro Cecchino, who had been recognized at Pesaro on his return, renewed concern about a Turkish invasion. Provision must be made now to capture Osimo, before it arrived. He was doing what he could, but he did not have enough troops with him. If things went wrong, it would be no fault of his.

A week later he reported on the lack of success Giulio Cesare Varano, sent by Venice, had had in his attempts to bring Boccolino to terms. Close watch was being kept on the coast for the Turkish fleet. He needed *money* – he had not given out 4,000 ducats that Innocent had sent to the troops, in case it should be spent to no purpose before the rest of the money arrived; when that came, the attack on Osimo could begin. Innocent could be assured that he would not fail to do anything to uphold the pope's honour, the dignity of the clergy[38] and the public good. The following day, 18 April, he wrote again with greater urgency, enclosing letters from the Turks, apparently taken from Cecchino. Bajazet had accepted all Boccolino's conditions, so Boccolino would not hear of negotiations now. Delay in sending money meant delay in launching the assault on Osimo. No one could blame him if the affair turned out badly.

The next surviving letter concerning the progress of the campaign is dated over a fortnight later, 5 May. Vincula had received a brief from Innocent of 24 April ordering him to attack Osimo, and was clearly injured by the implication that he was holding back. Everything possible was being done. He knew there was danger in delay, but a strong force was needed for the assault, and he had to wait for reinforcements to arrive. Even if the people of the province offered to serve, they would not be much use; they were doing what they could but they lacked military training. It would not be easy to get Venetian troops now they had become involved in a war with the Germans. Soldiers supplied by Milan or Naples would have to be used with the utmost care, and only if absolutely necessary. It would be both safer and more honourable to use the pope's own troops, and there would be no shortage of them if only the necessary money were forthcoming. Meanwhile, he would do his best, though he warned that the preparations needed would be very expensive. He would position the men available to the best advantage to lay siege to Osimo, and then go himself to Ancona to see to its defence.

On 12 May he reported the arrival of 4,000 ducats that

Innocent had sent, but he considered it pointless to spend this, or 5,000 ducats that had come earlier, before the arrival of the reinforcements, because until the cavalry was in order, money spent on the infantry would be wasted. He was sending the Bishop of Cervia to Innocent to explain the situation fully. Would Innocent please listen to him, because this business involved the honour of the pope, the dignity of the Apostolic See, and the reputation and interests of the Holy Roman Church – all of which should be of concern to Innocent, as supreme pontiff.

Some relief for Vincula's anxieties was in sight, however, for after a few days at Ancona he felt reassured that there was no present danger from the Turks, and he left for his own abbey of Chiaravalle a few miles away. Here his brother-in-law Gianfrancesco Franciotti arrived with a brief and a message for him from the pope. Rather wearily, Vincula wrote on 16 May that he had already, in several letters and by several messengers, told Innocent his opinion, but he had spoken freely about it again to Gianfrancesco, who would report back to Innocent. The pope could then make up his own mind about what needed to be done, and Vincula would always submit to Innocent's wishes.

By that time, Innocent had already made up his mind, and had written to him on 14 May to say he was sending Giangiacomo Trivulzio, a Milanese commander. Acknowledging the receipt of the brief on 19 May, Vincula reiterated that he had been doing all that was humanly possible. He had said what he thought about using Milanese troops, but if that was what Innocent had decided, he would work with Trivulzio. The dispute between Ascoli and Fermo had flared up again; the Ascolani were being difficult and trying to put the blame on Fermo, while the Fermanesi were being obedient and cooperative. He did not think that there would be peace between them until Osimo was settled.

Fortunately, when Trivulzio arrived, he and Vincula appear to have got on well together. On 5 June, Vincula reported that the siege of Osimo had begun in earnest. Infantry were arriving every day, bombards were on their way, and he hoped, with Trivulzio's help, that the city would soon fall. Money was needed to pay the infantry. If the efforts that had been made were left to go to waste now, and the siege failed, Boccolino could disrupt the entire province.

The following day, Vincula despatched another messenger, Alberto de' Magalotti, to Innocent, to speak of the danger that the whole campaign would fail if the pope did not make the necessary provisions immediately. If all went well, Innocent would win honour and glory, but failure would shame him. Once again, Vincula stressed that he personally could not be blamed if things went wrong. He concluded by asking Innocent to consider carefully what Alberto would say to him on his behalf, and to be sure of his own great devotion and affection. All that he had done and thought had arisen from his loyalty and desire to serve Innocent, who had had many proofs of this and should know him well by now.

This is the last surviving letter of this series. Vincula was soon recalled to Rome. By the end of the month, he was all but in disgrace with Innocent, and had been replaced as legate of the Marche by Cardinal Balue. About the time the brief recalling him was sent, Innocent was discussing him with a Neapolitan envoy, expressing a desire to be freed from 'such subjection' and saying that 'now he had white hair, he wanted to be at liberty.'[39] In the first weeks of his legation, the tone of Vincula's letters had revealed, through the constrictions of the formality appropriate in writing to a pope, genuine cordiality and a sense of mutual understanding between him and Innocent. Then the tone became at times exasperated, or self-justificatory. By the end, he was pleading with Innocent to believe in his loyalty and devotion. What had happened to sour their friendship?

The root of the trouble was that Innocent had become convinced that Vincula was procrastinating, spinning out the campaign and exaggerating the seriousness of the crisis in order to keep Innocent preoccupied and subject to him. In April he even suspected that he was conspiring to keep the pot on the boil with Calabria and then with Varano.[40] When he sent Trivulzio off to Osimo, Innocent sent a message to Vincula, saying that if he was finding the campaign too difficult, he should return to Rome.[41] The Milanese and Florentine ambassadors, if they had not planted these suspicions in the first place, certainly did their best to encourage Innocent to free himself from the cardinal's influence.

The dislike of the Sforza for Vincula was of long standing. Now Lorenzo de' Medici was trying to replace him as the pope's principal advisor. Soon after Vincula had left Rome for Osimo, Innocent had concluded a contract of marriage for his son Franceschetto with Lorenzo's daughter Maddalena. The Milanese ambassador heard that the pope had promised Vincula he would not make a marriage contract with Lorenzo until peace had been concluded between Florence and Genoa, and thought that the cardinal would be 'desperate' when he heard the news.[42] Word got back to Lorenzo that he was certainly not pleased, and it is notable that Vincula's letters to Innocent contain no mention of the news, let alone any hint of congratulations. It may be that a letter referring to it has not survived, or it may be that Innocent did not send word to him about the match, because he knew he would disapprove.

As Innocent began to express dissatisfaction with Vincula, something, perhaps this very attitude of the pope, seriously upset the Prefect. He took off from Rome without informing Innocent or his brother. Speculating as to why he should have done this, Vincula told Innocent that the basic problem was probably that he was in financial difficulties because his pay was in arrears.[43] Evidently the Prefect returned to Rome, only to leave again at the beginning of June, discontented, it was said, because he was not esteemed as captain of the papal troops: pique that Trivulzio, not he, had been sent to Osimo may have been the reason. Within a fortnight of the Prefect's leaving Rome, he was trying, so Ferrante informed Innocent, to reconcile his brother to the king, and had suggested that Ostia and the Castel Sant' Angelo, whose castellan was his other brother, Bartolomeo, Bishop of Ferrara, might be handed over to Ferrante.

Innocent had already been displeased with Bartolomeo della Rovere back in April, when he had blamed him for the escape of some prisoners. His behaviour when Innocent sought to take custody of the Castel Sant' Angelo from him only heightened the pope's suspicions. There were various reports over ten days or more that he was avoiding an audience with the pope; that he had refused Franceschetto Cibò entry to the fortress unless he was accompanied by only a few men; that (according to Infessura) he had said he had orders from Vincula to let the pope himself in only if he was accompanied by just four chaplains, and that he held the fortress for Vincula and the College. In the end, Bartolomeo obeyed a summons from the pope to the palace, and obeyed Innocent's order to surrender custody of the Castel Sant' Angelo.[44] The following day, Cardinal Balue was appointed legate of the Marche.

It is hard to believe that the Prefect could seriously have suggested to Ferrante that his brother would agree to hand over the Castel Sant' Angelo and Ostia to him. The king's own letters show that the Prefect was resisting his attempts to get some written statement about the fortresses from him, and had become even more coy about committing himself after he had consulted Vincula. Ferrante also recalled that the Prefect's man had told him that Vincula would never hand over Ostia, and never willingly agree to the Castel Sant' Angelo being handed over either, and that the cardinal would set the Papal States ablaze before he would surrender these fortresses.[45] That sounds as if there had been a suggestion that the pope would take Ostia from him, which would have been a serious mark of disfavour and distrust, for the fortress went with his cardinal-bishopric. There were no other reports or rumours that Innocent was considering this, though in mid-July Ferrante was trying to stir up Innocent's suspicions and saying he must secure Ostia. But the king had still been unable to extract anything in writing from the Prefect, and since his brother's man had been to see him, the Prefect had begun to claim that Ferrante was planning to attack him.

The Prefect had good reason for alarm, as did the other Neapolitan barons, for Ferrante, once he had felt certain that Innocent was estranged from Vincula, had arrested several of them. He claimed that they had been plotting with the cardinal and Salerno, and, he hinted to Florence, with the pope. This did not stop him from expressing pained surprise when Innocent held a public consistory to protest against the arrests. The pope had seemed very well disposed to Ferrante and firmly committed to the counsel of Lorenzo de' Medici and Virginio Orsini, having turned away from San Pietro ad Vincula and his followers and made clear to all the world his discontent with the cardinal, so it was astonishing, the king wrote, that he should now be making such a fuss about the barons.[46]

It may have been this culmination of Ferrante's cynical manipulation of Innocent that finally brought Vincula back to Rome. At first, he had gone to Ancona, for a rest, he said, and then to Urbino, where he fell ill. Innocent may have suspected that he would head for Genoa, or perhaps Avignon, because at the time he took the Castel Sant' Angelo from Bartolomeo della Rovere he asked Lodovico Sforza to stop Vincula if he tried to cross Milanese territory.

But his anger against the cardinal did not last for very long. Ferrante's brazen behaviour must have played a part in its abatement, and so may the fact that the new legate, Cardinal Balue, and Trivulzio did not find it easy to capture Osimo. Soon after he had arrived at Osimo, Trivulzio himself had echoed Vincula's insistence that more money and troops must be sent if the affair was not to end shamefully for the Church, saying that he had found the legate fully committed to the enterprise.[47] Perhaps Balue's letters began to sound like Vincula's had done and Innocent began to appreciate that Vincula had not been deliberately prolonging the campaign. Trivulzio's skill and determination, and the mediation of an envoy of Lorenzo de' Medici, finally brought about the surrender of Osimo, and Boccolino departed on 2 August.

Vincula arrived back in Rome on 18 July, suffering from heatstroke. He went to his palace at Santi Apostoli, rather than to the Vatican, and there is no record of how or when he was received by Innocent. He soon left for Ostia, but hurried back to Rome when Innocent arrested a chancellor of the Prefect on 17 August, though, again, he did not go to the Vatican. Infessura reported rumours that a plot by Vincula and the Prefect against the pope had been revealed, but speculated that they might simply be the result of the Orsini making insinuations.[48] Nothing seems to have come of this. In early September, Innocent was helping along negotiations for a Venetian *condotta* for the Prefect, to get him out of the way, he said.[49] By then, Vincula was reported to have left Rome again, and there is no report of his returning to the city until the following April. But this was not an indication that he was in disgrace: in October, Innocent was expressing pleasure at the possibility of a reconciliation between Vincula and Milan. Where he spent all the autumn and winter is not clear, but a couple of months at least were spent in his diocese of Bologna. In January he was in Bologna itself and in February he was at Cento, a possession of the bishopric.

The next news of him was of his return to Rome from Ostia on 8 April 1489, when he was greeted as though he were returning from a legation. Many courtiers went all the way to Ostia, and several cardinals and Franceschetto Cibò came some distance from Rome to greet him; nearer the city, he was met by a number of ambassadors and by more cardinals. 'As many Romans as there are in Rome'[50] flocked to see the sight. This was an extraordinary reception for a cardinal who was simply returning to the city, and was not only plainly on Innocent's orders, but intended as a mark of special favour.

Vincula would never recover the dominant position at Innocent's court that he had had until the summer of 1486, but nor would he lose Innocent's favour again. He may have been excluded from the major diplomatic business of the next few years, the interminable quarrel between Innocent and Ferrante: not until October 1491 is there a report of him handling negotiations with Naples.[51] There were hints that he was being difficult again about a proposed creation of cardinals in January 1489, when the Mantuan ambassador commented that he and his followers would have to be more accommodating to the pope if they were to be able to help their friends.[52] There was also a hint of possible trouble in May 1489 when Innocent was appointing Niccolò Orsini da Pitigliano to command the papal troops, with Vincula jealous as ever of his brother's reputation and title.

When the pope visited Ostia in November 1489, on what was perhaps his first visit since the troubles of 1487, there was a reminder of less happy days. When he went to see the fortress, he was presented with the keys on a silver dish, and greeted with a little formal speech on the cardinal's behalf. 'Cardinal San Pietro ad Vincula has had the fortress built for the benefit of Holy Mother Church and for the preservation of Your Holiness, to whom he gives all power and dominion over this fortress and all his other property.' Innocent replied graciously, saying, 'Our brother is true to his nature' ('nostro fratello non degenera da la natura sua').[53] Innocent paid several other visits to Ostia during the last years of his pontificate, and was always entertained lavishly there. This may have been politic, and, anyway, Vincula had changed since the days when Sixtus had had to force him to give banquets for visiting dignitaries, and was now a much more willing host. But they also seem to have been genuinely good friends, and by the last months of the pontificate Innocent's reliance on him was such that, when Vincula had the gout in February 1492, Innocent sent to him to say that he would not hold a consistory until he had recovered, 'because he needed him, as he well knew'.[54] Vincula's famous quarrel with Cardinal Borgia at Innocent's deathbed, when he defended Innocent's distribution of large sums of money to his family, was his last act of friendship. It was also a portent of still more bitter quarrels to come.

3

·

Exile

The next few years following the death of Innocent were critical ones in the history of Italy, and Giuliano della Rovere had a pivotal role in the drama. He was one of those Italian political figures who were ready to involve the French and other European powers in the affairs of Italy in order to further their own personal interests, and who thus contributed to the subjection of Italy to nearly four centuries of foreign domination. As pope, he would have an ambiguous attitude to the rulers of France, Spain and the Holy Roman Empire. One moment he would be collaborating with them, encouraging them to bring their forces to Italy; the next, he would be proclaiming his wish to rid the peninsula of all 'barbarians' from beyond the Alps. The policies he pursued as pope are foreshadowed in his actions during the pontificate of Alexander VI, a period that he was to spend largely in self-imposed exile from Rome.

For Giuliano della Rovere, during the next decade the enemy would not be the invaders of Italy – the French, the Spanish, and the Germans under Maximilian, King of the Romans. It would be Rodrigo Borgia, Pope Alexander VI. The result that he hoped would emerge from the French invasion in 1494 was the calling of a general council of the Church and the deposition of the pope.

It is often said that he had been hostile to Cardinal Rodrigo Borgia long before the conclave of 1492, but no evidence has been brought forward to support this. Information on the relations between the two cardinals is scanty; what there is points to their being on relatively friendly terms, at least during Sixtus's pontificate. When they were sent together to welcome and entertain Neapolitan visitors to Rome, there was no hint of any friction between them.[1] They may have been rivals in the conclave of 1484, and Cardinal Borgia was one of the critics of the involvement of the papacy in the Barons' War, but when the war was over, he was still to be found among the cardinals invited by Vincula on pleasure trips to Ostia.

Reports emerged of the spectacular row between the two cardinals at the deathbed of Innocent, when Borgia objected to the pope's distribution of all the reserves of cash (47,000 ducats) to his family, and asked him to put the Castel Sant' Angelo in the custody of the College of Cardinals. Vincula defended Innocent's gifts to his relatives, for which he had asked the cardinals' consent, and argued that the papal fortress should only be handed over to the new pope. He reminded Innocent that Borgia was a Catalan (a name with an unpleasant sound to Genoese ears) and had his own candidates in mind for the papacy. Borgia took this intervention as an affront to the dignity of his office, saying that, were they not in the presence of the pope, he would show them who the vice-chancellor was; Vincula retorted that he wasn't afraid of him. Retorts degenerated into the trading of insults, until Cardinals Sforza and Colonna intervened and calmed them down.[2]

That Vincula did not want Borgia to be pope need not mean they were enemies before the conclave. He had been his colleague in the College of Cardinals long enough – over twenty years – to have realized how clever, how ambitious and how unscrupulous Borgia could be. Perhaps Vincula, hoping to maintain or even increase his own influence, simply preferred a man who could be more easily dominated, but his behaviour from the first months of Alexander's pontificate suggests there was more to it than that. He plainly believed Alexander to be fundamentally untrustworthy, to be capable of treachery and violence – and this before any of the notorious scandals that were to make the Borgia papacy so infamous. Renaissance Rome was no community of saints, and Vincula need not have felt shocked or affronted by a man such as Borgia being a cardinal to feel he was not a man to be entrusted with the powers of the pope.

Cardinal Borgia was not, in fact, regarded as one of the front-runners before the conclave. The main battle lines were drawn up, not between him and Vincula, but between supporters of Milan and of Naples. Milan's interests were in the charge of Cardinal Ascanio Sforza. Those of Naples were represented, not by the cardinal usually referred to as 'Napoli', Caraffa – who was, indeed, one of Ascanio's main candidates – but by Vincula.

There had been some signs of reconciliation between him and Ferrante during the previous year. He had passed on to Ferrante a couple of hunting dogs that he had been sent as a gift from Charles VIII of France in October 1491. He had also had a hand in the conclusion of a peace agreement between Ferrante and Innocent, which explicitly guaranteed the security of the Prefect's Neapolitan estates. Nonetheless, it is still rather surprising to find him regarded as Ferrante's champion. True, since the death of his son, Cardinal Giovanni d'Aragona, in 1485, Ferrante had not had a spokesman in the College of Cardinals, and the friendlier inclinations of such a powerful cardinal as Vincula were most welcome. But it was as an enemy of Milan, rather than as a friend of Naples, that the king could turn to him. The quarrel between Naples and Milan – which was increasingly focused on Lodovico Sforza's clear intention to supplant the dissolute young duke, Gian Galeazzo Maria, his nephew, to the distress and indignation of the duke's wife, Isabella d'Aragona, and her grandfather Ferrante – dominated Italian politics at the time. Ascanio's increasing influence in Rome worried the king, and he looked to Vincula, as Ascanio's main antagonist in the College, to prevent him from bringing about the election of a pope favourable to the Sforza.

To this end, it was said, a large sum of money was put at Vincula's disposal by the king. Roman barons holding Neapolitan *condotte* were ordered to bring their troops near Rome and to obey his instructions. These barons included not only his friends the Colonna, but also Virginio Orsini. One of Lorenzo de' Medici's less celebrated, but in its own way dramatic, diplomatic successes had been the formal reconciliation of Virginio and Vincula in 1488. Virginio had said then that if Vincula did not fulfil his promises, he would treat him as a 'deadly enemy',[3] but by the summer of 1492 he was quite willing to cooperate with the cardinal. Rome now witnessed the curious spectacle of Virginio Orsini canvassing for support for Vincula's candidates in the conclave only six years after he had threatened to parade his head through the streets on the point of a lance.

Ferrante overplayed his hand. His display of force was too blatant. The cardinals, by no means reassured by the king's messages that his troops were at their command, were put on their guard and empowered Cardinal Riario to raise a force of their own to guarantee the security of the city and of the conclave. All that Ferrante achieved was to make Vincula's work more difficult.

Not that he was simply acting as the agent of the king. For some years, Vincula had had his own candidate in mind, his friend Cardinal da Costa. He was a worthy man and generally respected, but Ferrante did not trust him, and made it known to Vincula that he would prefer the Venetian Cardinal Zeno. On the eve of the conclave, da Costa was considered a leading contender, but once it opened, the main candidate of Vincula's group turned out to be another Venetian, Michiel. There is no evidence from before or during the conclave to indicate that Ferrante specifically opposed Borgia as a candidate. The contemporary historian and curial official Sigismondo de' Conti said that Ferrante feared Borgia and did all he could to prevent his election. Conti also said, however, that the king made every effort to have Vincula elected, but there was no hint of such an intention at the time, and Conti's interpretation sounds like guesswork based on later events.[4] The Milanese suspected Vincula of harbouring ambitions to put himself forward as a candidate, but their suspicions were probably unfounded. He was one of the longest-serving cardinals, but he was still, given his hale and vigorous constitution, rather too young – probably not yet fifty – to be a serious candidate. The cardinals rarely elected anyone who looked as if he would last for much over a decade. Ascanio, too, was far too young to be a candidate himself, but he and Vincula were unquestionably the power-brokers of this conclave.

Possibly in an attempt to reduce the time spent locked away in the conclave, the two cardinals had at least one meeting beforehand. There were reports that they had met for talks at Castel Gandolfo outside Rome even before Innocent had died, and had a long discussion on the morning of 4 August in the sacristy of St Peter's, which was interrupted by the arrival of the other cardinals. Ascanio told the Milanese ambassador, Stefano Taberna, that they had not gone beyond 'generalities' ('parole generale'), each trying to persuade the other that it was to their mutual advantage to work in harmony, and praising their own candidates. The hard bargaining was to be done the following morning. No report survives of that meeting, if it took place, but on the basis of Ascanio's account of the first one, Taberna reckoned it was possible that Vincula might even vote for Ascanio, if he saw the cause of his own candidates as hopeless.[5]

Whatever the outcome of their bargaining, and whatever its effect on the conclave, there was no question, once the cardinals were sealed in with their servants and the daily rounds of voting, the 'scrutinies', had begun, of Vincula voting for Ascanio. Indeed, Ascanio collected only one vote in the first three scrutinies. Each cardinal could vote for three candidates in each scrutiny; with twenty-three cardinals in the conclave, sixteen votes were needed for an election. Giuliano della Rovere collected five votes in the first and the second scrutinies, and six, perhaps more, in the third. In all three scrutinies, Ascanio's candidate, Caraffa, collected the most votes: nine in the first two, and ten in the third. Of Vincula's two candidates, da Costa received seven votes in the first, eight in the second, and fell back to seven again in the third, while Michiel received seven in the first two, and ten in the third, equalling Caraffa.

All that is known for certain about what happened after the third scrutiny is that Ascanio switched his support to Borgia, and at the next scrutiny Borgia was elected unanimously. Ascanio's sudden switch took everyone by surprise, and there was some speculation, as the unexpected outcome of the conclave was discussed and analysed in the following weeks, that he had been bribed by Borgia. The vice-chancellorship alone, which he now took on, was one of the most lucrative offices in the Church, and he also received Borgia's palace (though it could be argued that this went with the job) and some fine benefices too. Ascanio was already one of the wealthier cardinals. This does not mean that he could not be tempted by such rich prizes, but the pattern of the voting in the third scrutiny suggests another motive. Michiel had drawn level with Caraffa; Vincula himself had gained ground. Was Ascanio worried that the next scrutiny might see further gains by Vincula's party? Borgia had collected seven votes in the first scrutiny and eight in the second and third, Ascanio himself voting for him each time. If all ten cardinals who had voted for Borgia at least once were prepared to do so again, and if Ascanio could deliver all of those who had supported Caraffa and not Borgia, there would still only be a total of thirteen votes, not the sixteen needed. But when one cardinal looked as though he might be within sight of victory there was often a rush to support him. By switching the support of his own followers to Borgia, Ascanio made his election practically certain. Borgia openly acknowledged how crucial his support had been, and Ascanio took on the role of 'kingmaker' and chief advisor that Vincula had enjoyed during the early years of Innocent's pontificate. Within days of the election, however, there was speculation about how long such an experienced, intelligent and astute politician as Rodrigo Borgia would let himself be guided by Ascanio Sforza.

An experienced observer who had been in the conclave as an attendant of Cardinal Giovanni de' Medici, Niccolò Michelozzi, reported that Vincula and his faction had been forced to swim with the tide, and that though he had moved quickly once he had seen the danger, his standing with his colleagues had been diminished ('ha perso assai de conditione'), both because he had lost and because he had not been as firm as he had urged others to be.[6] A report written some months later by a less reliable source, Gianandrea Boccacio, Bishop of Modena, who had been in Rome at the time of the conclave but not in the conclave itself, said that Vincula, when he saw that Borgia had already got seventeen votes, which was more than enough, told him he wished to make him pope, and that Borgia then thanked him on his knees.[7] It is not impossible that in the euphoria of seeing his cherished ambition on the brink of realization, Borgia found himself thanking Vincula effusively for adding his support, but he would soon feel that he had little to thank him for.

Conflict between Giuliano della Rovere and the new pontiff was not inevitable, and certainly need not have arisen as rapidly as it did. It was said that Alexander made him offers, which he refused in order 'to preserve his good name and integrity', but that he remained a very powerful figure.[8] He had no objection to the first cardinal Alexander promoted, on 31 August, Juan Borgia-Lanzol, Bishop of Monreale; indeed, it was later reported that they had been close friends.[9]

It was not the influence of Cardinal Monreale, but that of Cardinal Sforza, that disturbed Vincula. Ascanio's manoeuvring in the conclave had reaped its reward, and his dominance at the papal court was clear and acknowledged by Alexander himself. It seems to have been Ascanio on whom Vincula focused his attention and distrust much of the time, and he was, if anything, more wary of him than of the pope. Conversely, it is not clear how much of Alexander's suspicion of Vincula was prompted by Ascanio. The pope was rather timorous by nature, for all his intelligence, experience and apparent self-confidence. Seeds of suspicion, whether or not they were sown by Ascanio, began to germinate in his mind within weeks of the conclave. The fertile soil was provided by the sale to Virginio Orsini by Innocent's son

Franceschetto Cibò of the lands, Cerveteri and Anguillara, that his father had granted to him.

This sale had been planned long before by Virginio with Franceschetto's father-in-law, Lorenzo de' Medici (who had died in early 1492), and it was Lorenzo's son, Piero, who maintained the pressure on Franceschetto to stick to his bargain when he showed signs of regretting it. Lorenzo, who had no very great opinion of Franceschetto's abilities, may have thought that the future of his favourite daughter, Maddalena, would be more secure if her husband's wealth was looked after by the Medici. For Virginio, it was a welcome opportunity to purchase lands in the middle of his extensive estates north of Rome. To Alexander, who claimed that the transaction was illegal without his permission, the sale appeared, or was made to appear, to be a plot by Ferrante to increase the grip of the most powerful Roman baron in Neapolitan service on the territory to the north of the city. The fact that the initial contract for the sale was drawn up and witnessed on 3 September in a palace newly built by Vincula outside the Porta Sant' Agnese indicated to Alexander that he was involved in this plot.

Vincula himself is not mentioned in the contract[10] as being present, and he may simply have made his palace available for the business, as a friend of Virginio. His part in the transaction seems to have been a very minor one, and there is no evidence that he was involved in any way in the conclusion of the final contracts relating to the sale, which were drawn up in Florence in early January 1493. Nevertheless, when news of them reached Rome, the pope blamed him. According to Sigismondo de' Conti, he accused him in consistory of encouraging this assault on the rights of the Church, 'which in the past he had been accustomed to defend with great constancy'. (To his friends, when they repeated this accusation, Vincula replied that it would have been worse if Cerveteri and Anguillara had gone to a Sforza relative of Ascanio, as he suspected they would have done.)[11] Alexander also demanded the surrender of Ostia and Grottaferrata. Calmly responding that His Holiness should know that, besides his fortresses, his person and all he possessed were at the pope's disposal, Vincula left the consistory and went home.[12] Almost immediately after, about 6 January, he left Rome for Ostia. Ostensibly, he went to prepare to receive Ferrante's son, Federico, Prince of Altamura, who was about to return to Naples after coming to Rome to swear obedience to the new pope on behalf of his father. Soon it became known, however, that he intended to stay at Ostia, claiming he did not feel safe in Rome.

Up to this point, Ferrante had had little if anything to do with the sale of Cerveteri and Anguillara, but now, because of Alexander's insistence that the transaction was a scheme cooked up for the benefit of the king, much of the burden of trying to find a settlement fell on him. Because Alexander also insisted that Vincula was acting as Ferrante's agent in this matter, the settlement of Vincula's affairs became linked to the solution of the problem of Cerveteri and Anguillara, and to the state of relations between the king and the pope.

Relations between Ferrante and Vincula had continued to be very cordial after the conclave, despite the setback to Neapolitan interests in Rome that Alexander's election under the auspices of Ascanio represented. The preparations that Vincula made to receive Federico as his guest in Rome in December 1492 were particularly magnificent. New hangings of silk and brocade were ordered, and silver trimmings for his chairs. A production of a play, *Amphitrion*, was to be staged, which 'everyone hopes will be one of the most beautiful entertainments to be given in Rome for many years, because no expense is being spared to make everything of the best'.[13] Sumptuous banquets were also prepared to greet Federico on his arrival on 11 December, and to honour and entertain him during the Christmas festivities.

Once Ferrante was drawn into the problem of Cerveteri and Anguillara, Vincula was frequently consulted by the Neapolitan envoys who were wrestling with the problem, and he was in direct contact with Virginio, whose cause he supported. For the king, the affair appeared to be the key to the resolution of all the current disputes between Naples and the papacy,[14] and he tried to persuade Vincula that it was the key to his affairs too. But by then the cardinal had his own quarrel with the pope. Alexander had been very worried when he had decamped to Ostia, and had tried to coax him back, had tried to pretend that he did not really care, and that, given a little time, the problem would solve itself. But there were reports that the pope was being encouraged to see Vincula as the major obstacle to his own control of the College, and that drastic steps needed to be taken to reduce his standing.[15]

On 15 January 1493 Alexander sent Cardinal da Costa to try to persuade him to come back to Rome; da Costa returned saying that he would be coming in a few days. Although he made a show of preparing to leave for Rome, Vincula did not return. Had he done so, he would have been arrested, for on the day on which he was supposed to be arriving back, Alexander stationed guards at the gates and bridges. At the hour Vincula had said he should reach his palace at Santi Apostoli, about 300 light horse appeared on the square, and more were waiting in the streets around, with two squadrons of mounted crossbowmen. 'If he had come, they would have taken him to the Castel Sant' Angelo before he had time to cry "God help me." ' [16]

After this attempted ambush, Vincula never trusted Alexander again. The presence of Ascanio in the Vatican was still an issue for him, and he claimed that he would not be safe in Rome so long as Ascanio was the acknowledged counsellor of the pope. It would be years yet before the two cardinals were reconciled. But the element of personal hostility between Giuliano della Rovere and Alexander was growing stronger, and eventually eclipsed even his enmity towards the Sforza.

There was considerable support and sympathy for Giuliano among his colleagues in the College of Cardinals. When the pope consulted the cardinals in consistory as to what should be done about him, their collective advice was that Alexander should seek a settlement, to avoid giving the impression of disharmony in the Church, but that Vincula should be allowed to stay in Ostia, where he was quite happy. His particular friends in the College were, indeed, determined that he should not return to Rome until he had received some more tangible guarantee of his safety than mere words, or a papal brief. [17] Such friends and allies made him a power in Rome even when he was ensconced in his fortress at Ostia.

Still, his absence from Rome left Ferrante without an advocate on the spot in the College, so signs that Cardinal Caraffa wished to be reconciled to the king were welcome. Once regular contact had been established with Caraffa, Ferrante had Vincula sounded out as to whether he wanted him involved in his own affairs. Vincula's response was favourable, and thus he gained another ally among the senior figures in the College. Soon, though, Caraffa began to replace him as the king's main advocate in Rome.

Ferrante had repeatedly instructed his agents in Rome to bring Vincula's affairs into their discussions with Alexander, and to reassure the cardinal of the king's concern for his welfare. But as he became increasingly anxious to settle the question of Cerveteri and Anguillara, he saw Vincula's advice as too hot-headed and self-interested. Distrust of the pope was behind Vincula's reservations about the king's too evident desire to bring about a settlement: he wrote to Virginio of his worries that Ferrante's anxiety would only make the pope prouder and his behaviour more high-handed, and he was concerned that the king's supporters in Rome were being gradually won over, which would leave Virginio and himself in still greater difficulties.[18]

Vincula clearly had, or was believed to have, considerable influence over Virginio, and was a key figure in the final round of negotiations. Federico d'Altamura was sent again to Rome in June, but went first to Ostia, where he had discussions with Vincula, Virginio and the other barons holding Neapolitan *condotte*, and with the Neapolitan and Florentine ambassadors. He eventually came to Rome on 10 July, but Virginio and the cardinal did not join him there until about a fortnight later, bringing troops for their protection. To Ferrante's exasperation, Vincula tried to insist that Ascanio should be turned out of his Vatican apartments, and when Alexander refused, left Rome for his abbey at Grottaferrata. The king dissociated himself from this demand, but it appears that some promise was made that Ascanio would go. At last, on 16 August, an agreement was drawn up – Virginio would keep the lands, and Alexander would get the purchase price. To save the pope's face, the lands were to be put in the joint custody of Vincula and Cardinal Monreale for three months, but the arrangement was really a fiction, and Virginio was in undisputed possession of Cerveteri and Anguillara by the end of August.

While the final agreement was being drawn up, Vincula was lying sick with fever, first at Grottaferrata and then, in search of 'better air' at Marino, which belonged to Fabrizio Colonna. He became very ill for a while, and his customary disobedience to doctors' orders led to another bout of fever when he had been on the road to recovery. Both the king and the pope professed great concern about his health. Alexander seemed genuinely pleased at his recovery, and sent him two briefs, one giving his household similar privileges to those enjoyed by the papal household, the other giving him 'such authority and independence ... that it makes him almost a second pope'.[19] Hints were dropped to Ascanio that he should leave the papal palace. Vincula was expected to return to Rome once the hot weather and its accompanying outbreaks of disease had passed.

But soon he would fall ill again with fever, this time brought on by news from Rome. The story that got back to the city was that he had been at Marino, gambling (a common occupation for a Renaissance cardinal), when he heard that Alexander had forced through the creation of twelve new cardinals, including his son Cesare Borgia and his mistress's brother, Alessandro Farnese (the future Pope Paul III). Trying, but failing, to carry on with the game, Vincula could not contain his rage; he rushed off alone to his chamber, where he could be heard 'shouting and bellowing'.[20]

Alexander had been seeking to push through a mass creation of cardinals for some months. When he first mooted the idea, soon after Vincula had left for Ostia, he said that such a creation was necessary for his own security, but he recognized that it was not the right moment to press for one. Backing from the Sforza encouraged him in the summer to try to force the creation of thirteen new cardinals on a College that was supposed only to number twenty-five members at most, and at that time had twenty-four. Opposition to this proposal was led by the senior cardinals, including Caraffa and da Costa. The final settlement with Virginio pushed the matter to the sidelines for a while, but in September, Alexander began putting pressure on the cardinals again. This time, some of the other senior cardinals adopted Vincula's tactic of staying away from Rome and ignoring papal briefs summoning them to return, and others simply stayed away from consistory. Alexander was not deterred. Suddenly deciding to hold a consistory on 20 September, he bullied and cajoled eleven cardinals who did turn up into agreeing to the election of his candidates. Vincula, da Costa and Caraffa were among the ten cardinals who not only refused to take part, but made known their intention of continuing to boycott the consistory, avoiding the pope and refusing to give the usual signs of recognition to the new members of the College. The one who particularly stuck in their throats was Cesare Borgia. They were also critical of the way in which the pope had openly accepted money from some of the neophytes. Alexander threatened to show them 'who Pope Alexander VI was',[21] and to make as many cardinals again at Christmas. Ascanio, meanwhile, set about winning over the newcomers, most of whom were, or he came to regard as, his men.

The cardinals who had tried to prevent the election did not reconcile themselves easily to their defeat. By continuing to refuse to attend consistory, they took the gloss off Alexander's triumph. He grew worried, and wrote briefs ordering all cardinals to be in Rome by 15 October for a discussion about the Turks. Still, eight individuals refused to come, including Raffaele Riario (who had voted for the new cardinals at the last moment and apparently regretted his compliance), as well as Vincula and Caraffa. Those who had opposed the election but who turned up to the consistory on 16 October said that they would obey Alexander's summons when there really was to be a discussion of matters of faith, but to discuss other matters would be to go against an agreement they had made. Faced by organized opposition in the College, based on principle at least as much as on politics, Alexander tried bribery, offering to create a cardinal apiece chosen by Vincula, Caraffa and Ferrante. Nothing came of this. A decree saying that absent cardinals could not share in the communal revenues of the College was believed to be aimed specifically at Vincula; Caraffa was to be exempt from its provisions. Caraffa did come back to Rome in January 1494, at Ferrante's request and on Vincula's advice, after Alexander declared that he could not definitely take the side of the king in the face of the looming threat of a French invasion if the 'Neapolitan' cardinals continued to absent themselves from Rome. Vincula himself, though he could be defined as a 'Neapolitan' cardinal, did not return, confident his control over important passages by land and sea (he may perhaps have been thinking of his brother's lands on the Neapolitan frontier as well as Ostia) meant that Ferrante could not afford to quarrel with him.[22]

Alexander also tried to persuade Ferrante to lend him troops for an assault on Ostia and Grottaferrata, and had his eyes on Ronciglione, another fortress held by Vincula, about thirty miles north of Rome, which he had a mind to give to one of his own family. Ferrante argued that the pope should be patient with Vincula and should not use force against him, but began to distance himself from him a little, saying he had no control over his behaviour and that it was for the pope to settle his own quarrels with his cardinals.

The death of Ferrante, on 25 January 1494, brought to the throne of Naples his son Alfonso II. At first, it seemed that he would continue his father's policy of trying to keep on good terms with Vincula while seeking an alliance with the pope. Vincula was believed to be responsible for Fabrizio Colonna's acceptance of a *condotta* with Naples, while Prospero took one from the pope and Milan. But when Alexander insisted that his priority in negotiations with the new king was the problem of Vincula, Alfonso at first argued, as his father had done, that he had no influence over him, and then made an agreement with the pope that left the cardinal at his mercy. Promises were exacted from Alfonso and Virginio that they would see to it that he came back to Rome.

Appreciating the danger that he was in, Vincula wanted guarantees of his safety not only from the pope and the College, but from Alfonso, Venice and Florence as well; Alexander was only prepared to agree to the demand for promises from himself and the cardinals. Intervention by some of Vincula's friends in the College at length brought Alexander to agree that once Vincula came to Rome, he could leave again when he pleased, and would not be treated as contumacious if he refused a summons to come back. This agreement was witnessed in Rome on 23 April.[23] That evening, San Pietro ad Vincula left Ostia – but not for Rome. Instead, under cover of darkness, he took ship for France.

He had already been in contact with France for some months. The Prince of Salerno, now the leading figure among the Neapolitan exiles who had taken refuge there after the Barons' War of 1485–6, had been planning to send an envoy to him back in October 1493. This man may have been Denis de' Vicarii, or 'Danese', whom Charles sent to Rome in February 1494 with a commission to Vincula: it was noted at the time that Charles was planning to send someone who had been on a previous mission to Italy, and that Danese had been brought up in Salerno's household. Danese was sent by the king in response to a message brought to France by one of Vincula's household prelates – a message stating that he was willing to come to France, leaving Ostia, Grottaferrata and the Prefect's duchy of Sora with orders to assist the invasion of Naples, and promising to bring over the Orsini and the Colonna to French service. While Charles found these offers attractive, he did not want to offend the Sforza, his most important Italian allies, nor the pope, and Danese was ordered to consult Lodovico on his way to Rome.[24]

In fact, both Lodovico and Ascanio Sforza had come to consider that it was highly desirable to get Vincula to France, for a number of reasons. He had several strategically important fortresses; he could help persuade the Colonna to accept *condotte* from France and Milan; and his presence in France would be a powerful check on the pope's behaviour. They did not hesitate to emphasize to the king the sacrifice of their own personal feelings this would entail – how they were ready to set aside their enmity towards Vincula to help the king to use him. If Alexander went along with the French, getting Vincula out of his way would be a service to him; if he opposed the French plans, a powerful and

disaffected cardinal could be used 'to beat him down'.[25] Although
the Sforza brothers encouraged the negotiations, some care had
to be taken to prevent their involvement from being obvious.
Ascanio's position was especially delicate – he did not want to
compromise himself with Alexander, and, in any case, it would be
difficult to persuade Vincula that any advice proffered by Ascanio
was given with his best interests at heart. Indeed, it is not clear
how the negotiations leading to the flight from Ostia were carried
on, for the Sforza agents in Rome complained of the timidity
of Danese, saying that he was afraid to go to Ostia. Vincula's
departure apparently took both the French and the Milanese by
surprise.

During the months that followed, Giuliano della Rovere
was one of a small group of advisers urging Charles VIII to
invade Naples, against the wishes of perhaps the majority of his
councillors and the nobles who would lead the army. Why?

One important piece of evidence needed to answer this question fully – first-hand information on his attitude to the prospect
of the French taking over the kingdom of Naples – is lacking. All
that can be done to try to understand his actions at this crucial
juncture in his career, and in the history of Italy, is to interpret
what he did, and what is known of his thoughts on what the
French invasion could bring about, in the light of what he had
done in the past and what he would say and do in the future.

It is clear from the reports from France that Vincula was
welcomed there primarily as an instrument for putting pressure
on the pope, and that he himself hoped Charles would summon a
council of the Church that would depose Alexander. Zeal for
ecclesiastical reform does not seem to have been uppermost in his
mind, although he may have felt Alexander was an unsuitable
man to be head of the Western Church, as well as regarding
him as a personal enemy. The Borgia pope's readiness to create
cardinals *en masse* to enforce his control over the College, and his
eagerness to endow his children with lands and titles, boded ill for
the affairs of the papacy. Nor was Vincula the only cardinal to
be looking to Charles to enforce reform – a French cardinal,
Raymond Peraud, a man of scholarly disposition who had no
personal grievance against Alexander, was also urging him to take
on this task.

If the price of humbling Alexander was the French conquest
of Naples, this may have been a price that Vincula was willing to
see paid. There is no evidence that he hoped this would happen,

but there would be likely gains for his family and friends to weigh in the balance. There was a good prospect that a French victory would lead to the return of the Prince of Salerno and other exiled Neapolitan barons to the kingdom, and to pickings for Giovanni della Rovere too. He had no particular reason to love the Aragonese dynasty of Naples – least of all, perhaps, Alfonso – and had already tried to encourage an invasion of the kingdom by Duke René of Lorraine.

But surely it must have been evident to him that encouraging the most powerful king in Europe to invade Naples was a different prospect from encouraging a Duke of Lorraine to do so. Soon after the French had conquered Naples, Vincula was expressing worries about the prospects for Italy, and urging upon Milan the need to keep Genoa out of the direct control of the French, but only a few years later, he was himself trying to take Genoa and Savona for the French king. When that failed, he made the settlement of the personal affairs of himself and his brother Giovanni an essential preliminary to any response to calls to be a 'good Italian'.[26] This lends credence to the notion that his actions were inspired by his personal dispute with Alexander as much as, if not more than, by concern for the reform of the Church.

If it seems a serious indictment of Giuliano della Rovere to say that he encouraged the French invasion of Italy in 1494 for personal motives, at least it can be pleaded in mitigation that he was not the only one to do so. In retrospect, the shortsightedness and selfishness of the Italian powers, their failure to reckon effectively with the long-term consequences of their actions or inaction, have baffled historians.

Lodovico Sforza once claimed that he would have invited the French into Italy solely to take revenge for efforts to have Ascanio turned out of his apartments at the Vatican.[27] Of course, he would not have done so, but how could a man who aspired to a reputation for political sagacity, as Lodovico did, even say such a thing? Lodovico urged the French to come to Italy in order to bolster his own position in Milan, and to further his quarrel with the Aragonese dynasty of Naples. He had moments of misgiving about where it might lead to, but then seemingly recovered his confidence that he could use the power of the French to accomplish what he wanted them to do, and then send them home again. The Venetians, determined to stay out of any war if they possibly could, obstinately refused, in the face of all the evidence of the French military preparations and of Charles's determination, to admit that the invasion would take place. While Piero de' Medici clung to his alliance with the Aragonese dynasty of Naples, many of his fellow citizens in Florence were anxious only to stay in the good graces of the French and preserve their trading interests in France, bolstered by the thought that they had never liked the Aragonese kings much anyway. Alexander VI shifted his position according to where he thought that his own advantage and security might lie – his alliance with Alfonso in the months before the invasion had much to do with the threat of a council and Vincula's presence at the French court.

Fears about where a French invasion might lead, about what it might mean for Italy – which were occasionally expressed – were not, for any of these powers, as potent a spur to action as their own short-term personal interests. If, as seems possible, Vincula encouraged the French to invade Italy primarily to strike a blow at Alexander, he was far from the only Italian to suffer from tunnel vision.

A few days after taking ship at Ostia, Vincula arrived at Savona. Here, he was visited by a delegation from Genoa, which included the Milanese commissioner and the French ambassador. After four days in his home town, he left for France, accompanied by 200 Savonese infantry. He may not have been sure what reception awaited him there, because he was reported to have paused at Nice until he had obtained a safe-conduct from Charles. Any doubts about how he would be received must soon have vanished, for the king was pleased and excited by his arrival, and sent the Prince of Salerno and one of his own most trusted counsellors, Etienne de Vesc, to Provence to escort him to Lyons.

Vincula's entry into Lyons on 1 June was a splendid affair. On the king's orders, representatives of the citizens, the foreign bankers and merchants and the principal courtiers went to greet him. His lodgings had been luxuriously decorated, with the floors as well as the walls spread with tapestry. Charles immediately summoned him to the palace, came down the staircase into the square to greet him, hat in hand, and took him to his chamber, where they talked for over an hour, before the king brought him out to the square again. The king continued to treat him with exceptional favour, visiting him at his lodgings on several occasions for discussions and even holding meetings of his council there. Emerging from one *tête-à-tête* with him, Charles, holding him by the hand, said, 'By God, this man has come for the good of Christendom.'[28] Perhaps they had been discussing the summoning of a council of the Church to challenge Alexander, the aspect of the Italian expedition that most interested the cardinal; perhaps the king was simply wrapped in his dreams of using the kingdom of Naples as a springboard for an expedition against the Turks.

Vincula's arrival breathed new life into the preparations for the invasion of Naples. Charles's councillors were divided on the wisdom of this scheme, with the majority against it. One of his principal advisors, Guillaume Briçonnet, Bishop of Saint-Malo, who had been among the most fervent instigators of the invasion, had had his fervour dashed when Milan had not obtained for him the cardinal's hat that he craved, and was now doing his best to obstruct and delay the preparations. Vincula's passion and energy, the assurances he gave of the readiness to serve France of his brother and of the Colonna, of the Duke of Urbino and the lord of Camerino, as well as his own potential usefulness as an instrument of pressure on the pope, did much to counter the effects of the cold water poured on Charles's dream of conquering Naples by those who thought of it only as an expensive, potentially disastrous folly, a waste of the new-found strength of the French monarchy.

One asset that his adherence to the French had offered them, the use of the fortress of Ostia, had, however, been lost before he even arrived. Ostia should be able to hold out for at least two months, he told the king, asking him to send ships and troops to support the garrison. Charles agreed, but news of the surrender of Ostia on 24 May came within a few days of Vincula's triumphant arrival in Lyons. At first, he found it hard to believe, hoping that his brother and Fabrizio Colonna, in whose charge he had left his lands near Rome, were merely feigning agreement with Alexander to win time.

Vincula had yet another asset that he could put at the service of the king: his contacts in Genoa. Lodovico Sforza had agreed that the French could gather a fleet there, and at the beginning of May, Charles had already sent his *grand écuyer*, Pierre d'Urfé, and other agents to raise money and prepare the galleys and ships. In August there was a plan for Vincula to go to Genoa to drum up money for the king from the Genoese bankers, but it came to nothing, possibly because he felt that it would be more useful to stay with the king to keep his easily distracted mind on the preparations for the expedition. The news that a successful plot by French agents and Prospero Colonna had put Ostia in the hands of the French on 18 September brought him hurrying to Genoa, on the king's orders. At first, it was proposed that he should go to Ostia, and join forces with Ascanio (who had now left Rome and taken refuge on the Colonna lands) in rallying the cardinals against the pope. Ascanio objected to the idea that he should recover control of Ostia, and Lodovico arranged that he should go to Genoa and seem to be preparing to take a fleet and troops to Ostia, but should not actually leave. It is not clear whether he himself knew that the Sforza were behind the change of plan.

Vincula arrived in Genoa on 27 September to a warm welcome from the people. Letters that he exchanged with Lodovico soon after his arrival discuss the preparations of the fleet for Ostia, but any notion that he would go with it had been abandoned. As well as helping Pierre d'Urfé with the assembly and arming of the fleet, Vincula occupied himself with appealing to his friends in Genoa to help supply money to the French, for the bankers were reluctant to lend any more money except on good security. These letters show that he was still very keen that the French expedition 'should go ahead with all speed', and betray no qualms about its consequences.[29]

Despite the lateness of the season, with the French army setting out for Naples at a time when the thoughts of Italian commanders were usually turning to winter quarters, despite the inexperience of the young king and his tendency to be distracted along the way by pretty women, and despite the bad advice that he received, according to the sage Philippe de Commynes,[30] from counsellors as young and inexpert as himself, the invasion took on the character of a triumphal progress, rather than a military campaign. Panic, an eye to personal survival and stunned disbelief at the speed of the French advance undermined what little resistance was offered. By November, Charles was in Florence, after Piero de' Medici's craven surrender of the major Florentine fortresses to him had brought about a revolt against Medici dominance and the expulsion of Piero from the city, and a revolt by the Pisans against the rule of Florence. By the end of the year, Charles was in Rome, negotiating with the pope. Having lost his two main Italian allies, Alfonso lost all heart and, with the enemy at the gates of his kingdom, abdicated in favour of his son Ferrantino; he then fled to Sicily with much of the royal treasure that was needed to pay the troops. Ferrantino, even younger than his opponent, made some attempt to put up a fight, but soon abandoned his capital and set sail too. On 22 February 1495

Charles entered Naples, to the acclamation and derision of the crowd. Charles, as he rode in state among his victorious army, looked like a hat on a horse. His huge head, with its long nose and pendulous lips, sat on a small, misshapen body with disproportionately large feet. This was not the romantic vision of the handsome hero–king, the successor to Charlemagne, that many Italians had cherished. When the French soon revealed themselves to be rapacious, exploitative, arrogant and uncouth, the disenchantment of the Neapolitans was complete.

For Vincula, disenchantment had set in some time before. Once the army was properly under way, he faded into the background to some degree, and little is heard of him in accounts of the progress of the French through Italy, until they began to draw near to Rome. Charles then sent him to Ostia with a large detachment of troops. It was planned that, with the help of the Colonna, these should encircle the Neapolitan troops south of Rome, but the plan came to nothing. This would have been the moment for Charles to restore Ostia to Vincula, but he did not, much to the cardinal's disappointment.

Worse still, although Vincula and Cardinal Peraud had been badgering Charles to take up the cause of reforming the curia, the king preferred to negotiate with Alexander. Far from returning to Rome in triumph, with Alexander humiliated, perhaps deposed, the 'French' cardinals – Vincula, Sforza, Sanseverino and Peraud – had to leave Rome with Charles for their own safety, for the treaty between the king and the pope contained few guarantees for them. Vincula, in fact, received more consideration than the others. Beyond the general clauses that Alexander was to restore to the cardinals who were 'the king's friends and servants' all their offices, dignities and property of which they might have been deprived, and not to rake up the past provided they promised to be loyal and obedient in future, and that they should be free to come and go from Rome as they pleased, special mention was made of the della Rovere brothers. Alexander was not to take any reprisals against the Prefect, and a major grievance that the pope nursed against him[31] was to be settled by the king within four months. Vincula was to be 'entirely reinstated in the legation of Avignon and in each and all of his properties', his castles, lands, lordships, liberties, privileges, offices and rights, granted by Alexander or his predecessors; and, henceforth, his possession of them could not in any way be troubled or revoked.[32] The king explicitly promised not to ask Alexander again for the Castel Sant'

Angelo – earlier requests that the pope should cede the fortress to him had been met with a firm refusal, on the grounds that Vincula would want to take command and thus Alexander would be left without a refuge.[33] Had he been left in charge of the fortress, perhaps Vincula might have stayed in Rome, but with no more tangible guarantee than a piece of paper, he had little choice but to follow the king.

Not much is known about what he did in the kingdom of Naples while Charles was there. His only recorded intervention in the campaign was to send someone to rescue the Prince of Salerno's son from his prison in Naples.[34] More is known about his state of mind – he was discontented with the French. By April he was warning the Milanese against French designs on Genoa, and offering to help reconcile Cardinal Campofregoso, Obietto Fieschi and other Genoese exiles with the Sforza. He was also feeling his way, with the help of the Venetians and Cardinal da Costa, towards an attempted reconciliation with the pope and Ascanio. Their initial response was favourable, but the negotiations seem to have foundered. When Charles left for France in late May 1495, leaving behind substantial forces to hold off the counter-attack of Ferrantino, Vincula went with him. By then, Lodovico Sforza had switched alliances, and a new league, of Milan, Venice, the pope, Maximilian, and the King of Spain had been formed. Venetian and Milanese troops were waiting for the French as they crossed the Apennines in the Lunigiana into the lowland plain. As the French forces were passing through the Lunigiana, Vincula proposed that an attempt should be made to raise a rebellion in Genoa. The king's council did not like the idea at all – if Charles won the impending battle, the Genoese would yield of their own accord, and if he lost, what use would Genoa be? Despite this advice, and to the consternation of many of his commanders, the king sent a large detachment of troops, including some men freshly arrived from France by sea, and Vincula went with them.[35]

Thus he missed one of the most famous battles in Italian history, fought at Fornovo on 6 July 1495. The Italians regarded it as a victory, revenge for their humiliation by the French, but Charles (who at one point was nearly captured) and the bulk of his army were able to make their escape. With the league's troops following at a discreet distance, the French proceeded to Asti. There was a pause while Louis d'Orléans and his starving troops were extricated from Novara, which Louis (who had been left behind in Asti) had taken, when the temptation to try his luck in the duchy of Milan, to which he had an hereditary claim, had proved irresistible. Once this was accomplished, the king crossed the Alps to safety. The attempt on Genoa was abandoned.

Vincula spent the winter in his diocese of Avignon. After the cardinal had fled from Ostia in April 1494, Alexander had written to his lieutenant in Avignon, Gianandrea Grimaldi, Bishop of Grasse, absolving him from all obligations to Vincula and appointing him governor of Avignon and the Venaissin in the name of the papacy. Grimaldi had complied with the pope's wishes and had begun enquiring after the cardinal's property, but as Vincula had made his way to the French court, accompanied by the Prince of Salerno and Etienne de Vesc, they had insisted that the papal territories should recognize him as legate. There was nothing that Grimaldi could do about this, so he delegated his powers to the vicar-general of the archbishopric, Pierre Albert, and left. The Avignonese were in a delicate situation, continuing to treat Vincula as legate while trying not to provoke the pope. Their dilemma was resolved when the agreement between Charles and Alexander in January 1495 officially restored Vincula to all his offices, including the legation. On 10 March 1495 Vincula appointed his *nipote* Clemente della Rovere, Bishop of Mende, lieutenant-general and governor of the Papal States in France. Grimaldi had retired to his bishopric; in order to vent their resentment against the cardinal, the members of his family named one of their mules Vincula.[36]

On his appointment as governor, Clemente had taken up residence in Avignon, and he continued to fulfil the functions of this office during his uncle's residence in the diocese. Vincula, meanwhile, kept in constant contact with the French court at Lyons, and would have gone there in March if the king had not left for a while. He did go at the end of April, and spent May in Lyons with the king.

Another expedition to Italy was being planned, and Vincula was again one of the leading instigators. He claimed that if he were given 2,000 Swiss infantry, he could deliver the whole of the 'Riviera di Ponente', the coast to the west of Genoa, including Savona.[37] Battistino Campofregoso, nephew of Cardinal Campofregoso, and an exile from Genoa, was also involved in the invasion plans. But, at the end of the month, Charles suddenly decided to go north to see his queen at Tours, and refused to discuss this decision with his council. Vincula had a long talk alone with the king, trying to persuade him not to go, but Charles was determined. Plans for an expedition faded away. Vincula probably spent the rest of the summer back in the diocese of Avignon – he was certainly there in late July – but still nursed schemes for an attack on the Riviera. When the king returned to Lyons in November, he quickly joined him, and, once again, there were reports of his taking part in councils to discuss Italian affairs.

The outcome of these discussions was an, assault on Genoa and Savona that was not only led by Vincula and Battistino Campofregoso, but also largely paid for by them. The possession of Genoa would be crucial to the success of another French expedition to Italy, but most of the French nobility and of Charles's counsellors had little enthusiasm for another Italian adventure, and regarded the Italian exiles and their plans with hostility. The king ordered Giangiacomo Trivulzio, who was in command of the French forces at Asti, to provide troops in support of both Battistino's attempt on Genoa and that of Vincula on Savona. Commynes argued that he could not supply them both with enough troops to be effective and, at the same time, leave himself sufficient forces to protect Asti.[38] Besides, Trivulzio had his own plans. He wanted to launch an attack on the duchy of Milan, where he had many partisans.

The outcome was a military fiasco, which cost Vincula a lot of money and some loss of reputation. But the affair had the important consequence of bringing him into diplomatic contact with Lodovico Sforza, the pope and Venice. The lengthy negotiations that ensued as they tried to draw him back into Italy reveal the importance that they attached to winning him over from the French, and also give some insight into how Giuliano della Rovere, only a few years before he became pope, responded to appeals to his patriotism as an Italian.

Ill-conceived the campaign may have been, but, nevertheless, it caused considerable alarm to Lodovico and his ally, Venice. In early December 1496 Vincula and Battistino left Lyons for Avignon, where they paused to gather troops and lay their plans. Vincula left Avignon on 24 December, and then wandered around a little, sowing confusion as to what his next move might be. On 6 January he entered Turin with Louis de Villeneuve, a French commander who may well have become involved in the enterprise as his friend. From a Provençal family with estates near Nice, Louis was described by Commynes as 'a friend of the cardinal and a bold talker', and by the Milanese envoy in Turin as 'crazy and vainglorious'.[39] Vincula was already in contact with another friend – and relative of Sixtus IV – Costantino Arniti, the regent of Monferrato, asking for victuals and a safe passage for the French troops. Monferrato controlled the passes over the Ligurian Alps leading to Savona and Genoa, so Costantino's cooperation was important. The Milanese envoy in Turin, Mafeo Pirovano, feared that his friendship with Vincula might swing his decision in favour of the French.[40] Indeed, the whole plan of campaign was founded on hopes that friendship and family links would make Savona and Genoa rise against the Milanese when the French troops appeared. The strategically vital, politically fragmented, territory between France and Italy was Vincula's home ground, and his contacts and influence there constituted one of the reasons why he was considered to be so dangerous to the peace of Italy.

A few days after reaching Turin, Vincula left for Asti, where the troops were already restive for lack of pay and the commanders at cross-purposes. He sent a man ahead to Savona to assess the strength of the forces there and open talks with citizens who he hoped would be favourable to his cause. Two men despatched to ask for the surrender of Savona were sent back by the Milanese commander, Lucio Malvezzi, with a threatening message. Vincula and the thousand or so infantry that he had brought do not seem to have managed to penetrate beyond Altare, about eight miles from Savona. When he did not get the response from the Savonese for which he had hoped, he lost heart, and withdrew to Monferrato in early February. The attempt on Genoa met with no better success.

Soon the leaders of the enterprise were quarrelling about what should be done next. In early March, Charles sent Pierre d'Urfé to try to restore some harmony to the command and some discipline among the troops, who were reported to be refusing to obey Trivulzio and Vincula. There was another, half-hearted, move towards Savona, which stopped at Cairo, about twelve miles away. On 9 March, Vincula sent a man to Lucio Malvezzi, saying how he wanted him to come over to the French and promising that he would be given money and estates. Malvezzi replied by pointing out that the Prefect's affairs were in a bad way and Ostia under siege, and that now it should be clear that 'Italy will be for the Italians, and France for the French.'[41] Soon the attempt on Savona was abandoned and the infantry disbanded.

Throughout this campaign (if campaign it could be called),

Vincula had been negotiating with Milan, Venice and the pope. Speaking to the Milanese agent in Savoy, Pirovano, in early January, he gave 'a long account' of his actions. 'Saying he had always intended to be on friendly terms' with Lodovico, he recalled, in particular, the reception that he had had in Lodovico's name when he had passed through Savona, having left Ostia 'so as not to fall into servitude under the pope'. Once in France, and when he had come to Italy with the king, he had always tried to follow Lodovico's advice. And yet there had been no mention of him or the Prefect in the league that Lodovico had made, nor in the agreement that it had reached with Charles, despite the offers that he had made to come to reside in Milan or Venice – whichever they chose – provided that he was safe and the Prefect was taken into their protection. He felt abandoned by all the Italian powers. Seeing no other way to save himself, he had been forced to go to his diocese in Avignon and seek the shelter of the king, without, however, scheming against the interests of Italy. But now, hearing that his brother's affairs had been given by the league into the power of the pope, and having been requested by the king to come to Italy to serve His Majesty in an enterprise that could also provide some remedy for his brother's predicament, he had come, with the intention, not of attacking Lodovico, but of serving the king, as a cardinal and not as a soldier. His duty was to carry out faithfully and diligently the commission given him by the king to the Duke of Savoy, the Governor of Monferrato (Costantino Arniti) and elsewhere as might be necessary. He declared that he personally would not go to any place of danger, and 'would be careful not to fall into the hands of whoever wished to take revenge' on him.

Urged by Pirovano to leave the French and come over to the league, Vincula said that he would like to do so, but he had gone so far that he didn't see how he could honourably change direction, and especially how he could do so without making an enemy of the king while finding all the league against him at the instance of the pope; this would mean disaster for his brother. He could see no other course than to press on

in the king's service, with fidelity and diligence, and in the habit of a cardinal, and for the preservation of his honour, and of his brother, commit his property, his life, his very soul to the task. And if the Lord God brought him on the right track, that is so that he could live in Rome as a good cleric and good cardinal, his wish for quiet and repose would be satisfied. If things turned out differently, he would regret it, but he would be content to have served the king well in the commission he had been given.

Should this involve offending Lodovico, he would take care not to fall into his power, so as not to be ill-treated by him. Pirovano, taking his leave, said Lodovico would do as he was done by; if Vincula acted like a soldier, he would be treated like a soldier. Vincula said he would be serving as a cardinal, with words only.[42]

He had been desperate about his brother's predicament for months. The Prefect was one of the last supporters of France still holding out in Naples, and Vincula's encouragement of a return by the French to Italy in the summer of 1496 had been fired by the hope that this would bring succour to him. As the prospect of a French return was fading, he asked the king to tell him if he did not intend to go, so that he could make provision for his brother.[43] By December the Prefect was describing his situation in a letter to his wife as dangerous, with all the new estates he had been given by Charles having rebelled against him and the loyalty of his other lands shaky, except for Arci, Sora and Rocca Guglielma.[44] The fortresses were defended for him by the Basque Gratien d'Aguerre, whose brother had served Vincula in Avignon in 1481 (Menaud himself was in Ostia.) As soon as Vincula reached Savoy, and had established contacts with the envoys of the league, he emphasized that a settlement for the Prefect was a *sine qua non* for ensuring his own agreement to leave the French. This would be the basis of all the negotiations with Vincula over the next year and more.

These prolonged negotiations were complicated, and are not worth following in close detail for the basic positions of the parties to them changed little. Nevertheless, they are significant, for they reveal what the leading Italian powers thought of Vincula. Still more significantly, they reveal how Vincula responded to appeals to him to think of the interests of Italy. The attitudes he adopted at this time accord with the policies that he would adopt a few years later after he became pope. As cardinal, he declared himself willing to behave as a 'good Italian', and that he 'loved his homeland, that is Italy, more than any other nation'.[45] But his priority was the security of his brother and himself, and to ensure that, he was ready to encourage and promote French rule in the peninsula. As pope, his first priority was the consolidation of the temporal power of the papacy; to achieve this, he was ready to use

French, Spanish, German and Swiss troops to fight on Italian soil, and to acquiesce in their claims on Italian territory.

The negotiations that began in Savoy in January 1497 were continued by a variety of intermediaries. One of the most important in the early stages, until his death in November, was the Duke of Savoy, Philip of Bresse, who had recently crowned a reckless and turbulent career by succeeding his young nephew. The duke's chief minister, the Treasurer of Savoy, Sebastien de' Ferreri, was on good terms with Vincula and was in frequent contact with him, in personal meetings or by letter – though by the summer of 1498, Vincula had begun to feel that he was too close to Milan to be really trustworthy. At an early stage, in the spring of 1497, Vincula's relative, Costantino Arniti, the Governor of Monferrato, became involved, but was too little trusted, and considered to be acting too much in the interests of Venice to be acceptable to the other members of the league. Most of the negotiating was done by the envoys and agents of Milan, Venice and the pope who were based in Savoy, sometimes talking to Vincula personally, sometimes to members of his household.

Two members of the household were particularly active: Coriolano Cippico, Bishop of Famagusta, a humanist of some repute, who was considered a partisan, indeed an agent, of Venice by the Milanese Pirovano; and Francesco Alidosi di Castel del Rio, Vincula's chamberlain and already one of his most trusted servants, a man destined for great power, and notoriety, during Julius's pontificate. Alidosi was sent on missions to Milan and to Rome at crucial stages of the negotiations. Another Francesco, Francesco Gonfalonero, was active for several months, and was also sent to Milan, but Vincula came to distrust him and it was only the fact he was related to the Treasurer of Savoy that saved him from dismissal from the household. A certain Piergiovanni da Forlì was sent to Venice on Vincula's behalf, but there was some doubt about whose service he was really in; Pirovano considered him to be a Venetian spy as well. Pierpaolo da Cagli, sometimes described as Vincula's secretary, sometimes as secretary of the Prefect, 'a skilful man in every sort of business',[46] helped the brothers to maintain contact and was also sent by Vincula to France. In Rome, Vincula's faithful friend Cardinal da Costa, a man above suspicion even by Alexander, was the chief intermediary.

From first to last, Vincula's central concern was his brother's safety, and the salvaging of as much of his lands as possible.

Affection for his brother was no doubt a powerful motive, but there was surely more to it. On Giovanni and his children rested the hopes of establishing the della Rovere as an Italian ruling dynasty, and Vincula fought hard for every fortress and estate that was, or had been, in his brother's possession. His lands in papal territory were as much at risk as his lands in Naples, for he had mortally offended Alexander by capturing, in November 1494, a Turkish ambassador and a papal envoy coming from Constantinople with documents that showed that the pope, the head of Western Christendom, was encouraging the arch-enemy of the Christian faith to make war on the Most Christian King of France. Worse, he had captured 40,000 ducats, the annual payment made by the Sultan to the pope to keep his brother, and rival for the throne, a prisoner in the Vatican.[47] This money constituted one of the most serious stumbling-blocks in the whole negotiations. Alexander could not bear to renounce it, and neither Giovanni nor Vincula could afford to pay it back. Without the support of his powerful brother, the Prefect would have been done for. As for Vincula's own position, essentially he required a guarantee that he could continue to enjoy his offices and benefices without being obliged to live in Rome, for he had no confidence that he would be safe from Alexander's vengeance, especially when Ascanio Sforza was still in the city.

Vincula's terms were set out on his behalf by Francesco Gonfalonero in Turin in late March 1497. First, he wanted his brother to have both his 'old' and his 'new' estates (his 'new' estates were those that had been given to him in Naples by Charles), and his office of Prefect. He wanted the restitution of his own offices and benefices, and Ostia to be placed in the charge of a cardinal whom he could trust. He wanted the remission of the 40,000 ducats that the Prefect had taken from Alexander, saying he didn't have the means to repay it at present. If the pope and the king accepted these petitions, Alexander should write a brief making explicit his goodwill, and Lodovico, Venice and the King of Naples should simultaneously send full mandates to their envoys in Turin to conclude an agreement. In return, he would come to Turin to make the agreement, and once this was concluded, settle in Italy, at a place acceptable to the pope and the other powers of the league.[48]

All he offered, in effect, was to leave the French. That was all he really had to offer. It is a measure of how much weight Milan and Venice believed him to carry in the councils of the French

king and among the other Italian exiles with the French, that this
was enough to keep them negotiating. They were not sure he was
sincere at first, not sure he was not playing them along. In
Venice, some senators said that if he could be won over, it would
be as great a miracle as the conversion of St Paul.[49] But the
opportunity to bring back to Italy the man regarded as the most
dangerous of the exiles was thought to be too good to miss. A way
had to be found, Lodovico wrote to Ascanio, to

> take away from the French the fomentors of these troubles. Among
> them the one who can do the most, because of his authority and his
> wealth, and on whom all the others lean, is this Cardinal San
> Pietro ad Vincula who, it should be borne in mind, because of his
> brother's situation, would risk his own life to find a way to save
> him. And so, since there's reason to hope he could be drawn away
> from this expedition if he knew it would make his brother secure,
> nor would he care by whose hands his safety was obtained, and
> since, if this were done, most if not all of these alarms would
> cease, considering our present danger, which is linked with that of
> others, we want every effort to be made to win over San Pietro ad
> Vincula.[50]

Lodovico, who stood to lose the most if the attack on Genoa and
Savona was successful, was the most vehement in arguing the
advantages of this plan of action, but it also made good sense to
many Venetian senators, and the Venetian envoy in Savoy was
instructed to negotiate with Vincula through whatever channels
the cardinal preferred.

The problem was that, while Milan and Venice were the
members of the league most ready to negotiate, they were not the
ones on whom the Prefect's fate depended. All that they could
offer Vincula was the free enjoyment of the income from his
benefices in their territory and promises of intercession with their
allies who were directly in conflict with the Prefect – Alexander
and the new King of Naples, Federico.[51] For these two, the
issue was not so straightforward. The pope was not keen to have
Vincula back in circulation in Italy, unless he was in Alexander's
power in Rome. He wanted Vincula's fortresses, he badly wanted
the 40,000 ducats, and he may well have wanted the Prefect's
lands for his own family. Federico was faced with the problem of
trying to reconcile all the conflicting claims to lands revived,
or caused, by the French invasion of Naples and its aftermath,
and was not inclined to disappoint those who had supported his

dynasty's recovery of the kingdom in order to satisfy Vincula's demands that the Prefect should hold all the lands he had held before 1494, and the lands he had been granted by Charles, or their equivalent as compensation. The fact that the Prefect was at the heart of the last resistance to his rule did not make the king any better disposed towards him. Both the king and the pope, however, came under considerable diplomatic pressure from their allies in the league to set aside their personal interests and misgivings for the common good. Even Alexander – at this time – was susceptible to arguments about the desirability of keeping the French out of Italy.

At first, the envoys from Milan and Venice and the papal nuncio in Savoy worked together in negotiating with Vincula, but by the beginning of April they were each acting separately. The Venetians wanted to put Vincula and the Prefect under an obligation to them, to increase their influence in the Marche through the Prefect and their influence in Rome through the cardinal. Alexander was playing a double game. To the ambassadors of the league, he insisted that Vincula was not to be trusted, that he must be forced to come to Rome, that there could be no compromise on the 40,000 ducats. Ostia was captured by Spanish troops for Alexander on 9 March from its French garrison, and he insisted on keeping it. He published a bull confiscating all Vincula's offices and benefices. But this bull may not have been put into effect, and to Cardinal da Costa he spoke of his willingness to be reconciled with Vincula. According to the papal nuncio in Savoy, the pope saw the cardinal as a useful future protector for his son Cesare.[52] The sticking-point was the money, but, eventually, Alexander was convinced that it could not be repaid immediately. In early June, without consulting his allies, he agreed terms with da Costa, which Vincula accepted. These terms, so Ascanio reported, were that the cardinal was to be in Italy within forty days, was to stay in places 'friendly' to the pope and acceptable to himself – Bologna and Senigallia were suggested – and was to be loyal to Alexander. If he came to Italy within the specified time, all his benefices and offices would be restored to him, and the past would be forgotten. If he came to Rome, a castellan acceptable both to him and to the pope would be put in Ostia, and he would pay 2,500 ducats for building work that the pope had had done there. Some terms relating to the Prefect's affairs – a full pardon, help with the recovery of his lands and some concessions on the repayment of the 40,000 ducats –

were also specified, but Alexander wanted the Prefect to send a man to Rome to settle these matters.[53]

These terms were considerably less favourable than those Vincula had been asking for in late March, and there is no direct evidence as to why he accepted them. They offered no guarantees for his brother, but it may have been precisely his brother's interests that he had in mind. The Prefect had had to come to terms with Federico (after asking his brother's permission), and it is probably no coincidence that about the time Vincula accepted the agreement with Alexander, the Prefect returned to Senigallia after spending two years in the kingdom of Naples. If Vincula had refused the agreement, how safe would his brother have been in the Papal States? Nor was there any mention of Vincula's having to renounce his connection with France.

In fact, he had gone to Lyons in May to ask for the king's permission to conclude terms with Alexander. Charles had wanted him to return to France – and had sent Pierre d'Urfé to persuade him – but he gave his consent, if somewhat reluctantly, so that when Vincula went to Avignon and reached agreement with the pope, this did not represent a breach with the French. And when he came into Italy, to fulfil his part of the bargain, he came no further than Savoy. This did not satisfy Alexander, nor reassure the other members of the league, but all suggestions that he should come further south were politely rejected.

For the next year, he divided his time between Savoy and Monferrato, doggedly insisting that the Prefect should have all his lands, or at least full compensation for those that could not be taken from their present holders. At times, he was acutely worried about his brother, but he was not prepared to see him stripped of his estates. Alexander continued to hold out for his money, and did not like Vincula's proposals that, for example, Federico should promise to pay him the cash, to set against the lands the king said he could not give to the Prefect.[54] By late March 1498 negotiations had been broken off completely between the pope and the cardinal.

Vincula also had to contend with a couple of bouts of serious sickness. In October 1497 he was dangerously ill. In the following April he was said to have colic brought on by anxiety about his brother, but, soon after, his malady was reported to be 'the bad sort of French pox', bringing sores on his face and pains in his bones.[55] These attacks of syphilis continued for several months.

There was some relief for his pain in the turn of events.

During the night of 7 April the young French king died, lying on a makeshift bed in a sordid corridor of his palace at Amboise, after banging his head on a door lintel. Neither of the two sons born to his queen had survived him, and his heir was his distant cousin, Louis d'Orléans. Vincula was pleased to hear the news, speaking of Charles with some contempt. Louis cut a very different figure from his predecessor – handsome and vigorous. He and Vincula had shared a common purpose in encouraging Charles to keep up his involvement in Italy. With the kingdom of France, Louis inherited Charles's claim to Naples, to which he added his own hereditary claim to the duchy of Milan through his Visconti grandmother.[56]

Vincula was at Chieri in Savoy when he heard the news of Louis's accession and received a letter asking him to come to France. He had been threatening to return to France, but he replied to the king that his legs were troubling him and he was not fit for travelling. Some observers in Savoy suspected that he was biding his time to see what would happen, before deciding whether to move. He sent Pierpaolo da Cagli, who reported from Paris that he had been graciously received by the king. Louis was, in truth, being gracious to everyone in this honeymoon beginning of his reign, but his comments that he would plan an expedition to Italy once his coronation was over, and that, in making his plans, he would follow Vincula's advice, were not intended as social pleasantries. Louis's closest adviser, Georges d'Amboise, the Archbishop of Rouen, was also very welcoming, and offered his services if there was any business that Vincula wished to transact with the king.[57]

This favour from the new king strengthened Vincula's position considerably, so that when Alexander began to seek an alliance with Louis, he found it necessary to be reconciled to the cardinal first. Papal ambassadors sent to Paris in July (who asked, among other things, that the French cardinals and Vincula should go to reside in Rome) were told that the king's attitude to the pope would depend on how the pope treated French concerns. After receiving this unfriendly response, they witnessed the audience accorded to envoys from Avignon, who asked for confirmation of certain privileges that they had enjoyed. The king was most willing to comply, he said, 'especially for love of San Pietro ad Vincula, whom he loved cordially and regarded as a special friend, and for whom he was ready to do as much as for any man in the world'; and he told Pierpaolo to report his words to his master.[58] Vincula was delighted at this news and made sure that these remarks were known in Rome, summoning the papal envoy in Savoy to tell him about them. Alexander took the hint, and soon negotiations were under way once more in Savoy and Rome. On 18 August, Francesco Alidosi was sent posthaste to Rome to get a brief giving Vincula permission to go to Avignon. Alexander had already written another brief telling him to have no fears for the Prefect. By the beginning of September all differences between the cardinal and the pope had been settled. The terms of the agreement that da Costa made this time are not known, except that Vincula was to come to Rome by Christmas. Since there was no further talk of any threat to the Prefect, this time his brother's differences with the pope may have been settled too.

One of the first outward manifestations of Vincula's formal return to the fold of obedient cardinals in 1497 had been a letter of condolence sent to Alexander after the body of the pope's son Juan, Duke of Gandia, had been fished out of the Tiber, with multiple stab wounds: he was as distressed, he said, with stunning insincerity, as if his own brother, the Prefect, had died.[59] One of the first results of the 1498 agreement concerned another of Alexander's sons, Cesare. His brother's death (for which many held him responsible) had given him the opportunity to renounce his cardinal's hat, which he had never wanted, and become the main secular, soldier *nipote* of the clan. Now he was coming to France in search of a bride, and Vincula was to receive him at Avignon (where he had arrived himself on 1 October), and to assist him at the French court. Cesare arrived on 28 October and stayed for just over a week, lodged with the cardinal in the archepiscopal palace. He was fêted with great magnificence, but the two principals did not appear to enjoy themselves very much. Neither had any reason to love or trust the other, and both were enduring attacks of syphilis. A week after Cesare left Avignon, Vincula followed him to the French court. Here he helped in the search for a bride willing to accept the pope's son, after the girl first chosen, a daughter of King Federico of Naples who had been brought up in France, flatly refused to marry an ex-cardinal. This took some months, and Vincula wrote several letters to reassure Alexander, saying how impressed everybody was with Cesare, and how Louis was sure to find some suitable girl soon.[60]

The delay before a bride was found meant that there was no longer any question of Vincula returning to Rome by Christmas.

During the next couple of years, there were occasional reports that he was planning to go to Rome, but he never did while Alexander was alive. He spent much of the summer of 1499 at Avignon, before going to Lyons to join Louis, who was making final preparations for his invasion of Milan. What part, if any, Vincula played in planning and preparing for this campaign is not known. The collapse of Sforza rule in the duchy of Milan was as swift as the conquest of Naples had been in 1495: on 6 October Louis entered Milan in triumph, with Vincula taking a place of honour in the procession. Vincula's old enemies Ascanio and Lodovico Sforza fled to the protection of Maximilian, King of the Romans. Their attempted return in February 1500 looked briefly as though it might succeed, but ended in their capture and imprisonment in France.

With the disappearance of the Sforza, the most important source of information on San Pietro ad Vincula's activities – the reports of Milanese agents and the letters from Vincula and his friends and servants that they intercepted and copied when they could – disappeared too. Consequently, not much is known of what he was doing over the next few years. Restless as ever, he spent much time wandering about in northern Italy, never straying very far from the areas under French rule or French protection.

While visiting his diocese at Lucca in July and August 1500, he tried, on Louis's orders, to find a solution to the intractable problem of the Pisan revolt from Florence. Pisa had rebelled against a century of Florentine rule when Charles VIII was staying there on his way to Naples in 1494, and the French had encouraged the Pisans in their fight for independence; but Florence was an ally of France and constantly demanding the French do something to clear up the problems that they had helped to create. Florentine and Pisan ambassadors visited Vincula at Cento (which belonged to his diocese of Bologna) when he moved there in the autumn, but by early October he had given up and referred the problem back to the king.

The next year or two he seems to have spent further north. He visited Milan several times – he was reported to be there in February and July 1501, and to be there with Louis in July and September 1502. He also stayed in Savona, perhaps in Genoa too. One reason for his wanderings may have been that he actually had nothing much to do. He had no role in the government of Milan and though still welcome at the French court, had no particular role there either.

He continued to keep a watch over his brother, negotiating a *condotta* with Florence for him in October 1500, though the Prefect, in fact, did not seem very keen to take it on. Giovanni was ill, and died in Rome in November 1501. Vincula did not get on very well with his brother's widow, whom he regarded as irresponsible, but he was the natural protector of his young nephew, Francesco Maria, and his sisters.

There was nothing that Vincula could do to ward off the attack by Cesare Borgia on Senigallia at the end of 1502. By then, the appetite of Alexander for lands for his children had become insatiable. The duchy of Urbino had been swallowed up in Cesare's new duchy of the Romagna,[61] and Giovanni's widow, Giovanna da Montefeltro, had incurred the pope's wrath by trying to help her brother the duke. Reports reached Rome that Francesco Maria – who was with Vincula – had, on his uncle's orders, instructed his mother to use all the resources of his state to help the Duke of Urbino in his attempt to recover his lands in November 1502. When Cesare Borgia drove the duke out a second time, Vincula wrote to the pope denying that he had instructed Giovanna to help her brother, and arguing that if she had done so, Senigallia, which belonged, not to her, but to her children, should not suffer.[62] Recognizing this would do little to deter the pope, he advised his sister-in-law that if Cesare Borgia did attack Senigallia, there should be no resistance. Only a couple of days were needed for Cesare to conquer Senigallia in the new year.

Louis was not in a position to be of much help to Vincula's family at this time. He was disputing possession of the kingdom of Naples with the King of Spain,[63] and the war was going badly for the French. He could not afford to use force to restrain Alexander – several other lords had already found that French 'protection' was no use against Borgia ambition. The pope was a little wary of proceeding against Vincula himself. In November 1502 he was reported to have annulled all the cardinal's privileges, but this order had not been made public because he did not know how Louis would react. Vincula's property was not confiscated; it was in the custody of da Costa. Earlier that year, in June, Alexander had attempted to capture the cardinal, sending Genoese galleys from Rome that were to try to lure him aboard on the pretext of a pleasure trip. In February 1503 he ordered him – with Cardinals Sforza, Riario and Colonna – to come to Rome, but there was no question of Vincula or the others being foolish enough to obey. In

March 1503 Vincula was reported to be in France, in May at Savona. It was at Savona in August that the news he must have been longing to hear reached him – Alexander VI was dead. His years of exile were over.

4

The Election

S an Pietro ad Vincula arrived back in Rome on 3 September 1503, after nearly ten years of self-imposed exile. He was honoured, reported the Venetian ambassador, as though he were the future pope.[1] With him were 100 mounted crossbowmen supplied by the Bolognese, to protect him from ambush by Cesare Borgia's men on his way to Rome. Initially, at least, he wanted to keep them with him, but they were not really needed, because Cesare Borgia had left Rome with all his troops the day before Vincula returned.

Cesare still had many men under his command, but his position was not a strong one. He later said that he had planned for every eventuality on the death of his father, except for the possibility that he himself would be gravely ill. Alexander and Cesare had both fallen ill on the same day: rumours circulating outside Rome had it that they had been poisoned by wine prepared by Cesare to kill the rich Cardinal Castellesi, which had been served to them by mistake. As they did not fall ill until a week after the party at which the poisoning was supposed to have taken place, a more likely explanation is that they both succumbed to a malarial fever that had already claimed the life of Cardinal Borgia-Lanzol on 5 August. Alexander died after about a week, on 18 August, while his much younger and stronger son was bedridden for several weeks.

Cesare had sufficiently recovered by the time his father died to give orders to his men, but his physical weakness helped embolden the cardinals to refuse to consider entering a conclave before all soldiers had withdrawn to a safe distance from the city. They did not want to choose a pope under pressure from Cesare, nor under pressure from the French and Spanish armies converging on the city. The French forces were making their way south in a rather leisurely way to confront the Spanish troops who now held most of the kingdom of Naples,[2] while the Spanish commander, Gonsalvo da Cordoba, was hurrying north to meet them. The Orsini were in arms, ready to take revenge on any Spaniard for the death of Paolo and Francesco Orsini at the hands of Cesare Borgia's executioners in January 1503, and the Colonna were on guard against the Orsini.

With French and Spanish armies nearing Rome, a strong contingent of Spanish cardinals in the College and Louis XII's chief minister, Cardinal d'Amboise – known as Cardinal Rouen – hurrying to Rome to take part in the conclave, there were real fears about how freely the cardinals would be able to make their choice of a new pope. Hence their refusal to consider entering the conclave before Rome was free of troops; hence too, perhaps, their decision to give time for those cardinals who were away from Rome to return for the election. At least three of them – Vincula, Ascanio and Rouen – came with the intention not only of participating in the conclave, but of trying to be elected themselves.

Vincula made no secret of his ambitions. The Ferrarese ambassador, Beltrando Costabili, heard that he had said he would do all he could to be pope this time, and that Rouen had no chance – as he would tell him when he arrived. If Rouen asked for his vote, he would give it to him only if he could show a list of enough cardinals who had promised him their votes to make him pope if Vincula added his own. Otherwise, he would say that he wanted to be pope himself.[3] Vincula told the Venetian ambassador Giustinian that he felt that the King of France should not back another candidate for the papacy, because of the promises that Louis had made to him for some time.

> 'I am here to look after my own interests, and not those of others, and I'm not going to give my vote to Cardinal Rouen, unless I see he has so many other votes that he could be elected without mine, which I don't believe he'll get.' And he said he wanted to be a good Italian, and if he couldn't be pope, would try to have a pope elected who would be good for the Christian religion and for the peace and tranquillity of Italy.

He also promised to bear in mind the interests of Venice, to which he declared himself to be very attached.[4] A few days later, he discussed with Costabili the previous conclaves in which he had participated. When Sixtus had died, he said, he had wanted Cardinal Barbo to be pope, but the others hadn't agreed. Innocent, 'if he had not been good, wasn't all that bad, but whatever he had been like, the one who had just died would have made him appear a saint.' When Innocent had died, Vincula had wanted da Costa, who was 'a good man', to be elected. In any case, there was no fear that any more 'barbari' (non-Italians) would be chosen.[5]

Indeed, the Spanish cardinals had quickly recognized that there was no prospect of one of them being elected, and Rouen, soon after he had arrived, had to come to terms with the fact that there was little enthusiasm for electing him either: some feared, it was said, that he would transfer the seat of the papacy to France. He complained to Giustinian that many cardinals had sworn not to elect a Frenchman or a friend of the French king, having taken oaths and signed undertakings to this effect. Contracts for votes were being made, he said, which was a disgrace to the faith.[6] According to the papal master of ceremonies, Johannes Burckhardt, Vincula was a leading conspirator.[7] Assessments of the front-runners varied, but the three most consistently mentioned were Vincula, Caraffa and another of the most senior and respected figures in the College, Piccolomini.

The cardinals, thirty-seven of them in all, entered the con-clave on 16 September; Vincula was allotted cell number thirteen. As usual, reports of the powerplay in the conclave varied. At one stage, according to Giustinian, Vincula had gathered twenty-two votes; according to both Modenese sources and Giustinian, he was scotched by Ascanio, who had pressed his own candidacy, but to small effect. This seems to have taken place before the first formal vote. After revising and subscribing the electoral capitulations, the cardinals finally held the first scrutiny on 21 September. Vincula got most votes, fifteen, Caraffa fourteen and Rouen thirteen; Vincula gave both of them his vote, and received Caraffa's in return, but not that of Rouen. The reports agree that after that, Rouen, recognizing that he had no hope of being elected himself, rallied support for Piccolomini, who had received only four votes in the scrutiny. Costabili reported that Vincula had tried to put forward da Costa to obstruct Piccolomini, but that the ambassa-dors who had the duty of guarding the conclave had warned the day before that the French army was anxious to pass Rome on its way to Naples, and that it would be unwise to delay the election much longer. Since Piccolomini, a quiet and scholarly character, was agreeable to everyone, Vincula's bid to have his old friend elected failed.[8]

It was fortunate for him that it did, for Piccolomini died within a month of his election, while da Costa, aged eighty-four and considerably older than Piccolomini, lasted for some years yet. Piccolomini, who took the title Pius III in memory of his uncle Pius II, was aged sixty-eight, and was sick and frail, tortured by gout. On 30 September, Vincula ordained him priest, and on the following day, he consecrated him bishop. A more demanding ceremony, his coronation as pope, took place on 8 October. Within a week, Pius had been taken ill. He died on 18 October. It is likely that the cardinals had, in electing him, taken into account his age and state of health; the fact that he was unlikely to last long was one of the qualifications that had made him an acceptable compromise candidate. Nevertheless, they must have hoped that he would last rather longer than he did. Now they had their work to do all over again.

Much work may have been going on behind the scenes already, because the coming papal election would be accomplished at record speed. In defiance of the old saying that he who entered the conclave 'as pope' (that is, as clear favourite) would come out of it still a cardinal, Giuliano della Rovere was confident – justifiably, as it turned out – that his time had finally come, twenty-four hours before the conclave was opened.

From the day of Pius's death he was clearly a front-runner, and by the time that the funeral ceremonies were over and the conclave was due to open, he was the only one in the field. How had he managed to do this, within two months of returning to Rome after ten years in exile?

Bribery, the cynics said. He had promised so much to so many that he would have trouble in making all the promises good, Rouen commented after the election.[9] This was not the carping of a disappointed rival, for Rouen, having recognized that he had no chance himself, had backed Vincula, and was in part responsible for his triumph. Venice had also backed him, and the Signoria had asked the Venetian cardinals to give him their votes. There were only two of them, not enough to have a crucial impact on the outcome. It was the Spanish cardinals who really held the key to success. It was their votes Vincula had needed; none of them had voted for him in the previous conclave. This had meant that he had had to come to terms with Cesare Borgia, who could command the votes of several of them who owed their promotion to his father.

Vincula's bargain with Cesare and the Spanish cardinals was struck on 29 October, at a meeting in the papal palace.[10] Rouen may have been present as well.[11] While the fact that the meeting had taken place became known by the morning after, few details of what passed there emerged. Burckhardt heard that Vincula had promised that if he became pope, he would make Cesare captain of the papal forces and help him to maintain himself in his Romagnol dominions. In return, the Spanish cardinals promised to give him their vote.[12]

After this agreement became known, Vincula was a clear favourite in the betting in the banking quarter. That he should be outpacing all rivals so clearly did not please all his supporters, who feared that there would be a reaction. Vincula himself was wearied by the incessant bargaining, complaining to Giustinian: 'See the problems which the mess Pope Alexander left behind him is leading to, with so many cardinals. Necessity forces men to do what they don't want to do, so long as they're in the hands of others; but once they're free, they can behave differently.'[13]

Observers in Rome thought it an extraordinary conclave. No one could remember a cardinal entering a conclave with everyone, including himself, so confident that he would be elected. According to Machiavelli, who was in Rome at the time, Ascanio made a last ditch attempt to put up Cardinal Pallavicino as a competitor,[14] but no one else reported any disagreements. Since the cardinals had already made up their minds whom they wanted to be pope, they agreed to cut the preliminary proceedings short, hear the Mass of the Holy Spirit, and get on with the election. They had already, on the evening of 30 October, as was customary, gone in a body to Vincula's cell to tell him that they intended to elect him. When the scrutiny was held the next day, he was duly elected unanimously (he himself voted for Caraffa, da Costa and Rouen). After the results of the scrutiny were read out, the cardinals crowded round the new pope to congratulate him. He announced the title he would take: Julius II. He was seated in the papal chair and given the papal ring, the 'fisherman's ring', of Pius III, but so confident had he been, that he had come prepared with his own 'fisherman's ring' and took that instead. Seated on the altar, Julius received the reverences of the cardinals and others, and was then carried in the papal chair to St Peter's for the singing of the *Te Deum*. It had been, and still is, the quickest conclave on record.

Bribery alone could not explain the speed and unanimity of this election, though it figures large in the explanation that Francesco Guicciardini, that most astute of political commentators of early Cinquecento Italy, suggested.

> Great, certainly, was the universal amazement that the papacy should have been given up, without a dissenting voice, to a cardinal who was notorious for his very difficult nature, which everyone found formidable, and who, always unquiet, and having spent his life in continual turmoil, of necessity had offended many and aroused hatreds and enmities with many important men. But on the other hand, the reasons were clear why, having overcome all difficulties, he was raised to such an elevated position. Because, having been for a long time a very powerful cardinal, and owing to the magnificence in which he had always outshone all others, and to his rare spirit, he not only had many friends but also deep-rooted authority in the court, and he had gained the reputation of being a leading defender of ecclesiastical dignity and liberty. But much more influential in his promotion had been the excessive and infinite promises he made to cardinals, to princes, to barons and to anyone who could be useful to him in this business, of whatever they cared to ask. And besides, he had the means to distribute money and many benefices and ecclesiastical dignities, both of his own and those of others, because with the reports of his liberality many, of their own accord, vied to offer to put at his disposal their money, their name, their offices and their benefices; nor did anyone consider that his promises were much greater than, as pope, he could or should observe, because he had for a long time had such a name as a generous and truthful man that Alexander VI, bitterly critical of him in other ways, admitted he was a man of his word. This good repute he did not mind besmirching in order to obtain the papacy, knowing that no one can more easily deceive others than one who is accustomed to, and has a reputation for, not using deceit.[15]

Of course, Julius had made promises, lavish promises, promises that, as Rouen had predicted, he would find difficult to reconcile, difficult to keep. Most problematic of all would be the promises that he had made to Cesare Borgia. But since he had returned to Rome, he had had the opportunity to remind his colleagues of the force of his personality, of his vigour and determination. He had been a cardinal and an important political figure for over thirty years; he knew the world and its ways, and yet had preserved a reputation as one who defended the interests of the Church and would not willingly see her rights diminished. His years with the French had not deprived him of the reputation of being an independent man, and though he was expected to be a friend of France, which was the leading power in Italy, no one could fear that he would be a French puppet. It was still a gamble for the cardinals, for he was known to be quick-tempered, unpredictable, stubborn. But whatever else he might be, he would not be weak, and the papacy stood in need of a strong hand at that hour.

The political map of Italy had been irrevocably changed in the previous decade. As a cardinal, Giuliano della Rovere had helped to bring this about, encouraging the French to come into Italy and to press their claims to Italian territory. The incursions of the French had brought the Spanish into the peninsula, at first to help restore the Aragonese dynasty dislodged by the French from the kingdom of Naples, but then to take its place. At the time of Julius's election, the French and Spanish armies were facing one another across the River Garigliano, near the northern borders of the kingdom – the real contest being who could keep their morale in the incessant rain and muddy bivouacs. To the north of the Papal States, the French were the masters of Milan, and the pole of power to which the smaller Italian states turned for protection. Among the states that found it hard to escape the force-field of French domination was Florence, now reduced to a second-rank power in Italy, weakened by the weary struggle to recover Pisa, which had been lost to her since Charles VIII's invasion in 1494. Of the five powers that had formerly dominated Italy – Milan, Naples, Venice, Florence and the pope – only Venice and the pope still preserved their full independence of action and the ability to influence the course of events. It was France and, increasingly, Spain, that were the major players of Italian politics. Maximilian, King of the Romans (he could not properly be called Emperor because he had not been crowned by the pope), was ready to assert the Holy Roman Empire's rights in Italy as well. His congenital poverty and fecklessness and indecision made it difficult for him to make his pretensions good, but, nevertheless, he had more weight in Italian affairs than any Emperor had had for a century.

The new balance of power in Italy had yet to be decided, and would not be for another thirty years. The task that faced Julius was to maintain the power and authority, temporal and spiritual, of the papacy in this uncertain new world. What remained of the spiritual authority of the papacy had been compromised by the scandals and cynicism of the Borgia pope and his family, and the restoration of the dignity and authority of the Church was one of the tasks that Julius was to set himself. But for him the dignity and authority of the Church were inextricably associated with the temporal power of the papacy, and throughout his pontificate, he saw his primary task in the defence of papal territory and the consolidation of papal control over the temporal government of that territory.

The major weak spot in the temporal authority of the papacy was still the tradition of semi-independence of many of the major towns and leading families of the northern Papal States. Cesare Borgia's campaigns to eliminate the signorial dynasties of the Romagna and the Marche had cut a terrible swathe through their ranks, but were too recent for his new duchy of the Romagna, conferred on him by his father, to have snuffed out old political loyalties and habits. Within weeks of Alexander VI's death, his son's authority was crumbling away in his new duchy, and surviving members of the old families were coming back to try to revitalize their rule. Some found this easier than others. While Guidobaldo da Montefeltro recovered his duchy of Urbino with no trouble at all, the Malatesta of Rimini and the Manfredi of Faenza, who had already been in decline, had little prospect of reconstructing viable regimes. They needed protectors to help them to survive, but effective protectors were rather harder to find than they had been. Now there were no resident dukes of Milan or kings of Naples to provide troops and pensions. While the new master of Milan, Louis of France, was willing to accept major families such as the Este of Ferrara, or major cities such as Bologna, under his tutelage, he was not interested in propping up petty dynasties of *signori* in small Romagnol towns. Florence still wanted to exert influence in the region, but was hamstrung by the financial and military burden of the war with Pisa. Venice, the remaining traditional prop of the lords of the Romagna and the Marche, was very ready to lend an ear to appeals for help, even if the answer to those appeals was not what the remnants of once powerful families such as the Malatesta, the Manfredi or the Ordelaffi wanted to hear. The Venetians saw little advantage in trying to support these broken reeds when presented with what seemed a golden opportunity to take the Romagnol towns directly under Venetian rule.

So, ironically, for much of Julius's pontificate, the greatest threat to the papacy that he perceived came, not from the ultramontane powers, but from the only other remaining independent Italian power of any substance, Venice. Hostility to Venice, and the obsessive urge to recover the territory that she had taken from the Church, would be the fulcrum of his policy for the first six years of his reign.

5

·

The Patrimony of the Church

Julius had no time at all to settle in and enjoy the extraordinary turn that his fortunes had taken before he had to confront the problem that would dominate much of his pontificate. Even as he was planning to celebrate his coronation in lavish style, and to make the ceremonial journey to take possession of the ancient palace and basilica of the bishops of Rome, the Lateran, the Venetians were busy taking possession of as much of the papal province of the Romagna as they could grab.

To the world outside the lagoons, the Venetians presented their activities in the Romagna as a move against their enemy, the common enemy, Cesare Borgia. They had watched his campaigns in the Romagna with a jealous eye, fearing that he might turn his attention to the recovery of Ravenna and Cervia, papal towns they had taken more than half a century before. A debilitating and anxiety-provoking war against the Turks had prevented them from seriously considering using force to contain Cesare Borgia's expansion, and they had limited their interference with his plans to giving refuge to members of the signorial families who had been fortunate enough to escape being captured or murdered by him. Within the walls of the senate, the real motives of the Venetians were clearly expressed. While some patricians, particularly the older ones, advised caution, others felt that the opportunity to realize long-held territorial ambitions in the Romagna and the Marche was too good to miss. By early September 1503 the powerful Committee of Ten had some negotiation afoot in 'all the lands of the Romagna'.[1]

The first major prize was Rimini. Pandolfo Malatesta, who had been lord of the city and a Venetian client before Cesare had forced him out in 1500, was soliciting the protection of Venice in early October, even before he had recovered his *stato*. If the peasants in the country around Rimini felt some loyalty to the Malatesta, most people in the city were not very keen to have them back, and Pandolfo was a typical representative of the fag-ends of the Romagnol signorial dynasties in being a weak, ineffective and cruel man. The Venetians wasted little energy on supporting him, concentrating instead on persuading him to agree that Venice should take over Rimini for herself. The day after Julius's election on 2 November, Pandolfo came in person to offer himself, his son and his *stato* for their service. By the middle of the month, he had agreed to surrender Rimini to them, in exchange for cash, a small *condotta* and an estate in Venetian territory; and by 22 November the Venetians had control of the city and its fortress, described by the new Venetian castellan as 'very beautiful, and the key to the Romagna'.[2]

At about the same time as they were clinching the agreement for Rimini, the Venetians were achieving another major objective, the seizure of Faenza. This they accomplished, not by agreement, but by force. The fortress was obtained by negotiation with the castellan early in November, but the people not only wanted to keep their young lord Astorre Manfredi, they were looking to Florence, not Venice, for protection. In order to have their way, the Venetians brought troops to camp outside the city, and when the Faentini sent envoys to the camp to declare that they had no intention of abandoning Astorre, they were bluntly told that Venice did not want him to stay. If the citizens submitted without a fight, Venice would be kind; if they were obstinate, Faenza would be sacked. A few days after the agreement with Pandolfo Malatesta, the Faentini negotiated a rather less generous settlement in lands and cash for the Manfredi, as well as terms for themselves, and the Venetian commissioner entered the city, received, he claimed, with joy. Faenza, he reported, was a very large and populous city, a good acquisition.[3]

Before Faenza was bullied into submission, the Venetians had already gained the Val di Lamone, the valley of the upper reaches of the River Lamone, which flowed to Faenza from the mountains. Here the decisive factor was winning over some of the faction leaders, especially Dionigio Naldi, an infantry captain who had been in Cesare Borgia's service. Not only did the acquisition of the valley block one route of Florentine penetration into the Romagna, it gave Venice control of several mountain passes and more fortresses, including one major one, Brisighella, and of a recruiting ground for the prized Romagnol infantry. Other valleys and fortresses were targeted too, such as Verrucchio and Montefiore, south of Rimini. Several of these smaller places sent to Venice to offer to surrender. Not all their offers were taken up. The rectors of Ravenna refused to accept the surrender of Savignano in early October, because they had been told to take only the larger places, and Savignano was small and had no fortress. The place was in Venetian control by early December, so presumably there was a change of heart.

Fano, which was considerably more important than Savignano, also volunteered to submit to Venice, in late October just before Julius was elected. There was some opposition in the senate to accepting Fano's offer, because the town had been directly under the government of the papacy, not held in vicariate, before it had been given to Cesare, but after some debate, it was decided to agree to it. The envoys carrying this reply back to Fano, however, reached the city two hours after the news of Julius's election had come making the people decide against raising the Venetian standard.

The Venetians were surprised when they heard the people of Fano had not raised the banner of San Marco; Julius, when he heard that it was the news of his election that had made them change their minds, was delighted.[4] His view of what was happening in the Romagna was very different from that of the Venetians, as anyone who knew him and his reputation as a defender of ecclesiastical rights and property could easily have anticipated. Collective self-conceit seems to have blinded many of the senate to how he was likely to react, and their suspicion and indignation at his response looks genuine. As a cardinal, he had been friendly with Venice for many years, as both he and they recalled during the early days of his pontificate. The Pregadi decided that his election warranted a special letter of congratulation in Latin, because he had been so much the friend of Venice; and Julius, at his first meeting with the Venetian ambassador after his election, told him not to stand on ceremony, that he would be the same friend to Venice as before.[5] Each side saw the implications of the long-standing friendship differently, however. The Venetians argued it should make the pope readier to accept that they should hold on to the lands that they had taken, while Julius argued it should make them readier to help him to maintain the honour of the Holy See.

Barely a month after his election, Julius had already made it clear that his duty as head of the Church took precedence over any earlier friendship. Displeased by reports of Venetian progress in the Romagna, he said he was sorry that he had cause to quarrel with Venice at the beginning of his pontificate, 'but he could not, with honour nor in good conscience, let them take the lands of the Church.'[6] He said it and he meant it, and against this resolution, to their surprise and indignation, none of the arguments that the Venetians put forward – that they were only taking the lands from Cesare Borgia; that they were preventing Florence from taking them; that they were taking only lands that had been held by others from the Church, not lands that the Church had ruled directly, and that they were willing to pay the due census for them – none of these prevailed. It was no excuse, Julius told Giustinian, to say that Venice had simply taken the lands from Cesare Borgia. It was no business of hers to do that, the papacy could see to it. When asked to grant Venice the vicariate of the lands she had occupied, he replied that the pope could not alienate the property of the Church without the consent of the cardinals; that he didn't want to do it as pope; and that if he were a cardinal, he wouldn't vote in favour either.[7]

The attitude of the Venetians was equally uncompromising. When Angelo Leonino, Bishop of Tivoli, the legate Julius sent to Venice, told them the pope wanted the lands back, the Doge told him bluntly that Venice had no intention of giving them up, no matter what the cost. This was not, he said, the behaviour they had expected of Julius.[8] Such was the arrogance of the Venetians, so adamant their refusal to believe that Julius could not be willing to let them keep the territory that they had occupied, that they accused the legate of forging the briefs he brought before the government reiterating the pope's demand for their return, and asked for him to be recalled to Rome. Convinced that the legate was unpopular just because he was pressing the papacy's case so determinedly, Julius refused.[9]

Uncompromising his words might be, but, for the moment, they were the only means that he used to defend the Church's lands from the encroachment of the Venetians. It was only his patent sincerity and concern for the loss of the Romagnol lands that convinced Cardinal Rouen and the Florentine representatives in Rome, Cardinal Soderini and Niccolò Machiavelli, that he was not secretly in collusion with Venice. The Florentines, who had sent some troops to the Romagna to support what resistance there was to Venice, were annoyed and frustrated that he was not doing more, and sent regular reports of the latest Venetian moves to try to stimulate him into reinforcing his words with action. Part of the reason for his delay in sending troops himself seems to have been a stubborn hope that words alone could convince the Venetians that he was not prepared to use the Church's lands to buy their friendship. There were important practical reasons too: a shortage of money and men. Cesare Borgia's campaigns had used up the papal revenues and exhausted the treasury. What was left on Alexander's death, Cesare had appropriated for himself. He had been the papal commander, his troops the papal troops, and his men were all but dispersed. Those of them that were left were stripped of their weapons in Tuscany when he sent them north to try to save the remains of his disintegrating dominions. When Julius did, at last, send commissioners to the Romagna, they had difficulty in reaching it through the snow-blocked passes of the Apennines, in an exceptionally severe winter. His inability to respond effectively in this crisis was a lesson he did not forget. He would spend years building up the papal treasury to ensure that he would never be so helpless again.

The question of what was to become of Cesare Borgia was a major complicating factor in the whole Romagnol problem. He was no longer really a free agent, and to those who had known him in his prepotent days of glory, he sometimes seemed a confused and even pathetic figure. At other times, his old arrogance returned, but his threats and bluster were little more than posturing. His two remaining cards (apart from the remnants of his fearsome reputation) were the fortresses of Cesena, Forlì and Bertinoro in the Romagna, which were still held for him, and the continued loyalty of the group of Spanish cardinals who had bargained for him before the conclave. The first meant that he still had some potential to cause trouble; the second meant he could not simply be executed or quietly eliminated. Besides, in order to smooth the way to his election as pope, Julius had made an agreement with him, promising, among other things, to make him captain of the papal troops. While Julius had no intention of fulfilling that particular promise, he did feel some compunction about breaking his word, and certainly did not want to be seen to break his word without a good pretext. He even toyed with the idea of using Cesare to stem the Venetians in the Romagna, for Cesare could still attract loyalty not only from the Spanish commanders of his fortresses but also, to some degree, from the people

of the province, among those who did not relish the thought of
being ruled either by Venice, or by their former lords or directly
by the papacy. This notion did not attract the pope for long,
especially with the Venetians claiming that all they were doing in
the Romagna was taking the lands of their enemy, Cesare Borgia.
Instead, Julius concentrated on forcing Cesare to hand over the
fortresses being held for him, as the price of being allowed to leave
Rome.

After Julius's election, Cesare had surrendered the Castel
Sant' Angelo to him and come to live in the Vatican, but he did
not feel safe there and wanted to depart. Julius was prepared to
let him go, for this was the moment when he considered using him
in the Romagna. If Cesare was to go to the Romagna with the
connivance of the pope, there was a swift change of plan, for only
a couple of days after he left Rome for Ostia on 19 November,
Julius sent to him to ask for the countersigns of the fortresses that
he held. Ten days later, he was brought back to Rome by the
papal guard. Julius summoned a congregation of cardinals to
explain, especially to the Spanish, why he had ordered this.
Venice, he said, has claimed to be acting against Cesare, so in
order to remove this pretext, he had asked Cesare to surrender the
lands and castles that he held. After much debate, he had agreed
to give up the countersigns, but in case he did not give the true
ones, he would be kept in a safe place until it was clear that the
fortresses would be yielded by his castellans.[10]

This proved to take several months. Either acting on secret
instructions from their master, or hoping to raise their own price
for surrendering the castles in their charge, or out of genuine
concern for Cesare's safety, the castellans took some convincing
that he really intended them to leave. About the time he was
brought back to Rome, the troops that he had sent north were
surrounded and stripped of their weapons by Tuscan peasants
and the soldiers of Gianpaolo Baglioni. Julius was particularly
pleased by the capture of Michelotto, one of Cesare's most notorious
commanders, whom he thought could reveal all the crimes and
extortions of the Borgia. Cesare, his position weakened even more
by this blow, handed over the countersigns and received in return
a brief dated 8 December saying that he could go where he liked,
once the fortresses had been surrendered.[11] His castellans, however, refused to surrender them while their master was being held
against his will. In early February, Cesare was sent to Ostia, in
the custody of one of the Spanish cardinals, Carvajal. The object

was to prevent the castellans from saying that he was a prisoner in Rome, but, in fact, he was more closely guarded at Ostia. Negotiations with the castellans of Cesena and Bertinoro were making more progress than those with the commander at Forlì, who was demanding 15,000 ducats. It was agreed that Cesare could go once Cesena and Bertinoro had been handed over and he had deposited 15,000 ducats for Forlì. Carvajal stood by these terms, letting him leave on 19 April, as soon as news of the surrender of the two fortresses arrived.

Julius was not pleased: he was said to be in no hurry to free Cesare, thinking every day of new dangers that he could cause.[12] He had already extracted a formal promise from him that he would not attack papal territory, but it is difficult to see what threat Cesare could pose, once the fortress at Forlì was out of his control. Carvajal, who seems to have felt a little sorry for Cesare, argued that he was no danger – he had no money, he was ill with syphilis and he would not get any help from the Spanish, with whom he had taken refuge.[13] He had gone to Naples, where the viceroy Gonsalvo had at first made him welcome; but he had begun to try to recruit troops, and when Ferdinand and Isabella heard of their unwelcome guest, they ordered their viceroy to arrest him. He was held in Naples until the castellan of Forlì was finally persuaded to yield, in August, and was then transferred to Spain, passing out of Italian history.[14]

As if Julius did not have enough to deal with, outmanoeuvring his former friends the Venetians and his old *bête noir*, Cesare Borgia, members of his own family had ambitions in the Romagna. Cardinal Riario, his cousins, the sons of Girolamo Riario, and their mother Caterina Sforza, had their sights on the recovery of Imola and Forlì, from which they had been expelled by Cesare. Mutual dislike between Caterina and the cardinal was too intense to be buried even in this common cause: Caterina backed the claims of her eldest son, Ottaviano, while the cardinal backed Galeazzo.

In the early months of his pontificate, Julius made much of Cardinal Riario, taking him into his confidence. Apparently, he did not wish to upset him by rejecting out of hand the idea of a restoration of the Riario, and initially the cardinal was quite optimistic. This optimism was probably ill-founded. Julius had no reason to love the sons of his old enemy, nor did the people of Imola and Forlì. The Forlivesi much preferred to have their former *signori*, the Ordelaffi, back, despite the fact that

Antoniomaria Ordelaffi was sick and had no obvious heirs. At Imola, too, there was another family of former *signori* who wanted to return, the Alidosi. Their claim to Imola was weaker than that of the Ordelaffi to Forlì, because it was several decades since they had ruled there and their record as *signori* had been impressive only for its violence and incompetence. Their trump card was Francesco Alidosi, a favourite servant of Julius in the years of his exile and marked from the early days of the pontificate as one of the key figures at court.   .

Against this competition, no outstanding personal qualities strengthened the claims of the Riario. Very few people in Imola and Forlì had any desire to see Girolamo Riario's widow, the virago Caterina Sforza, back; her eldest son, Ottaviano, was obese, stupid and reputed to be under his mother's thumb; the middle son, Cesare, was a cleric, and out of the running; and there was little to recommend the youngest, Galeazzo – Julius himself thought that there wasn't much to him.[15] But when a match was arranged between Galeazzo and the sister of one of the pope's favourite nephews, Galeotto della Rovere, the new Cardinal San Pietro ad Vincula, in January 1504, the Imolesi interpreted this as a sign of favour, decided that they had better make the best of it, and staged a demonstration in the streets asking for Galeazzo to be made vicar of Imola.

Over the next few months, the Imolesi continued to refer to Galeazzo and Cardinal Riario as though they expected Galeazzo to be given the vicariate under the cardinal's supervision, but Julius gave no sign that this was his intention. Meanwhile, Imola was troubled by faction-fighting, with the Alidosi backing the Sassatelli and their followers, who gradually gained the upper hand. It began to be said that Francesco Alidosi would succeed in getting Imola for his brother; the papal governor of Imola was reckoned to be an Alidosi man. The governor, however, reported to Julius in August that the people really wanted to be under the direct rule of the Church. With this request, genuine or not, Julius was ready to comply.

He had already granted a bull to the people of Forlì in June, promising that their city would not be given to any other papal vicars.[16] When Antoniomaria Ordelaffi had died, in February 1504, they had been prepared to consider accepting an illegitimate Ordelaffi, Lodovico, as *signore*, or possibly to turn to Venice, but had sent envoys to Julius to say they did not want the Riario back. Julius was not prepared to accept Lodovico, was certainly anxious not to drive the Forlivesi into the arms of the Venetians, and did not try to persuade them to change their minds about the Riario. He floated the idea of giving Forlì to his nephew Francesco Maria della Rovere, but the Forlivesi did not take to the suggestion, and he did not insist. Just as he was quite prepared to forgo any family ambitions in order to secure Forlì, so, perhaps, he had been biding his time with Imola, unwilling to give a direct repulse to either Cardinal Riario or Francesco Alidosi, but waiting until the Imolesi asked to be immediately subject to the papacy.

Initially, Cardinal Riario refused to agree to the bull for Forlì, saying that he could not sign away the rights of his *nipoti*, but soon, to his great discontent, he began to realize the game was lost. A month later, he signed the bull and also ceded his family's rights in Imola, for a promise of compensation, including repayment of 6,000 ducats that he had given to Borgia's castellan of Imola to get him out of the fortress. The Riario boys were not happy with this arrangement, but there was nothing they could do. All vicariates over the city, including that granted to their father, were definitively revoked by a bull promulgated in October, promising that Imola, like Forlì, would stay under the direct rule of the Church. Francesco Alidosi was promised compensation for his family's claims too, but he did not give up hope that one day, perhaps after Julius's death, the Alidosi would once again rule in Imola.

By the autumn of 1504, then, Cesare Borgia was out of the way, the last Ordelaffi had been forced out of Forlì and the Riario had been pushed aside. Of the major towns of the Romagna, Cesena, Imola and Forlì were back under papal rule. Faenza and Rimini, however, were still in the hands of the Venetians, as were many smaller places, including much of the territory of Cesena and Imola.

The Venetians were given a warning of what might be in store for them if they continued to brush off Julius's protests. On 22 September 1504, as part of a series of agreements between Louis XII, Maximilian, King of the Romans, and his son, Philip, Duke of Burgundy, known as the Treaties of Blois, an alliance specifically directed against Venice was concluded. Its object was to recover from her, territories claimed by the pope and by Maximilian and Louis. Representatives of the pope were present at the conclusion of this alliance, and he was mentioned as its promoter, but he was not formally a party to it.[17]

Some cardinals were not sure it was wise for the pope to be

associated with a treaty that was liable to upset the King of Spain, but Julius hoped for great things from it. He had been working since the beginning of his pontificate, soliciting the support of the major powers against the Venetians. From the first, he had declared himself ready to 'arouse all the Christian princes against them'.[18] The problem was that the leading Christian princes – Louis, Ferdinand and Maximilian – were preoccupied in trying to resolve a complex web of conflicting claims and grievances among themselves, and regarded Venice as a potentially useful counterweight.

Reconciling France and Spain had been Julius's first aim in the early months of his pontificate, when he had argued that this would be to the advantage of everyone except Venice. Papal briefs asking for help might be couched in terms of 'defending the Church',[19] but Julius knew that self-interest was the most powerful spur. Speaking to the Mantuan envoy, Gianluigi Cataneo, he told him, 'If peace is made between them, as I hope, I would like to make use of them both, because if they don't take steps, in time one of them will have trouble in Milan and the other in the kingdom [of Naples]';[20] for wherever the Venetians went, 'by sea or land, especially in Italy, they are too overbearing... I know what's in my interests', he said, 'and [those] of the Church and of my family, but it's also in the interests of Italy and of the world.'[21] He was sure that if peace were made, Venice would return Rimini and Faenza.

It was principally to the French that Julius looked for help, even if he thought 'sometimes they don't seem to care for anyone, and they can't be relied on much.'[22] Louis and Cardinal Rouen, his chief minister, took the line that Julius was legally in the right in demanding the return of the Romagnol territories, and that it would be desirable for Venice to comply, but made it clear France did not intend to attack Venice or even lose her alliance. Ferdinand of Spain took a similar view. He made a token offer to lend Julius some of his troops from Naples, while naming Venice as an ally in the truce with France concluded in February 1504, claiming to have done this before receiving the papal brief that asked him not to. So neither France nor Spain was prepared to go to war with Venice to get Julius's lands back for him. After all his efforts and all his hopes, they did not even mention him in the truce they agreed, and he thought that neither side showed much respect for his concerns.

Nevertheless, he did not feel strong enough to act on his own, and continued to solicit support from the major European powers. Now it was on a prospective peace between Louis and Maximilian that he pinned his hopes. He found his position as a suppliant galling, complaining to the Duke of Urbino that 'he had to be everyone's slave.' When the duke said that it was his own doing, Julius took the hint, replying that 'to recover these lands, he had to make himself a slave to France, Spain, Germany and all the world.' Urbino argued that if he came to some agreement with Venice, from being a slave he could become master of all. This was true, the pope responded, but he couldn't do it with honour, and 'did not want to do anything for which he could be blamed, and which would give his successor grounds to complain he lost the way to recovering the Church's property'.[23]

Cultivating Maximilian proved as thankless and fruitless as asking for help from Louis and Ferdinand. Julius found the letters that Maximilian sent to Venice on his behalf far too weak and conciliatory, but purported to blame his advisers, and urged him to come to Italy. Perpetually hard-up, Maximilian wanted to use money that had been collected in Germany for a crusade. This was sacrosanct, Julius told him, and could only be used for the defence of Christianity or (pointedly) the recovery of the cities of the Church.[24] Maximilian showed no signs of a serious intention to come to Italy, and even baulked at sending an envoy to Venice at the pope's request. All that Julius accomplished was to make Ferdinand nervous. Afraid that a war against Venice would merely present Louis with an opportunity to extend his power in Italy, the king ordered his ambassadors in Rome and Venice to try to settle the quarrel over the Romagna peacefully, in such a way that Julius would abandon the idea of forming a league with France and Germany, and Venice would feel grateful to Spain.

The treaty of Blois concluded in September 1504, with its alliances specifically directed against Venice, seemed to be the realization of Julius's hopes and efforts, but, once again, they were to be disappointed. Maximilian, though the terms agreed had been very favourable to him, delayed in ratifying them, and the pope's optimism that, once he had ratified the treaty, he really would attack Venice with Louis began to fade. Something had been achieved, nonetheless, for the Venetians had been alarmed at the news of the alliance and were ready to listen when hints were dropped in Rome that some sort of compromise might be on the cards.

It was Francesco Alidosi who seems to have been the first to broach the subject with the Venetian ambassador, Giustinian. Assuring him that Maximilian was coming to Italy with a powerful army, Alidosi said that he personally would like there to be peace between the pope and Venice, because 'he knew well that the pope only stood to lose if the barbarians came to Italy', but, he said, necessity was driving Julius on, because he could not back out with honour. You Venetians, he remarked, laughing, 'want to hold our lands and then you want us to keep quiet about it. Start by giving back the *contado* of Imola, and the other things you have no shade of justification at all for keeping – then, as for the rest, it will be as God wills.'[25]

Once the Venetians took the hint, it was only a matter of weeks before agreement was reached on the principle of a settlement. The details took a little longer, because the Venetians hoped to extract a formal grant of Rimini and Faenza from the pope. He made it clear this was out of the question, and refused to put anything in writing, refused even to send a friendly brief, until the Venetians had fulfilled their promises. While the Venetians discussed the matter in secret meetings behind closed doors, Julius was much less discreet, speaking openly about the negotiations that the Duke of Urbino was handling for him in Rome. Both sides were keen to settle the business, however, so in early March 1505 Venice agreed to hand over to the pope eleven fortresses and villages, including the territory belonging to Cesena and Imola that those towns had been clamouring to have back, in return for Julius ceasing to press for the return of Rimini and Faenza. This was not much of a concession by the pope, in truth, which is perhaps why the Venetians tried to put it about outside Italy that they had been granted the investiture of Rimini and Faenza, to his great annoyance.

Discord over this point somewhat marred the harmony of the grand embassy that the Venetians sent to Rome, with eight ambassadors, to swear obedience to Julius as the 'new' pope. At the ceremony, on 5 May, the Florentine ambassador reported, 'Their oration was high-flown and full of flowers and curlicues, in commendation and praise of His Holiness the Pope and of their city.' All that they got from Julius in return was a short, purely conventional response.[26]

Neither the pope nor the Venetians regarded this as the final settlement of the matter. The Venetians would continue to press for investiture with the two cities that they had hung on to, and Julius, if he ceased for the time-being to urge the ultramontane powers to attack Venice, was by no means reconciled to their loss. Lack of cash and lack of troops had hindered him from taking command of the situation in the Romagna in the first months of his pontificate. Appeals to the ultramontane powers for help had borne little real fruit. For the next two years, Julius concentrated on ensuring that in future he would have the resources to act when he wanted to, alone if need be.

Chafing at his inability to counter the loss of papal territory, as early as February 1504 he had clearly decided that he needed a long-term strategy. He described the papacy as 'poverty-stricken and run-down'. For the honour of God, for his own honour, he could not rest until he had brought about some proper settlement. He knew that it would be difficult to do anything quickly, but the time would come when even the troubles with Venice might have an end.[27] Soon it was noticed that he was gathering money from every possible, legitimate, source – 'not by the sort of tricks Pope Alexander used to get up to'. He had been heard to say 'that he wanted to accumulate 200,000 ducats, which appeared to him to be essential for any pope to face up to every adversity and problem which might confront him, by raising some troops'.[28] Expenses were pruned to such an extent that his stinginess began to excite remark – he cut the papal guard by two-thirds, and had had more people in his personal household when he was a cardinal.[29] Generous and free-spending then, now he began to be described as avaricious. Debts went unpaid or were paid in other ways than with cash. By the end of the year, he had already garnered over 100,000 ducats; by May 1505, his initial target of 200,000 ducats had been reached. Still he did not relax his purse-strings, and by late August, when he spent two days in the Castel Sant' Angelo, doing nothing but look over his treasure, he had over 300,000 ducats and was planning to raise more by granting 'expectatives' (privileges giving the right to succeed to a benefice after the death of the existing incumbent). By the following January, according to Alidosi, he had 400,000 ducats between cash and plate, and was accumulating more every day. 'Believe me', Alidosi said, 'he is holding this to undertake some fine expedition and not to give it to his *nipoti*, nor does he want other popes to have it.'[30]

Money and the troops that money could buy were not the whole solution to the problem of guarding the territorial integrity of the Papal States. They could help to combat threats and drive off intruders, but what was also needed was more effective government, to make it harder for other powers to turn papal subjects into political clients. Papal rhetoric might speak of the 'mild' and 'sweet' rule of the Church, but in Italy, 'government by priests' was synonymous with weakness and oppressive inefficiency, with a chronic instability and lack of control generating disorder that could spill over into neighbouring territories. Factions flourished, and, all too often, the response of papal officials was not to attempt the difficult task of pacification, but to allow one to prevail over its rivals. Dynasties of *signori*, some with their rule sanctioned by the grant of vicariates, others simply party bosses with no legal authority for their dominance, had become so rooted a feature of life in the north and east of the Papal States by the later fifteenth century that they regarded the cities they ruled as their own property. This was why Pandolfo Malatesta could 'sell' his 'right' over Rimini to Venice. Even the Riario, Julius's own relatives, were ready to promise Venice the 'reversion' of Imola and Forlì if the Riario died out, when they were casting about for support for their attempt to return.[31] Giovanni Bentivoglio, who had no legitimate sanction for his power over Bologna, and despite the fact that the city was the seat of papal government for the area, conducted an independent 'foreign policy', forming his own alliances with scant regard for whatever policy the pope might be pursuing at the time.

These conditions positively invited interference in the Papal States by other powers. Julius found it intolerable. His famous campaign against the Baglioni of Perugia and the Bentivoglio of Bologna in 1506 – the foundation of his reputation as the 'warrior pope' – was only the best-known manifestation of his desire to strengthen the hold of papal government over its territory and to focus the obedience and loyalty of its subjects on the pope, not on some local faction leader or external power. The campaign was just the climax of a concerted effort to pacify the Papal States, and to reform and stabilize the government of its cities, which had been under way since the first year of his pontificate.

The scale of the task that he was taking on can be gauged just by considering a list of towns in the Papal States where faction-fighting, boundary disputes or other quarrels seriously disturbed public order during the period from the summer of 1504 to the summer of 1506, before Julius launched his campaign against the Baglioni and Bentivoglio: Imola, Spoleto, Foligno, Ascoli, Ancona, Jesi, Forlì, Rieti, Fano, Terracina, Pesaro, Todi, Cesena, Rocca Antica, Civita Castellana, Viterbo, Trevi, Norcia, Gallese and Otricoli. In some cases, notably that of Forlì, there were several reported episodes of fighting. And these are just the towns for which reports of disorder survive; there may have been others too.

A closer look at three principal trouble spots in three different provinces of the Papal States – Rieti in Umbria, Forlì in the Romagna and Ascoli in the Marche – reveals the kind of problems that had to be tackled.

Rieti was traditionally one of the Ghibelline strongholds of Umbria, with ties to the Colonna family. The persecution of the Colonna in the later years of Alexander VI's pontificate, during which their lands had been confiscated and given to members of the Borgia family, and the close association of the Orsini with Cesare Borgia until the final dramatic year of his father's reign, had brought about a resurgence of the Guelfs in Rieti, and the exile of some leading Ghibellines. The nemesis of the Borgia permitted the return of a leading Ghibelline family, the Poiani, and the prospect of a revival of their party's dominance. The Guelfs responded by introducing some troops of the Orsini party leader, Bartolomeo d'Alviano, into the town in January 1504, who killed about twenty Ghibellines. Fabrizio Colonna, when he heard of this, came swiftly, with many armed men. About forty Guelfs were killed, Bartolomeo d'Alviano's troops thrown out and all the Colonna's exiled friends readmitted.

A year later, the Guelfs entered Rieti by night and seized control of the main square. When morning came, the Ghibellines took arms, gathered 1,000 men and attacked the Guelfs, but were repulsed with heavy losses. For two days, the triumphant Guelfs rampaged through Rieti, killing, looting and burning, but on the third night, Ghibelline leaders from neighbouring Piediluco and Terni arrived; gathering their men and those who had fled Rieti, they attacked and defeated the Guelfs, who fled in their turn, leaving 100 dead. A few days later, Muzio Colonna arrived, and told the general council of the city that he had been sent by Fabrizio and Cardinal Giovanni Colonna to protect Rieti and offer troops and money. He was asked to stay until all danger had passed, and to guard Rocca Sinibalda in the city's territory; fifty Colonna horse were put at the disposal of Rieti for its defence.[32]

In view of the scale of the forces involved (including professional soldiers), the savagery of the fighting, and the scale of the casualties, such conflicts between opposing factions in Umbria were not just a matter of street-fighting between rival gangs. They seemed more like a minor civil war, with the forces of the nominal government, the papacy, nowhere to be seen.

Where papal officials, even papal troops, were rather more

in evidence, they sometimes failed to command the respect of
factious papal subjects. Forlì was one of the towns in the Romagna
that Julius was most anxious to secure under the direct rule of the
Church, and months before Cesare Borgia's castellan surrendered
the fortress, a papal legate and commissioner had formally taken
possession of the city, on 6 April 1504. The papal castellan who
took charge of the fortress later that month, Giustiniano Moriconi,
Bishop of Amelia, was well-behaved and well-liked in the city,
and there were papal troops stationed in the province. This
was not enough to secure public order. No Guelf and Ghibelline
parties on the Umbrian model survived in the Romagna, and
there was little cooperation between the faction leaders of the
different towns. The faction-fighting here had more of the character of family feuds.

Much of the fighting involved members of the Morattini
family. The entry of the legate had been facilitated by the calculation of the Morattini that they would benefit more by helping to
turn Forlì over to the Church than by continuing to support the
Ordelaffi, whose return they had backed. A Morattini was beside
the legate as he made his formal entry, a Morattini handed over
the keys of the city, and a Morattini placed the legate's standard
at the gate of the public *palazzo*. Only weeks before, they had
assaulted and sacked the houses of a rival family, the Numai, for
failing to support the Ordelaffi. The feud between them was
rekindled the following year, and the fighting, said to involve
thousands of men (and to have included the murder of one seventy-
year-old Morattini canon in the cathedral itself), caused some
citizens to abandon Forlì in search of a more peaceful life. The
following summer, the Morattini, some of whom had been exiled
from the city, returned in strength, with 800 infantry and 200
horse, and sacked over fifty houses belonging to their rivals.[33]

Ascoli provides an example of another kind of problem – the
citizen who aspired to become *signore*. Astolto Guiderocchi, a
leader of the Ghibellines in Ascoli, had been driven from the city
by returning Guelf exiles in 1498, his house burned, he himself
escaping, half-dressed, with his wife and two small children. Not a
man to be easily intimidated, he determined to return to the city
as its *signore*. The Ascolani, however, after twenty years of self-
government,[34] which had been twenty years of fierce internal strife
for power, decided that life might be easier if they returned to
direct subjection to the papacy. A papal governor arrived early in
1502. Only Astolto was not prepared to accept the new situation.

In 1504 he made a surprise return to a city distracted by an epidemic. Cardinal Farnese, the legate, sent troops and siege weapons, but could not dislodge him and had to make a truce. Astolto lorded it over Ascoli, exiling his major Guelf opponents. But his family's behaviour became intolerable. One of his older sons, Gian Tosto, killed four citizens in the communal palace and tossed their corpses into the piazza. Julius ordered the arrest of Astolto and his imprisonment in the fortress of Forlì. Astolto's sons continued to conspire against the papal government, and it was not until after Julius's death that the problem was resolved and Astolto and his sons returned to Ascoli.[35]

On top of such problems, for about a year a leading *condottiere* from a family of minor barons allied to the Orsini, Bartolomeo d'Alviano, who had a record of participation in faction-fighting (as at Rieti), caused Julius serious concern. He was ostensibly in the service of Spain, and had enhanced his reputation by playing a prominent part in the decisive victory of the Spanish over the French on the Garigliano in Naples in late 1503. At this point, he was at something of a loose end and came with his troops to the Papal States, lodging near his own lands and the Orsini territory to the north of the city.

Within months of his return to the Papal States, Bartolomeo had become involved in some skirmishing and stock-raiding against the Ghibelline-dominated town of Amelia, and was reported to be involved in a plot at Montone with his Vitelli relatives and to be planning to cause trouble in Perugia, so giving another relative, Gianpaolo Baglioni, the opportunity to strengthen his own position there. Julius became very annoyed, describing him as a 'disturber of the peace of the Church' and recalling the trouble Bartolomeo had caused in the Papal States in the past.[36] When Bartolomeo complained about a scheme that the Colonna were hatching to return Carlo Baglioni, an exiled rival of Gianpaolo, to Perugia, Julius warned him not to involve himself in the affairs of the Papal States.[37] Bartolomeo took no notice. He began preparing his men, declaring his readiness to defend the Orsini, Baglioni, Vitelli or any other relatives against anyone who might attack them, including papal forces.[38] So seriously did Julius take him that he began spending some of his precious reserves to raise troops to deal with him if necessary.

In the event, there was no confrontation. Suspicions that Bartolomeo was involved in plots at Orvieto and Viterbo made Julius determined to make him leave the Papal States, but he was

becoming less of a threat all the time. Having quarrelled with his
Spanish employer (in large part because the Colonna were also in
the service of Spain), he was running short of funds, and his
men were drifting away, with those that remained in bad order.
Nonetheless, he did have an ambitious scheme in mind – the
restoration of the Medici to Florence. After only a few weeks of
campaigning in Tuscany, he was routed by the Florentines in late
August 1504, to Julius's pleasure. But when he went to visit the
pope at Viterbo in September, he was well received, and he was
also summoned to Rome and welcomed there in December; he
was even promised a *condotta*. How seriously either side took this
offer is not clear. Bartolomeo really wanted to return to Venetian
service, which he had left in 1503, and by the end of March
negotiations were completed and he was back in Venice, and out
of Julius's hair.

If Julius's worst fears about Bartolomeo d'Alviano's intentions and capacity for creating disorder were not realized, the
presence of this restless, talented and partisan *condottiere* in papal
territory had raised the temperature – though there were those
who thought Julius attributed too much importance to him. It
helped to make Julius more anxious to quell the disorder so rife in
the Papal States.

How did he set about this?[39]

The most straightforward method was by reminding the
officials and legates responsible for areas of the Papal States of
their duty to keep the peace, and making clear his personal
interest – telling Cardinal Farnese, legate for the Marche, that
he wanted that province cleared of troublemakers, for example,
ordering the local *signori* not to give refuge to malefactors on their
lands, or urging Cardinal Sanseverino to take effective steps to
pacify Viterbo. He was aware of the causes of fighting and would
issue direct orders to deal with them. Thus he ordered Farnese
to enquire into an apparently mundane complaint about stock-
raiding. He did not want this sort of trouble between papal
subjects, he said, because it could lead to greater problems. Concerned by reports of the many private feuds and quarrels in the
Romagna, he told the governor of the province that he must try to
pacify them, punishing the intransigent. On several occasions, he
sent out commissioners with special powers to tackle specific
problems. When he heard that no effort had been made to find the
murderers of two men in Terracina, for instance, he ordered
Giovanni Ruffo to go there, make enquiries and punish the guilty

parties, and also to settle the differences dividing the citizens, to help keep the peace in future.

The Romagna merited special attention, for its persistent violence and its political sensitivity. Julius sent his relative Costantino Arniti there as lieutenant-general in July 1504, and then Giovanni da Sassatello to back him up in January 1505. In August 1505 he appointed the astute nuncio to Venice, Angelo Leonino, Bishop of Tivoli, as commissioner, with instructions to settle trouble in Fano, Forlì, Cesena, Bertinoro (and all other places in the province), giving him powers to pardon and to restore the property of those who had left those four cities during the recent turmoil, but also to exile any of their citizens he thought fit. A few months later, having learned that the worst malefactors were often in ecclesiastical orders, Leonino was given powers to punish their crimes according to their severity, disregarding the privileges of the clergy.

The initial instructions Julius gave to Leonino highlighted one of the most tricky and recurrent dilemmas that his attempts at pacification of the Papal States involved – what to do with the internal political exiles. Exiles, particularly if they had left the city *en masse* following fighting, often banded together, watching for an opportunity to get back at their enemies or force their way back home, and constituted a perpetual threat to public order. Bringing them back without provoking further bloodshed required a difficult combination of diplomacy and a firm hand.

In the past, popes and their agents had often not been impartial in their handling of political factions: Julius himself, as a cardinal, in his campaign against Spoleto and Città di Castello, had clearly been favouring the Ghibellines against the Guelfs. Bartolomeo d'Alviano, for one, evidently expected him to discriminate against the Guelfs as pope, but Julius did not want to rely on an alliance with either faction to uphold the authority of the papacy in its own territory.

Instead, he seems to have tried to deal with each group of exiles on its merits. Those who gathered together, threatening the peace, were to be dispersed and discouraged. He rebuked his *condottiere* Giovanni da Sassatello for taking exiles from Pesaro into his service and then bringing them near the city; he ordered that they should be dismissed. Disruptive as exiles could be, some papal subjects could be even more disruptive if allowed to stay at home, and Julius was ready to order them into exile himself, as he did with Astolto d'Ascoli and his sons, and the citizens of Narni whom he heard had been plotting to disturb the peace. His preferred solution was the return and reintegration of exiles, at least of those who had not been ringleaders, but this could be very difficult to achieve. Threats of drastic penalties were needed to bring the community of Norcia to accept the return of their exiles in the summer of 1505. Julius told the envoys they sent to ask him not to insist on this that he wanted all those exiled for political reasons to return; but he ordered a commissioner to investigate who, of those inside and outside the city, really merited punishment. Despite solemn pledges of peace and exchanges of hostages, within a few months of their return some of the exiles had been murdered by poison.

One measure of Julius's personal interest in bringing good order to his dominions is the frequency with which he summoned troublemakers to come to see him in person. Men from at least a dozen cities, including Acquasparta, Fermo, Narni, Norcia, Spoleto, Benevento and Forlì, were called to Rome between the summers of 1504 and 1506. Sometimes they were ordered to stay in Rome until they were given permission to leave. Unfortunately, no account of the reception that he gave to the small town bully-boys who appeared before him has come to light, but it can easily be imagined that the full force of one of his famous rages would be enough to take the edge off the most swaggering bravado. Failure to obey a summons would not bring escape. The pope would write to remind the men or the official responsible for seeing that they came, and the penalties threatened would increase in severity. When only two of the citizens of Terracina whom he wanted to come to see him turned up, the governor of the city, Tommaso Feo, received a blistering brief in which Julius's anger glows through the conventional formulae of his secretary. The appearance of just two men was not sufficient to enable Julius to settle the peace of the city. He wanted Feo to send at least two others from both of the parties, on pain of their incurring the penalties of rebellion for non-compliance, and warned him that 'If you don't use the necessary prudence and diligence in this matter, we will judge you to be unfit to govern such a city.'[40]

Well aware that, where there was a degree of self-government, the administration of the public revenues could be a fertile ground for political squabbles, Julius sometimes took some or all of their financial control from the communal councils. Fano was one place where he thought that money was at the root of the discord between the citizens, and he approved Leonino's measure to bring the communal revenue under the control of the Apostolic Chamber. Cesena and Orte also lost control of their revenues because of civic strife, though the citizens of Cesena were given back some degree of control over their finances, on condition that they stayed peaceful and united.

Another aspect of civic government that Julius was concerned about in Cesena was the distribution of offices. Nominations to the council had been carried out inequitably, he wrote to Leonino: some families had several representatives, some loyal citizens had been excluded. Leonino must reform the council, bringing on to it those who loved peace and were loyal to the Church, and there must be only one member from any family. In other cities, such as Città di Castello and Viterbo, he intervened even more directly, sending lists of the officials that he wanted to be appointed, or approving the list of names from which appointments were to be drawn by lot.

Only limited use was made of force to back up these measures to re-establish order and papal authority in the Papal States. Costantino Arniti and Leonino had some troops at their command in the Romagna, but Julius, intent on garnering his war chest, was not keen to spend very much on them. In February 1505 he ordered Cardinal Riario, the head of the Apostolic Chamber, to reduce the garrisons of papal fortresses so that no more men were retained than were needed for security and the Chamber was not burdened by unnecessary expense. 'Diligent enquiries' had been made, and the numbers to be retained in each fortress in future had been settled: a list of nearly fifty papal fortresses was attached, with the size of the garrison specified for each one.[41] Economy was not the only motive for Julius's reluctance to order large-scale military activity to bring the provinces to order. He wanted to make the rule of the papal government acceptable and attractive to his subjects, above all in areas where Venice constituted a rival pole of attraction.

Two cities, Perugia and Bologna, demanded special attention.

Perugia was the largest city in Umbria, a centre of papal administration and a base for one of the major provincial treasuries. Within the city, power was shared between the local papal officials and the members of the Baglioni family and their allies. The Baglioni had never managed to set themselves up as *signori* of Perugia, partly because there were many of them and they were riven by endemic family quarrels. An oligarchy of about thirty families had a monopoly of the more important posts in Perugia, and although the Baglioni's main opponents, the Oddi and Ranieri, were under-represented, they were not completely excluded. Indeed, the papal officials exercised more influence on appointments to the offices in Perugia than the Baglioni did. This was a state of affairs that Julius might well have been able to tolerate, but there was a complication. The Baglioni were a family of *condottieri*, and the paymasters of the leading members of the family often expected to benefit from the resources of Perugia, as a recruiting ground, a billet for their troops and a source of supplies. In the fifteenth century other Italian powers would make separate agreements with Perugia, of friendship, even alliance, through the Baglioni, treating the city as quasi-independent and hoping that if they were at war with the pope, they could use Perugia against him. This was a state of affairs that Julius could not tolerate. The Baglioni had to be put in their place.

Bologna, too, despite the fact it was the seat of the most important legation within the Papal States, was treated as a quasi-independent city by other Italian powers. Just as the communal church, San Petronio, far surpassed the cathedral of Bologna in size and magnificence, so the papal legates and their lieutenants were outshone by the Bentivoglio. Giovanni Bentivoglio was accounted one of the most fortunate men in Italy, because he had effectively dominated Bologna, while only being a private citizen, for forty years, without ever showing any outstanding qualities of intelligence, or political or military skill, or personality.[42] He had enjoyed a series of *condotte* and pensions from neighbouring states, eager to establish an interest in the city. Then as now, Bologna was situated on major communications routes of immense strategic importance, standing on the road running from the Adriatic to Milan and at the head of the most frequently travelled pass through the Appenines between northern and central Italy. For Giovanni Bentivoglio to pursue an independent 'foreign policy' under the eyes of the papal legate was not just an affront to the papal government. It was, in the uncertain political climate of early sixteenth-century Italy, a danger to the integrity of the Papal States – one that Julius could not afford to ignore. For the rest of his pontificate, securing control of Bologna would be one of his constant cares.

While Julius took a personal interest in the settlement of all the Papal States, to Perugia and Bologna he devoted particular care. Monitory briefs and special commissioners would not be enough. Even sending a few hundred papal troops would not be enough – the cities were too big to be overawed by a small force. If military action were to be needed to put Giovanni Bentivoglio in his place, a full-scale campaign would be required. The value that Julius put on securing Bologna was shown not only by the size of the forces he was prepared to commit to the task, but, above all, by his decision to lead them personally.

For a cardinal to lead or accompany a military expedition was commonplace, virtually normal practice. For a pope to do so, was unheard of. Julius's martial behaviour was one of the features of his pontificate that most upset his critics. In his satire *Julius Exclusus*, Erasmus portrayed the pope arriving at the gates of heaven at the head of an army, demanding to be admitted, only to be turned away by St Peter.[43] Yet when Julius announced his decision to go to Bologna, none of the cardinals is reported to have tried to dissuade him on the grounds that this was unseemly behaviour for a pope. Perhaps the military aspect of his expedition was masked by his decision that all the cardinals fit to travel, and the whole of the papal court, officials and all, should come too. The Bentivoglio and Bologna were to be confronted by the full authority of the Holy See, made as visible as it could be.

Such an expedition would not have been mounted for Perugia alone. Steadily increasing pressure had been applied to Gianpaolo Baglioni and Perugia for the past few years, as Julius sought to diminish his standing in the city and bring it more firmly under the rule of the papacy. His first scheme had been to restore the Perugian exiles to counterbalance Gianpaolo. There was some opposition from his own family to this idea. They were afraid that the return of the exiles, who were linked to the Colonna faction, might strengthen Fabrizio Colonna's hand if he decided to challenge Francesco Maria della Rovere for the succession to the duchy of Urbino. The Duke of Urbino himself was a friend of Gianpaolo, and acted as a mediator for him with the pope. It was thought that Urbino might hold back if Julius ordered him to attack Perugia, which may have discouraged Julius from using force when he appeared to be considering doing so in the autumn and winter of 1504.

In February 1505 Gianpaolo came to Rome and made an agreement with Julius. He promised to be a good 'vassal', to be obedient to the pope and to accept the appointment of a new papal governor 'who would have the authority . . . which befits a governor of His Beatitude in one of his subject territories'.[44] Exiles who had been involved in violence, and who could not return to

Perugia without danger of further bloodshed, were to remain outside the city. The others were to be permitted to return – Urbino and Gianpaolo were to decide who should be allowed back. One condition on which Julius insisted was that Gianpaolo was on no account to accept any contract with Venice, and he protested vigorously about reports that Gianpaolo had offered Venice his own services and to put Perugia under her protection. An effort was made the following year to make clear that it was the papal government that was in charge. The Perugians were ordered to await the arrival of the new legate, Cardinal Antonio Ferreri, before they renewed the list of names of those eligible for office. In June, Ferreri, on orders from Julius, dismissed the members of one of the main governing councils, the Dieci dell' Arbitrio, and selected their replacements himself. Gianpaolo, who had enjoyed great influence over this council, did not protest. He was behaving like the obedient subject he had promised to be. Julius's expedition merely provided an opportunity to set the seal on the new situation in Perugia; it did not create it.

Bologna was, in fact, the only declared goal of the campaign. As Bishop of Bologna for nearly twenty years, from 1483 to 1502 (and legate for some months, from December 1483 to September 1484), Julius had had ample opportunity to learn about the workings of Bolognese politics. Judging from his surviving correspondence with the communal government, his relations with it as the city's bishop were fairly formal but reasonably affable, in spite of a persistent problem with two territories of the bishopric, Cento and La Pieve, which had a running feud with their neighbours in the Bolognese *contado*.

Unfortunately, there is very little evidence concerning his relations with the Bentivoglio while he was a cardinal. In April 1485 he had lodged Giovanni Bentivoglio in his own palace at Santi Apostoli when he came to Rome, and he had acted as Innocent's representative in drawing up the *condotta* that Giovanni was given. In December 1500, while he had been staying at Cento for some months during his wanderings around northern Italy in the final years of his exile, there had been a confused report that Francesco Alidosi had been held in Bologna on suspicion of planning to poison Giovanni. According to Guicciardini, he had had to flee from Cento at night, having heard that Giovanni was about to imprison him at the request of Alexander; but the contemporary report when he left Cento in January 1501 was that he did so because Cesare Borgia's troops were to be billeted there.[45]

On his return to Rome in September 1503, he was accompanied by a force of Bolognese crossbowmen.

Julius's election as pope was greeted with apparent pleasure by those in the governing council of Bologna, the Sedici Riformatori (Sixteen), who wrote to their ambassador in Rome about what a wonderful pope he was going to be, and how they had no doubt that his pontificate would bring Bologna profit and repose.[46] No serious cause for quarrel arose between the Bolognese and the pope during the next few years. There were, however, clear signs of dissatisfaction on the part of Julius with Giovanni Bentivoglio. If there was a legacy of personal hostility between them from Julius's years as a cardinal, it was not thought significant at the time. The problem was, rather, that Julius was determined to assert his authority over Bologna and its leading family, and that Giovanni did not like this. Told by Julius in June 1504 that he and his sons should not accept *condotte* from anyone, but should stay at the disposition of the pope, Giovanni replied that his sons, young and practised in arms, could not remain without some sort of provision and that he could not prevent them from trying to get something. A few months later, the pope was reported to have spoken angrily to Giovanni's chancellor about his master.[47] Giovanni then made the mistake of looking to Venice for support. This could have been his fatal error.

The Bolognese had got wind in July 1506 of reports that Julius was planning to expel Giovanni Bentivoglio and take Bologna. Protests by their envoy in Rome met the response from Julius that he would not be doing wrong in recovering the lands of the Church. But he also wrote to Giovanni, saying that he should either come personally to Rome, with some of the Sedici Riformatori, so that Julius could arrange with them how Bologna was to be governed in future and what would become of him; or he should send his four legitimate sons to Rome, and Julius would go to Bologna without troops. Julius would promise Giovanni that he would not be expelled from Bologna, and that any accusations brought against him would be pardoned, but 'he did not want him to be greater than the others whom His Holiness would appoint to that government.' Plans for the expedition were not suspended while Giovanni's reply to these proposals was awaited. Julius was not only planning to use his own troops, and to hire 3,000–4,000 of the formidable Swiss infantry mercenaries, with perhaps twice as many Italian infantry, but was also confident that he would have the support of French, Florentine and Ferrarese troops as well. Louis, he said, had promised to ensure his Venetian allies would not try to interfere with the pope's plans.[48] Giovanni told the Venetians that he had sent to say that the pope would be welcome if he came with the curia alone; if he came in arms, the Bolognese had arms too, to defend themselves.[49]

On 17 August the pope announced to the cardinals assembled in consistory his intention of personally leading an expedition to Bologna. Speaking of all the misdeeds of Giovanni and the other Bentivoglio, he told them that he was 'compelled to go to save his people'.[50] Now he dismissed the idea of leaving Giovanni in Bologna as out of the question, telling Machiavelli[51] that Giovanni 'would be mad to stay there as a private citizen', and that he didn't want him there on any other terms. When Giovanni had gone, Julius would so settle matters that he would not return to Bologna, at least while Julius was alive.[52]

The cardinals had been warned that Julius expected them to accompany him. Caraffa and da Costa were excused because they were too old; three others were excused because they were ill, and one, Sangiorgio, was to be left in Rome as legate. At first, all the curial officials were to come too, but it was soon decided that some would stay behind. With twenty-six cardinals and their households, and a crowd of officials and their servants – about 3,000 horses were required for the *curiali* alone – and the papal household, including the chapel staff and singers, all having only a matter of days in which to prepare for an absence of several months, the confusion in Rome for the next week can only be imagined. Julius gave the cardinals permission to go before him, to ease the problems of finding provisions along the road.[53]

Leaving Rome on 26 August, Julius kept up such a swift pace as he made his way north through the Patrimony that those travelling on foot, including the groom leading the horse carrying the sacrament, found it difficult to keep up with him. Some cardinals' grooms died, because they were having to run all the time in the heat of late summer. If it was not much fun for the people accompanying him, Julius was enjoying himself. He always loved travelling, and often went on pleasure trips in the Patrimony.

One of his favourite activities was inspecting his fortresses, and he had the chance to see a number of them along the way. At Civita Castellana, which he reached on 28 August, he spent a day admiring the beauty of the fortress and ordering repairs and new works. He inspected a derelict fortress at Montefiascone (which the local people avoided, believing it to be inhabited by evil spirits), and ordered it to be repaired at a cost of 3,000 ducats. When he reached Lake Trasimene, he took the opportunity to indulge another favourite pastime, fishing – sailing in five boats with some cardinals and prelates and members of his household, as well as fifty Swiss infantry with their trumpets and drums.

The serious business of the expedition can never have been far from his mind. Even if he had been inclined to forget it, a stream of envoys and messages that reached him on the road acted as a constant reminder. It was at Civita Castellana that he received the first of a series of envoys whom Giovanni Bentivoglio, trying to bargain his way out of trouble, was to send to him. Julius offered some conditions, which were rejected; the pope complained that Giovanni 'does not want to accept terms from us, but to impose them on us and give us orders'.[54] The next day, Julius sent Antonio Ciocchi, one of the auditors of the Apostolic Chamber, to announce to the Bolognese that if they did not receive the pope and drive the Bentivoglio out, they should expect ruin. Giovanni's position was weaker than he realized, as he prepared to defend himself in Bologna. Forced to choose between supporting him and offending the pope, those to whom he looked for aid and protection were promising to help the pope against him. Machiavelli joined Julius at Civita Castellana to tell him that Florence would make available the troops that he wanted. The pope had already heard on the road that Louis had also agreed to his request for troops, and soon sent his majordomo, Pierre Le Filleul, to Milan to bring 600–800 French horse to Bologna, giving him money to raise 4,000 Swiss infantry.

Meanwhile, there was other business to be dealt with along the way.

First, on reaching Viterbo, Julius set out to reinforce earlier efforts that he had made to reconcile the warring factions of the town. In 1504 he had sent one of the younger and more forceful cardinals, Sanseverino, to Viterbo as legate to enforce order, but even he had found it a tough nut to crack. Julius had taken over the negotiations with the head of the factions himself, and in January 1505 had issued a decree that everyone was to observe a true and perpetual peace and to forgive all injuries. Property seized during faction-fighting was to be returned, as far as possible, to its rightful owners, and all weapons were to be surrendered. Those who contravened the decree would be guilty of *lèse-majesté*, all their property confiscate, their houses razed to the ground. They and those who helped them would be excommunicate.[55]

Julius had come to Viterbo in person in September 1505,

entering the city in full pontifical robes, with the sacrament borne before him. Having listened to many citizens and settled some feuds between individuals, he had held a solemn ceremony in San Francesco, at which he had made many of the faction leaders swear peace. Another decree had been read out, repeating and reinforcing the earlier one, and some men had been sentenced to exile.[56]

As he returned to Viterbo in September 1506, Julius knew that the provisions of this decree had not been fully observed. He changed all the officials, appointing one of his *nipoti*, Cardinal Leonardo Grosso della Rovere, as legate. To try to cement the peace between the factions, he arranged two marriages between members of the leading families, attending the weddings himself when they were held in the fortress.

The second piece of business was to settle what would happen to Perugia and Gianpaolo Baglioni. This was easily solved, because envoys from Perugia came to see the pope at Viterbo to urge him to visit their city. Gianpaolo himself came to meet Julius soon after, at Orvieto, to offer his submission. He was to help in the campaign against Bologna, and to surrender to the pope all the fortresses in the jurisdiction of Perugia. According to Machiavelli, Julius had decided that either Gianpaolo should leave Perugia, or he could stay there only as a private citizen, and without soldiers. Machiavelli considered that necessity would force Julius to realize that it would be better not to try to take Perugia by force, if he could get Gianpaolo's assistance in the major goal of driving the Bentivoglio from Bologna, and he noted that Gianpaolo had many friends in the papal court.[57] Just before Gianpaolo arrived in Orvieto, the Duke of Urbino, who had helped him before, came there with the papal legate of Perugia, Cardinal Ferreri, and they both interceded for him with the pope. When he left to see to arrangements for Julius's arrival at Perugia, they went with him.

The pope made his solemn entry into Perugia on 13 September, with the ceremonies and paraphenalia usual on such occasions. He was met at the gates by the priors of the city government, dressed in new rose-coloured robes, who handed him the keys to the city. They and other officials, together with a crowd of doctors from the university, accompanied him as he was carried to the cathedral in his papal chair. Their progress was slowed by the performances of various Latin songs (Julius began to chafe at the delays), and the dispute over precedence that was almost as much a part of the routine of such formal entries as the interminable songs and mimes – the dispute on this occasion being between the Dominicans and canons regular. (Another customary diversion that Julius might happily have done without was the seizure of his mule, when he dismounted near the gates, by a group of youths who had met him outside the city: it cost him fifty ducats to ransom it.) On reaching the cathedral, he prayed and heard a *Te Deum* sung by his own choir, and was then carried to the palace of the priors.

Julius's entry into Perugia was the occasion for Machiavelli's famous – and, it has to be said, fatuous – comment that Gianpaolo Baglioni missed the opportunity to win eternal fame, or infamy, by seizing Julius and all his cardinals. In his *Discorsi*, in a chapter headed 'It is very rare for men to be either all bad or all good', he describes this episode, saying that Julius 'with his guard alone put himself into the hands of the enemy'. 'Prudent men who were with the pope', he wrote, meaning himself, 'noted the rashness of the pope and the cowardice of Gianpaolo, and could not imagine how it happened that, to his perpetual fame, he had not at one stroke abased his enemy and enriched himself with booty, as all the cardinals with all their finery were with the pope.' Gianpaolo had not scrupled to kill his own relatives to win power, and his incestuous relationship with his sister was common knowledge, so it could not be fear for his reputation that had stopped him from seizing this 'chance to be remembered forever', as 'the first who had shown the prelates how little those who lived and governed as they do are to be esteemed'.[58]

In his original despatch from Perugia on 13 September, Machiavelli had described the pope and cardinals as 'being at the discretion of Gianpaolo', and had remarked that if Gianpaolo did no harm to the man who had come to take his power from him, it would be because of his own good nature. Gianpaolo himself, he went on, had said that he knew two ways to save his position – by force, or by humility and trusting the advice of his friends – and that he had chosen the second alternative, and had followed the guidance of the Duke of Urbino.[59] This surely is the point. The advice and intercession of the Duke of Urbino had stood him in good stead so far. He had already been to meet Julius at least twice, making the show of obedience that the pope desired, and had accepted a more assertive attitude on the part of the papal officials in Perugia. If he continued to play his cards right, there was a good chance that he and his family could stay in Perugia and hold on to their property and at least some of their authority, and hope that easier days would return.

Machiavelli thought that Julius and his cardinals were at the mercy of Gianpaolo because most of the papal troops were stationed at the gates to the city, while Gianpaolo's troops were a little outside it; in the *Discorsi*, he describes Julius as entering 'unarmed'. Another eyewitness, who described the scene in a letter to the Marquis of Mantua, tells why Gianpaolo's troops were outside the city – because, four hours before Julius's entry, the legate had ordered him to send them out of Perugia and they had left without any fuss. This eyewitness describes Julius as entering 'with all his men at arms in order, and 150 light horsemen, and 300 crossbowmen and handgunners etc.'.[60] According to the usual detailed account by Paride de' Grassi, the papal master of ceremonies, Julius was surrounded by his Swiss guard and his military commanders, including the Duke of Urbino and Costantino Arniti. Among the nobles riding with them was Gianpaolo Baglioni.[61] Had there been any attempt to capture the pope, Gianpaolo was in a very dangerous position – unless one assumes that all Julius's commanders would have been privy to the plot.

There was a problem with Gianpaolo before Julius left Perugia, but one of a rather more mundane order than a suicidal attempt to capture the pope. He was just making difficulties about the return of the exiles. A number of Perugian exiles had come with Julius, expecting to return to the city with him. But two days before his entry, he told them that he would leave them behind, and send for them when he had been in Perugia for a few days. They were not to worry, he told them, because he wanted to humble Gianpaolo and make it safe for them to come home; he would take Gianpaolo's troops with him. He had no intention of executing him for any past crimes, but if he erred even a little in the future, he would be hanged. For the present, he wanted him to stay with the Duke of Urbino. Far from reassured by the pope's words, the exiles believed that Gianpaolo's friends were, step by step, winning him over, and that they would be left in the cold.[62]

While not openly opposing the return of the exiles, Gianpaolo dropped some very unsubtle hints that if they came, there might well be trouble. Let them come back, he said, but he could not be held responsible if they were cut to pieces. Perhaps as a compromise, only the 'old' exiles, those who had been driven out before 1500, were allowed in; those involved in an attempt to massacre Gianpaolo and his family in that year had to stay out. With the return of the 'old' exiles, Gianpaolo might have to disgorge much property that had been confiscated from them, though he tried hard to avoid having to do this. He also made it difficult for the exiles to find guarantors for their future good behaviour, by asking their friends to stand surety for him. As for assurances that the exiles would be safe, he again stressed that while he could make promises on behalf of himself and his family, he could make none on behalf of other citizens or any outsiders.[63] Eventually, however, these hitches were straightened out, and there was a ceremony of public reconciliation, orchestrated by Julius.

He gave orders for a solemn mass to be said on Sunday 20 September. This was to be held in the church of San Francesco because, he said, that was where he had been initiated into letters and had begun his life in the Church, of which he was now, by the grace of God and Saint Francis, the head. A famous preacher, Fra Egidio da Viterbo, was asked to give a sermon exhorting the congregation to keep the peace; to Julius's annoyance, he preached instead in praise of the pope. Then followed the ritual of peacemaking, along the lines of the one that Julius had presided over in Viterbo the year before. Two hosts were consecrated, and one kept back after the mass. The leading members of the rival factions came before the pope, and a papal notary read an injunction ordering them not to offend each other. After exchanging kisses of peace, they went, two by two – each pair comprising men from either faction – and, joining hands over the reserved host, took an oath, and then kissed the pope's foot. At the end, Julius gave a blessing.[64] But he obviously did not place complete faith in the efficacy of this ceremony to hold the factions in check. When he left Perugia the following day, he took hostages from both sides with him, as well as Gianpaolo and his men-at-arms.

As Julius was making his way from Gubbio to Urbino, two envoys from Bologna came to ask for safe-conducts for an embassy of six – two sons of Giovanni Bentivoglio, two members of the Sixteen, and two other leading citizens. Refusing to give any written safe-conduct, on the grounds that he did not regard them as his enemies, he said he would give them an audience if they went to Urbino to meet him there.[65]

At Urbino, where Julius was delighted by the beauty of the ducal palace, and the curia revelled in an abundance of supplies, there was no sign of the Bolognese envoys, but he was joined by the man whom he had sent to Bologna in the early stages of the journey, Antonio Ciocchi. He was more optimistic than Julius that the envoys would appear, although he had not had much success in his mission. The Venetian ambassador with the pope wrote that he had been sent to ask for three things: the troops that the Bolognese were obliged to give whenever the pope requested; the communal palace as a residence for the cardinal legate; and that Giovanni Bentivoglio should come to Julius. The Sixteen had replied that they wanted their palace for themselves and the troops for the security of Bologna; Giovanni would not come himself, but would send a son. When Antonio came to report to Julius in Urbino, he said the Bolognese were ready to defend themselves if Julius was intending to alter their government, and that Giovanni was making great preparations for defence.[66]

These preparations, Machiavelli heard, were perhaps causing discontent among the citizens, who were being made to arm themselves at their own expense.[67] And there was confirmation at the time that they would not be faced just by the papal troops: letters from France saying that Louis offered to send 700 lances,[68] and word from Lombardy that even more troops were on the move. A papal chamberlain was despatched northwards to tell the French that 700 lances and 5,000 infantry would be quite enough.

Leaving Urbino on 29 September, Julius pressed on through roads made treacherous by the autumn rains. As his wretched train struggled through the mud, 'Some cursed Giovanni Bentivoglio, others the pope, or God and Heaven.' Julius heard them, but did not take offence.[69] News came to him at San Marino that the six Bolognese envoys, and the two who had been with him and had gone to meet them, had been warned by Giovanni Bentivoglio to flee, because Bernardino Gozzadini, the father of the papal datary, had been murdered in Bologna. Three had been captured as they fled, the others had reached Rimini. Julius sent to reassure them that they had nothing to fear; he did not want the Church's supporters in Bologna to be put in any more danger. At Cesena, which he reached on 2 October, the envoys finally had an audience with him.

They spoke of the loyalty of the Bolognese to the Church, and of how peaceful and God-fearing they were, and reminded him that he had confirmed the form of their government that had been agreed with several of his predecessors. The vehemence of his reply stunned them. If the Bolognese were devoted to the Church, so they should be, because it was their duty to be so. He was coming in person to free them from tyranny, and he did not care what arrangements other popes had agreed with them, nor what he had himself confirmed, because they had all been forced to make such agreements by necessity, not of their own free will. Now the time had come when he could correct these provisions, and he could not find any excuse before God if he failed to do this. If, when he came, he liked the way in which the city was run, he would confirm it; if he didn't, he would change it. In case he could not accomplish what he wanted by peaceful means, forces had been prepared that could make all Italy tremble, let alone Bologna.[70]

Julius was not relying on military force alone to frighten the Bolognese. The day before he left Cesena on 8 October, the consistory considered a bull threatening them with an interdict. A few days later, at Forlì, a new, more severe, draft of the bull was approved by the cardinals, whose indignation had been aroused by hearing the terms that the Bolognese envoys had put to the pope. These included the stipulation that if he were to come in person to Bologna, he should be accompanied only by his personal guard of Swiss infantry, and he should tell them how long he wanted to stay. A fierce bull excommunicating Giovanni Bentivoglio and laying down harsh penalties for those who followed him or helped him was also approved. Bentivoglio's secretary was sent packing by Julius, who accused him of being a troublemaker, of inciting resistance. Only his status as envoy saved him from condign punishment, he was told, and he was warned to leave the Papal States. All the Bolognese ambassadors had asked permission to leave, as they saw the storm clouds thickening, but Julius told them he did not advise them to go. They took the hint, but had to endure a public scolding from the pope in front of a large crowd, as he told them that they should be ashamed of themselves for defending Giovanni.[71]

Already, papal troops were moving through the *contado* of Bologna, and some villages were declaring their allegiance to the pope. At this time, little news was coming through from the city, but there were hints of growing disquiet, and that Giovanni was reluctant to spend enough to organize effective defences. A letter from Louis, written on 11 September, had probably reached the Sixteen by now, telling them that he was willing to act as a peacemaker – in so far as he could do so without contravening his obligations to the Holy See.[72] Mediation, not the active protection that they had hoped for, was the best they could expect from the

French, and the approach of the French troops was a ground for apprehension, not reassurance.

Julius had his own apprehensions about the French. He did not want to be upstaged by them, and he was eager to press on with his journey through the Romagna. Nevertheless, he stayed in Forlì for a few days, inspecting the fortifications, ordering repairs, and trying to promote peace between the factions in the city. His tour of the fortifications made him weary – perhaps the strain of travelling was beginning to tell on him – and he had pains in his knee, possibly gout, possibly a recurrence of syphilis. This did not prevent him from choosing to take a circuitous route to Imola through the mountains in Florentine territory, rather than to travel the straight route along the Roman road in the plain, which would lead through Faenza, held by the Venetians. He would not be beholden to the Venetians for hospitality in his own lands. Machiavelli warned him that provisions and shelter might be sparse and hard to find, because the Florentines would have little time to prepare for him, but he said that he would be satisfied with whatever was available.[73] Still, he took heed of the warnings, and decided to take with him only his personal attendants, the cardinals – who were told to bring only two servants each – and some bodyguards. The rest he sent to Imola by way of Faenza. Julius took his mitre and precious vestments with him, in case, he told de' Grassi with a laugh, they should fall into the hands of the Venetians. He preserved his good humour on the trek through the mountains, even when he had to walk because the track was too difficult for him to ride or be carried in his litter, quoting Virgil to keep up the spirits of his attendants.[74]

He enjoyed his entry into Imola, too, when he reached it on 20 October, praising a mime and songs that execrated the Bentivoglio. He even was amused, rather than annoyed, by the pretensions of Giovanni da Sassatello, who had had his own coat of arms stuck up with those of the pope all over the city. The scandalized Paride de' Grassi, with the support of Cardinal Alidosi, sent men to tear them down before the pope saw them, but there was not enough time to remove them all before his entry. Julius noticed some of them, but just smiled.

He had also smiled when he had heard the latest terms proposed by Giovanni Bentivoglio a day or two before, but that had been a mark of speechless anger rather than amusement. Proposed through Francesco Gonzaga, Marquis of Mantua, who was one of Julius's commanders, these 'unworthy and iniquitous' terms were considered more appropriate to a victor triumphing over his enemy.[75] Gonzaga, who was related to Giovanni by marriage, kept coming to see the pope to speak for him, and when Julius rebuffed him, asked permission to leave for Mantua, which was refused. A request from the Bolognese envoys to allow the people time to think an agreement over was dismissed with contempt. Instead, Julius sought to increase the psychological pressure on Bologna by ordering all the Bolognese in the curia to write to their relatives and friends exhorting them to fulfil the terms of the interdict, and either bring Giovanni as a captive to the pope, or expel him from the city. If they failed to do this within four days, the French troops who were now near would be unleashed on them. The envoys were ordered to send this message to Bologna, but they only pretended to do so, and also tried to prevent the letters written from the curia from being sent.[76]

But the threat of a French attack had been communicated directly to the Bolognese, who were sent a warning by Chaumont, the French commander, that if they did not obey Julius within two days, all Louis's obligations to protect the city and the Bentivoglio would be nullified, and he would treat them as enemies. The Bolognese sent to Julius promising obedience, but still hesitated to do what he most desired of them, drive out the Bentivoglio. Chaumont represented the gravest threat to Giovanni, but also his best hope of safety for himself and his family. When he was finally convinced that the game was up, he turned to Chaumont for a safe-conduct from the city.

On 2 November, as Julius, in the fortress of Imola, was preparing to go to mass, he received three messages. The first was that, the night before, Giovanni Bentivoglio and his sons had fled from Bologna. The second was that four of the Sixteen were coming to commend Bologna to him, and to ask that the French troops be kept out of the city and the interdict be lifted. The third message, from Chaumont, was that the Bentivoglio had come to him, and that he had promised them that they would be safe. Bonfires were lit in the streets of Imola, and cannon fired from the fortress, to celebrate the liberation of Bologna from the tyranny of the Bentivoglio.[77]

But Julius's problems with Bologna, with the Bentivoglio, and, above all, with the French, were just beginning.

6

The Papal Court

Like any other temporal ruler, the pope governed his dominions
with the aid of a host of clerks and officials, some based in the
capital and some in the provinces. Unlike other temporal rulers,
he was also head of the largest international organization in
Europe, the Roman Church, and many more officials were
engaged in its central administration, under the pope's command.
Men came from all over Europe to make a career in the papal
administration, though Italians were generally in the majority.[1]
Cosmopolitan the Roman curia may have been, but it would be
the Italians who set the tone. Popes such as Alexander VI who
were not Italian themselves encountered some hostility from
the papal bureaucracy for that reason alone. The Flemish pope
Adrian VI, who reigned for only two years, from 1521 to 1523,
was so at odds with the ambience of the Roman curia that afterwards, until the election of Pope John Paul II, there was a tacit
understanding that only an Italian could be head of the Roman
Church.

Most of the papal officials and clerks, even those based in
Rome, would not be known to the pope by face or name. Many of
them would only ever see him over the heads of the crowd lining
the route of a papal procession, or glimpse him at a distance as
they went about their business in the papal palace. Those working
for the papal chancery were not even based in the Vatican, but in
a palace on the other side of the Tiber, in Julius's time – at the
palace later called Sforza–Cesarini – and the chancery scriptors,
who engrossed papal bulls, worked in their own homes. Julius
planned to move the other offices of the administration, including
the Apostolic Chamber and the increasingly important office of

the datary, into a vast, new, purpose-built Palazzo dei Tribunali
on the Via Giulia. Bramante designed it for him, and construction
was begun but never got beyond the ground floor.[2]

It is in the nature of bureaucracies to be constantly expand-
ing unless deliberately cut back, and the papal bureaucracy was
no exception. Since the pontificate of Sixtus IV, that expansion
had been accelerated by the creation of offices whose sole purpose
was to provide revenue to the popes through their sale. None were
yet – quite – a sinecure, but the need to find something for these
new officials to do made transacting business with the curia still
more time-comsuming and expensive than it had, notoriously,
been for centuries.

From the point of view of the officials, these offices were
essentially a form of investment. In return for payment of a
capital sum, they got nominal duties and a steady income, about
eleven or twelve per cent a year return on their capital at the start
of the sixteenth century. From the point of view of the popes, the
offices were a way of raising loans, bringing useful cash bonanzas
and a variable, but sometimes substantial, annual revenue from
the sale of offices that had fallen vacant for one reason or another,
but also imposing a burden of interest payments, in the form of
salaries, which became a heavy charge on papal finances. Julius
used the sale of offices to raise money. Much of the war chest that
he was garnering in the early years of his pontificate came from
this source. He also created offices for sale, notably a college of
101 Scriptores Archivii Curiae Romanae, in 1507, which raised
70,000 ducats, and 141 Praesidentes Annonae or Praesidentes
Ripae (who were supposed to supervise the import of food stuffs to
Rome), in 1509, which raised 90,000 ducats.[3] Like any financial
market, that for venal offices was subject to outside influences
and political disturbances. In December 1511 Julius had 40,000
ducats' worth of offices to sell that no one wanted to buy because
the income from them had been halved by the wars.[4]

Selling the right to hold offices in the curia restricted the
range of those who could be appointed to men able and willing to
pay. But, for most of the offices affected, this was less a restriction
on the pope's powers of patronage – for he would rarely, if ever,
have been personally concerned in appointments to minor offices
anyway – than on those of the higher officials who had controlled
the appointments. There could still be an element of choice, in
that there would usually be several candidates for an office. The
more important the office, the more likely it was that the pope

would be directly involved in choosing who would fill it, and the more likely it was that it would not necessarily go to the highest bidder. Antonio Ciocchi da Monte San Savino was made one of the auditors of the Apostolic Chamber in July 1504, although he only offered 6,000 ducats while others had offered up to double that amount, because Julius 'wished the good name of this man to be worth more than what others were willing to pay'.[5] Other considerations, besides money and personal merit, could be taken into account. A request from the government of Bologna that one of its citizens, Alessandro Palleotto, should be appointed an auditor of the main papal judicial tribunal, the Rota, was turned down by Julius on the grounds that one of the incumbent auditors was a Bolognese and, as there were only twelve of them altogether, he did not want to have two from the same 'patria'.[6] A few months earlier, Ferdinand had reminded the pope that he had promised to appoint a Spaniard to this tribunal.[7]

The money to be made from the disposal of offices always loomed large, however, and could affect appointments to benefices too. Most office holders aspired to hold important, and lucrative, ecclesiastical benefices, but most of these benefices could not be held in conjunction with offices at the curia. Appointment to them could involve, therefore, the sacrifice of a man's offices. For the right benefice, it was a sacrifice willingly made. When someone could be found who would accept an abbey such as that of Santa Cristina in Pavia, which provided an income of 3,000 ducats a year, in exchange for relinquishing offices worth 13,000 ducats, which the pope could then sell,[8] the 'merits' of such a candidate were hard to ignore.

Occasionally, protests could be heard, even from those at the heart of the system, against the practice. In consistory in December 1509 the bishopric of Perugia, said to supply an income of 800 ducats a year, was given to a protonotary Spinola, a *nipote* of Cardinal Riario, who would surrender a secretaryship worth 4,000 ducats. Cardinal Briçonnet 'rose to his feet and said, "Holy Father, I don't believe this is a good way to proceed, that benefices are not given except to those who leave offices. I believe this is to the discredit of the Holy See. For the love of God, some thought should be given to this." His Holiness replied that it was something that could be done ... and that could be tolerated, being done for the benefit of the Apostolic See.' Cardinal Vigerio, a theologian, who had been in Julius's service for many years, began to argue in support of what the pope had said, but

Briçonnet stood his ground, saying that if he read his books carefully, he would find that it was against all the canons. It was thought to be astonishing that such a challenge should be made to the pope in public (and a measure of the current prosperity of French fortunes that it had been done at that moment), but then, the Venetian ambassadors who reported the episode remarked, it was amazing to see how benefices were being given out at that time, with none being awarded except to those who would relinquish offices worth four or five times the value of the income from the benefices.[9]

Money could buy an office in the curia, in the administration, but not at the political heart of the papacy, in the circle of the pope's servants and family and favourite cardinals, with whom he worked and passed his hours of leisure. There were, of course, various degrees and kinds of intimacy with the pope, which could bring various degrees and kinds of influence with him. His barber, Tommasino, was described as being 'one of the pope's intimates, especially when he's relaxing',[10] and had sufficient interest in politics to prompt him to write to the new regime in Bologna in 1507, exhorting it to obey the legate: he was made a citizen of Bologna the following year.[11] There is no evidence, however, of Julius ever turning to him for advice, and it seems highly unlikely he would ever have done so. Other members of the pope's household, particularly the majordomo and the treasurer, evidently could be figures of political significance, and were entrusted with important missions. A French majordomo, Pierre Le Filleul, Bishop of Aix, for example, was sent to France to see Louis in 1507. Francesco Alidosi served as papal treasurer for nearly two years before he was made a cardinal in December 1505, and, from the first, was recognized as being one of the most influential figures at the court. Members of Julius's family would on occasion offer him advice on political affairs, which was not always well received. He was very fond of some relatives, such as his nephew Galeotto Franciotto della Rovere, whom he made Cardinal San Pietro ad Vincula in November 1503, and disliked others, particularly his sister-in-law, Giovanna da Montefeltro, but he was always wary of any of them trying to assume the role of a Girolamo Riario or a Cesare Borgia, and none of them had real political influence. As for the cardinals, who were supposed to be the counsellors of the pope, only some were regularly at his side, even of those that usually lived in Rome, and by no means all of them can truly be accounted members of the inner circle of the court.

The papal court was an amorphous entity, whose boundaries were as unclear to contemporaries as they are to historians. Such vague boundaries, and the difficulty of defining who was, and who was not, a member, are common problems in the study of courts, but, again, the dual nature of the papal government – the temporal aspect, and the spiritual aspect with international competence – complicate the picture. Ambassadors in Rome sometimes spoke of 'the court' thinking this or commenting on that in a way that implied they were speaking of a wide circle of people with an interest in public affairs but who would not necessarily have any influence on them. They seem to have been reporting the climate of opinion in the Vatican, the offices of the curia, the banks, the households of the cardinals and major officials. To an ordinary cleric in England, say, or in Germany, the 'papal court' would be the curia, the administrative bodies that levied dues and taxes on benefices or to which certain judicial business had to be addressed. For the King of France or the Signoria of Venice, this aspect of the papal court was one that they could not, unfortunately, forget, and rulers who had much routine business with the papal administration often kept a 'procurator' in Rome to steer it through the labyrinthine complexities of the curia procedures. But they had also to be aware of the papal court in the more restricted sense – the group of men whom the pope knew personally, with whom he worked and to whom he might turn for advice or information, men who could be awkward enemies or useful friends to a secular ruler. Membership of the papal household, even, did not make a man forget other loyalties or his own interests. Early in Julius's reign, for example, the Spanish cardinals had good contacts in his household and were told 'everything'.[12]

At the beginning of a pontificate, ambassadors were always on the alert to spot who the influential servants of the new pope would be, whom it would be worth approaching, to whom it might be worth giving a present, or a benefice in the ruler's gift. They would also assess which cardinals were likely to enjoy the pope's confidence, and observe which relatives of the pope seemed likely to enjoy his special favours, and whom it would be worth cultivating. A large consignment of carp that the Marquis of Mantua sent to his envoy in Rome for distribution arrived at a very timely moment, the Mantuan envoy reported, because he could give some to the pope, who was giving a sumptuous banquet to the envoys of Genoa and Savona. Some of the rest he shared among several cardinals: Caraffa, Pallavicino, Trivulzio, da Costa and Riario, 'because of their authority, and friendship' with the Gonzaga; Sangiorgio, because he was in charge of the *segnatura di giustizia*, supervising the signing of documents recording the pope's personal response to petitions; Sanseverino, because he dealt with French affairs (and so he could give them to the Princess of Bisignano, with whom he was in love – which he did); the two cardinal *nipoti*, Clemente and Galeotto della Rovere, for obvious reasons; and Farnese, Fieschi and Soderini, for reasons that he did not explain. Two lay relatives of the pope also received a share: the Duke of Urbino, uncle (and about to be adoptive father) of the Prefect, Francesco Maria della Rovere; and Francesco Maria's mother, Giovanna da Montefeltro – negotiations were beginning for a Gonzaga match for the boy, which would come to fruition a few years later. The datary, Fazio Santorio, who (among other duties) controlled the sale of offices, collected the money obtained in this way and held it for the personal use of the pope, had come to be one of the most powerful figures in the administration, and he and the pope's personal secretaries, such as the historian Sigismondo de' Conti, were men who could be of use 'every day'. Thus they too got a share of the carp. So did the treasurer, Francesco Alidosi, because 'he is the leading figure close to the pope of his familiars and household.'[13]

This list provides a snapshot of the inner circle of the court at the beginning of Julius's pontificate, and it helps to illustrate two other peculiar features of the papal court: the virtual absence of women and, among the men, the very small proportion of laymen.

Celibacy among the Roman clergy was probably more honoured in the breach than in the observance. It was common for cardinals to have mistresses, and frequently to acknowledge the children that they fathered. Such conduct was no bar to the papacy, though it was considered scandalous that Alexander VI should have a mistress, and father children, while he was actually pope. Julius himself had at least one daughter, Felice, whom he brought to Rome and lodged near the Vatican. Near the Vatican, but not in it, for the etiquette of the court frowned on the pope even dining in public with women, let alone sharing his domestic life with one. One of the characteristics of his sister-in-law Giovanna that Julius found exasperating was that she did not always observe the unwritten rules governing the behaviour of the female relatives of the pope: for example, on one visit to Rome she caused a stir by paying formal visits to the cardinals. His daughter did keep to the rules, and her occasional presence in the Vatican gave rise to no scandals or critical comment. She can be considered a member of the papal court, though scarcely one who had any formal position or function, as the daughter of a secular ruler would have.

Male relatives of the pope by blood or marriage were virtually the only laymen of any political significance at the papal court, apart from the ambassadors of other powers accredited to the pope. None of Julius's male relatives, however, had any substantial political influence. The major lay *nipote*, Francesco Maria della Rovere, spent much of his time in the duchy of Urbino, even before he inherited it, making only occasional visits to Rome. A much more permanent presence was a cousin of Julius, Bartolomeo della Rovere, but his role appears to have been that of trusted servant, rather than confidential minister, and there is no evidence that he had any say in the determination of papal policy. Military commanders, who might have constituted another group of influential laymen, could never feel at home in the papal court. In any case, Julius followed the pattern set by most Quattrocento popes, of appointing relatives to the major military commands. Nor was there any role for lay members of the Roman baronial families, apart from some ceremonial duties guarding conclaves. They were certainly not expected to attend upon the pope, like the nobility of a lay ruler would be. Leading bankers associated with the curia, such as Agostino Chigi from Siena, who held the lucrative monopoly rights to exploit the papal alum made at Tolfa, or the Genoese Sauli, who acted as the pope's bankers, are rarely recorded as having much to do with the pope personally, however important their role in running the affairs of the papacy.

The laymen who saw most of the pope were probably the ambassadors and other agents of the secular rulers accredited to him. It is their despatches that provide the best picture of life at court, and of the environment in which Julius himself lived and worked, the atmosphere he created around him.

This was not a restful one. To begin with, he was physically restless. When he was in Rome, he moved frequently from his apartments in the Vatican palace to the Castel Sant' Angelo or the Belvedere, or into the city to stay at a cardinal's palace, especially one of those that he had built himself at San Pietro in Vincoli and Santi Apostoli. But he could never stay in Rome for long without taking trips outside the city.

His favourite refuge was the fortress at Ostia, which he seems to have treated as his own even though it had been given to Cardinal Caraffa and, after his death, to Cardinal Riario. One of the great attractions of Ostia for Julius was the sailing and fishing he could do there. He loved ships and the sea, and even just watching ships from the shore always gave him pleasure. Was this a passion that had developed when he was a boy at home in Savona, on the Ligurian coast? Not everyone shared his affection for Ostia and its pastimes. A Mantuan who went there for two days with Federico Gonzaga (the son of the Marquis of Mantua, who was being held hostage in Rome) complained of the great inconvenience to which everyone had been put, because it was such a small place and there was little to do, except look at the shore and watch the ships passing in the distance.[14] The fact that there was no room for anybody but the pope, his servants and a few guests was probably another attraction of the place for Julius. He could escape from routine business, and ambassadors or cardinals who wanted an audience with him had to make a special trip to obtain one, and soon learned not to put themselves to the trouble of going to bother him about anything that could wait.

While Ostia was his favourite retreat, there were others. In the last years of his pontificate, he stayed several times at the villa at La Magliana near Rome that had belonged to Francesco Alidosi, Cardinal Pavia. Civitavecchia, which could be reached quickly by sea from Ostia, offered the opportunity of watching the progress of the building works at the fortress there, as well as the delights of its harbour. A trip to Civitavecchia could also be combined with an extended tour of the countryside round Rome, which offered an escape from the heat and disease that made Rome so uncomfortable and unhealthy in the summer.

Reluctant to stay in one place for long, Julius found it hard to keep still as he went about his daily business either. Except when he was laid up (as he quite frequently was) by an attack of fever, or gout, or syphilis, or haemorrhoids, when he would give audiences lying in or on his bed, he often strolled about as he talked to officials or ambassadors. He might just walk up and down the room or a loggia, or in a garden, but sometimes the ambassadors would be taken off to inspect some building works with him, for example, or to look at ships. This was a sign of goodwill and special favour; for an envoy to be left kneeling throughout the interview was a mark of the pope's displeasure with him or his master.

Quite apart from the physical activity they might involve, audiences with Julius were rarely very relaxed affairs. Anyone who had anything to do with the pope soon learned that it was

fatal to contradict him, and extremely difficult to tell him anything that he did not want to hear. His temper was on a very
short fuse, and his rages were notorious. Servants who displeased
him could find themselves driven from the room with blows of his
cane. He had sufficient self-control not to mete out that sort of
treatment to ambassadors, but they might find, if he did not like
what they had to say, or if they happened to chance upon him in a
bad mood, that they had to endure prolonged outbursts of invec-
tive and expostulation and insults. Once the storm had blown
itself out, however, he would sometimes apologize, explaining he
simply had to let off steam, and they shouldn't mind too much
anything he might say when he was angry. He could then become
quite tractable, and discuss the matter in hand amicably. But this
did not make the experience any more pleasant, and as he grew
older, he became harder still to reason with. Bernardo Dovizi da
Bibbiena, the secretary of Cardinal de' Medici, who had to spend
much time with Julius while his master was legate with the papal
troops in the Romagna in 1511–12, found it an ordeal. 'It kills
you trying to negotiate with this man; when somebody says something he doesn't like, either he refuses to listen to you, or he loads
you with the worst insults ever heard.'[15] According to Dovizi, the
Venetian ambassador Girolamo Donà, who had just died, had
said in his last illness that death would be sweet to him, because it
meant that he wouldn't have to deal with Julius any more.[16]
Encountering Julius in a good mood could be something of an
ordeal too – ambassadors might have to put up with being clumped
affectionately on the head or made to stagger under good-natured
claps on their shoulders.

Although there were times when he liked to get away and go
fishing, and he did not want to be bothered with business during the carnival season, Julius was passionately absorbed in
the pursuit of his political goals. So absorbed was he once in
a conversation with the Venetian ambassador that he failed to
notice that the hangings near the bed on which he was lying had
caught fire. (When he did notice and called for help, he became so
excited that he lashed out with his cane at those trying to enter
the chamber, until he was finally persuaded that he was in danger
of burning to death if he did not calm down and let people in to
extinguish the flames.)[17] When affairs were not going well, he
would lose his appetite and be unable to sleep, getting up to walk
about the room, or reading and re-reading the latest letters, which
he liked to keep with him. He liked to read letters himself, though

he needed eyeglasses to help him and would lose his temper if he came to a word that he could not decipher. He would read out letters to those around him, interrupting himself to comment on what they said. Sometimes he did this without checking their contents first, so that he might find himself indiscreetly reading out news or opinions that would have been better kept private. Bad news could make him furious, even bring on a fever; good news would be greeted with cries of delight. Once, a Mantuan envoy who brought Julius some letters watched him leap out of bed in his nightshirt to read them and then, finding that they gave news of a victory, cavort around the bedchamber crowing, 'Giulio e Chiesa'. All that day, he was laughing and joking, and seemed half out of his mind; anyone who came near him needed body armour on their shoulders.[18]

Inevitably, a man who could cut such a figure attracted some ridicule. 'You can imagine that there has never been a greater fool than this one holding the Holy See ... As for myself, I've never known a greater madman', was but one of Dovizi's reflections on the pope.[19] His well-known liking for drink did not help him to acquire a reputation for dignity, at his own court or with other princes. But Dovizi, like others who began by mocking Julius, came to feel affection for him. No one could be more lovable than Julius, wrote one member of his household, Alessandro di Gabbioneta, 'he doesn't know how to harbour anything bad in him, and anyone who says otherwise doesn't know what he's talking about.'[20]

But by the end of his pontificate, there were few who were loyal to him. When he lay dangerously ill in August 1511, 'anyone who saw what the *palatini* [those who lived in the palace] are doing, would think he was dead, not just that he seems to be dying.' They were busying themselves clearing out of the palace both their own goods and much that belonged to the pope. At times, during the night, he was left completely alone, with no one to look after him, for all the servants and relatives that he had.[21] But this behaviour was common to ecclesiastical households. 'It's really pitiful to see the death of priests', commented one observer of the behaviour of the servants of Cardinal de' Gabrieli as he lay on his deathbed, 'and the greater lords they are, the worse they are treated: even before they're dead their servants are killing each other over their property ... and they don't give any thought at all to their master.'[22]

If Julius was no more successful than other princes of the

Church in attracting true loyalty from the self-seeking career clerics by whom he was surrounded, he himself did show gratitude to those who had served him during his years as a cardinal. In the second creation of cardinals of his pontificate, in December 1505, he promoted nine men, five of whom are known to have served him before he became pope. The first, Fazio Santorio da Viterbo, had been in his service since at least 1485. During the years of his patron's exile, he had stayed in Rome to look after his property, and he had been one of his attendants in the conclaves of 1503; soon after, he had been made datary. Marco Vigerio da Savona, castellan of the Castel Sant' Angelo and a distant cousin of the pope, had been a protégé of Sixtus IV. He had been made Bishop of Senigallia about the time that it had been given to Giovanni della Rovere, and had served Julius when he was a cardinal.[23] Francesco Alidosi, Julius's treasurer and a favourite, had been one of his most trusted agents during his exile. Carlo Domenico del Carretto, Marchese del Finale, had also been one of his household prelates and been sent on missions to France; his family was related to the della Rovere by marriage. Lastly, Gabriele de' Gabrieli da Fano had served Julius since at least 1493.

Two of the others in this promotion were members of the papal household, and may have served Julius before his election too. Antonio Ferreri, who was from Savona, and was allowed to use the surname della Rovere, was his majordomo. Robert Guibé, a Breton, who acted as a French envoy in Rome, was made a cardinal, Julius said, not because of his connection with Louis, but because he had long been a member of his own household.[24] Of the two remaining members of this promotion, one, Leonardo Grosso della Rovere, was related to the pope, and the other, Sigismondo Gonzaga, brother of the Marquis of Mantua, was about to be, for his niece was betrothed to Francesco Maria della Rovere.

All in this creation, therefore, were men with whom Julius had close personal connections. There were rumours on several occasions later in the pontificate that he intended to make other familiars cardinals, but it was only in the final creation, in March 1511, that he promoted two more men who had done him personal service. Francesco Argentino, the datary since 1507, had been one of Julius's chamberlains in the first years of the pontificate, and Antonio Ciocchi da Monte San Savino, the man to whom Julius had given the office of auditor of the Apostolic Chamber because he thought him the best candidate, though others had offered more money,[25] had been used by the pope several times since then on special missions in the Papal States.

Julius was not so much given to making members of his family cardinals. There were still two of Sixtus's half-dozen family cardinals, besides Julius himself, surviving when Julius was elected pope. One was Girolamo Basso della Rovere, who had never made much of a mark, and the other was Raffaele Riario, a leader of the College. In the first stages of the pontificate, Riario seemed destined to be one of Julius's inner circle of counsellors, but it did not happen. Perhaps his disappointment at his nephews not being given Forlì and Imola estranged him from the pope a little; perhaps he was shouldered out by Alidosi: he certainly strongly opposed Alidosi's promotion to the College in 1505.

Four della Rovere *nipoti* were made cardinals by Julius, but there were never more than two of them in the College at one time. Two were among his first promotion, in November 1503, but they both predeceased him. Clemente, Bishop of Mende, who had served as his lieutenant in Avignon, died in August 1504, without having made an impact in Rome. His companion, Galeotto Franciotto della Rovere, a son of Julius's sister Luchina, was an attractive, mild-mannered and popular figure, and his uncle's favourite; he had replaced Clemente as lieutenant in Avignon in March 1502. He was heaped with benefices and given the title of San Pietro ad Vincula. Appointed legate of Bologna in 1504, he was not tough enough to deal with such a politically demanding appointment, and he lost the legation after his uncle's campaign against Bologna. His future prominence had been guaranteed, however, by the grant in 1505 of the important office of vice-chancellor of the Church. By 1507 he was said to have an income of 40,000 ducats a year. His death, in September 1508, grieved Julius deeply – he wanted Galeotto to be reburied with him in his own tomb. The pope's only consolation was to transfer immediately all his offices and honours to his brother, Sisto, who was said to be as ignorant and clumsy as Galeotto had been learned and accomplished.[26] The new San Pietro ad Vincula was never as close to his uncle's heart as his brother had been, nor was he entrusted with any important mission. The fourth della Rovere *nipote*, Leonardo Grosso della Rovere, promoted in 1505, was given a number of legations – of Viterbo in 1506, of Perugia in 1507, and in Rome during Julius's second prolonged absence in the northern Papal States, in 1510–11. He was also given Julius's old office of Grand Penitentiary when it fell vacant in 1511. But, again, his real influence was always limited.

It was not a shortage of candidates among the della Rovere that stopped Julius from making more of them cardinals. Indeed, he apparently wished to avoid doing so. Before the final creation of his pontificate, he was anxious to find a cover for his promotion of the Venetian Francesco Argentino, whom he did not want to be thought of as 'his' man, and arranged for the Doge of Venice to ask for it. He would then have some excuse to make to his family for not promoting two relatives – Orlando del Carretto, his treasurer; and a son of Bartolomeo della Rovere – who were regarded as being in line for the College: he could tell them that he was not promoting any personal candidates this time around.[27]

It was accepted practice for cardinals to be created at the request of secular powers, who kept a jealous watch on the numbers of their rivals' subjects who were in the College. Lesser Italian dynasties, such as the Gonzaga and the Este, regarded having a cardinal in the family as an important status symbol, and would lobby tirelessly for years to achieve this. Juggling all these claims called for considerable diplomacy on the part of the popes.

Julius's first creation consisted of his two *nipoti*, Galeotto and Clemente; a Frenchman, François de Clermont, Archbishop of Narbonne, a *nipote* of Cardinal Rouen, whose promotion was part of the agreed price for Rouen's support in the conclave; and a Spaniard, Juan de Zuñiga, whose promotion balanced that of Clermont and was a reward for Spanish support in the conclave. At the time of the second creation, Julius was careful to point out that he was promoting Robert Guibé as his man, and not to please the King of France, but the third promotion, in December 1506, was an entirely French affair, with three *nipoti* of Rouen – Jean François de la Trémoille, Archbishop of Auch, his sister's son; René de Prie, Bishop of Bayeux, another sister's son; and Louis d'Amboise, Bishop of Alby – all created cardinals at once. This was a reward for French support of the campaign against Bologna, though Alby had to wait for years before his promotion was published and he was formally accepted into the College.[28] Julius withheld full recognition of him for political motives, first to induce his brother Chaumont, the viceroy of Milan, to take tougher action against the Bentivoglio, and then to symbolize the cooling of relations with Louis. Publication of the promotion of the other two was delayed as well, until May 1507, when a Spaniard, Francisco Ximenes Cisnero, Archbishop of Toledo, was made a cardinal to please Ferdinand. It was thought that Julius also wanted to create a counterweight to Rouen, for

Ximenes was a very influential prelate in Spain, and extremely wealthy.

Ferdinand was not satisfied, and when there was talk of an impending creation in the winter of 1510–11, he proposed three candidates, saying that the pope should not deny him a little thing like that.[29] Julius did deny him. There were no Spanish – or French – cardinals in the batch promoted in March 1511. But it did include four men promoted primarily from political motives: Christopher Bainbridge, the Archbishop of York and English ambassador in Rome; Matthaeus Schiner, Bishop of Sion, who had been of great assistance in recruiting Swiss infantry; Matthaeus Lang, Bishop of Gurk, Maximilian's right-hand man; and Alfonso Petrucci, whose father, Pandolfo Petrucci, dominated Siena and had been assiduously cultivating Julius for some time.[30] Rumours continued that another promotion was in prospect, and Ferdinand continued to suggest candidates. A list of twelve prospective cardinals circulated in late 1511 included two Spaniards, a Portuguese and a Venetian, but Julius did not create any more before his death.

Apart from personal connections and political favours, one other motive for promoting men to the College began to be mentioned in the later years of the pontificate: money. Alexander VI certainly sold cardinals' hats; it is not certain that Julius did. His defence of the practice of giving benefices only to those who would vacate offices that could be sold makes it credible that he may have done so. Girolamo Donà, the Venetian ambassador, assured the Doge that if a Venetian patrician were prepared to spend, he could easily become a cardinal. He listed details of the cash given by those spoken of for promotion in March 1511, and the offices that they would leave vacant. Bandinello de' Sauli was said to be giving above 25,000 ducats, for instance, while Francesco Argentino would relinquish offices worth 8,000 ducats and put up 4,000 ducats in cash.[31] Nonetheless, there were personal and political reasons for the promotion of every candidate on the list.[32] Dovizi also spoke of prelates lending money to the pope on the strength of promises of a hat,[33] but none of those whom he mentioned in this connection appeared on the lists of potential candidates. So, while some observers, and some prelates, believed that a cardinal's hat could be bought, there is no evidence that Julius ever promoted anyone to the College solely for financial gain, although there are grounds to suspect that he may have been prepared to accept 'gifts', and certainly that he would have been well aware of the possibilities for gain represented by the offices that candidates would vacate. When he was on his deathbed, his confessor told him that he must return any money he had accepted for such promotions.[34]

One distinct category of candidates that can be seen in the promotions of other popes – even of Alexander VI – but that is missing from those of Julius is that of scholars. No one was ever made a cardinal by Julius simply in recognition of his learning as a canon lawyer or a theologian, nor because of his literary skill, nor because he was the head of a religious order. Ximenes was an austere, learned man, a great patron of education in Spain, but that was not why he was made a cardinal.

One reason for this omission may have been that scholars and heads of religious orders were liable to be comparatively poor men, and Julius would have had to provide them with a subvention so that they could live in a manner befitting a prince of the Church. He was prepared to do this if he had to. When the impecunious Cardinal Raymond Peraud arrived in Rome in October 1504, the pope gave him money and furnishings, and paid for the lease of a house for him for a year. He felt responsible for providing poorer men of his own creation with enough benefices to provide a respectable income, but he did not think that he had to make it possible for them to live in the lordly style of the richer cardinals. Scions of princely houses such as the Gonzaga and the Este were expected to make a show; cardinals of less distinguished family could live more modestly. Discussing arrangements for Cardinal d'Este to come to Rome, Julius said he thought that the palace of Santi Apostoli would be suitable for such as him. Recalling the time that he had lived there himself, he said it was fitting for a 'signore' to live in a palace where he would be able to withdraw from the press of visitors, and come and go quietly if he wished. It was not for such a one as his own man Cardinal de' Gabrieli; he and his small household would be lost in it.[35]

Those promoted to the College by Julius out of his household continued to serve him in their new dignity. Men from this group became the principal *palatini* cardinals, the men who had rooms in the Vatican and helped the pope in the transaction of daily business. So many cardinals had been given lodgings in the palace towards the end of Alexander's pontificate – twenty-three, according to the Ferrarese ambassador – that there was no room for Julius's household, he claimed, and he asked them all to leave. He did not scorn all of Alexander's cardinals: three of them,

Gianantonio di Sangiorgio, a learned man who published books on canon law, Lodovico Podocataro, a Cypriot, and Francesco Soderini, a secular-minded man, brother of the elected permanent head of the Florentine government, Piero Soderini, were among his confidants in the early years after his election. Da Costa, who had stood so long his friend, was given rooms very near the papal apartments, and was recognized by everyone as enjoying the pope's special respect. During a serious illness in October 1504, when Julius was refusing all food, da Costa was brought to his room because it was felt that he, if anyone, could persuade him to eat.

By the middle of the pontificate, this core of advisers had changed. Podocataro died in August 1504, da Costa was very old and increasingly infirm, Soderini became somewhat suspect, as a partisan of France like his brother, and Sangiorgio seems to have lost some favour. Cardinals that Julius himself had promoted now formed the majority of the group that he liked to have around him.' His favourite *nipote*, Galeotto della Rovere, was one of them, and, inevitably, Francesco Alidosi was another. Two other long-standing servants who had been made cardinals were brought into the palace: Fazio Santorio and Marco Vigerio. Both kept the pope's confidence, Santorio until his death in March 1510, Vigerio for the rest of the pontificate.

The allocation of rooms was an index of papal favour. In June 1507 Galeotto della Rovere was assigned new rooms in the Vatican, after Julius had decided that he needed his help to relieve some of the burden of routine business. As Galeotto was given rooms that had been occupied by Alidosi, including some of the apartments Alexander VI had lived in and the Torre Borgiana, this was seen as a sign of declining favour for Alidosi, who did not give them up without a fight. This was but one of several episodes during which it was thought that Alidosi was losing his hold over Julius, but he kept a special place in the pope's affections and his counsels, until he was murdered in 1511 by Francesco Maria della Rovere, who had hated and resented him for years.[36]

No one succeeded to his special position with the pope, though Cardinal Ciocchi fancied that he did. Another man from the same, last, creation, Pietro Accolti, also became a palatine cardinal after their promotion. Both enjoyed the pope's confidence; neither of them was very popular with their fellows.

There were other cardinals whom Julius liked to have with

him when he was relaxing, generally men from noble or baronial families. Among the more frequent guests on hunting trips were three cardinals: Giovanni Colonna, a good man but not very learned; Alessandro Farnese who was the amiable brother of the beautiful Giulia, Alexander VI's mistress, and who later became Pope Paul III; and Luigi d'Aragona, a natural son of King Ferrante of Naples. These leisure companions were never among the pope's closest political advisers: he seems simply to have found them congenial company, especially on his trips outside Rome.

If Julius turned to individual members of the College for friendship and companionship as well as help with business, he was not willing to allow the College as a body much say in how he ran the papacy. Theoretically, the cardinals' function was to act as counsellors of the pope, and important decisions were formally recorded as being made with their advice and consent. In practice, Julius was no more prepared to receive advice that he did not want to hear from the College than from anyone else. For him, the function of consistory in general was to approve decisions that he had already taken, not to help him formulate policy. Sometimes it suited him to emphasize the support of the College for his policies; and he would summon a special meeting of consistory to discuss the Venetian offer to surrender the Romagnol towns in May 1509, for example, or the peace terms on offer from France in April 1512.[37] The public backing of the College was naturally important to him when a group of dissident cardinals, backed by Louis, summoned a council at Pisa in 1511, and there were times when he had to temper his response to reflect the wishes of the College in a way that he would not normally have bothered to do – in the measures taken against the schismatic cardinals themselves, for instance.[38] It clearly irked him to have to do this.

He did make use, as other popes had done, of special commissions, which often represented each order of cardinals, so that there would be, say, two cardinal-bishops, two cardinal-priests, and two cardinal-deacons. It is not clear how much say the cardinals had in the appointment of such commissions or whether it was up to the pope to choose whom he wanted. They often included at least one of his *nipoti*, and other cardinals in his confidence, but usually at least one senior and independently minded cardinal as well. Cardinal Caraffa, one of the longest-serving members of the College, and one not afraid to speak his mind, was frequently included. How much notice Julius took of what such commissions reported is not known, but, at the least, they provided him with a sounding-board of opinion in the College, without the potential embarrassment of holding a full-scale debate in which divisions among the cardinals, and disagreement with his own policies, might come into the open.

However much they might mutter in private, most of the cardinals were too scared of Julius to risk publicly opposing him. Julius expected them to regard him as their 'padrone', their master, and not their 'compagno', their colleague.[39] He could tolerate polite, tactful disagreement, but he did not like cardinals to boycott sessions of consistory to show their disapproval. When a consistory was asked to approve a grant of three estates – Frascati, Monticello and Sant' Angelo – to Niccolò della Rovere, brother of Galeotto and Sisto, in November 1508, only Grimani, of those present, raised any objection; and he did it 'modestly', saying that he left it to Julius's own judgement. Cardinals Sanseverino and Briçonnet, having heard what would be discussed, did not turn up. Julius had been told that Sanseverino was going to disagree, and had said he would fix him with cash. Briçonnet had promised to come and give his consent, but then had been persuaded by Sanseverino to stay away. Julius was not very concerned about him, but he was angry with Sanseverino.[40] Occasionally, a cardinal would speak up in defence of his home government, as the Venetian cardinals Grimani and Corner repeatedly did, but Julius could prevent them from voicing their opposition. The two Venetians were not summoned with the other cardinals to the meeting that was to consider the war against Venice in March 1509, and although they were present in consistory when the bull of excommunication against Venice was read out on 26 April, Julius formally imposed silence on them.[41]

Only in defence of their own interests would most of the cardinals find the courage openly to oppose his wishes. Nothing aroused more determined resistance to the pope by the cardinals than the prospect of an addition to their number. One of the bargains that Julius had struck with the other cardinals in order to secure his election to the papacy had been that he could create three new cardinals immediately – one of his own *nipoti*, a *nipote* of Cardinal Rouen, and a third, to be agreed – and that then there would be no more promotions for a long time, and not until the numbers in the College had fallen below twenty-four. In the event, he proposed four candidates – one for France and one for Spain (to encourage them to assist the Church against those who had invaded her territory, he said), and two of his *nipoti*. He recalled his promise to create only three new cardinals, but explained that he wanted to promote both *nipoti* at some stage, and that by promoting them together now, he would avoid being pestered by those who hoped to come into the College on the coat-tails of the second. He promised, on the word of a pope, not to create any more cardinals until the College asked him to do so.[42]

Within a year, however, he was quarrelling with the cardinals because he wanted to promote some more and they did not like either the idea or the men that he had in mind. It was not until a year later that he finally did make a second creation. He only achieved that by working on the cardinals individually first, and, even so, he claimed that several had promised him their votes in private, only to come out against the promotion in public. Only Leonardo della Rovere and Sigismondo Gonzaga were not opposed as candidates; objection was fiercest to Alidosi and Antonio Ferreri. It took Julius several hours to browbeat the College into submission in one exceptionally stormy consistory, with fourteen cardinals led by Caraffa and Riario standing out against him, while only twelve were ready to agree. As one cardinal after another spoke against the idea, Julius exploded into rage, crying, 'I want to make them and I'm going to make them.' He called the captain of the guard, and said that the cardinals would not leave until they had agreed, threatening to make thirty new cardinals.[43] At length, he wore down nearly all of them, except Riario, who stood out because he hated Alidosi, and Caraffa, who was said to want a *nipote* of his own to be cardinal.[44]

Battered into submission, the cardinals eventually crawled out of the consistory, and Julius never had that degree of trouble with them again. Fears were expressed when the three French cardinals were promoted in 1506 at the danger of increasing the French presence in the College so much that the curia might be drawn back to France, but Julius dismissed the notion. There was some unease at the promotion of Ximenes, too, until the cardinals reflected that he was old, rich and unlikely to come to Rome. When Galeotto della Rovere died, the cardinals readily agreed to his brother's appointment to take his place. They did not want to agree to the creation in March 1511, not to all the candidates named, anyway, but by then – except for those cardinals who were refusing to come to court and were beginning to plan the council to be held at Pisa – they lacked the spirit to put up a fight. Fears of setting an uncomfortable precedent did rouse them to object to Julius's plans to demote the schismatic cardinals, but those who tried to plead for delay in consistory were cut short by Julius, and he forced them to agree.

One of those who tried to avoid taking part in this decision was Sisto della Rovere, the second San Pietro ad Vincula. He sent to say that he was ill; Julius replied that if he did not turn up at the consistory, he would regret it.[45] He came. Julius did not expect his cardinal-nephews to take an independent line on important matters of policy, and, in general, they showed no signs of trying to do so. Nor did he expect much from them by way of trying to influence their colleagues: there is no evidence that he used his *nipoti* to help him to manage the College. If there was any opposition to overcome, he relied on his own formidable personality to do the trick.

His lack of reliance on help from his family was in marked contrast to the example of his own uncle, or of Alexander VI, or of many of the popes who followed him over the next three centuries. He gave his clerical *nipoti* honours and offices and benefices, and arranged prestigious marriages for some lay members of his family. But he would not permit them even to appear to have any influence over him. Unlike other popes, he did not encourage those seeking favour to approach him through the agency of his relatives.

Julius's only known child was his daughter, Felice.[46] She was brought to Rome from Savona by his sister, Luchina, in June 1504. He openly acknowleged his paternity – but was discreet. Felice was not loaded with money and jewels from the papal coffers, and, though she came to the palace to dine privately with her father, she had no public role. Julius set about finding a husband for her. She had been married at least once before, and was apparently not eager to repeat the experience; she had objected to several prospective husbands in the past, and flatly refused to marry one man favoured by her father: Roberto, Prince of Salerno.[47] In 1506 she did agree to marry the eccentric Giangiordano Orsini, bringing him a large, but not lavish, dowry of 20,000 ducats, and went off to live with him at the great, gloomy castle of Bracciano. From there she made occasional visits to her father, and sometimes tried to speak to him about public affairs. One attempt that she made to settle the bitter dispute between Julius and the Duke of Ferrara by proposing a match between her daughter and the duke's son was harshly dismissed by her father, who sent her away, telling her to attend to her sewing.[48] Representations that she made to him at the request of Anne, Queen of France, about making peace with Louis were received more patiently but were ineffective.

Felice's marriage to an Orsini was complemented shortly after by the wedding of another della Rovere girl, Luchina's daughter Lucrezia, to a Colonna, Marcantonio, who had originally been spoken of as a prospective bridegroom for Felice herself. Julius had welcomed the suggestion from the Orsini of giving Felice an Orsini husband instead, because he had felt that it would provide greater future security for Francesco Maria, presumably on the assumption that linking the della Rovere to both major baronial families might help to protect them against persecution by a future pope. The marriage of Luchina's son Niccolò to Laura Orsini was not a reinforcement of this policy, because her family was not truly a branch of the powerful baronial clan.[49] But she was the sole child and heiress of her father, Orso Orsini, and she had inherited the exceptional beauty of her mother, Giulia Farnese, so Niccolò had no cause to complain. Julius also provided the couple with three small fiefs near Rome in 1508,[50] although three years later he made Niccolò give one of them, Frascati, to Marcantonio Colonna, whose family had held it in the past, and gave him two former Orsini places, Gallese and Soriano, instead.

Niccolò was thus well looked after but, like Felice, was not so favoured as to cause a scandal, or to give rise to accusations that Julius was making improper use of the resources of the papacy to endow his family. Fortunately for him, the future of the della Rovere family as a signorial dynasty had already been secured by Sixtus, when he had endowed Giovanni della Rovere with Senigallia and other lands in the Marche. Giovanni's marriage to one of the daughters of Federico da Montefeltro had turned out to open up even better prospects for his heir, Francesco Maria, for Federico's only son, Guidobaldo, had proved unable to father children, and thus his death would raise the question of who was to inherit the duchy of Urbino. Federico had married off several daughters into Italian noble families, including the Sanseverino and the Colonna.[51] Had Julius not become pope, there might have been stiff competition for the inheritance, but with his accession, there could be no contest, for the della Rovere were sure to win. All that Julius had to do was to have the ailing Guidobaldo formally adopt Francesco Maria as his son, and to have the adoption approved by the College of Cardinals, which was accomplished in May 1504. Francesco Maria was now set up as the heir to one of the most desirable quasi-independent fiefs in the Papal States. On the death of Guidobaldo, in April 1508, the eighteen-year-old della Rovere boy took peaceful possession of the duchy. In later years, there were reports that Julius was considering giving other lands to his nephew – Ferrara and Modena; and Parma and Piacenza, when these were taken from the French – but it is unlikely he ever seriously intended to do this. Under pressure from his family, just before his death, he did give him Pesaro, after refusing to give the vicariate to Galeazzo Sforza, uncle of the young *signore* Costanzo, when the boy died in 1512.

Despite his good fortune, Francesco Maria grew up to be ungrateful, discontented and disloyal. While Guidobaldo was alive, he was put under his tutelage, and spent much of his time with him in Urbino. He was betrothed to Eleonora, daughter of Francesco Gonzaga, Marquis of Mantua, and of Isabella d'Este, sister of Alfonso d'Este, Duke of Ferrara. The boy was being groomed to take his place among the second-rank ruling families of Italy, but he learned his lesson too well. He identified himself with the interests of his adoptive family, and of his wife's family, rather than with those of the pope.

Julius was fond of the boy and took pleasure in seeing him master the skills of horsemanship and preparing for the military career for which he was destined. He gave him *condotte*, though the effective command of the troops that he was given was exercised by the senior professional soldiers put by his side to educate him. Francesco Maria relished his life as a young prince – so much so, that both the pope and the Gonzaga warned him that he should begin to pay more attention to serious business and think about something other than riding and enjoying himself. As Guidobaldo lay dying, Julius decided that it was time to build up Francesco Maria's status and reputation. He gave him a house in Rome, and ordered papal *condottieri* to apply to him if there was anything they wanted. In September 1508 he made him Captain of the Church.

But soon the relationship went sour. Francesco Maria spent most of his time out of Rome, away from the pope, and never had any influence over papal policy. He became jealous and resentful of his uncle's favourite, Alidosi. When he was asked by the pope to undertake some military action, he was usually slow to obey, quick to complain that he could not do anything effective without more money or more men. In the war against the Duke of Ferrara, which was so close to Julius's heart in the later years of his

2 The arms of Julius II, as they appear above the door leading from the *anticamera segreta* to the Stanza d'Eliodoro in the Vatican. (© Courtauld Institute)

3 The fresco by Melozzo da Forlì, commissioned by Sixtus IV, commemorating the foundation of the Vatican Library in 1475. Giuliano della Rovere is the central figure; the other figures standing around the seated pope have been identified as Girolamo and Raffaele Riario, and Giovanni della Rovere; the kneeling figure is the librarian, Platina. (© Musei Vaticani)

4 The façade of the Palazzo della Rovere built for Giuliano della Rovere at SS. Apostoli in Rome. (© M. Hirst; courtesy of the Courtauld Institute)

5 The courtyard of the Palazzo della Rovere at SS. Apostoli. (© M. Hirst; courtesy of the Courtauld Institute)

6 As cardinal and as pope, Giuliano della Rovere frequently emphasized his relationship to Sixtus IV, as in this inscription accompanying a Roman relief he placed in the porch of the church of SS. Apostoli. (© Courtauld Institute)

7 One of Julius's favourite fortresses, and places of relaxation, at Ostia Antica, which belonged to him as Cardinal Bishop of Ostia. (© Professor Sir John Hale)

8   The entrance to the stairs out of the courtyard of the fortress at Ostia Antica; as pope, Julius still treated this fortress as though it were his own, as the inscription above the doorway illustrates. (© H. Burns; courtesy of the Courtauld Institute)

9   The tomb of Sixtus IV, commissioned by Giuliano della Rovere from Antonio Pollaiuolo. (© Reverenda Fabbrica di San Pietro)

10 The Palazzo della Rovere in Savona, designed for Giuliano by
Giuliano da Sangallo. (© J. Shearman; courtesy of the Courtauld
Institute)

11 Julius's first commissions as pope, such as this loggia at the Castel Sant' Angelo, were on a small scale; Julius often preferred to stay at the Castel Sant' Angelo rather than at the Vatican, when he was in Rome. (© H. Burns; courtesy of the Courtauld Institute)

12 The tomb of Cardinal Ascanio Sforza in S. Maria del Popolo in Rome, commissioned by Julius from Andrea Sansovino in a generous gesture to a former enemy. (© Courtauld Institute)

pontificate, he was particularly dilatory, under the influence of the Gonzaga, who were doing all they could to help Ferrara. In the last year of Julius's life, at a critical stage of his war against the French, he openly, if briefly, switched his allegiance to Louis.[52] The delight Julius displayed when he received Francesco Maria's message that he once again wished to serve the pope, and that he was ready to live and die with him, showed that he still felt great affection for him. On the whole, however, his nephew must have been a sore disappointment to him, a source of irritation and worry, rather than of support and solace. He was also responsible for one of the greatest scandals of Julius's pontificate, when he murdered Cardinal Alidosi in the street in Ravenna – as in 1507 he had murdered his sister Maria's lover, a favourite of Guidobaldo.

Had Julius lived much longer, and Francesco Maria continued on his erratic course, he might have had cause to be jealous of some other della Rovere *nipoti*. In the later years of his pontificate, Julius became close to Bartolomeo Grosso della Rovere, a brother of Cardinal Leonardo. Bartolomeo had served as the governor of Spoleto for several years before coming to live at court. By late 1510 he was an increasingly influential figure; by 1512 he was said to be with Julius day and night, to be the only man whom the pope trusted. Julius planned to make one of his sons a cardinal. But Bartolomeo had the misfortune to lose three children in a year, including his only son who was still a layman, Galeazzo, a youth of considerable ability and promise, in November 1512. Julius himself died a few months later without having given the promised cardinal's hat.

In secular courts, the prince's major military commander would often be part of the innermost circle. Leadership in war, with the dispensation of justice, was traditionally at the heart of the prince's duties, and in the early sixteenth century it was still the exception for a secular ruler to play no practical military role. In contrast, military command was not supposed to be a function of the pope – not that this stopped Julius from taking personal charge of military operations – and soldiers would only be a part of the papal court if they were also members of the pope's family. It had become the practice for popes to appoint a lay *nipote* as captain of the papal troops, although, usually, the *nipote* had little or no military experience and effective command would be exercised by professional soldiers at their side. Part of the trouble with Francesco Maria della Rovere seems to have arisen because,

having received some military education, once he had been made
captain of the papal troops he felt competent to take charge, while
his uncle apparently did not agree. Julius was constantly looking
for a reliable, tested senior *condottiere* to command the papal troops
in war.

He had little luck in his quest, even though the della Rovere
could count among their relatives by marriage some of the leading
condottieri of the day. His first captain, Francesco Maria's adoptive
father, Guidobaldo da Montefeltro, did not inherit his own
father's military skills with his gout, and was so ill with this
affliction and with syphilis that for much of the time he could
not even mount a horse. Francesco Gonzaga, Francesco Maria's
father-in-law, whom Julius tried to employ in campaigns against
Bologna and Ferrara, proved treacherous and idle. The Colonna
were a family of soldiers, and two of them, Prospero and Fabrizio,
were among the most sought-after soldiers of the day. Prospero,
however, pitched his demands too high, was not willing to share
command with anyone else and, besides, Julius felt, if sage
in counsel, was insufficiently bold in the field. Fabrizio's disappointment at the exclusion of his Montefeltro wife's claims
to the succession to Urbino made him somewhat resentful and
unreliable, as his behaviour during the campaign against Ferrara
in 1510–11 showed. Julius liked Marcantonio Colonna, who
married his niece, Lucrezia, but though he did serve the pope
faithfully in the tasks with which he was entrusted he was too
junior to be given supreme command. The Orsini too had a long
military tradition, but the only member of the family competent to
exercise an important command, Niccolò da Pitigliano, was
committed to serving Venice, with whom he had a contract for
life. Felice's husband, Giangiordano, was an honourable but
strange man, and did not have the military skills of his father
Virginio. Costantino Arniti, a relative of Sixtus IV, held *condotte*
from Julius for most of the pontificate, but he only exercised
subordinate commands and was more interested in politics.
(He spent much of the pontificate shuttling between Julius and
Maximilian, acting as a papal ambassador in Germany and an
Imperial ambassador in Rome.) When, in 1511, Julius at last
secured a competent commander for his troops – the Duke
of Termini, who came from Naples and was 'lent' to him by
Ferdinand – he fell ill and died on his way north.

This lack of success in finding a competent, reliable – not to
mention healthy – commander for his troops, is mirrored by

Julius's difficulties in finding competent, reliable – and honest – men to share the burden of government with him. Sheer bad luck may account for this in part, but cannot be the whole explanation. Bad judgement of men, such as he had shown as a cardinal,[53] was at the root of his problems too. He did try to choose men to serve him on the basis of their suitability for the task, not just on whether he found them personally congenial. He took away the legation of Bologna from his favourite *nipote* in 1507 to give it to a man whom he did not much like, but whom he had recently made a cardinal, because he believed that he was tough and able. The appointment turned out badly: Cardinal Ferreri was corrupt and oppressive, and, within six months, was recalled and shut up in the Castel Sant' Angelo.[54]

The outstanding example of Julius's bad judgement of men was his loyalty to Francesco Alidosi. Fortunate the favourite who does not attract jealousy and spite in a court, but the universal odium in which Alidosi was held was quite exceptional. Few pitied him when he was cut down in Ravenna by Francesco Maria; few mourned his death, except Julius. Even the usually detached Guicciardini denounced him as 'thoroughly deserving, because of his enormous and infinite vices, of every kind of bitter torment'.[55] Perhaps the best measure of how much he was hated is how little disturbed the other cardinals were by the manner of his death. Generally, the least assault on the dignity of a cardinal brought them rallying to the defence of their honour and privileges; nothing else could rouse them so. Yet they made no difficulty at all about absolving Francesco Maria, and this was not just to please the pope – Julius himself was more inclined to punish his nephew than they were.[56]

Why was Julius so loyal to Alidosi? Inevitably, there were accusations that his hold over the pope was a sexual one, but this was the common currency of insult and innuendo about figures at the papal court. Maximilian and Louis both made comments on Julius's supposed designs on the young Federico Gonzaga when he was a hostage at the papal court,[57] but the boy's mother and his attendants had no fears on that score. Julius may have had homosexual lovers in the past, and had certainly had at least one mistress, but there is no evidence that he was sexually active while he was pope. He was prepared to send Alidosi away from court for long periods, to be resident legate in Bologna.

The explanation for Alidosi's influence over Julius is, rather, that he knew how to handle him. He knew that Julius's wishes must never be opposed directly; he could withstand anger and insults, and even blows. Alidosi flattered the pope with public displays of devotion, putting up an inscription describing himself as 'Julii II Alumnus' over the entry to the chapel in his villa at La Magliana and making the della Rovere oak and the arms of the pope, with his own arms, the basis of the decoration of the chapel of his Roman palace.[58] Such signs of affection and recognition must have appealed to the pope's warm and loyal heart. Even when he came to know of Alidosi's misgovernment in his legation, and of his intrigues with the French, he could not bring himself to turn his back on such a friendship.

Moody, impulsive, unpredictable, with a violent temper, hard to advise and even harder to dissuade from a course of action on which he had set his mind, Julius was obviously difficult to work with. As the years went by, he was more than ever inclined to keep his own counsel. This may have contributed to his strength, his extraordinary determination to carry on against all odds. But he paid the price of increasing isolation. The sight of the indomitable old man directing siege operations in the middle of a bleak winter because there was no one around him who could be trusted to carry out orders properly, or lying mortally ill in the Vatican in 1511, deserted by his servants and his family, aroused pity in the envoys who reported the scenes. At such moments, this warm-hearted, generous, irascible, impossible man was almost a tragic figure.

7

·

'Julius Caesar Pontifex II'?

'Julius II operated as a patron on a scale and on a level of quality that make him equal to the artists we associate with him: Bramante, Raphael, Michelangelo. If, as many believe, this was the greatest assembly of talent ever to work for one man at the same time, we must hail Julius as the most perspicacious as well as the most fortunate patron the world has ever known.'[1]

Among the works of art commissioned by Julius are some of the most famous in the world – the Sistine Chapel ceiling, painted by the reluctant Michelangelo; the Vatican Stanze, painted by Raphael; the new St Peter's, begun by Bramante. But these are just the tip of the iceberg. As cardinal and as pope, he was one of the most active patrons at the papal court, both within and outside Rome. A bare catalogue of his major commissions shows the extraordinary scope of his patronage.

In Rome, before he became pope, he had built the best part of three palaces, restored two ancient basilicas, and paid for extensive works at a third. In the garden of one of his Roman palaces, he had amassed a fine collection of antique sculpture; and in Sixtus IV's chapel in St Peter's, he had placed a masterpiece by a contemporary sculptor, the bronze tomb of his uncle, by Antonio Pollaiuolo.

Two of the palaces that he built in Rome were associated with one of the three ancient basilicas that he repaired and embellished. His titular church, San Pietro in Vincoli, naturally benefited from his patronage. Some of the money for this came from a legacy left by Cardinal Nicholas of Kues, who had held the title before Sixtus. Giuliano della Rovere covered the transepts and the side aisles with vaults, and restored the roof of the basilica; he also rebuilt the main entrance, and put an arcaded portico before the façade. For the niche on the altar containing the chains believed to be those that had bound the captive St Peter, he had Antonio Pollaiuolo make beautiful doors of gilded bronze, with reliefs showing the imprisonment of St Peter and his release by an angel. These doors, made in 1477, bore the papal arms and an inscription with Sixtus's name, as well as the arms and the name of Giuliano.

On the southern side of the basilica, he built a cloister for the clergy who served it. Work on this seems to have been interrupted; it was finished while he was pope. To the north, he constructed a comparatively modest palace to serve as a residence for the titular cardinal; work on this was not begun until after 1481, when the restoration of the basilica was complete. It apparently had three storeys, with an arcaded loggia running the length of the upper floor. Every internal door on the *piano nobile* still bears his coat of arms. He seems to have been fond of this palace, and often stayed there for a few days when he was pope, though it had its drawbacks. An envoy described the chambers that he was using there as small and stuffy, uninhabitable in the heat of the day.[2]

It has usually been thought that this palace did boast of one famous amenity, a lovely garden containing the cardinal's collection of antique sculpture and inscriptions, but recent work suggests that this may have been found at the palace that was in fact his main residence in Rome, at Santi Apostoli.[3] By contrast with the palace at San Pietro in Vincoli, the one he built at Santi Apostoli was considered one of the most luxurious in the Rome of his day. It had two distinct halves, on either side of the basilica. That on the south had been begun by Pietro Riario, and included some rooms from an earlier palace on the site built by Cardinal Bessarion, which are now incorporated in the Palazzo Colonna built on the site in the eighteenth century. The part that Giuliano della Rovere built to the north of the basilica survives, and the windows of the *piano nobile* still bear his arms. This block of the palace was not large, and the façade is not imposing, but the decoration of the three rooms on the *piano nobile* was particularly fine, and much still survives. They have carved marble cornices and elaborate sculpted window frames and benches supported by carved balusters. These windows have no parallel in Rome, but do resemble some to be found in the ducal palace at Urbino, which were completed a few years before the Santi Apostoli palace: a porphyry slab in one of the window recesses at Santi Apostoli carries the date 1482. This floor of the block was linked to the corresponding floor on the other side of the basilica by a two-storeyed loggia running across the façade of the church; the upper loggia was closed in the seventeenth century. A similar loggia was built on the first floor of the southern and western sides of the small courtyard of the palace, with a ground-floor arcade on all sides. After he became pope, Julius built another block behind this, and a second, larger courtyard.

To the east of the basilica, extending southwards, lay a large garden, with a beautiful pavilion built about 1485. This may have joined on to the southern block of the palace, but it was incorporated into the eighteenth-century Colonna palace, and its relation to the earlier one is uncertain. Originally, it had an arcade with seven bays opening into the garden, with rooms above it; the standard of the decorative detail is very high. The quality of the '*palazzina*', as this pavilion is called, has led to speculation that it was designed by a famous architect, but no documents survive to furnish any information on this.

The portico of the basilica has been attributed to the Florentine architect Baccio Pontelli. Much altered, this is now the oldest surviving part of the church, which was substantially rebuilt in the eighteenth century. Inside the church, there is a very personal memorial of Giuliano della Rovere: the tomb of his father, Raffaele. As on many Roman tombs of this period, a marble relief depicts the dead man lying on a bier. Unusually, at either end of the bier stand two weeping *putti*, holding a shield with the della Rovere arms. The inscription, dated 1477, recalls that Raffaele was the brother of Sixtus IV, as well as the cardinal's father; it does not mention his other children. Originally placed in the choir of Santi Apostoli, in the nineteenth century the monument was moved to the crypt.

Of the third palace that Giuliano della Rovere built in Rome as a cardinal, nothing seems to remain. In the document recording the sale in September 1492 of Cerveteri and Anguillara by Franceschetto Cibò to Virginio Orsini, which was signed there, it is referred to as the palace outside the Porta Sant' Agnese newly built by Cardinal San Pietro ad Vincula.[4] From this description, it is not clear if the palace was associated with the basilica of Sant' Agnese, which lies over a mile from the gate, along the ancient Via Nomentana. Giuliano is known to have restored the basilica in 1479, though what connection, if any, he had with the church, remains obscure.

Exile from Rome presumably brought about a suspension of the cardinal's building activities there. Perhaps the last major commission to be completed before he left was the wonderful bronze tomb of his uncle, Sixtus IV, made by Antonio Pollaiuolo, which is now in the Treasury of St Peter's. Originally, it was placed in the chapel that Sixtus IV had built in the old St Peter's – where Julius would also be buried – the last addition to the old basilica and the last part to be demolished in 1606. The free-standing bronze monument has a life-size, recumbent figure of the pope, lying on a platform surrounded by representations of the virtues and of the liberal arts. Beautiful as the monument is, it seems a little inappropriate for a pope whose field of study was theology to be surrounded by female figures in classical draperies. 'Theology' is represented by the goddess Diana, reclining, nearly nude, and looking into a sunburst surrounding the Trinity. It is not known what part, if any, the cardinal had in deciding on the design of the monument, but he must have at least approved of it. His arms appear on it, together with those of the pope, and the inscription records his responsibility for the commission.

In the vicinity of Rome, Vincula held the abbey of Grotta-ferrata from 1473, and the bishopric of Ostia from 1483. The buildings at Grottaferrata were in a ruinous state: he restored the monastery and enclosed it with a wall and defensive works that gave it the appearance of a fortress. It was used, against his will, as a military base by Girolamo Riario's soldiers in the campaign against the Colonna in 1484. He visited Grottaferrata occasionally, but Ostia became a favourite residence. There he built one of the most advanced fortresses of the day, designed in large part by Baccio Pontelli. No documents concerning its construction survive, and it has been argued that the basic design of the fortress was established while Cardinal d'Estouteville held the see, and that Vincula simply continued the work that he had begun.[5] A more recent study argues that d'Estouteville never began the improvements to the fortification that Sixtus had wanted him to make.[6] The design of the fortress was influenced partly by its site – its unusual triangular shape was determined by its position on the river, which has subsequently changed its course. Its great bastions put the fortress in the forefront of military design in Italy in the late Quattrocento, and it has been much admired for its beauty.[7] When it came under siege in the

1490s, however, its defences were criticized – 'the experts don't consider the fortress to be strong' – and Alexander was told that Ostia could not hold out for a week against artillery because the fortress was very cramped and its defences deficient.[8] In the attack in May 1494, the new cathedral of Sant'Aurea that Vincula had built was burned, together with the old episcopal palace. The cardinal apparently preferred to stay in the fortress anyway.

Vincula's long tenure of the legation of Avignon prompted him to undertake building there too. No trace survives in the papal palace of the work that he had done there, but his reconstruction of the south side of the archiepiscopal palace has not been obliterated, and the façade still has an inscription bearing his name and titles. Breaches in the city ramparts, caused by flooding in 1471, were repaired on his orders, but not at his expense: the money was raised by a local tax. He does not seem to have commissioned any restoration or alterations at the cathedral, but he did give fine vestments and jewels and plate, including a crucifix and candelabra, almost all bearing his arms. He also established a choir of six boys to be instructed in plain chant by a master.[9]

In Savona, his home town, Vincula largely followed the example of Sixtus IV in his commissions. Sixtus had paid for extensive alterations to the cathedral (which was demolished in the mid-sixteenth century by the Genoese to clear the way for a fortress) while Vincula rebuilt the presbytery. Throughout his years as a cardinal – particularly when he held the see of Savona, from 1499 to 1503 – and even when he was pope, he continued to pay for the embellishment of the cathedral. In the late 1480s he commissioned a large polyptych of the Madonna in majesty for the main altar, executed by the Brescian painter Vincenzo Foppa, assisted by Lodovico Brea. After he became Bishop of Savona in 1499, he paid for the decoration of the apse in 1501–2, and contributed to the construction of fine choir stalls, which bear portraits of him as pope and of Sixtus IV at the sides of the central stall. Six silver statues of the Apostles and two candelabra of silver and crystal that he gave to the cathedral have been lost. A portrait of himself that he gave to the episcopal palace in 1493 also disappeared. The Franciscan monastery in which Sixtus had begun his ecclesiastical career was chosen by Sixtus as the site for the funerary chapel that he built for his parents, and after his death, Vincula continued the work, paying for frescoes and a polyptych of the Nativity for the high altar, which his uncle had probably commissioned in 1483. Dismantled in the eighteenth century, the three central parts of the polyptych are now in Avignon; the left-hand wing has a portrait of Sixtus IV kneeling in his pontifical robes, the right-hand one a portrait of Vincula in the habit of a Franciscan.

Most notable among the surviving works commissioned by Giuliano della Rovere in Savona is the palace that he asked Giuliano da Sangallo to build for him, which was begun in 1495. Never completed to the original plan, and subsequently altered, with its façade patterned with white marble and grey stone, it is still the most elegant and imposing palace in the city. Vincula also bought from the Fregosi (it is not clear when) a palace in Genoa, which he described as 'our house of San Tomasso',[10] but it was claimed in 1498 as a traditional residence of the governor of the city. Vincula denied this, saying that he wanted the governor to leave it, and that he was not prepared to accept any rent for it. He had not bought it to let it out, he said, but to put it in order for his own use, and to make it an ornament to the city.[11]

After he became pope, although he continued to contribute to the embellishment of Savona cathedral, he largely confined his patronage to Rome and the Papal States. Within Rome, apart from work at Santi Apostoli and San Pietro in Vincoli, which was a continuation of earlier projects interrupted by his exile, his patronage was largely confined to the complex of St Peter's, the Vatican and the Castel Sant' Angelo. The exceptions to this were commissions in and for the favoured Roman church of the della Rovere, Santa Maria del Popolo, and the abortive project to build a huge Palazzo dei Tribunali to house many of the offices of the curia.

If the compass of his interests in building in Rome was comparatively limited, the scale of some of his commissions, and the quality of all of them, were not. So grand were several of the schemes, notably those planned for him by Bramante, that they were not completed during his lifetime, usually never completed at all. Julius's primary interest was always in building; ironically, as a patron he is best remembered for the paintings by Michelangelo in the Sistine Chapel and by Raphael in the papal apartments, for the 'tragedy' of the great tomb commissioned from Michelangelo, which dogged the artist for decades, and for the destruction of the old basilica of St Peter's.

Not all his projects were on the grand scale. Some of the first works that he had done as pope were improvements to his living quarters at the Castel Sant' Angelo, including a loggia looking out over the Tiber, perhaps designed by Giuliano da Sangallo, and a bathroom in which he could take medicinal baths, whose construction he took the Venetian ambassador Giustinian to see in March 1504.[12] Towards the end of his life, he began a covered way from the fortress to the Vatican, which would be shorter and straighter than the one Alexander had built.[13]

Work on the Vatican began in 1505, with the Belvedere courtyard. This was the first of Bramante's great designs for Julius that were destined not to be finished. The villa built on high ground 300 yards from the Vatican by Innocent VIII was to be linked to the palace by three terraces, flanked by covered porticoes serving as corridors, with the top storey providing a link between the second storey of the wing of the palace built by Nicholas V and the ground floor of the villa. The lowest court would provide an open-air theatre, for entertainments such as the bullfights put on there in 1509.[14] The two upper courts were to be laid out as formal gardens with fountains; they were to be linked by ramps framing a nymphaeum. At the Belvedere, a special garden was constructed for the pope's collection of classical sculpture, which was augmented during his pontificate by newly discovered pieces, including the *Laocoön*, dug up on the Esquiline hill in 1506.

This sculpture garden, and the right-hand portico corridor leading to the Belvedere from the palace, were the only parts of the plan to be substantially realized during Julius's pontificate, and, even so, much remained to be done on the portico. They may well have been the aspects of the project that interested him most. He went frequently to the Belvedere, and to have a convenient means of reaching it out of the rain or the glare of the sun would be very appealing. Much has been read into Bramante's grandiose designs, and it is claimed that Julius was trying to emulate the Imperial villas of the Caesars,[15] but the fact is that no one knows how much of the inspiration for the project came from Bramante, and how much from the pope. Julius's huge inscription, and the medal that he had struck to commemorate the Belvedere scheme both refer to it as a 'via': the inscription on the Belvedere itself records that he constructed this 'via' for the convenience of the popes.[16] This suggests that, for him, its prime purpose was to be a way of getting from one place to another, not the recreation of a piece of Imperial Rome. Vasari[17] records a story that, if it is true, throws light on the question of who, artist or patron, was allowing himself to be carried away by visions of Imperial grandeur. Bramante, he says, proposed to Julius a hieroglyphic emblem for the frieze of the courtyard. A profile of Julius Caesar, a bridge with two arches, and an obelisk were to stand for JULIUS II PONT[IFEX] MAX[IMUS]. The pope received this proposal with derision, calling it a folly.[18]

Bramante devised another grandiose plan to restore and rebuild the Vatican, including remodelling the façade overlooking the square before St Peter's, the only part to be built. This was being constructed about 1508–9. In August 1508 Julius summoned Alfonso d'Este's envoy to an audience 'high up near the roof, where he is having corridors and loggias, very delightful, made';[19] these works may have been those on the new façade. Was it as somewhere to take the air while conducting business on a summer's day, near the new apartments to which he had recently moved, that this appealed to Julius too? Or was it as a new Septizonium, an echo of the huge palace of Septimius Severus on the Palatine, as some art historians would argue?[20]

The façade was completed, after both Julius and Bramante were dead,[21] by Raphael, who, with assistants, painted the vaults of the loggia on the second floor. This loggia leads from the suite of rooms now known as the Stanze of Raphael, the papal apartments that he decorated for Julius II and Leo X. The two rooms painted by Raphael for Julius – the Stanza della Segnatura and most of the Stanza d'Eliodoro – contain some of his finest work. Julius moved to these apartments in 1507, when he decided he could no longer bear to live in the chambers that had been decorated by Alexander VI and that included a portrait of his loathed predecessor, saying he didn't want to have to see Alexander all the time. But he rejected the suggestion that he could have this portrait and the Borgia arms removed, saying that wouldn't be right, but he didn't want to live there and be reminded of Alexander's wickedness.[22]

The iconography of the frescoes painted for Julius by Raphael in the pope's new apartments has been much discussed, particularly that of the ones in the Stanza della Segnatura, which may have served as Julius's private library. The four major frescoes on the walls, painted in 1508–11, are: the *Disputa*, representing the discussion of, or the triumph of, the mystery of the Eucharist; the *School of Athens*, representing the triumph of philosophy; *Parnassus*, celebrating poetry; and, on the wall around the window, representations of civil and canon law (with Julius portrayed as Gregory IX) and of the three cardinal virtues. Such a programme was a common one for the decoration of Renaissance libraries, and interpretations that link, for example, the figure of Apollo in *Parnassus* with the *Apollo Belvedere* in Julius's sculpture collections, and with the fact that the Mons Vaticanus was believed by Roman humanists to have been sacred to Apollo,[23] are ingenious, but perhaps over-strained. Nothing is known about who devised the details of the programme for the paintings, let alone what part, if any, Julius had in it; there is some evidence, from preliminary drawings, that Raphael himself added as many figures, and grouped them in such a way, as best suited the needs of his composition.[24]

Of the major frescoes in the adjoining Stanza d'Eliodoro, begun in 1512, two were completed for Julius. The painting of the story from the Apocrypha of the expulsion of Heliodorus – who had been sent by his master to seize the treasure from the temple at Jerusalem – by a horseman assisted by two angels has two portraits of Julius: one as himself, observing the scene from the left, and another as the high priest Onias, praying before the altar. It is seen as an allusion to the expulsion of foreign powers from the Papal States. The second fresco is an oblique reference to an episode during the expedition against Bologna in 1506, when Julius, in the cathedral at Orvieto, venerated a relic of a thirteenth-century miracle whereby a priest who had doubts about the doctrine of Transubstantiation had his faith confirmed by seeing the host bleed. The pope himself is shown kneeling opposite the priest. Both frescoes could be seen as depictions of the power of prayer, and would accord with Julius's frequent insistence that God would help to overcome those who tried to take the property of the Church or doubted her authority. Once again, though, it has to be said that nothing is known about who devised the programme for the room, or what part Julius had in its choosing.

Something is known about the elaboration of the programme for the other major series of frescoes that Julius commissioned for the Vatican, those on the ceiling of the Sistine Chapel. By Michelangelo's own account, 'the first design consisted of figures of the Apostles within the lunettes, while certain portions were to be adorned after the usual manner.' As soon as he began work, he realized that 'it would come off a poor thing' and told the pope so. 'Then he granted me a new commission to do what I wished, disposed to satisfy me, and told me to paint down to the stories underneath.'[25] Some art historians have argued that this must not be taken to mean that he did not have the guidance of an iconographic programme drawn up by a theologian;[26] but, in fact, the programme, though rich and suggestive, is relatively straightforward. Even the various Sibyls could easily have been inserted into their appropriate places in the ceiling with the help of the little books of illustrations of the Sibyls and the prophecies associated with them that were popular and easily obtainable at the time.[27]

If, as seems possible, he had little or no part in devising the programme, Julius was certainly interested in the work itself. According to Condivi, a friend of Michelangelo, during the painting of the ceiling the pope often wanted to see how it was progressing, and would climb up a ladder and be helped by Michelangelo onto the scaffolding beneath the vault. His impatience to see it completed, Condivi wrote, prevented the final touches from being put to the fresco. When Julius asked one day when he would have finished, Michelangelo replied 'When I can'; the pope, furious, demanded 'Do you want me to have you thrown off the scaffolding?' After he had left, Michelangelo had the scaffolding dismantled.[28]

The ceiling occupied Michelangelo from 1508 to 1512. It is probably his best-known work, but he did not want to paint it. He was not a painter, he maintained, but a sculptor, and he already had a major commission from the pope, one much more to his taste. This was for Julius's own tomb. Julius had summoned Michelangelo to Rome in March 1505, and in April the artist left for Carrara to quarry the marble for the huge, free-standing monument that he had projected. This was to be about twenty-three feet wide and thirty-six feet long, with three separate levels and around forty statues, as well as bronze reliefs depicting the deeds of the pope. He returned to Rome in December, but while he was waiting for the marble to arrive, Julius was already losing interest in the project, and Michelangelo could not obtain the payment that he needed to go on with the work. He fled home to Florence in April. Julius sent briefs summoning him back, but he was afraid to return, and did so only when the head of the Florentine government, Piero Soderini, compelled him to obey the pope's summons. After an unsuccessful attempt to meet him at Viterbo, he eventually appeared before Julius in November 1506, by which time the pope had sent another brief saying he wanted 'to have some works done by him' in Bologna.[29] Condivi's famous account of his reception has the ring of truth. When he was brought into the room where Julius was dining, the pope looked at him angrily and said, 'You ought to have come to us, and you waited for us to come to you.' Falling on his knees, Michelangelo asked for pardon, saying he had left because he could not bear to be turned away from the palace by the pope's men, as he had been. Julius, his head bowed, said nothing, but was roused by a prelate who tried to make excuses for the artist, saying he had erred through ignorance. He turned on the unfortunate man, saying he was the ignorant one for abusing Michelangelo while the pope himself said nothing, and drove him from the room. Then he called the artist to him, pardoned him and told him not to leave Bologna.[30]

But he had not brought him to Bologna to work on the tomb, and it was not until the last months of the pope's life, after the completion of the Sistine ceiling, that Michelangelo turned his mind to that project again. On his death, Julius left 10,000 ducats to continue the work. A new contract was signed in May 1513 with Julius's heirs; the tomb, to a new design, was to be finished in seven years, and Michelangelo was to be paid a further 13,000 ducats.[31] He worked furiously for the next few years; it was during this period that he produced the powerful statue of *Moses*, the centrepiece of the monument to Julius that was finally erected in San Pietro in Vincoli. In this statue, he perhaps paid tribute to the character of the pope whose commissions had blighted so much of his life: the *Moses* is a far better evocation of Julius than the bland recumbent figure on the monument produced by a pupil of Michelangelo. The miserable saga of the tomb dragged on until 1547, when the botched compromise was finally completed to the satisfaction neither of the artist nor of the della Rovere. After all those years, and all that effort, apart from the *Moses*, only two statues by Michelangelo were included in the monument – rather characterless figures of *Rachel* and *Leah*, personifying the contemplative and the active life.

Julius had not intended his tomb to be erected in San Pietro in Vincoli, but in St Peter's itself. According to Condivi, it was the scheme for the tomb that led to Julius's project for the destruction of the old Constantinian basilica of St Peter's and its replacement by a new church conceived on the grandest scale,[32] a story that fitted comfortably into conceptions of a megalomaniac pope. Careful recent scholarship has shown that the genesis of the idea, and Julius's plans for St Peter's, were rather more complex than this. The first bull offering indulgences – commutation of punishment for sins – in return for financial contributions to the rebuilding, promulgated in February 1507, states that Julius had cherished hopes, since he had first been a cardinal, of renewing the church of the Prince of the Apostles.[33] This statement may be more than a rhetorical flourish of the official who drafted the document. The need to do something about the crumbling basilica had been apparent for years, and Nicholas V had begun work on the reconstruction. The foundations of the choir that he had begun in 1451 were to be used by Julius as the basis for the choir that he asked Bramante to construct, which was to be the site for the tomb by Michelangelo.

In his plans for the reconstruction of St Peter's, Julius was following in the footsteps not only of Nicholas V, but of his uncle, Sixtus IV. Sixtus had built on to St Peter's a chapel intended as a combination of choir chapel and a site for his own grave: it was here that Julius had erected the tomb that he commissioned from Antonio Pollaiuolo. The tiles on the floor bore the della Rovere arms; the ceiling was decorated with oak branches and acorns in green and gold. It became a della Rovere burial chapel – Julius himself was eventually buried there, near his uncle, following his *nipoti* Clemente and Galeotto della Rovere and his sister Luchina. Julius planned to build a new choir chapel for St Peter's, to be dedicated to the Virgin, where his own tomb was to be erected. Michelangelo's grandiose scheme for a free-standing tomb required a generous space; the foundations for a choir chapel already laid by Nicholas V provided an obvious solution. But a conflict arose between Michelangelo's requirements for a site for the tomb and Bramante's plans for a wholesale reconstruction of the church.

Bramante became rather carried away, and put before the pope a plan that would have meant reorienting the church so that it faced south, on to a new piazza with, at its centre, the obelisk popularly known as 'Caesar's obelisk' and believed to contain the ashes of Julius Caesar. The pope rejected this idea outright. To carry out this plan would have meant shifting the tomb of St Peter, and Julius would not hear of it. The building work that was undertaken was on such a large scale that it required so many workmen that Julius joked there were enough for him to hold a military parade.[34] For Julius, the construction of the new choir had priority; he did not set himself the impossible task of rebuilding the whole basilica in his lifetime. In his will, he left 30,000 ducats for his tomb, his chapel and to endow a choir of twelve singers, the Capella Giulia, that he had founded only a month before.[35] It took over a century for the new St Peter's to be completed, with many changes of plan in which the work undertaken during Julius's lifetime became lost. But, thanks in part to Bramante's enthusiastic demolition of large parts of the old fabric in preparation for his own building, which ensured that the ancient basilica would have to be replaced, it is Julius who is regarded as the founder of the St Peter's that now stands.

Another, far smaller, choir combined with a funerary chapel, both designed by Bramante, was finished during Julius's lifetime, that of Santa Maria del Popolo. This church had been rebuilt by Sixtus IV, and had become associated with the della Rovere; several members of the family were buried there, including Cardinals Cristoforo and Domenico della Rovere. Julius was fond of it and used it for important public ceremonies, such as the publication of treaties, and private devotions, such as his prayers for his dying *nipote* Galeotto. To his uncle's church, Julius added a fine new choir, which still survives, with its simple, shell-shaped apse, a tribune with frescoes by Pinturicchio, and stained-glass windows by Guillaume de Marçillat. This provides the setting for two of the finest Renaissance tombs in Rome, that of Cardinal Ascanio Sforza, who died in 1505, and that of Julius's cousin, Cardinal Girolamo Basso della Rovere, who died in 1507. Both were commissioned by Julius from Andrea Sansovino. It was a magnanimous gesture on the part of the pope to provide a resting-place of such dignity, in a church so dear to the della Rovere, for a man who had at one time been a bitter enemy, but who had become reconciled with him, and whose own family had been scattered by the French conquest of their duchy of Milan. To this church, Julius also gave a masterpiece by Raphael, painted in 1511–12: the portrait of the pope as an old, sad but resolute man, that now hangs in the National Gallery in London. Its original purpose was to be hung in the church on feast-days, perhaps as a pair with Raphael's *Madonna of the Veil*. (In the last year of his life, Julius also commissioned another picture of the Virgin, the *Sistine Madonna* (now in Dresden), in which the pope kneels at her feet.)

In his commissions at St Peter's and Santa Maria del Popolo, Julius was consciously following his uncle. He tried to follow him in other projects too, improvements to communications within Rome, and the erection of a building to house the offices of the curia, but with mixed success. Sixtus had replaced an old, ruined Roman bridge over the Tiber, building the Ponte Sisto to connect what was then one of the most populous areas of Rome with Trastevere. Julius also planned to replace an old Roman bridge, Nero's Pons Triumphalis, but this plan was never realized. The bridge was to have linked two new, straight, wide streets running either side of the Tiber, to be laid out by Bramante. One, the Via della Lungara, running from Trastevere to the Borgo near the Vatican, succeeded in enticing a number of wealthy men, including Agostino Chigi and Cardinal Riario, to build palaces and villas along it. The scheme for the corresponding street on the other side of the river, the Via Giulia, was realized only in part, for the focus of the street was to have been a square with the massive new Palazzo dei Tribunali on one side, opposite the palace, now known as Sforza–Cesarini, where the chancery then was. Sixtus had also planned to build a huge, new office building, near St Peter's. Work was begun on the Palazzo dei Tribunali in 1508; it was designed as a powerful, fortress-like building. After two or three years, however, work was stopped. Much of what had been built was later dismantled, and gradually the site was filled up with other buildings, though remnants of the ground floor can still be seen on the Via Giulia.

Outside Rome, most of the building activity that Julius sponsored involved the repair or extension of fortresses in the Papal States. He was much taken with the fortress–palace that had been under construction by Antonio da Sangallo for Cesare Borgia at Civita Castellana when he saw it in 1506, and ordered that it be completed.[36] At the port of Civitavecchia, he ordered the construction of a fortress. Having seen the model of the design, probably by Bramante, he decided to go himself to lay the foundation stone, in December 1508. He took great interest in the building of this *rocca*; he was reported to be spending 70,000 ducats to make it beautiful and strong.[37] Bramante was also asked to design a new courtyard in the mediaeval fortress of Viterbo, and was consulted on the project for a port at Recanati that Julius planned in 1511.

It is not certain if Bramante had a hand in designing the new, ill-fated fortress that Julius built in Bologna, which was demolished by the citizens in 1511, but since he was with Julius in 1506 when it was being planned, it is likely that he was at least consulted. The papal palace in Bologna, which itself had the aspect of a fortress, was strengthened with new defences, but

Julius also had a grand stairway made (attributed to Bramante), ordered some purely decorative alterations and had a new chapel hastily constructed – 'like the papal chapel in Rome', but with wooden screens rather than screens of marble and ironwork.[38] During his second stay in the city, in 1510–11, before he became finally disenchanted with the Bolognese, he spoke of his plans for the communal church of San Petronio, which faces on to the same square as the papal palace (now called the Palazzo Comunale): he wanted, he said, to make it the first church in the whole of Italy, in revenues, in magnificence and in privileges.[39]

One contribution that he had made to the magnificence of San Petronio was the bronze portrait statue, larger than life, that he ordered Michelangelo to make when he summoned him to Bologna in 1506. Michelangelo agreed with reluctance, and it took him over a year of toil to produce the statue – only for it to be destroyed a few years later by the Bolognese, in an act of vandalism that Julius found hard to forgive. Practically all that is known about this statue before its destruction comes from Condivi's biography of Michelangelo, which recounts another exchange between pope and artist that sounds as though it contains a kernel of truth. Before the pope left Bologna, the story goes, Michelangelo showed him a clay model of the statue, but said he was not sure what the figure should hold in its left hand. Did the pope wish to be shown holding a book? A book? Julius replied, a sword rather, for 'I am no scholar.' He then joked about the figure's right hand, which was raised in a vigorous act of benediction. Did this statue of his give a blessing or a curse? Michelangelo replied that it threatened the Bolognese lest they be foolish.[40]

The only other place in the Papal States to benefit from a large-scale commission by Julius was the shrine of Loreto, built around what was believed to be the house of the Virgin Mary, miraculously transported there from Nazareth in 1294. Cardinal Girolamo Basso della Rovere, who had been Bishop of Recanati, in which diocese Loreto lay from 1477, spent much of his income on decorating the shrine, which was not many miles from Senigallia. Julius commissioned Bramante to do some work in the church there, including the design of a beautiful screen surrounding the Santa Casa itself, and ordered the construction of a papal palace, which was begun in 1510. Once again, Bramante set about the work with a will; de' Grassi, recording Julius's inspection of 'the ruins and the buildings' that Bramante was creating at Loreto in June 1511, recalled the architect's nickname of 'Ruinante'.[41] Once again, the work was not completed for many years.

Arnaldo Bruschi, the Bramante scholar, believes that Bramante devised a spectacular plan, with a huge courtyard uniting the church and the palace: an evocation of Caesar's forum, with its temple of Venus.[42] Such an interpretation of a project to honour and dignify a shrine to the Virgin Mary that had acquired special family significance for the della Rovere stems from the idea – which has become an orthodoxy for art historians – that the artists who worked for Julius were seeking to echo Imperial themes and emulate Imperial glories, and that they did so to please Julius, because he saw himself as heir to the Roman emperors, as reviving the glories of the Roman Empire, as well as restoring the Church.

The scale of some of Bramante's projects for the pope, and perhaps also of Michelangelo's plans for his tomb, indicate that they, at least, were consciously trying to emulate the ancients – but Julius's reaction to some of Bramante's ideas show that he was not so taken with the notion. In Latin poems urging him to reconquer Jerusalem and the East, in sermons telling him that, thanks to the discovery of the New World, he governed wider realms than Julius Caesar had, the pope was exhorted to emulate Caesar, and even told that he surpassed him.[43] Satirists, too, compared the warrior pope and his Roman namesake. But how much direct evidence is there that Julius saw himself in this way?

There is, in fact, very little. Essentially, it comes down to one inscription – IULIUS CAESAR PONT. II – on one of the medals issued to commemorate the expedition to Bologna in 1506, which presumably had been authorized by the pope. None of the other medals or coins that he is known to have issued, none of the inscriptions placed on the buildings or paintings that he commissioned, carries such a title. There was a report in July 1510, from Maximilian's envoy in France, that the commanders of an expedition that Julius had sent against Genoa were using the words 'Papae Julii Caesarii', but none of the detailed reports of this abortive enterprise from those who actually took part in it mention this.[44] The choice of the title Julius II is not in itself evidence that the pope identified himself with Julius Caesar. At first, he thought of taking the title Sixtus V, but then decided on Julius – perhaps simply because it was the nearest that he could come to his own name, Giuliano, without evoking memories of the Emperor Julian the Apostate, who turned from Christianity back to the old Roman gods.

What was said of Julius by other people, cannot be taken as evidence of his own motives. If writers in and around the Roman court liked to think of themselves as the heirs of the ancients, if satirists could not resist using an obvious weapon against a warrior pope apparently obsessed with the things of this world, it does not mean Julius saw himself like that.

The small medal bearing the inscription IULIUS CAESAR PONT. II was issued in connection with Julius's triumphal entry to Rome on his return from Bologna in 1507. The inscription on the obverse was 'Blessed is he who comes in the name of the Lord', the text for Palm Sunday, the day on which he entered Rome. Paride de' Grassi had raised objections to making too much of the pope's return, saying that it was an inappropriate point in the liturgical year for celebrations. Julius did not take kindly to this – his self-esteem was in need of some nourishment, after a rather hurried departure from Bologna.[45] De' Grassi noted that the Romans themselves did not enter into the spirit of the celebrations; only courtiers close to the pope erected triumphal arches with laudatory inscriptions.[46] At least one of these made an indirect reference to Julius Caesar, incorporating Caesar's renowned comment 'Veni, vidi, vici' in a couplet praising the pope as the author of peace and liberty.[47] No such references were recorded in the account of his entry to Bologna, which was organized by de' Grassi along the lines of the procession that the popes made to take possession of the Lateran at the beginning of their pontificates. The inscriptions on the triumphal arches hastily erected in Bologna had celebrated Julius as a liberator, the expeller of tyrants. Specially minted coins thrown to the crowds during the procession carried the inscription 'Bologna freed by Julius from the tyrant' and, on the reverse, IULIUS II PONT. MAX. There was no mention of Caesar.

Echoes of Roman triumphs were commonplace elements in ceremonial entries in Renaissance Italy. One of the most frequently invoked figures was Julius Caesar, whom the triumpher would be said to have surpassed. Cesare Borgia had paraded through the streets of Rome, with the motto 'Aut Caesar aut nihil' – 'Caesar or nothing'; Charles VIII had been compared to Caesar in his triumphal entries into Italian cities.[48] There is nothing exceptional about the references to Caesar made in connection with Julius II, no good reason why the use of this favourite, and somewhat stale, motif should be considered of special significance when applied to him.

In all the thousands of surviving accounts of conversations and discussions held with him, there is no hint that he saw himself as the heir to, or the reviver of, the glories of ancient Rome. He was not a tactful man. If he learned in later years to keep his own counsel rather better than before, he was still given to outbursts of enthusiasm in which he would talk of wild plans, such as going to Paris to crown Henry VIII as King of France.[49] If he had had any desire to emulate Caesar or the Roman emperors, had in any way identified himself with them, surely some hint would have emerged at some time?

Nor did he ever say he wanted to be the monarch of all Italy, another ambition that cultural historians have ascribed to him.[50] The direct evidence of his political aims reveals more modest aspirations. Indeed, how could he dream of ruling over all Italy, when he could not even assert or maintain papal control over Bologna without help from the troops of other powers, could not capture Ferrara in nearly three years of trying?[51] Driving the 'barbarians' out of Italy was an ambitious enough aspiration, and one that he never accomplished. To the end of his pontificate, he depended on the military help of others to hold on to the Papal States.

The one piece of political iconography in which Julius is known to have taken a direct interest, which was created following the expedition to Bologna of 1506–7, was a stained-glass window that he had erected in a hall in the Vatican near the chapel. Julius was depicted enthroned in a public consistory, with the cardinals around him, and the King of France kneeling before him. He may well have ordered this to be made in anticipation of a meeting with Louis that had been supposed to take place that winter, but which he had avoided for fear he might be held prisoner by the king.[52] This window was criticized because the episode depicted had never taken place; if Alexander had had himself portrayed with Charles VIII, they had actually met in Rome, with the king paying the pope all the elaborate courtesies that etiquette demanded.[53]

The inscriptions on Julius's coins, medals and buildings do give clear evidence that there was a figure and a place with which he wished to be identified. The figure was Sixtus IV; the place Savona, or, more broadly, Liguria. The great inscription running along the outer wall of the Belvedere that still greets those entering the courtyard from the Porta Sant' Anna – IVLIVS II PONT. MAX. LIGURUM VI PATRIA SAONENSIS SIXTI IIII NEPOS VIAM HANC STRVXIT PONTIFICVM COMMODIDATI – is the most striking example of this: it records that he was the nephew of Sixtus IV, that he came from Savona, that he was the sixth Ligurian pope. References to his relationship to Sixtus were frequent in the inscriptions on the works that he commissioned as a cardinal, such as the fortress at Ostia.[54] Some small portraits of the pope in manuscripts written and illuminated for his private library also couple the name of Sixtus with his own.[55] References to Savona, and especially to Liguria, were a very common element in his inscriptions,[56] although it was not customary for popes to celebrate their place of birth in this way. In conversations with ambassadors, too, when he was discussing the affairs of Genoa, he would refer to it as his 'patria'.[57]

To deny that Julius saw himself as a second Caesar or the reviver of the splendours of Imperial Rome is not to say that he could not appreciate, perhaps even enjoy, the literary parallels of his courtiers, or the grandeur of Bramante's dreams. But Julius, for all his impetuosity and excesses of enthusiasm, was a pragmatic politician who lived in the real world. There is no evidence that he encouraged comparison of his deeds with those of Caesar, nor that such comparisons inspired him. He was a patron of discrimination and taste. He loved building, and had a keen sense of beauty – whether in a palace, or a painting, or a fortress, or a ship. Much less attention is paid to the fortifications that he commissioned or improved than to his palaces or churches, but he took as much delight in watching the progress of the work at Civitavecchia as he did in inspecting the building site at St Peter's – and certainly more than in triumphal arches, or stilted formal praise and flattery.

8

———— • ————

The League of Cambrai

Julius made a magnificent formal entry into Bologna on 11 November 1506. Carried through the streets in his *sedia gestatoria*, wearing a purple cope shot through with gold thread and fastened by a jewel set with emeralds and sapphires, and a large jewel-encrusted mitre, he was the focal point of a huge procession that slowly made its way to San Petronio, the great communal church of Bologna, through streets filled with crowds and decked with tapestries and pictures and flowers. Triumphal arches had been erected along the route, celebrating him as the expeller of tyrants, the bringer of peace, the liberator of Bologna from tyranny. Specially minted gold and silver coins were thrown to the people, bearing the inscription 'Bologna freed by Julius from the tyrant'.

Whether the Bolognese who thronged the streets in holiday mood were rejoicing at being freed from the 'tyranny' of the Bentivoglio is a moot point. Giovanni Bentivoglio had become increasingly suspicious and autocratic, his wife had been arrogant and haughty, and his sons were given to swaggering around the city with groups of bravos, but there were still plenty of supporters of the family left. Administration by papal officials, untempered by the political influence of the Bentivoglio, would soon feel more irksome to the citizens than the high-handed ways of Giovanni and his sons had been. For the moment, though, as the sun shone on the soldiers and officials and ecclesiastics processing through the streets, and on the watching crowds, relief at the removal of the threat of the French troops, who had taken a few days to accept that they would lose the opportunity to sack the prosperous city, made Julius a welcome sight to the

Bolognese. Celebrations went on for three days, with bonfires and the ringing of bells.

Within a week of his arrival, Julius had reorganized the city government. Cardinals Galeotto Franciotto della Rovere, who was legate of Bologna, and Francesco Alidosi had been sent ahead when news of the departure of the Bentivoglio had reached the pope; and they had already deposed the Sixteen and elected twenty men, all merchants without a political following, to replace them. Warned that there could be trouble unless the Bolognese were provided with an effective civic government, on 17 November Julius announced the creation of a Council of Forty to replace the Sixteen. Some continuity was provided, because all but four of the Sixteen were to be members of the new council. They were to sit alongside some returned exiles of the Malvezzi and Marescotti families.[1]

One of the first acts of the Forty was their unanimous decision that Giovanni Bentivoglio and all his sons, and his male heirs to the fourth generation, should be exiled as rebels against the commune of Bologna, and banished to wherever Julius should choose, at least 200 miles from its jurisdiction. With only one dissenting vote, they also decided that all those who had left with the Bentivoglio and were at that time absent from the city were to be exiled for life, if Julius wished.[2] As a further token of their devotion to the pope, they decided to present him with a gift worth 1,000 ducats, which they would have to raise a loan to pay for.

An expense that the Bolognese were unwilling to meet was the cost of rebuilding a fortress at the Porta Galliera, on the road leading to Ferrara, which had fallen into ruin. Julius pressed on enthusiastically with the scheme once he had decided that that site was best. Plans were completed by the New Year. By the middle of January work had begun on the foundations, and, before he left Bologna on 22 February, Julius laid the foundation stone. No doubt, he saw the citadel as strengthening the defences of the city – he had every expectation that the Bentivoglio would try to return – but the Bolognese regarded it as a symbol of the reinforcement of papal control, of a diminution of their liberties, and did not like it.

Already, Julius had decided that some concessions had to be made to keep the Bolognese from looking to the Bentivoglio. At first, he had decided that he would leave the taxes as they were. When the citizens sent representatives to ask him to relieve the tax burden, he replied he hadn't made any promises to do so, and that the expedition to Bologna had cost him 100,000 ducats.[3] He did, however, remit one particularly vexatious toll, and soon withdrew some more, trying to recoup lost revenue by imposing taxes on cronies of the Bentivoglio who had hitherto enjoyed exemptions. But he foresaw the need for sticks as well as carrots, and said he felt that he had better leave the government of Bologna to others. Some matters called for severity, he said, and when tearful petitions were being made to him from all sides, he was too yielding. Perhaps the legate whom he would leave behind would not be so soft-hearted.[4]

The legate whom he had chosen to replace his nephew Galeotto – too mild himself to provide the kind of direction that Julius thought might well be necessary – was Cardinal Antonio Ferreri, who was legate of Perugia. Julius did not actually like him very much, but he thought him tough and spirited.[5] How the new legate would work with the Forty had yet to be settled. The Forty formally recorded their protest that if the bull defining the powers of the legate gave him authority to decide disputes without their knowledge and agreement, this would be prejudicial to the papal government in Bologna and to the peace and order of the city.[6] This was not Julius's view of the matter. He wanted the bull to stipulate that the Forty should not be involved in fixing tolls, and he wanted the legate to have judicial powers, even in criminal cases, without consulting them. The Forty stuck to their guns, and Julius apparently hoped that the problem could be resolved by not spelling out the powers of the legate in writing.[7] But then he deputed three cardinals – Riario, Ferreri, and de Clermont – to talk the problem over with the Forty, and it was agreed that they and the legate should consult on difficult affairs. In fact, Ferreri bribed the officials drawing up the bull, so that he was awarded powers that he had never been intended to have. His corrupt and despotic behaviour would do little to recommend the new regime to the Bolognese. Within a few months, he would be recalled to Rome, and imprisoned in the Castel Sant' Angelo, but the disaffection that he had helped to brew persisted.

When Julius had been describing himself as too easily swayed by tears to be as severe as might be necessary, he had been putting this forward as one reason why he was leaving Bologna earlier than he had originally planned to do. He gave other reasons too. The air didn't agree with him, he said. Papal revenues were suffering to the tune of 10,000 ducats a month because of his absence from Rome. Besides, the curial officials were nagging him to return. Costabili, the Ferrarese ambassador to whom he was listing these reasons for an early departure, knew quite well that the real reason had not been mentioned. Was not Louis still intending to come to Italy? he enquired, innocently. This had not been decided yet, the pope replied, and if he did come, he could still get on with what he wanted to do even if Julius was in Rome.[8]

The point was that one of the main reasons why the French king had planned to come to Italy was to have a meeting with the pope. Louis had spoken of this plan in October 1506, saying that Julius wanted to meet him, and in late December was still saying that the pope was urging him to come. French troops had played an important part in securing the submission of Bologna: according to the king nothing would have been accomplished there without his help.[9] And he had had his reward. Three French cardinals had been created a month after the pope's arrival in Bologna – Jean François de la Trémoille, Archbishop of Auch, René de Prie, Bishop of Bayeux and Louis d'Amboise, Bishop of Alby. The promotion of all three was supposed to be kept quiet and the status of Alby was unclear. His full promotion was to be postponed until the following year, and the question of when he would formally be given his cardinal's hat would become a bone of contention between king and pope as their relations deteriorated.

This deterioration set in soon after the promotion had taken place. The root cause was the rebellion of Genoa against the French in January 1507. Louis was persuaded that Julius was supporting, if not actively fomenting, this rebellion, and threatened to retaliate by putting the Bentivoglio back in Bologna: all it would take was one letter, he said. It was in order to allay the king's suspicion that he was interfering in Genoa, Julius told the French, that he would leave Bologna for Rome.[10] Indeed, if he wished to see his '*patria*' freed from French rule, he gave the rebels little encouragement, let alone material support.

The real reason for Julius's avoidance of the meeting with Louis was that he had been persuaded that it would be dangerous for him to meet the king in person. The idea had been implanted in his mind, it was thought, that no pope had ever had a personal meeting with so powerful a king without being forced to make exorbitant concessions, or having a serious row with him. Word got back to France that he had been made to believe that he would be in personal danger if he met Louis, that he had been warned by a secret envoy from Maximilian that Louis was planning to carry him off to Milan and make Cardinal Rouen pope in his stead.[11]

His decision to return to Rome, turning his back on his projected meeting with Louis and leaving important questions about the future shape of the government of Bologna still unresolved, caused dismay among the Bolognese and great surprise to the cardinals and *curiali*. It savoured of panic: he was behaving as though 'he fears the sky will fall on him.'[12] Protestations that 'he wasn't going to die for anybody',[13] that the air of Bologna disagreed with him so badly that it would kill him if he stayed, only reinforced the impression of flight.

He hurried through the Romagna, eschewing any welcoming ceremonies in the towns that he had visited on the outward journey. Once again, he avoided Faenza, though the Venetian governor based there came to greet him privately on the road. As his train laboured its way through the hills into the Marche, with many being forced to sleep in stables and sheepfolds, the local people came to look at the pope, with those from Rimini lamenting that he had avoided their territory too. Only when he was out of the Marche and into Umbria, did Julius slacken the pace a little. At Foligno, there was a formal entry during which the keys of the city were handed to him, and a ceremony in the cathedral. At Orte, which he reached a few days later, he ordered a solemn entry, despite warnings from Paride de' Grassi that this was a hick town and not a suitable venue for papal pomp. De' Grassi speculated that he might not have realized how small the town was,[14] but perhaps Julius wanted to soothe his pride, which must have been hurt by scurrying out of the reach of the French. He certainly wanted his entry to Rome to be celebrated in style. When de' Grassi, discussing what ceremony there should be, suggested that it would be inappropriate at Passiontide for Christ's vicar to be acclaimed in triumph, Julius became very frosty, and asked what more appropriate cause for celebration there was than the return of the pope to Rome from a long journey. It would be quite appropriate, he said, if he made his entry on Palm Sunday, that he should be greeted with cries of 'Blessed is He that comes in the name of the Lord.'[15]

Thus the famous triumphal entry to Rome on his return from Bologna was at Julius's express wish. It was mostly the *curiali* who rejoiced at his return – they had feared that he would be away for a couple of years – and it was they who put up the triumphal arches with the inscriptions glorifying his expedition. The representatives of the Roman commune, the *Conservatori*, did not take part in the procession (claiming that they did not want to give precedence to the Venetians or other non-royal ambassadors), and had not made any speech of welcome to him as he disembarked from the galley that had brought him to Rome along the Tiber. De' Grassi thought their lukewarm welcome – of which Julius took note – was due to guilt that they had not sent any message to the pope while he was away, not even to congratulate him on the expulsion of the 'tyrant' from Bologna.[16] Perhaps they were thinking that the reinforcement of papal authority over the second city of the Papal States boded ill for them, and that further erosion of their already limited powers of self-government was in the offing.[17]

In a formal address to the consistory, Cardinal Riario spoke of how Julius's success had immeasurably increased the honour and consideration in which the Church was held and would give immortality to his own name and reputation. He 'deserved to be ranked among those illustrious popes who, casting aside all personal considerations or family interests, proposed no other end for themselves but the care of preserving and augmenting the authority and majesty of the Holy See.'[18] Certainly, Julius had accomplished the main purpose of the expedition – to enforce the authority of the papacy over Bologna – and the other powers in Italy had taken due note of his determination. Nonetheless, they were well aware that French military power had made a significant contribution to that success, and Julius had returned to Rome on considerably worse terms with Louis than those he had been on when he left. The future of Bologna, as it turned out, had not been settled by this expedition, and much of the trouble in store would be owing to French intervention and support for the Bentivoglio.

Julius's dilemma – which had, if anything, been intensified by the circumstances of the submission of Bologna, and of his departure from the city – was this. In order to recover the papal lands held by Venice, he needed the help, or at least the neutrality, of France, the major military power in northern Italy. The purpose of the meeting with Louis that he had first sought and then avoided had been to discuss joint action against Venice. But he was also wary of the French, and considered them untrustworthy. Above all, he did not trust Cardinal Rouen, Louis's chief minister.

When the Ferrarese ambassador suggested that Louis and Julius could easily be on stable good terms, and that the differences that had grown up between them might be being caused by Rouen in pursuit of his own private interests, Julius said that he was right.[19]

Rouen's consolation prize for not being elected pope, a grant of full powers as papal legate in France, had not satisfied his appetite. From the early months of the pontificate, it was believed at the papal court that the French were trying to manipulate Julius and his desire for help against Venice, because Rouen 'wants to force the pope to confirm him in the legation on his own terms, and in this way he wants to remain pope in France for his lifetime, seeing that he couldn't be pope of the universal Church'.[20] In June 1504 Julius wrote assuring him that he was confident that he acted with the best interests of the Church in mind, and that he wouldn't listen to those who tried to slander him.[21] If this letter was sincere, the pope came to change his mind. Rouen continued to press to be given the legation of France for life, and it was widely rumoured that his desire to be pope was as strong as ever, and that he was not necessarily prepared to wait for Julius to die. Reports that he had consulted astrologers to find out when Julius would die, true or not, cannot have been very reassuring. Some thought that, knowing Julius's choleric and excitable temperament, he was trying to annoy him as much as possible, so as to drive him to an early grave.[22] Maximilian, at one of the recurrent low points in his relations with Louis, wrote to Rome in June 1507 accusing Rouen of aspiring to be pope in Julius's lifetime. When Rouen wrote formally denying the charge, Julius said that he believed him, but the suspicion persisted. He would trust Louis personally as much as any prince in the world, he told Vich, the Spanish ambassador, but Louis relied so much on Rouen; and for the pope's distrust of Cardinal Rouen, Vich commented, there was no remedy.[23]

If the French were wary of interference by Julius in Genoa, he was equally wary of French interference in Bologna. The very expulsion of the Bentivoglio had provided France with the means to engage in it, for they had left under French safe-conduct and Giovanni and his family took refuge in the Milanese. Julius became almost paranoid in his pursuit of the Bentivoglio. There was some justification for his fears: they still had many supporters in Bologna, while the corrupt and oppressive administration of the papal officials who now ruled the city fostered nostalgia for the old regime, and the younger Bentivoglio, Giovanni's sons, were constantly plotting and scheming to return. But while he wanted Chaumont, the French commander in Milan, to keep a watchful eye on them, he made the terms of their exile, and the penalties to be visited upon anyone helping them when they failed to observe those terms, so severe that it would be almost impossible for them to settle anywhere. He did not want them to join their relatives by marriage in Ferrara or Mantua, and he certainly did not want them on Venetian territory. The French could be effective guardians – enabling Giovanni to live in reasonable comfort, but, when his sons were planning an assault on Bologna, as in early May 1507, being prepared to arrest him to signal their dis-approval. On the other hand, if Louis were to be at odds with Julius, the presence of the Bentivoglio in his territory gave him a useful instrument to harass him. If Julius was trying to make waves, said Louis at the moment when Julius had just left Bologna and mutual suspicion between the king and pope was high, he could immediately restore Giovanni Bentivoglio. It would be easy to do, and Giovanni would pay him at least 100,000 ducats to boot.[24] As relations between Louis and Julius deteriorated into outright hostility, a few years later, interference by the pope in Genoa would be matched by rather more suc-cessful interference by the king in Bologna.

There was an element of exasperation in the attitude of Louis and his ministers towards Julius. Ingratitude, he was sometimes accused of: after all the years that he had spent in France as a cardinal, receiving honour and shelter and protection, helping to plan the expeditions to Italy, it rankled with the French that he should be critical of the extent of their power. Perhaps they knew him too well as a person, knew his foibles and his weaknesses, and, in a way, did not take him quite seriously enough. 'He's the son of a peasant', Louis told the Florentine ambassador in February 1507, 'and it takes a stick to make him go.'[25] It was some years before the French stopped expressing confidence that, in the end, Julius would have to do what Louis wanted.

Part of Julius's dilemma was that there was no other power on which he could rely for support against the French. The only other Italian power of any substance, Venice, was out of the question, at least until the papal lands that she held had been returned. Florence was so closely linked to France that the Florentines could scarcely be said to have an independent foreign policy at the time. The only other possible counterweights to the

13 Julius frequently recalled his Ligurian origins in his inscriptions as pope, as in this one over a window on to the Sala Regina in the Vatican. (© Courtauld Institute)

14 The fortress at Civita Castellana, originally commissioned by Alexander VI. (© Professor Sir John Hale)

15 A view of the Belvedere courtyard in the Vatican; commissioned by Julius from Bramante, it was much altered by other architects for subsequent popes, but the original plan of tiers of loggias is still evident. (© Courtauld Institute)

16 One of the medals issued by Julius in connection with the laying of the foundations of the new St Peter's; this portrait by Caradosso was frequently copied and became a standard representation of the pope. (© Ashmolean Museum, Oxford)

17 An exterior view of the Vatican apartments, the Stanze, decorated
for Julius by Raphael. (© J. Shearman; courtesy of the Courtauld
Institute)

18 The Stanza della Segnatura, with Raphael's fresco portraying Julius as Pope Gregory IX. (© Courtauld Institute)

19 The Stanza d'Eliodoro, showing the portrait of Julius in Raphael's
fresco of the *Mass of Bolsena*. (© Courtauld Institute)

20 The south window embrasure of the Stanza d'Eliodoro, with Julius's arms and inscription. (© Courtauld Institute)

21 The shrine of the Holy House at Loreto, designed for Julius by Bramante. (© Courtauld Institute)

22 An inscription put up by two Roman officials praising Julius's achievements. (© Courtauld Institute)

23 Michelangelo's statue of *Moses*, part of the monument finally erected to Julius in San Pietro in Vincoli in Rome. (© Courtauld Institute)

French were Ferdinand of Aragon and Maximilian, and Julius
had difficulty in establishing an equable relationship with either of
them.

Ferdinand had been willing to write letters to Cesare Borgia's
castellan, and to make representations to Venice to help Julius
recover papal fortresses and lands in the Romagna, but this had
been as far as he was prepared to go. He had not been willing to
jeopardize his own friendship with the Venetians. Even though
they were holding on to coastal cities in the kingdom of Naples
that they had received as pledges against help for the deposed
Neapolitan Aragonese dynasty, their potential usefulness as an
ally against the French was given priority.

One trait that he shared with the Venetians was what may be
called a 'more-pious-than-the-Pope' attitude towards the curia,
which gave him more than a tinge of self-righteousness in the
routine bickering about the disposition of benefices. His pride in
his record as victor over the Moors of Granada, and as defender
of the faith as patron of the Inquisition, was shared by many
Spaniards, and made them regard the ways of Rome very critically. A note of scorn sometimes crept into the remarks that the
Spanish ambassadors in Venice and Rome made about the pope
in their conversations with other envoys. All popes followed the
same path, the Spanish envoy told the Venetian one in Rome in
February 1504, and if Julius was out to acquire new lands, it was
for personal motives, not out of zeal for the Church.[26]

Ferdinand refused to let the nuncio whom Julius sent at the
beginning of his pontificate, Cosimo de' Pazzi, into the kingdom,
saying that a nuncio wasn't needed and a Florentine nuncio,
who was bound to be a partisan of France, was certainly unacceptable to his people.[27] He delayed sending an embassy to
swear obedience to Julius for several years – not until April 1507
did he finally do so for Aragon and Naples. He may only have
sent one then because it seemed a good moment to try to extract
the investiture of the kingdom of Naples from the pope. Not until
he sent the embassy did he finally agree to allow Francesco Maria
della Rovere to hold the key fortress of his Neapolitan estates,
Rocca Guglielma.

The king's attraction for Julius as a counterbalance to Louis
was obvious, but the pope could never be sure of him. It was his
intention, Julius told the Spanish ambassador in February 1508,
to trust no prince in the world so much as Ferdinand, because he
knew that he was a Catholic prince, directed by his own prudent

intelligence and not by any other person, and that his deeds were worthy and sincere, and he felt that he could rely on him.[28] Unquestionably, Ferdinand was his own man – there was no minister who had anything like the power over him that Rouen had over Louis – and he was a pious Catholic. But he was quite ready to threaten to withdraw the obedience of his kingdom from the papacy when Julius sent a brief to Naples that the king interpreted as an attempt to extend papal jurisdiction there.[29] Julius paid great honour to the ambassadors who came to swear obedience on behalf of Ferdinand's daughter, Queen Joanna, for the kingdom of Castille in July 1508, which was considered to be a sign of good understanding between pope and king; but 'fine words and ceremony' were all he got from Ferdinand, the pope complained.[30] Ferdinand was one of the wiliest and most experienced players in the diplomatic game, and it was not just Julius that had trouble developing a firm mutual understanding with him.

Similarly, it was not just Julius who found Maximilian impossible to pin down. This was not due to any marked diplomatic skill on the part of the King of the Romans. He was far from stupid, and had some capacity as a soldier, but his good qualities were cancelled out by his congenital instability and his chronic inability to hold on to money or to spend it usefully. To have Maximilian as an ally was to be subjected to a continual stream of requests for cash and other assistance, and trying to coordinate any military action with him was a nightmare. He was given to making sudden changes of plan, to unexpected and inexplicable withdrawals. Conducting diplomatic negotiations with him was difficult too, because he had a habit of forbidding the ambassadors who had been sent to his court to follow him as he moved ceaselessly about, and even envoys of friendly powers could be kept waiting for weeks or months before he gave them an audience.

During the first year of his pontificate, Julius had hoped that Maximilian would come to Italy to help against Venice, but he had been disappointed by his response. Maximilian's main interest had been in trying to get the pope's consent to his taking possession of money that had been collected in Germany for a crusade. After that, Julius never placed any real hopes in him again. He could have his uses, if he could be brought to attack Venice, and when there was talk of his coming to Italy, Julius was given to dropping hints that the Venetians had better watch out. But when he began to talk about coming to Rome to be crowned Emperor by the pope (and not until he was crowned by the pope could he rightfully be called Emperor), Julius was circumspect in his response. His general line was that Maximilian would be welcome to come for his coronation, if he came without troops. It was, however, very unlikely that Maximilian would ever venture into Italy without troops, so this response was tantamount to telling him to stay away from Rome.

Maximilian was very conscious of his position as Emperor-elect, and would, when it suited him, recall that one of the duties of the Emperor was the protection of the papacy: of the papacy, but not of the pope. 'For Pope Julius himself, I wouldn't move three steps', he told the Venetian ambassador in April 1507, 'but to keep the Holy See in Italy, and not let Italy be taken over by the French, more than they've done already, that's a different matter . . .'.[31] He never professed much respect for Julius personally, and nursed a curious ambition – it is hard to tell how seriously he took it – to become pope himself.[32] For his part, the more Julius had to do with Maximilian, the less he thought of him. '*Bestia*' – 'fool', 'blockhead' – was the epithet that he usually applied to him.[33]

In temporal politics, the pope was at a considerable disadvantage to Louis, Ferdinand and Maximilian. The papacy was only at the margin of the European power game, and the pope not really a major player. In most of the problems that concerned these rulers – such as French support for the Duke of Guelders in his rebellion against Maximilian, the fate of the duchy of Milan, or Ferdinand's determination to continue to direct the government of Castille after the death of Isabella, when that kingdom was inherited by their daughter, the demented Joanna, wife of Maximilian's son Philip – the papacy had no direct interest and no voice. The only dispute between the three leading European powers in which the pope was directly concerned was the question of their conflicting claims to the kingdom of Naples. Militarily, the question had been decided by the Spanish victory over the French, but this did not stop Louis from continuing to claim it. The card that Julius held was the right to confer the investiture of the kingdom, to give formal recognition of which claim was the rightful one. It is symptomatic of the papacy's weakness that Julius could not afford to make a decision. His failure to do so was especially irksome to Ferdinand, who regarded *de jure* recognition of his *de facto* possession of the kingdom as an indispensable sign of goodwill. To confer investiture on Ferdinand, however, would be regarded by Louis as an unfriendly act. The best solution that Julius could devise for several years was to accept the token census payment, the white horse presented on 29 June, St Peter's Day, from each party, using the non-committal formula 'We accept this without prejudice to our rights or those of others.'[34]

The pope, of course, had a unique position in Europe, in that he was not just a temporal sovereign, but also head of the Western Church. This gave him a link with every other European ruler. Unfortunately, the negotiations over appointments to benefices and conflicts of jurisdiction and the levying of taxes that were the basis of the everyday diplomatic traffic centred on Rome often became prolonged and contentious. If the pope's position as head of the Church gave him interests throughout Europe, these frequently became a source of tension, rather than a basis for understanding. In general, the less a prince had to do with the papacy, the easier it was for him to see the pope as the Holy Father, rather than as just another ruler with personal interests and weaknesses, who also happened to have unique powers in matters of faith and of jurisdiction.

As cardinal and as pope, Julius was noted for his defence of the property of the Church. It was a quality that earned him respect, from those whose interests it did not lead him to cross. His defence of papal rights, or papal claims to rights, over benefices did not evoke the same respect, for it inevitably cut across the interests of secular rulers. Both pope and secular powers looked on ecclesiastical benefices as a reserve of patronage, a way of rewarding or maintaining their own men or satisfying petitioners. Some benefices, such as bishoprics or important monasteries that were strategically situated, were considered by the secular powers to be politically sensitive and to require an incumbent who was a trusted subject, not an importunate curial official or papal favourite who would regard it as solely a source of income. For the pope, too, benefices could be a source of income, not just from the fees that a new incumbent had to pay, but because of the opportunity to sell again the venal offices that appointees to certain benefices had to resign.[35] Much of Julius's war chest of treasure in the Castel Sant' Angelo was garnered in this way. There could be a lot at stake for both parties claiming authority to appoint to a benefice.

This conflict of interest had been a feature of relations between the pope and secular governments for several centuries.

Although the boundaries had shifted from one period to another, and different states had struck up different working arrangements with the papacy, in practice it was generally recognized that both sides had legitimate rights, and compromise was possible. But it could be more difficult for the pope to strike a compromise with a friendly power, or a nominally friendly power, than with one with whom political relations were not so close. Friendly rulers, 'obedient sons' of the pope, tended to consider that they should get their own way over benefices. Ferdinand spelt out his feelings on this matter very explicitly when he professed shocked disappointment in April 1504 that Julius had not accepted his candidate for the see of Malta.

> We feel this to be a great injury on the part of the pope, seeing that all we are asking for is just and reasonable, and that he denies us everything as though it were unjust, and that His Holiness has so little respect for us and for the great affection we have for him, and our desire to do things for him and the Apostolic See . . . we do not know what more a pope can do to offend us and show himself our adversary, than provide to the churches of our kingdoms without our petition, undermining our royal powers of patronage, which are enforced in the most minor kingdoms of the world, and refusing to do what we have asked in order to protect the public weal of our kingdoms. If, for this, we want to do what all other kings do, the remedy is in our hands, and we have very little need of what we have asked His Holiness for. And we can use this remedy with much more justification, since we put our request to His Holiness out of reverence and honour for the Church, and he didn't grant it, than can other kings, who without so much justification and without petitioning His Holiness, or having such regard for the Church, take the remedy into their own hands.[36]

On the other hand, Julius considered that 'obedient sons' showed their obedience by accepting the nominations of their 'loving father' the pope. He spelt out his views to the ambassador of Philip, the young King of Castille (taking a sideswipe at Philip's father-in-law, Ferdinand, along the way).

> Write to the King of Castille, your master, that I am resolved to love him, and that he should always wish to behave well to me and bear my honour in mind, and that he should not behave like the King of Aragon. And when he does behave well to me, I promise you that I shall always have his concerns and his honour as much at heart as mine.

What the pope wanted above all, the ambassador explained, was that he should have free disposal of the benefices that fell vacant in the court of Rome,[37] as he claimed was his right. In return, he would take care not to appoint anyone suspect to Philip, and would comply with his requests concerning all other benefices falling vacant in his dominions. If the king wanted an important benefice at present held by a cleric resident in Rome to go to one of his servants when it fell vacant, he should let the pope know well in advance. Julius promised to agree to such nominations – 'and I'll do it in such a way that my honour and the privileges of the Church of Rome will be protected, because I'll provide those he has nominated, pretending that it's on my initiative as well as on his.' The ambassador's next remarks, however, made it clear that he considered the assurances that he gave the pope that Philip would observe these conditions to be purely conventional, as he reminded Philip, 'You should not allow any benefices, especially bishoprics, wherever they may fall vacant, either in Rome or elsewhere, should be given except at your request.'[38]

And this was the attitude of rulers who were, or wanted to be, on good terms with the pope. Those who were on bad terms with him found that the interests he and his courtiers had in benefices throughout Europe provided them with a useful set of sanctions against him to demonstrate their displeasure. They could, for example, confiscate the revenues from benefices held by residents in Rome. They could forbid payments to be sent to the Roman court. They could order those who held benefices to come to take up residence in them (as canonically they were obliged to do), threatening them with the confiscation of their benefices if they failed to come. And they could, of course, fail to accept papal nominations to benefices, and install their own candidates in their place. It was a brave cathedral chapter or religious community that refused to accept the nominee of a determined ruler and stood by a papal nominee. As the ultimate threat, a disaffected ruler could invoke a general council of the Church, citing the failure of the Holy See to provide for the reform of the Church as his justification – as Louis was to do against Julius.

There was not a great deal that the pope could do in response, except use the weapons of excommunication and interdiction. These spiritual sanctions, which should have been terrifying for the pious Catholic forbidden the comforts of the rituals and sacraments of the Church, had been blunted by over-use. In-dignation, rather than terror, was the response of those who felt that the pope had banned them unjustly. Nevertheless, if the clergy observed papal decrees (which they did not always do), the lack of the consolations of the Church could sap the morale of a people whose rulers had quarrelled with the pope. If the sanctions were in force for some time, discontent could spread and might force the government to seek an accommodation with the papacy. One aspect of the sanctions made them particularly unwelcome to cities heavily dependent on banking and foreign trade, such as Venice and Florence. Goods belonging to a citizen of an interdicted state or city could be seized, according to ecclesiastical law, so that merchants or bankers trading away from home were vulnerable.

As an ally, Julius did not have a great deal to offer. The papacy was not a first-rank military power. Like most popes, Julius was very reluctant to spend much money on keeping an effective standing force, and tended to rely on hastily recruited infantry, and last-minute contracts with whatever military commanders were available, to provide the bulk of his forces when he was at war. Ironically, at a period when most of the leading *condottieri* in Italy were from the Papal States, the papal troops were often badly commanded. Guidobaldo da Montefeltro, Duke of Urbino, who was the overall commander of the papal troops during the early years of Julius's pontificate, was too crippled by gout to be effective in the field. His successor in the duchy, Francesco Maria della Rovere, was incapable of providing proper military leadership either. Francesco Maria's father-in-law, Francesco Gonzaga, Marquis of Mantua, was even less use. On the two occasions on which he was appointed to lead the papal troops, he was more sympathetic to the enemy (in 1506, the Bentivoglio, in 1510, the Duke of Ferrara), than to the pope.[39] Julius never really had an effective and capable commander. As when he secured the submission of Bologna, he was usually dependent on the troops of his allies to help him attain his military objectives. But he insisted on having his own army, and was not willing to act as a paymaster for his allies and leave them to do all the fighting for him. Requests for subsidies were generally refused.

All in all, in aspiring to deal on equal terms with the leading European powers, Julius had to contend with severe problems. His role as head of the Church gave him some weapons to compensate for the comparatively small territory that he ruled and his lack of military power, but it also made him vulnerable to sanctions against the revenues of the papacy, and to the threat of a general council. Respect for the spiritual head of the Church was tempered by an all-too-vivid awareness that the present incumbent of the see of St Peter was a fallible individual, involved in the same political world – and playing by much the same rules – as other princes. Nor could Julius compensate for the weaknesses of his state by his diplomatic skill. He was not a good diplomat; he was far too impulsive and quick to anger for that. Though he learned in later years to keep his own counsel, he was not skilled in bluff or deception. He did not know how to compromise. All too often, he could only get what he wanted from his allies if their interests happened to coincide with his. He simply did not have the 'clout' to dictate his own terms.

The other powers were, of course, well aware of his problems. As one Spanish ambassador saw it, in February 1507, the pope could not upset any plans of the French and Spanish kings, 'because, whether he wants to or not, His Holiness is forced to concur with them, as a consequence of the greatness of these princes'.[40] How little regard might be shown to him, was never demonstrated more humiliatingly than in late June and early July 1507, when Louis and Ferdinand met in Julius's own home town of Savona. He himself had just evaded meeting Louis because he feared to do so. He had invited Ferdinand, who had been in Naples for some months, to visit Rome before he returned to Spain, but Ferdinand had refused. Julius was so eager to meet him that he went to Ostia as the king sailed north, but Ferdinand's galley did not call there. A legate, Cardinal Antoniotto Pallavicino, was with Louis, but he was given little honour in the ceremonies of greeting and exchange of courtesies between the two kings, and was excluded from their negotiations, except for a two-hour meeting that he had with them on 1 July. Little is known about what the kings discussed, but they are known to have talked about something in which Julius and his legate would have had a peculiar interest – the reform of the Church. When Julius heard how his legate had been treated, he was naturally furious, but there was nothing that he could do.

But Julius had one great personal strength, which sometimes could, on its own, counterbalance all the weaknesses of his position. He never knew when he was beaten. Certainly, there were times when he was discouraged, times when he was afraid, but the slightest fresh hope or favourable circumstance would restore his spirits and his confidence and he would once again be predicting the downfall of his enemies and the triumph of the Church. His refusal to admit defeat was rooted in his own character, his obstinacy and courage, and his sheer animal spirit, as well as in his physical strength and endurance; but he was also fortified by his belief that he was about God's work. Many people, from his time to our own, find the concept of a pope fulfilling the will of God by leading an army hard to accept, but Julius was quite sincere.

Guicciardini compared him to Antaeus, the son of Mother Earth who wrestled with Hercules, and whom Hercules could defeat only by lifting him clear of the ground because every time that he touched the earth he derived fresh strength from it.

> Adversity had the same effect on the pope, so that when he seemed to be at his lowest and most trampled down, he would rise up again with a still more steady and determined spirit, more hopeful of the future than ever, but having no other foundation for his optimism than his own resources, and the assumption (as he said openly) that, as his enterprises were not undertaken for private interest but solely from a desire to liberate Italy, they would be brought, by God's help, to a prosperous conclusion.[41]

Yet in spite of his anxieties about French ambitions to bully or even depose him, and the humiliation of the Savona 'summit meeting' between Louis and Ferdinand, liberating Italy would still have to wait until he had accomplished his first aim, the recovery of the Romagnol territories lost to Venice. This was still the focus of his diplomacy, the underlying agenda of his negotiations with other powers.

The Venetians were not making conspicuous efforts to conciliate him. In their handling of the ever-thorny matter of appointments to ecclesiastical benefices within their lands, they at times did not even show much tact, let alone any wish to appease. All princes and republics kept a jealous eye on the benefices in their jurisdiction, but Venice was markedly reluctant to allow strategically or financially important benefices to be held by anyone who was not a Venetian patrician, citizen or subject. Venetian clerics who spent much time in Rome were often viewed with some degree of suspicion back at home, as if they had 'gone native' and were not to be trusted to have a proper appreciation of where their loyalties should lie. Sometimes when the governing councils were debating a point of controversy with the pope, the '*papalisti*' – those who were believed to be tainted with a degree of dependence on Rome through holding offices or benefices or through family connections – were excluded from the chamber for the duration of the discussions.

Religion and religious ritual were integral to Venetian culture. The periodic wars with the Turks that they became involved in through the defence and extension of their maritime trade and colonies in the eastern Mediterranean gave them a role as defenders of Christendom against the infidel of which they were proud. There was a nexus of pious and thoughtful supporters of religious reform among the patricians. Contempt for the less edifying features of the life of the papal court was scarcely disguised, and there was a current of feeling (not peculiar to the Venetians) that they were better Christians than the men who were running the central administration of the Church. All this gave added strength to the tenacity with which they fought to have their candidates appointed to benefices. The Venetian senators considered themselves to be perfectly capable of assessing who would be the best man for the job, and they rarely felt that they had to look beyond their own dominions to find him. One of their own men was not only more likely to be politically reliable, and less likely to extract the income from the benefice to be spent elsewhere, but was at least as likely to be a good cleric.

One dispute about the disposal of a major bishopric, Cremona, in the years following the Venetian return of some territory to Julius in 1505, was given a sharper edge by the fact that the new incumbent whom Julius had in mind was his favourite nephew, Cardinal Galeotto Franciotto della Rovere. He would have thought, Julius remarked to the Venetian ambassador after the dispute had dragged on for nearly two years, that, knowing he loved Galeotto more than anyone else, they would not only have given him the possession of Cremona but offered other benefices to him as well.[42] But the Venetians dug their heels in, and unwisely gave Julius another grievance against them.

By the time that the news that Julius had given the bishopric to Galeotto reached Venice, the Venetians had already decided to appoint a member of a Venetian patrician family, Girolamo Trevisan. In the opinion of the senate, 'in our lands, as we have always done, the senate, not the pope, should elect the bishops, and so His Holiness ought to give' the bishopric to Trevisan.[43] From the pope's point of view, since the bishopric was a benefice that had fallen vacant by the death of a cleric resident in Rome he had the right to appoint the bishop. Neither side was inclined to yield.

Cremona was important, rich and in a strategically sensitive position near the duchy of Milan. When the bishopric of Padua, worth a little less and much less politically sensitive, fell vacant, a compromise was suggested – Galeotto should have Padua, and Trevisan Cremona. Julius later said the Venetians had proposed it, but contemporary Venetian reports indicate that it was the pope's idea.[44] This might have been a basis for agreement, had not the question of the investiture of Rimini and Faenza come up. It is not clear if the Venetians were trying to exploit Julius's increasingly evident anxiety about the French or whether Alidosi had planted the idea in the Venetian ambassador's mind, by suggesting that he could persuade the pope to give a verbal promise that he would leave Venice in peaceful possession of Rimini and Faenza for his lifetime.[45] Julius himself indicated that he was prepared to make a verbal promise to Venice, but insisted he would not put anything in writing and did not want Venice telling other powers that he had given them the investiture.[46] But when the Venetians still did not give Galeotto either benefice, any hint of concessions on Rimini and Faenza was out of the question – instead, Julius threatened to take them by force.

By his own account, he had told the ambassador that he would sooner let go every benefice that Galeotto had, and Galeotto himself, and every *nipote* and relative that he had, than give them one property of the Church. If they did not give Cremona to Galeotto within a certain period, he would put it under interdict, and give the bishopric of Padua to one of their gentlemen of his choosing; he knew well how to sow division among them, he said.[47]

Meanwhile, a third benefice had been brought into the equation, that of Vicenza, because the Venetians had decided to give Padua to Piero Dandolo, the Bishop of Vicenza. Again, it is not clear which side first proposed that Vicenza might be given to Galeotto, and it took several months for this solution to be adopted. In the end, the Venetians got their way, because in consistory in late October 1507 the bishopric of Padua was given to Dandolo, that of Cremona to Trevisan, and Vicenza to Galeotto della Rovere.

It may be significant that at the time at which this settlement was being concluded, Julius was worried that the Bentivoglio might be planning to return to Bologna, and that they might have

French support. That autumn, only a few months after the Savona 'summit', he had small hope of any support from France or Spain, and, as usual, could place little reliance on Maximilian, so he may have decided that it was worth making some concession to Venice to have a little more security on that flank at least. Earlier that year, he had been pleased when the Venetians had forbidden any of their subjects to take service under the Bentivoglio and had sent away some Bolognese exiles who turned up at Faenza. But only ten days after the consistory in which the bishoprics were assigned, Julius was complaining bitterly about the Venetians giving shelter in Faenza to exiles from Forlì, who were using it as a base to launch assaults on Forlì. He knew the Venetians, he said, 'they cannot stay quiet, and they're too stubborn [*accechati*] and I'm not going to lose the property of the Church, if I can help it, and if they think they can wear me down in this way they'll find they're mistaken.'[48]

Throughout the following year, Julius's animus against the Venetians was open. He hated the Venetians more than the devil himself, a Mantuan agent reported, but even more he hated anyone who was dependent on them in any way.[49] Alfonso d'Este, Duke of Ferrara, on a visit to Venice, wrote to Rome of how well disposed the Venetians were to the pope: Julius responded that they were suspicious of him, because they were holding his property; if they restored it, they would have no further grounds for suspicion.[50] But Julius was fostering suspicions of his own against Venice, which he aired in consistory in July: that they wanted Cardinal Corner to reside in his diocese of Verona and have the powers of a legate; that they were giving refuge to rebels from Bologna; that Bartolomeo d'Alviano, who was now one of their senior commanders, was to be billeted in the Romagna – all for no good purpose, he implied.[51] Tactlessness on the part of the Venetians after the death of Galeotto della Rovere, in September 1508, exacerbated his feelings. The grief-stricken pope had immediately conferred all Galeotto's offices and benefices, including the bishopric of Vicenza, on his brother Sisto. Not only was Sisto della Rovere denied the possession of the diocese by the Venetians, they appointed their own candidate in his stead. Julius took this as a personal injury, and his determination to free himself from 'these Venetian tyrants'[52] became still stronger.

'Venetian tyranny', as Julius saw it, was not directed only against himself. The Venetians aimed to 'occupy and tyrannize over all of Italy',[53] he maintained, when a proposal was being mooted by King Ferdinand for a league against the infidel in February 1508. No expedition against the infidel could safely take place, he argued, until Venice had been forced to disgorge all her ill-gotten gains: the lands she was holding that rightfully belonged to the papacy, to Louis as Duke of Milan, to Ferdinand as King of Naples, to Maximilian as head of the Empire. If the Christian powers were occupied in a crusade, the Venetians would look for an opportunity to seize more land in Italy. The best preparation for a crusade would be for Ferdinand and Julius and Louis and Maximilian to unite, so that each could recover his own territory from Venice; then they could jointly launch a great expedition against the infidel.[54] Ferdinand replied that it would not be possible to form a league of those four powers, excluding Venice, but suggested there could be a treaty between the five powers, including Venice, and then a separate understanding among the four about the recovery of the lands that Venice was holding.

Ironically, when these ideas bore fruit at the end of the year in the League of Cambrai, Julius was not directly involved in the negotiations. This was partly his own fault. He had become displeased with his legate in Germany, Cardinal Carvajal – who was trying to curry favour with Maximilian, having fallen out with his earlier patron, Ferdinand – and had sent orders recalling him to Rome in July 1508. Carvajal had hung on, and persuaded Maximilian to write to Julius praising the cardinal and saying that it would be good if he could stay to take part in the negotiations,[55] but, at last, he had to leave in October. A replacement, Bishop Achille de' Grassi, was supposed to be sent, but, even when word was sent to Rome of the preparations and arrangements for the discussions at Cambrai, there was no sense of urgency about his despatch.

In Maximilian's instructions to his daughter Margaret, the regent in the Netherlands, who would represent him at Cambrai, there was no mention of admitting a representative of the pope. She was to ensure that the English ambassador was present at all sessions, and Ferdinand's ambassador, if he had instructions to take part.[56] According to the French, Ferdinand's ambassador had agreed not to take part, in order to appease the Venetian ambassador, who was to be excluded. But at least both Ferdinand and Venice had representatives on the spot. Julius was still thinking about sending Pietro Griffo to Cambrai on his way to England, where he was to be the collector of papal taxes, when he heard of the conclusion of the treaty. Even if Griffo had arrived in time, he might not have been admitted to the discussions. The Spanish ambassador in Rome, for one, considered him to be a person of too little authority to be suitable to take part in negotiations at such a high level, with the likes of Margaret and Cardinal Rouen.[57] This negligence by Julius meant that he was 'represented' by Cardinal Rouen, who undertook to obtain the pope's ratification of the terms that he had agreed in his name.[58]

Thus the irony was heightened, for the self-appointed guardian of the papacy's interests at Cambrai was the very man whom Julius most distrusted, and it was suspicion of French intentions in urging an attack on Venice that had kept Julius aloof from the negotiations in the first place. There had been discussions about a campaign against Venice in the summer, when Cardinal de Clermont had been sent to France, ostensibly to see his uncle Cardinal Rouen; but the pope had been very wary. In a conversation with the Florentine ambassador, Roberto Acciaiuoli, he had confided that the French had already approached him three times through different people, on the last occasion through Massimo, de Clermont's secretary,

> and I see that they want to make me come out into the open, . . . against the Venetians, [so that] they can manipulate me to suit themselves, and make me do what they want, seeing I have need of them. And because I've had so much to do with them, that I know them, and I've been deceived many times . . . I want to see what I'm getting into and know for sure how I ought to handle myself with them. They are so proud that they don't treat anyone with respect unless it suits them [*che e' non fanno stima di nessuno, se non a posta loro*]. . . .
> I've replied that they should show their hand, and that, when I see they're being sincere, I'm ready, and . . . that I won't hold back . . . because I am very keen. But I don't want to be the first.[59]

For all his doubts, before de Clermont returned to Rome in October Julius was becoming quite optimistic, saying he was sure that the French would not let him down this time, and that they wanted the honour of being the ones to restore the Church's lands to her.[60] But he did not like the proposal that the cardinal brought – basically that the French would provide the troops, and he should provide the money to pay for them. 'These French are behaving badly', he told the Ferrarese ambassador,

> worse than the Venetians (by which he meant that they couldn't be behaving worse) . . . they say they want to raise a powerful

army, such that they can invade the Veneto, [and] they want a great deal of money from His Holiness, but he realized that, thanks to Cardinal Rouen, they wanted to get his cash from him, and then they would have him at their discretion. His Beatitude did not want to find himself in that position, indicating he didn't trust them, and he said he had replied that he wasn't asking for any help in the recovery of the lands of the Church, nor was he inclined to want to take Venice, but when the French wanted to see to recovering their own lands which had been occupied by the Venetians, they would be helping His Holiness in that way and, vice versa, His Beatitude would be helping them, because the Venetians couldn't defend themselves on two flanks. And as Auch [de Clermont] persisted that the French wanted to recover the lands of the Church themselves, he [Julius] had arrived at another arrangement, and had decided that if the French wanted to be the ones to recover the lands of the Church, he would agree, but they should ask His Beatitude for a reasonable sum of money they would need for this, that he would put it on deposit and undertake to give it to them as soon as they had attacked and had restored to him one of his towns.[61]

If Louis did not like the idea of being paid by instalments, with Julius handing over a prearranged sum for every town that Louis restored to him, the pope proposed another arrangement. A coordinated assault should be launched against the Venetians by French troops in Lombardy and papal troops in the Romagna, and whoever recovered all their lands first would help the other. But Julius was still afraid that the French wanted to involve him in so many problems that he would have to spend all the treasure he had accumulated, so that then they could make him do as they wanted – as he was sure they would be able to do if he had no money any more. All this sprang from his conviction that every action and every plan of Rouen was motivated by his ambition to be pope. Consequently, Julius was trying for every guarantee and security he could obtain, so that he did not have to trust himself to the French.[62]

Because he had delayed in sending a representative to Cambrai as even Rouen had urged him to do, Julius was faced with a difficult decision after the treaties were concluded. Should he ratify terms agreed on his behalf by the man who, he was convinced, was out to ruin him? Or should he lose the opportunity that he had been trying to bring about for years of taking part in a concerted attack on Venice with a good chance of recovering the Church's lands?

One of the two treaties did not concern him much, that between Maximilian and his grandson Charles of Austria on one side, and Louis XII and Charles of Egmont, Duke of Guelders, on the other. Julius was named in the treaty as a guarantor, together with the Kings of England and Aragon and the princes of the Holy Roman Empire, but apart from pious noises about a crusade against the infidel, the treaty was concerned with regulating various disputes between Louis and Maximilian.

It was the second treaty that really concerned the pope. This was an agreement that there should be a league between the pope ('on whose behalf Cardinal Rouen . . . has promised to have and to show his ratification of this present treaty of league and confederation'), Maximilian, and the Kings of France and Aragon, against the Venetians, 'for the conquest and recovery of all that they have lost' to Venice. The pope and the two kings were obliged, with a 'sufficient number' of infantry and horse and artillery, to attack the Venetians before 1 April, and none of them was to abandon the war, until: 'the Holy See had entirely recovered Ravenna, Cervia, Faenza [and] Rimini with their dependencies and appurtenances, and the towns of Imola and Cesena, with all their rights and appurtenances whatsoever, together with all other territories belonging to the Holy See that the said Venetians are holding and occupying'; the Emperor had recovered all the territory belonging to the Holy Roman Empire and to his own house of Austria; the King of France had recovered the lands held by Venice that had once belonged to the duchy of Milan; and the King of Aragon had recovered all the towns that the Venetians were holding in the kingdom of Naples.

As Maximilian had only recently agreed a three-year truce with the Venetians, which 'without some honest cause he cannot break', it was agreed that he should send troops to help the pope, who would write to him, 'as advocate and protector of Holy Church' for assistance in recovering its property. These men were to be at Julius's disposal by 1 April. If he wanted them, then Maximilian would be obliged to join in the attack on Venice on his own account within forty days.

The Duke of Savoy, who had a claim to the kingdom of Cyprus, which was held by the Venetians, the Duke of Ferrara and the Marquis of Mantua, could be included in the league for the purpose of regaining lands lost to Venice. Henry of England could also join if he wanted, and the King of Hungary would be specially invited to participate.

The person of the pope, his dignity, jurisdiction and authority, and that of the Holy See, were to be defended against any enemies who sought to trouble them, and Julius's nephew, Francesco Maria della Rovere, was to be received into the protection of the league. Julius was to proceed with ecclesiastical censures and the interdict against the Venetians and their subjects and all who gave them aid and assistance; and he should call upon the Emperor, the King of France and the other allies to use their complementary secular powers, taking reprisals against the persons and property of the Venetians and their subjects to help to give effect to the ecclesiastical censures.[63]

Two clauses would be frequently invoked against Julius later. If one of the signatories recovered his lands sooner than the others, he was bound to help them until everyone had won back all that they claimed; and none of the signatories could make any peace or truce with the Venetians without the express consent of his allies. They could be invoked against him because he did, indeed, ratify this treaty, although after considerable hesitation. What did Ferdinand think of the terms? he wanted to know. Was he going to ratify? If he was not going to do so, Julius would like to form a separate alliance with him. Ferdinand assured him that he thought the terms good, and that Julius should ratify them, although he thought that Maximilian should join in the attack from the beginning, to forestall any separate agreement between Venice and the Emperor. He also thought that the pope should supply his own troops, not just pay those of Ferdinand and Louis to do his fighting for him.[64] Eventually, on 23 March, Julius signed the bull making public his adherence to the league – but also announced that he would not send his troops against Venice until after the French had opened up hostilities. And he was not going to pay them any money, but use his own troops.

Julius, so Maximilian heard, suspected that the French were coming to Italy to attack him, not Venice. Ferdinand suspected that Maximilian was ready to come to terms with Venice. Maximilian thought that the French were trying to prevent him from attacking Venice so that France and Venice could attack Maximilian or Julius, or come to a separate peace. Such distrust was a poor foundation for a successful alliance and a coordinated campaign. Yet within weeks of the opening of the campaign, the Venetians had lost most of the lands in Italy that they had spent a century acquiring, and were desperately trying to detach Julius from the league.

For the first three months of 1509, as Julius hesitated over the decision to adhere to the league, many Venetians had been hoping that his distrust of the French, and of Rouen in particular, would be stronger than his desire to recover the Romagnol towns. Hopes were nurtured by reports from the Venetian ambassadors in Rome describing long conversations with the pope. True, he had forbidden papal subjects to take service in the army of any other power, a measure that the Venetians recognized as being aimed at preventing them from hiring the Roman barons with whom they were negotiating *condotte*. True, he had also told the ambassadors that Venice would do well to raise a big army, because she was going to need it.[65] Still, they hoped that he would at least stay neutral, and as late as 19 March, the ambassadors reported (according to Sanuto) that Julius had told one of them, Pisani, that he wanted to look over the terms of the treaty again, and that if there was anything in it that was hostile to Venice, he would not sign it.[66] As the whole *raison d'être* of the treaty was hostility to Venice, this remark was disingenuous, to say the least, if Sanuto's report of the despatch was accurate.

Only three days later, Julius summoned a congregation of cardinals to discuss what reply should be made to the pressing requests by the French for a decision on ratification, without inviting either the Venetian cardinals Grimani and Corner, or others known to be friendly to Venice. This was the meeting that finally decided on adherence to the league. Even without knowing what had been said at this congregation, the Venetians recognized that it boded ill for them. Turning the '*papalisti*' out of the discussion of the matter did not make it easier to agree on what response should be sent to Rome. Already, however, one obvious course, that of returning the Romagnol lands to the pope, was being considered. Sanuto heard that the senate had discussed what he, perhaps significantly, referred to as 'the lands of the pope, Rimini and Faenza',[67] but that it had decided to wait before taking further action. All of Venice was uneasy, he noted, because there was no good news from any side and the Venetians were being left on their own.[68] Soon the Venetians began to be afraid that Julius would excommunicate them, as he had threatened to do, and as he was being urged to do by the French cardinals and ambassadors.

An offer to return Rimini and Faenza to the pope, on condition that he 'did something' (Sanuto does not specify what) about the threat from Louis, was rejected.[69] Papal troops began to muster at Castel Bolognese, about five miles from Faenza. Over dinner with Cardinal Grimani, Julius raged against Venice. As they talked, he already had in his pocket the text of the 'terribilissima' bull of excommunication.[70] On 26 April the bull excommunicating the Venetian Signoria because its members had refused to give back the papal lands was read out in consistory. Unless all the possessions of the Church in the Romagna, and the revenues that had been taken from them, were restored within twenty-four days, the excommunication would take effect.

Poorly led and in bad order, as usual, the papal troops were having some minor successes in the Romagna, picking up some of the smaller fortresses. Their greatest success was the capture of Brisighella, when a prized Venetian commander, Gianpaolo Manfrone, fell into their hands. Francesco Maria della Rovere was in overall command; he was joined by Cardinal Alidosi as legate. Bitter rivals, they did not work effectively together, and the Venetians could well have held out against any force under their command for a long time. Fortunately for Julius, the decisive action was taking place on another front. He would owe the recovery of his lands to French arms after all.

The crushing defeat of the Venetians by the French at Agnadello on 14 May 1509, when half their army was destroyed and one of their most senior commanders, Bartolomeo d'Alviano, was captured, terrified the Venetians. So rapid was the advance of the French and Imperial troops that within three weeks even Padua had fallen.

One of the first things that the Venetians did, when news of the defeat reached them, was to write to the Venetian cardinals Grimani and Corner (the ambassadors had been instructed to leave Rome) requesting them to ask Julius not to wish to see the ruin of Venice, and to tell him that 'his' lands (as Sanuto now generally referred to them) would be offered to him before the date set in the bull of excommunication.[71] As the heads of the government discussed late into the night what could be done to remedy their desperate situation, one source of hope was the belief that the pope, once he had his lands back, might be appeased. Meanwhile, in Rome, Julius was delighted by the news of Agnadello, held celebrations in the Castel Sant' Angelo, and ordered the cardinals to celebrate as well. He planned to send further troops and money to the Romagna, confident, now, that the territories would soon be his. Sooner even than he thought. Before the letters to the Venetian cardinals reached Rome, a message arrived from Cardinal Alidosi, telling of the arrival of a Venetian secretary with instructions to surrender Rimini, Faenza, Cervia and Ravenna to the papacy; Alidosi asked for the pope's consent.

Julius did not hesitate to accept. He wanted to keep the Venetian prisoners who had been taken, and he wanted the artillery and munitions in the cities to be left behind by the Venetian garrisons. In the Romagna, Alidosi was promising the Venetians that their prisoners would be freed, and that they could take the artillery and munitions with them as they wanted; but then he ordered the shipments to be halted until he had further instructions from Rome. Alidosi may have been trying to make the most of his good fortune in being in the right place at the right time, by making the Venetians feel as obliged to him as possible. If the present storm blew over, Venetian patronage could be useful to him in future, after Julius's death. He even promised to procure Julius's agreement to the Venetian request that he should write to all the Christian princes telling them that the Venetians had obeyed the papal *monitorio*, and he also promised the Venetians that they would be absolved from the excommunication.[72]

Submissive sons of Holy Church was how the Venetians now wanted to represent themselves to Julius, and Cardinals Grimani and Corner were instructed to tell him that the Venetians were undone, and to ask him for mercy. Let the pope do as he pleased, the ambassadors in Rome were told when the diocese of Padua fell vacant, this was not the moment to argue over the nomination of a successor. (It was given to Sisto della Rovere, and his bishopric of Vicenza to a relative of Costantino Arniti.) Significantly, since the defeat of Agnadello, the *'papalisti'* were no longer excluded from discussions, and could hear all the letters that were read out in the councils. An honourable embassy might soften Julius, the Venetian cardinals reported that they had been told; six new ambassadors were elected immediately, and ordered to leave for Rome without delay.

But Julius was not being gracious in victory. He refused to see the two Venetian ambassadors who were still in Rome, because they were excommunicate; and he revoked the licence that he had given them to go. He refused to lift the excommunication, threatening, instead, to publish it throughout the world to make the Venetians outcasts everywhere, calling them heretics and schismatics. His temper cooled, but he was still preparing to exploit the trouble of the Venetians for all it was worth to him. While they were optimistically hoping that the excommunication would be lifted once the special embassy arrived in Rome, Cardinal Sigismondo Gonzaga, the legate in the Marche, had heard that Julius had said he wanted the Doge himself to come to Rome with a halter around his neck to beg for mercy and absolution, as an example to all Christians not to rebel against the Holy See.[73]

Most Venetian diplomatic correspondence for this period has perished, but fortunately two copybooks of the ambassadors' despatches from Rome from mid-1509 to mid-1510 have survived, and it is possible to follow the progress – or, for much of the time, lack of progress – in the negotiations closely, and to observe how Julius handled them.

No red carpet was rolled out for the six ambassadors when they arrived, in early July. Julius was leaving for Ostia when he was told that they were near, and saw no reason to postpone his trip, saying he wanted them to enter Rome at nightfall, without pomp (as befitted the representatives of an excommunicate state). On returning to Rome, he refused to see them as a group. Indeed, he went on refusing to see them all together even when it was agreed in consistory on 17 July that the ambassadors should be given personal absolution. One of them, Girolamo Donà, had already been absolved by Julius, who had sent for him a week before saying that, although he knew most of them, he was the one whom he knew best. Subsequently, he would agree to see Donà, with whom he got on well personally, a few more times. Generally, however, he communicated with them through the two Venetian cardinals, Grimani or Corner, or the commission that he appointed to handle the negotiations, consisting of Cardinals Caraffa and Riario, Sigismondo de' Conti, his secretary, and Pietro Accolti, the senior member of the main papal judicial tribunal, the Rota. Part of his reluctance to deal with all the ambassadors in person may have stemmed from the fact that two of them were men with whom he did not get on, Domenico Trevisan and Paolo Capello, and that one, Paolo Pisani, had taken part in drawing up an appeal to a future council of the Church against the censures that Julius had imposed on Venice.[74]

Initially, Julius attached four conditions to granting the absolution: there were to be no more arguments about appointing the men whom Julius chose to Venetian benefices; no taxes were to be imposed on Venetian clergy without papal consent; all papal subjects were to have the right to sail freely in the 'gulf', the Adriatic north of a line from Ancona to Zara where the Venetians imposed tolls and severe trade restrictions on all shipping (this condition was included at the request of the Anconitani); and the Venetians should be bound to contribute a certain number of galleys and other aid to support a crusade, if one were launched.[75] None of these were conditions to which the Venetians would willingly agree; the demand for freedom of navigation in the 'gulf' would be notably contentious. Julius also wanted the ambassadors to have a mandate to seek absolution, but they were not at all keen on the form of mandate for which he was asking. They maintained that Venice had not incurred any censures, because she had complied with the terms of the bull within the set time-limit: Julius said, no mandate, no absolution. Discouraged by this unpromising beginning, scarcely a week after they had arrived the ambassadors suggested to Venice it was not fitting that they should all stay in Rome while Julius was being so unforthcoming.

In Venice, the form of mandate that was being asked for was considered unacceptable; but the form that was sent was not acceptable to the papal commission nor to the pope. There was, for example, no mention of navigation rights in the Adriatic. Julius told Cardinal Grimani that a mandate such as the one for which he was asking was necessary because it would help him to argue to his allies that he had no alternative but to absolve a properly contrite Venice.[76] Negotiations were deadlocked on this issue until early November, when news that Louis was planning to come to Italy the following year with an even larger army than in the previous campaigning season made Julius more anxious to come to a settlement with Venice. Meanwhile, however, he had been raising the stakes, the most important new demand being that Venice should drop all her claims to jurisdictional privileges in Ferrara. Since the beginning of the fourteenth century the Venetians had imposed trade restrictions on Ferrara and had kept an official there, the *visdomino*, who had jurisdiction over all Venetian citizens working or trading there. This was not a situation that Julius was prepared to put up with any longer.

The conditions that Julius was now attaching to the absolution of Venice were spelt out at a meeting on 3 November between the commission and the ambassadors. Accolti, acting as spokesman for the commission, said that there were 'three spiritual matters and four temporal'. The spiritual were: firstly, that Venice should be obedient in giving possession of benefices to those whom Julius appointed to be incumbents; secondly, that ecclesiastical causes should be tried before the Rota, in Rome; and thirdly, that the tax known as the '*decima*' should not be imposed on the clergy without papal authorization. The primary temporal condition was that concerning Ferrara, for Julius did not consider it fitting that Venice should exercise such authority in papal territory and have a representative with a title such as *visdomino*. These privileges had been gained by war and could be lost by war too. Secondly, there were agreements that the Venetians claimed to have with Ancona, Fano and other papal towns; again, it was not fitting that papal territories should have made any such pacts without the knowledge and consent of the pope, and thus they should be rescinded. Thirdly, there was the question of the 'gulf': the seas were free, and Julius did not like restrictions being imposed on his subjects. The Anconitani had complained that Venetian galleys came to the very mouth of their port and imposed tolls on ships that wished to enter. Lastly, there was the question of the revenues taken from the Romagnol lands while the Venetians held them. Julius wanted these paid now to him; and he wanted reparations for the expenses that he had incurred in the campaign.[77]

By this time, Venice had sent permission for five of the six ambassadors to leave; Girolamo Donà was to stay. Told of this decision, Julius was offended and gave another ultimatum. Either all six stayed or all six must leave – and he wanted twelve ambassadors to be sent when Venice was finally granted absolution. 'We know the wiles of the Signoria', he said: the Venetians want to leave just one ambassador, so that it will look as though we have come to a settlement.[78] The ambassadors thought that he wanted them all to stay just to strengthen his hand with France, because Louis would wish to avert the threat of Julius making a separate peace with Venice. In fact, Julius genuinely wanted an agreement with Venice, though he was ready to threaten that he would join France in attacking her if he did not get the answer that he wanted soon.

The issue of Ferrara was a complicated one. Julius insisted that the Venetians must relinquish their privileges in Ferrara, and they were beginning to recognize that these would have to be sacrificed. Yet he was angry with Alfonso d'Este, the Duke of Ferrara, for having put himself under the formal protection of the French, and for having become involved in the attack on Venice, provoking a Venetian counter-attack on his lands. Pleas from

Alfonso for help against the Venetians were rejected – Julius said that if he had got himself into trouble it was his own responsibility[79] – but, at the same time, repeated warnings were given to Venice not to attack those parts of Alfonso's lands that were held from the papacy, including Ferrara itself. The ambassadors were warned that Venice's assault on the Ferrarese was seriously harming her prospects of an agreement with the pope. Yet when Alfonso routed a Venetian fleet on the Po, Julius was displeased, because he believed that it would be an encouragement for Louis to press home an attack on Venice in the next campaigning season, and this was a very unwelcome prospect.

In order to bring pressure on Venice to come to terms, on 1 January 1510 Julius summoned Girolamo Donà and Cardinal Corner and set out to them the position of Venice as he saw it. Despite the threat from Louis, who was planning to come to Italy with a large army in the spring, he said, Venice was refusing to accept the conditions that had been set for her absolution. If they were relying on the support of the King of England, they were mistaken. The young King Henry VIII might have written on their behalf to Rome and to France, but he had done so on the advice of only a few of his counsellors, and a combative reply from France and the advice of sager members of his council had made him return to his father's firm policy of maintaining peace with France. If they had hopes of the Swiss, they were again mistaken, for they could not hire one Swiss infantryman while they were still under interdict. It was said that they were angling for help from the Turks: if they stirred up the Turks, they would turn the whole world against them. Perhaps, he said, they thought they could make peace with Maximilian, but he would just use them to extract more money from the French. And if they did manage to make peace with him before they obtained absolution, Julius would put him under interdict too, and draw closer to Louis. France and the papacy united, he warned, were far more powerful than Venice and the Emperor united. From Spain, they had nothing to hope. He was sure Ferdinand would not welcome their ruin, but even if he did not attack Venice, he had many interests that would hold him to the French. In conclusion, he told them,

> You want to stick to your position; if you would have some respect
> for our honour and that of the Holy Apostolic See and cede what
> we are asking of you, it would be good for you and for us, and for

the whole of Italy. And we'd join with you and with Maximilian and we would drive the French back over the mountains, and you would recover your reputation and your lands. When you don't do this, the same thing will happen to you as happened with the Romagnol lands: when you wanted to give them to me, it was too late for me to accept them and not oppose you. By the grace of God, we have men at arms and we can raise more with money, and we needn't lack for infantry. You know well your best troops, that you have had in the past and that you have now, especially infantry, come from our lands, and the captain of your infantry, Dionigio di Naldo, is our subject, and we won't mind if he and the others stay with you ... You know very well what my attitude was to your affairs before the business of the Romagnol lands. I will return to my natural inclination, and be better disposed than ever to your concerns, and we'll free ourselves of the French – we know well what their attitude is to you and to everyone and to the whole of Italy.[80]

Reluctant though they were to make concessions, as the new campaigning season drew near and the threat of renewed assaults on what lands they had managed to retain or to recover loomed larger, the prospect of having one enemy the less and of the lifting of the ecclesiastical censures, looked ever more attractive, and the Venetians at last braced themselves to meet Julius's demands. In consistory on 4 February, Julius promised to lift the sentence of excommunication against the Venetians, because they had obeyed him and done as he asked. Of the twenty-six cardinals present in consistory, fifteen were said to have voted in favour and eleven, six of them French, against. When the news was brought to Venice, there was, initially, great rejoicing – until the ambassadors' letters were read more closely and it became clear that there would be difficulties and there would be terms that some Venetians considered dishonourable. There was some hesitation too about the terms of the mandate that Julius required, but on 15 February a mandate for the ambassadors to conclude the agreement was finally drawn up, containing the acknowledgment the Venetians had been trying to evade – that the ecclesiastical censures had been justly imposed – and instructing them to ask for pardon.

The agreement itself was dated the day the ceremony of absolution took place in Rome, on 24 February. By it, the Venetians renounced the appeal to a future council against the ecclesiastical censures; acknowledged the justification for the censures and sued for pardon; promised never to impose any taxes on the clergy or on ecclesiastical benefices; undertook not to impede any promotions to benefices, or to interfere with ecclesiastical courts or appeals to Rome. No tolls or restrictions were to be imposed on traffic by river or sea to the Romagna, the March of Ancona or Ferrara. They promised always to be obedient sons of the Church in future. All pacts and conventions that they had with any places in the Papal States to the prejudice of the papacy were to be null and void. No rebels or enemies of the papacy were to be admitted to Venetian dominions. No papal vicar or baron, even if he bore the dignity of a duke, was to be received into the protection of Venice without the pope's permission. All claims to keep a *visdomino* in Ferrara and exercise other jurisdiction there were renounced. Any ecclesiastical revenues that had been seized under colour of the interdict were to be reimbursed.[81]

No wonder that there was some restiveness in Venice at accepting these terms, even when it was recognized that 'we have to agree to what the pope wants since we can't do anything else.'[82] Julius effectively had his way on every point. The Venetians were not even given any concrete assurance of future support. A hint from them that he might form a league with Venice brought the immediate response, 'We are willing to have a good understanding with the Signoria, but not, on any account, in writing, because it would be bad for them and for us, as the others [that is, the French and their allies] would draw still closer together.'[83]

At least the five surviving ambassadors (Paolo Pisani had died in early February) were spared the humiliation that they had feared might be inflicted on them at the ceremony of absolution on 24 February. They came dressed in scarlet before Julius and the cardinals, who were seated on a tribune erected under the portico of St Peter's, knelt on the steps of the tribune and kissed the pope's foot. Domenico Trevisan, speaking on behalf of all of them, asked for Julius's absolution and blessing. Then all the terms that had been agreed were read out, in such a low voice, they were pleased to note, that even Julius could scarcely hear. This took about an hour, with the ambassadors having to stay on their knees throughout, a posture made no more comfortable by the press of people against them, with some spectators leaning on their shoulders. One by one, they then took an oath on behalf of Venice to observe the terms, with their hands on Julius's hands resting on a missal. After the ambassadors had been blessed by

Julius, and kissed his foot and his cheek, the doors of the church were opened and they were led up to the high altar of St Peter's, where they knelt in prayer, and then to the chapel of Sixtus IV, where they heard a high mass. Julius did not come with them, 'because His Holiness never stays at such long services'.[84] Returning to the portico, they found the papal master of ceremonies and the papal household waiting for them, with the households of several cardinals and many Venetian prelates. To the music of trumpets and fifes and other instruments, they made their way home, where the celebrations went on in a throng of visitors and musicians and buffoons.[85] All the court, all of Rome, was rejoicing, it seemed – except for the French.

9

— · —

'*Fuori i Barbari*'

Until Faenza, Rimini, Cervia and Ravenna were once more under the direct rule of the Church, the central reference point for Julius's relations with other powers had, from the first months of his pontificate, been Venice. Now that obsession had been satisfied, it was replaced by another: driving the French out of Italy. There may be no record of his ever having uttered the actual words 'fuori i barbari', but he was quite explicit, on many occasions, about his desire to be rid of the French.

In the past, he had sometimes expressed distrust of the French, and been wary of their power, but he had needed that power to help him to achieve that which he most desired. Within a month of the Venetians withdrawing from the Romagna, he was denouncing the French as insatiable, not content with their own possessions, and declaring it necessary for him to guard against their insolence.[1] But it took him several months before he finally came out in open hostility to them. Absolving Venice was the prelude to an attack on French power in Italy that would last until they were driven from the duchy of Milan, the pro-French regime in Florence had been overturned and their other most loyal Italian partisan, the Duke of Ferrara, had come as a defeated supplicant to Rome. Before this was achieved, Julius himself would face humiliation and defeat, and lose control of his great prize, Bologna.

There were several reasons for Julius's hesitation before he began an open assault on French interests. One was his wish to keep up the pressure on Venice, to enable him to extract all the advantage he could in exchange for her absolution. Another was the desire to see Louis back on the other side of the Alps with much of his army: in July 1509 he was 'counting the hours until the King of France leaves Italy'.[2] A third was his calculation that, for all Maximilian's failings, it would still be better to try to woo him from his alliance with France. Not the least important reason was sheer confusion about what to do next.

The French may not have suspected the full extent of his hostility to them at first – they may still have been working on the assumption that, however much he might kick, in the end Julius would always have to throw in his lot with them. They were not too pleased by the news of the Venetians yielding up the Romagnol towns, suspecting that there might be more to the transaction than met the eye, and Louis was very upset that the Venetian ambassadors were to be received in Rome. Rumours reached France of the pope's wish to divide Maximilian from Louis. 'The pope could not be behaving worse towards us', lamented Florimond Robertet, Treasurer of France and one of Louis's most trusted counsellors.[3]

Until Louis was safely out of Italy, however, Julius's policy seems to have been to maintain some appearance of friendship for France, and to win over Maximilian – and free himself from his remaining obligations under the Treaty of Cambrai – by exhorting Venice to surrender Treviso and Friuli to him. Once these lands had been restored, a league against the infidel could be formed, comprising Julius, Maximilian, Venice and Ferdinand of Spain. France, he said, was not apparently interested in a crusade.[4] In fact, Louis declared that he was interested in a crusade, very interested, and was ready to be first in the field with an army and a fleet. But first he had to escape the summer heat of Italy, which was making him ill. Before he crossed the mountains, however, he wanted to know if Julius intended to abide by the terms of the League of Cambrai. Not only did Julius reply immediately that he did intend to do so, he made a new bilateral agreement with Louis, for the mutual defence of each other's lands in Italy and for the regulation of disputes over benefices.[5]

This agreement had been negotiated with Louis by Cardinal Alidosi, who had been sent to join Louis in Milan. On his entry to Milan on 12 July he had been much honoured, though the French anticipated that there would be more than a few arguments with him. Negotiations proved to be more amicable and easier than expected. No details leaked out, but 'from all the external signs, one can see great satisfaction on each side, and it's believed they are working out a clearer understanding to live with one another

better than they have done up to now.'[6] The cooperative attitude
on the papal side came from Alidosi, not Julius. In Rome, Julius
was rejoicing in unfounded reports that Rouen, who had been
very ill, was dead, and declaring 'I don't want to be the chaplain
of the French.'[7] In Milan, and as he accompanied the king to the
foot of the Alps, Alidosi, who favoured an alliance with France
and asserted that Julius did too, was working hard to arrive at
an agreement with Louis. He claimed to have been so successful
that, in future, those who had been working against the French in
Rome would no longer be given any credence.

As a result of his efforts, Alidosi maintained, relations between the pope and the king could not be on a better or firmer
footing. Louis had promised to use all his power to defend the
Church and to help in all matters in which the pope had an
interest, and, in return, Julius had promised to defend the states
of the king (who was prepared for him to come to similar arrangements with other princes, including Maximilian). Alidosi claimed
that Julius was no longer suspicious of Rouen, for experience had
shown that he had made no attempt to depose him, and he could
not reasonably hope to become pope when Julius was alive
anyway: the other Christian princes would never agree, and no
council would elect someone such as Rouen pope; they would look
for an independent figure. Julius had received from the king
everything that Alidosi had asked for. All the disputes about
benefices had been settled as the pope wanted.[8] In future, Julius
was resolved to stick with France, rather than Maximilian, who
was too unstable and unquiet. The French, too, said that the
agreement had cleared away all possibility of further dispute on
the question of mutual obligation to defend each other's territory,
and that Julius would have his way in outstanding disputes about
benefices. 'They set great store by this agreement with the pope',
a Florentine envoy reported, after a conversation with Cardinal de
Clermont, who was hurrying to Rome on the orders of the king to
have the agreement ratified.[9]

De Clermont arrived in Rome on 20 August, and was fêted
by the pope, treated 'like the beloved disciple'.[10] Within three
weeks, the new agreement was already on the rocks, with Julius
accusing Alidosi of having been duplicitous in the negotiations –
the many fine words that he had written were not proving true.
The French, too, blamed Alidosi, saying that much of what he
had promised them was not being fulfilled.

What seems to have happened is that Alidosi exaggerated to

the French the pope's readiness to make concessions in order to
secure harmonious relations with them. If, in the short term,
Julius wanted to preserve at least outwardly friendly relations
with them, his intentions in the long term were anything but
friendly. Alidosi, his closest confidant, must have known this.
Perhaps he relied on his influence over the pope, thinking he
could bring him round to the policy of friendship with France
that he himself favoured. Such was Alidosi's reputation, that
the general assumption was that he had simply sold out to the
French: his personal haul from the negotiations was the bishopric
of Cremona, worth 5,000–6,000 ducats a year, and an abbey
worth 2,000 ducats in the Bresciano.

The main bone of contention was what exactly Alidosi had
promised Louis concerning the disposition of benefices that would
fall vacant in his dominions in future. Julius had been given
his way in the current disputes, so that Cardinal Farnese was
promised possession of the bishopric of Parma, for example, and
the rich abbey of Chiaravalle near Milan would go to San Pietro
ad Vincula. In return, Louis d'Amboise, Bishop of Alby, nephew
of Cardinal Rouen and brother of Chaumont, the viceroy of
Milan, would at last be given the cardinal's hat that had been
withheld since the publication of his election in May 1507.[11] Louis
was 'adamant that [Alidosi] had given him an absolute assurance,
in the pope's name, that His Holiness would dispose even of
benefices which fell vacant at Rome as the King pleased'.[12] This
was not what had been reported to Rome. There it was said that
Louis had promised not to interfere in appointments to benefices
in the Milanese, at least.

It is hard to believe that Julius would have authorized
Alidosi to give such a sweeping assurance as Louis maintained he
had been given. It is also hard to believe that Alidosi, however
confident he may have been of his influence with the pope, could
have given such an undertaking in good faith. No matter how
anxious he may have been to ingratiate himself with the French, if
he had made such promises cynically, he must have been aware
that it would soon become clear that Julius would not comply
with Louis's requests, and he himself would lose any credit he had
hoped to gain with the French by lying to them. Even at the
French court, it was believed that Louis was mistaken, that he
had taken literally, as a firm commitment, what had been meant
as a polite general remark: that Julius would never elect anyone displeasing to him.[13] But he could not be budged from his

opinion, and Rouen, Robertet and other French officials tried discreetly to limit the damage to relations with the pope. When Louis, for example, ordered Chaumont to withhold the income from all benefices held by cardinals in Lombardy, Rouen wrote to countermand the order. For his part, the papal nuncio was careful not to report Louis's outbursts against his master, so as not to pour oil on the flames.

At the papal court, no one seems to have been trying to cool Julius's anger, and he was just as obstinate as the king. When the French ambassador, Gimel, spoke to him about a number of benefices that Louis considered to be politically sensitive appointments, Julius became furious, ending up by saying that if Alidosi had made any promises, he was the one whom he should go to see. 'Holy Father', the ambassador said, 'since my king can't ask for anything from Your Beatitude, there's no point in him keeping an ambassador here. I can go away.' 'Go when you like', Julius replied, 'We can manage well enough without you.' He was just as annoyed with Ferdinand, who was asking for men of his choice to be given benefices that had fallen vacant at the papal court. The Spanish ambassador, Vich, unwisely became over-insistent, and Julius drove him out of the room with insults. Vich came back a few days later to speak about yet another benefice, and Julius, in great indignation, exclaimed, 'These two kings . . . aren't content with being king, they want to be pope as well, and give benefices and occupy lands and do what they please. By the body of Christ, the Venetians are not ruined yet, they're not ruined yet.'[14]

The French cardinals and ambassadors did not let up, importuning Julius to give way to Louis over the benefices and to give the hat to Cardinal Alby, mixing promises about what Louis would do in return with threats about how he would be coming to Italy with a powerful army. Julius would not be moved, believing that 'if he gave way, it would be no small ruin to his reputation, because not only would he not have power over the benefices of that kingdom, but the other Christian princes would take example from this and want to follow the same road.' He wanted all the benefices in question to be disposed of as he chose, and 'then he would not fail to show his clemency and kindness.'[15] He still refused to receive Alby as a cardinal, although he did receive another French cardinal who had been elected at the same time and was making his first visit to the papal court, René de Prie, yet another Amboise *nipote*.[16] Hearing that the French might come to attack Siena, at the request of Florence, did not improve his temper, because he had Siena under his protection. He spoke of sending his own troops to defend Siena, and ordered Cardinal Alidosi, who had returned to his legation of Bologna, to refuse transit through Bolognese territory to any French troops. Louis 'wants to make us his chaplain but we'd sooner be martyred', he told Prospero Colonna. 'The King of France is a powerful king, but God is more powerful and greater than he.' And then he repeated the refrain 'The Venetians aren't ruined yet.'[17]

The Venetian ambassadors who reported these diatribes did not allow their hopes to be raised too high by such remarks. They believed that Julius thought Venice was wasted and exhausted, that he had little use for Maximilian, holding him to lack both strength and political skill, and that he felt he had to persevere with France, although he was still very wary of Rouen. In their opinion, his own pusillanimity, and avarice, were preventing him from deciding on any other course. He was just living from one day to the next, hoping that Rouen or Louis might die, or that something else would turn up in his favour. Despite repeated denunciations of the French by Julius – that they aspired to the monarchy of Italy, that Louis was too powerful in Italy now – the ambassadors held to their view that he would not break with France. Even when he spoke of joining with Venice and Maximilian to drive the French over the Alps, they still believed that he was too afraid of losing the revenues from France, afraid that the French might withdraw their obedience from Rome, might summon a council.[18]

The French, however, did not dismiss the possibility that Julius might mean what he said, and made some attempt to win him round. A sequestration order on some benefices in Milan (it is not clear whose) was lifted in late December 1509, and, in return, the inoffensive Cardinal Alby, who had been sitting in Rome not knowing what to do, was given his cardinal's hat at last on 9 January 1510. Louis decided to send a new ambassador to Rome, 'to sweeten the Pope'.[19] The new man, an Italian, Alberto Pio da Carpi, had instructions to consult with the pope about Louis's plans to come to Italy in the spring; it was hoped that this would alleviate his suspicions. If he persisted in his hostility, Alberto's mission would justify the French in the eyes of God and man. Louis declared that he could not believe Julius would unite with others against France, but 'should he be so mad, I believe God would allow him to do this for the punishment of his sins.'[20]

News of Julius's decision to absolve Venice was greeted at the French court with anger at first, but then Rouen decided to make the best of it, arguing that the only one whose interests would suffer was Maximilian, and this would only serve to make him draw closer to the French. Attempts to look on the bright side were encouraged by letters from Cardinal Alidosi assuring the king and Rouen that Julius would stand by the agreement made at Milan, that he would continue to regard the Venetians as political enemies, and that he wanted to be united with Louis.[21]

The papal nuncio in France, Angelo Leonino, was also trying to maintain the alliance, and urged Julius to write to Louis assuring him that he intended to abide by the provisions of the League of Cambrai. As far as the pope was concerned, however, his only remaining obligation under the league was to join in an expedition against the infidel, and he wanted nothing to do with anything else. To the French envoy, Alberto da Carpi, he said that he was prepared to observe the agreement made with Louis before his departure from Italy, at least the provisions for the mutual defence of each other's states; but to the Venetian ambassador, he admitted that he had only said this to play the French along. By confiscating the income from benefices, he argued, the French had already breached that agreement, and it was no longer in force.[22]

Now he was going to set about cutting the French down to size, he said. First he was going to try to disrupt negotiations in train between England and France. In this, the English ambassador in Rome, Christopher Bainbridge, the Archbishop of York, who was eager for papal favour (desperate for a cardinal's hat, the Venetians believed), would be a useful instrument. Bainbridge suggested the outline of a brief to King Henry to dissuade him from an alliance with France, which Julius then asked the Venetian ambassador to work up into a draft. Precautions were taken to ensure that Alidosi should not hear of it, and when the draft was ready, and Julius had edited it himself, he made his own secretary, Sigismondo de' Conti, swear, as he held his life dear, that he would not reveal the contents to anyone, but draw the brief up personally.[23] Because the French were intercepting letters and keeping all travellers passing through France on their way to England under observation, Bainbridge had the brief bound up in the cover of a book so that it could be carried safely. Another brief to Henry was also prepared, probably one that could be safely shown to the French. Bainbridge was kept supplied with useful news items, such as the report from Leonino that Louis was sending 20,000 scudi to suborn Henry's councillors.

In Germany, Julius was planning to stir up opposition both to French influence and to that of Maximilian. He wanted to distract Maximilian and impede the grant of subsidies to him by the Imperial diet. Here he hoped to use another ecclesiastic as his instrument, Matthaeus Lang, the Bishop of Gurk, one of Maximilian's chief ministers. Great rewards, rich benefices and a cardinal's hat had been offered to him, and Julius had written to him, trying to win him over. Lang proved singularly resistant to such blandishments, both at this time and in the future.

More direct action against the French was soon being planned: an assault on Genoa. Julius may have had such an enterprise in mind for some months before he began active preparations for it. In January 1510 he had remarked to Bainbridge, who was using the Genoese bankers, the Sauli, to transmit letters from France, that 'they are good men, but still subjects of the King of France, although we hope one day they will be free.'[24] Asked by Alberto da Carpi to agree that Genoa should be included in the lands of the King of France covered in the agreement that Alidosi had negotiated with Louis, he refused, saying that 'it would not be fitting', if the Genoese were to rise against the French, 'that I should take arms against my own homeland.'[25] It was not until the middle of May 1510 that he proposed to Venice a joint expedition to provoke a rebellion in Genoa. He expounded the reason for his scheme to the Venetian ambassador Donà at great length, and with great enthusiasm, telling him about the Genoese factions and how he believed they would unite against Louis to recover their liberty, and about the impact the loss of Genoa could have on the French. It could, in his opinion, ultimately lead to the French losing Milan.[26]

So confident was he of success, and of the readiness of the Genoese to revolt, that he predicted that everything could be over before the galleys that the Venetians had agreed to send even arrived. Ottaviano Campofregoso, who hoped to be installed as Doge if the enterprise were successful, came to Rome secretly to discuss how to incite the rebellion; and Julius gave Marcantonio Colonna a *condotta* and sent him to put his troops in order in Tuscany, while himself seeing to raising several hundred infantry in Rome.

Initially, the enterprise looked promising. There were signs of unrest in Genoa, and Marcantonio Colonna took La Spezia, Sestri and Chiavari on the Ligurian coast, while the French seemed to be making few preparations to defend the city. Appearances were deceptive. At least two of the major Genoese families, the Adorno and the Spinola, sided with the French (it was said because Julius had refused to give them money), while Louis soon began vigorous preparations to raise large numbers of troops, 10,000 infantry, as well as men-at-arms. The papal force comprised about 80 men-at-arms, 60 crossbowmen and 600 to 800 infantry, scarcely enough to take a city the size of Genoa unless they were joined by partisans of the Fregosi exiles, and there were no signs of them. Some of the papal troops embarked on the galleys at Chiavari in mid-July, and then the fleet kept near the shore to protect the rest of the troops as they advanced up the coast. On 19 July the fleet approached Genoa, to be met by a more powerful fleet of Genoese and French vessels, and by bombardment from the shore. After an exchange of fire, the Venetian and papal fleet went to Sestri to protect the troops. While they were hesitating about what to do next, they heard that 400 French horse were approaching, which they felt unable to confront. The expedition retreated south, and many of the men making their way back by land lost their horses and arms as they struggled to reach safety. With a superior French fleet on the alert, and 3,000 infantry having entered Genoa itself, the French were confident that it was secure.

Undaunted, however, by what had been little short of a fiasco, Julius was eager for a second attempt. Thinking that the Genoese had been reluctant to act in concert with what looked like a Venetian fleet, he put on board a papal commissioner, Francesco Ghiberti, and gave the Venetian commanders papal banners to fly. A message came from Genoa that the Genoese were ready to revolt, but wanted substantial forces nearby on land before they would do so. Julius had been trying to raise thousands of Swiss infantry all summer, and promised that they were on their way to Genoa. Relying on them, he raised even fewer troops to go with the fleet than the last time. Enthusiastic as ever, he told the Genoese exiles to leave all the planning to him, assuring them that he knew what he was doing. They were not too sure that he did, but nobody had the nerve to challenge him. Julius went up to Civitavecchia with the fleet, made final arrangements there and sent it off on 24 August.

This second expedition had even less success than the first. No foothold could be taken on the Riviera; it was well guarded by the French fleet, which also discouraged partisans of the exiles from showing themselves. The leaders of the expedition decided to try their luck at Genoa, but changed their minds when they heard that reinforcements had entered the city. They sent a messenger to find the Swiss that Julius had assured them were on the way, and contemplated filling in the time before the reply came, and finding some fresh supplies, by raiding the coast of Provence. (In fact, the Swiss, claiming that they had not been paid all that had been promised, turned back before they ever got near Genoa.) An encounter with the French fleet put an end to the idea of raiding. By this time there were, it was said, 5,000 French infantry in Genoa, Savona and along the coast; and with no sign of the Swiss, and the fleet running out of food and fresh water, the expedition withdrew to Piombino, and then to Civitavecchia.

Still Julius did not give up; instead, he insisted that another attempt should be made. The papal commissioner, Ghiberti, claimed to have intelligence that the Genoese would rise if the fleet appeared offshore. Leaving Civitavecchia in great secrecy, the fleet kept away from the coast, to try to prevent the French from learning of their coming until the last moment. On 24 October several Venetian galleys advanced into the port of Genoa carrying infantry, but as they approached the land, the Genoese exiles, seeing the harbour filled with armed men who gave every indication of being prepared to resist them, and not detecting any hint of a rising in their favour, changed their minds at the last minute and asked to be taken away again. They had obviously lost all heart for the entire enterprise, but continued to make a number of unrealistic demands on the Venetian commanders, in the hope, as the Venetians believed, that their requests would be refused, but that it would be the Venetians, not themselves, who would take the blame. By now, the weather was breaking, with the first winter storms making the seas unsafe, and there was nowhere on the Ligurian coast where the fleet could take shelter. The Venetian commanders – no doubt to the relief of the Genoese exiles – insisted on turning south. By the time that they were off Tuscany, Julius was desperately ill, and was in no condition to insist that they try again, even if he had wanted them to.[27]

Had he been well, even he might have conceded that it was not the moment to make a fourth attempt, for he was now openly at war with the King of France, and the campaign that was being fought around Bologna and the duchy of Ferrara was going badly for him.

Julius's main motive for attacking Alfonso d'Este, Duke of Ferrara, was basically the same as his main grievance against Giovanni Bentivoglio had been. Although Alfonso was subject to the papacy, he was acting independently of, and to Julius's mind, against the interests of, the papacy in his relations with other states. More specifically, he had sought the protection of France, and become a virtual client of France at the moment when Julius was meditating a campaign to expel the French from Italy.

Up until the summer of 1509 relations between Julius and Alfonso d'Este had been fairly friendly. Even the problem of Cento and La Pieve, the former lands of the bishopric of Bologna that Alexander VI had given to the Este as a dowry for Lucrezia Borgia on her marriage to Alfonso, had not generated as much heat as might have been expected. Julius had resigned the bishopric of Bologna in 1502 rather than consent to their loss, but as pope, he did not want to lean on Alfonso's father Ercole too heavily in order to get them back for the bishop, who was now Cardinal Ferreri. In November 1506 Alfonso, who had succeeded to the duchy in January 1505, came to terms with the pope over Cento and La Pieve. He was to keep them, in return for other property that he would cede to the bishopric of Bologna worth 2,000 ducats a year, and a payment of 20,000 ducats to the pope.[28]

After the expulsion of the Bentivoglio from Bologna in 1506, Julius was worried that they might find refuge in Alfonso's lands. Annibale Bentivoglio was married to Alfonso's half-sister, Lucrezia, the natural daughter of Ercole d'Este, and did, indeed, go to Ferrara. Julius suspected that he was being visited there by many Bolognese. It was an awkward position for Alfonso, for he had either to turn away his brother-in-law or bring down an interdict on his city. He chose to pretend that he did not know that Annibale and his brother Ermete were there, refusing to receive them; and they played the game by staying hidden. Ermete soon left for Mantua, and Annibale and Lucrezia followed: Francesco Gonzaga's wife, Isabella d'Este, continued to defend her half-sister, Lucrezia, and cared less about placating the pope than Alfonso did at this time. Alfonso shouldn't pay any attention to the fact that he was related by marriage to Annibale, Julius told him: it was much better for him that Bologna should be in the hands of the pope than in those of a tyrant who, to keep his position, would always be hand-in-glove with the Venetians, and might even consider giving Bologna over to them. Giovanni hadn't shown much respect for their relationship, he said, referring to a persistent dispute over Cento between Bologna and Ferrara.[29] Nagging by the pope at length prompted Alfonso to take action against a gathering of Bentivoglio supporters on Ferrarese territory at Spilimberto. On several occasions in 1507 and 1508 Julius expressed satisfaction with support sent by the duke or his brother Cardinal Ippolito to the legate in Bologna when the Bentivoglio were on the prowl. The Golden Rose, an exquisite jewel awarded annually to a ruler who had deserved well of the papacy, was given to Alfonso in April 1508, because of his loyalty in helping to keep Bologna subdued. When he came to Rome, supposedly incognito, on a pleasure trip in September 1508, the pope welcomed him and wanted him to stay in the Belvedere.

In his efforts to persuade Alfonso that it was not in his interests to give succour to the exiled Bentivoglio, Julius tried to play on his fears of Venice. Just after Alfonso had succeeded to the duchy, Julius had been worried that the new duke would be too friendly to the Venetians, and Alfonso had written to assure him that a visit that he was to make to Venice was a purely ceremonial affair, customary for the Duke of Ferrara after his succession. He had already paid a visit there a few months before his father died. Julius had thought that this made him appear too submissive to Venice and he had warned him against encouraging the Venetians to increase their demands on Ferrara. Thanking him for his concern, Alfonso had replied that he had to cultivate the Venetians, because the French were so unreliable.

It is ironic, in the light of Julius's later assault on Ferrara because Alfonso was too close to the French, that in the early years of Alfonso's rule, he was almost encouraging him to cultivate Louis. He warned the duke not to make the French suspicious of him, and said that he did not mind him using Louis's intercession with Cardinal Ferreri in the wrangle over Cento and La Pieve.[30] It was after he became uneasy about Louis's ambitions in Italy that he began to worry about Alfonso's contacts with the French. Just at the time when Julius was avoiding meeting Louis in early 1507, the duke went to see the king. Told of this visit, the pope said that he could see Alfonso had to go, but he plainly wanted the visit to be as short as possible, and was concerned that Louis might ask Alfonso for money or troops to use against Genoa.[31] A little later, he was afraid that the French might be encouraging Alfonso to interfere in Bologna on behalf of the Bentivoglio.

By the summer of 1509 Alfonso was one of Louis's most

reliable Italian allies, and Julius was thoroughly annoyed with him. The duke had seized the opportunity of the disastrous turn in Venice's fortunes after the defeat at Agnadello to rid himself of the Venetian official, the *visdomino*, who had been the symbol of her pretensions to treat Ferrara as a virtual client state. Perhaps it would be better if he left Ferrara for a little while, Alfonso told the *visdomino* disingenuously, saying that he didn't want to turn him out but he would not be able to guarantee his safety. In the circumstances, Venice instructed the *visdomino* to pretend to be ill, and leave.[32] The Ferrarese ambassador was withdrawn from Venice, stressing Alfonso's filial devotion to her as he took his leave, and receiving a gracious reply from the Doge. Joining in the general plunder of Venice, Alfonso took possession of places that his predecessors had lost to her, including Este, the one from which his family took their name.

The Venetians were determined on revenge: for the Duke of Ferrara to behave in this way really did add insult to injury. As they began to recover the lands that he had taken, and seemed to threaten an attack on Ferrara itself, Julius was unsympathetic to appeals for help from him. Alfonso should never have got himself mixed up in the fighting in the first place, he said. If Venice did attack, he would send help, but he didn't think that she would, and Alfonso shouldn't provoke her.[33] He did warn the Venetians repeatedly that he would not tolerate their moving on Ferrara and other territory that Alfonso held of the Church, but also said that he would not concern himself if they confined their assault to the lands that he held of the Empire. At the same time, he was insisting that Venice should renounce all claims to special privileges or jurisdiction in Ferrara. Illogically, he even wanted a papal *visdomino* to replace the Venetian one. Apparently, he was not claiming that there should be a papal official exercising the jurisdiction over Venetian subjects and Venetian interests in Ferrara that the *visdomino* had had; and he did not need to create the office as a sign of the dominion of the Church, for the duke himself was the representative of the papacy. His reasoning seems simply to have been that Venice had had a *visdomino*, so he wanted one.

Alfonso managed to keep the Venetians at bay himself, inflicting a humiliating defeat on a river fleet that they sent against him up the Po in December 1509. Little help had been forthcoming from the pope. He had ordered his nephew Francesco Maria to take all his troops to Ferrara as the Venetian fleet

approached it, but this was only because he had heard that
French troops had entered the Ferrarese, and he countermanded
the order when Francesco Maria claimed that he needed 3,000
paid infantry if he were to make an honourable appearance and
asked for the money to pay for them.[34] This did not stop him from
wanting Alfonso to hand over the ships that he had captured from
the Venetians. Louis wanted them too. If Alfonso had been ready
to hand his prize over to anybody, it would have been to Louis,
because, by then, he was firmly committed to France, having paid
a high price for French 'protection'. At the time the agreement
promising Alfonso protection against all aggressors was made, in
July 1509, it was said to have cost him 45,000 ducats; a few
months later, Julius estimated that the duke had spent 80,000
ducats in what he called his 'mania' to have protection against
everybody.[35]

Once Venice had renounced all claims to keeping a *visdomino*
in Ferrara or exercising any jurisdiction there, as part of the
concessions that she made in return for absolution, Alfonso began
to flex the muscles that had been cramped for so long by the
constraints on ducal power imposed by the Venetians. One such
restriction had been their insistence that the dukes should not
make salt at the salt-pans at Comacchio. Salt was a very valuable
mineral, used for preserving food and in industrial processes, and
monopolies of its trade and taxes on its supply furnished some of
the most lucrative revenues of governments of the day. Alfonso set
about restoring the salt-pans at Comacchio, but Julius did not
want him to begin salt production – for one thing, it would
compete with the salt-works that he had just taken over from
Venice at Cervia. An increase in tolls that the duke imposed
on goods passing through the Ferrarese from Bologna or the
Romagna infuriated the pope. He showed himself to be 'very
dissatisfied with the Duke of Ferrara, because all the Romagnol
territories which have just been acquired have complained to him
that since they came under the government of the Church the
Duke is making them pay a third more than the tolls they paid
under the Signoria of Venice'. Julius 'has protested forcefully,
with bitter and ominous words'.[36]

Underlying the pope's anger, was his resentment that Alfonso
should have turned to Louis for protection. By April 1510 he was
saying 'that if he had the opportunity he would make him repent
having accepted the protection of France against His Holiness'.[37]
On receiving a report from the papal commissioner whom he had

sent to Ferrara that Alfonso had prevented some goods from passing through his territory from Bologna to Venice at the instance of Louis and Maximilian, Julius sent back the reply 'that if he didn't let these goods and everything else through without hindrance, he would make him understand his displeasure'. Neither Louis nor Maximilian 'had the right to give orders in Ferrara, but only His Holiness, and on this theme he spoke some very angry words, indicating such a bad disposition towards the duke that it is impossible to think how it could be worse'. He was clearly of a mind to bring Ferrara under the immediate government of the Church at the first opportunity.[38]

Julius openly admitted that this was true in early May, saying he had a mind to punish Alfonso and take his state from him, but now was not the time, and he didn't want the duke's subjects to suffer. He wanted them to be well disposed to the papacy, and ready to drive Alfonso out, so he couldn't make any moves with the help of France or others against Julius or Venice. Reports had reached him that Alfonso had said that he cared little for the pope, since he had the protection of France.[39] Louis refused to renounce this protection. Punishing, even deposing, Alfonso, and containing the threat from France, became closely linked in Julius's mind. 'These French have taken away my appetite and I don't sleep', he told the Venetian ambassador Donà, 'and last night I got up to walk about the room because I couldn't sleep, and I felt in my heart all would be well. I have hope things will turn out well, I've been very troubled in the past', concluding, 'It's God's will the Duke of Ferrara should be punished and Italy freed from the hands of the French.'[40]

It took some time for the Ferrarese ambassador in Rome to realize how serious his master's position was, partly because he could not understand why the pope was so annoyed. Perhaps it was mainly because of the salt at Comacchio, he thought; perhaps Alfonso should stop manufacturing it for a while. Neither he nor the French cardinals and ambassadors in Rome seem to have recognized how much Julius resented Alfonso's relationship with Louis – though Cardinal Aragona warned him that an assault on Ferrara was to be the first stage of a campaign against the French waged by the pope in alliance with Venice and Ferdinand of Spain.[41]

Aragona's information was accurate. Stirring up the Spanish ambassador with tales of Louis's ambitions to take the kingdom of Naples, Julius promised Ferdinand the investiture of the kingdom

if he would provide troops to be used against Ferrara. Cardinal
Alidosi was instructed to let the Venetians use their fleet on the
Po against Alfonso, provided they did not burn the countryside or
treat the people cruelly. The duke had many enemies in Ferrara,
he claimed, and Alidosi had contacts with them. Alfonso offered
to come to Rome to justify himself. Nothing could be more dis-
tressing to him, he said, than to hear that the pope planned to
settle their differences by the sword. Nothing would induce him to
use force to defend himself against the pope. He was ready to fly
to Julius's feet to clear up the misunderstandings that had grown
up between them.[42]

It was difficult for his friends in Rome to advise him, because
the signals from Julius were contradictory. At one moment, he
would say that he wanted Alfonso to come to Rome; at another,
he would say that if Alfonso came, he would be put in the Castel
Sant' Angelo. He said that he wanted to proceed against Alfonso
only judicially, that it would not be necessary to fight; and then
he sent infantry to seize Comacchio. Clerks were set to work
searching out documents to prove that Comacchio belonged to the
Church; he dismissed documents sent by Alfonso to show the
Este's rights to Comacchio as worthless, and was not pleased by
claims that they held it by virtue of a grant from the Emperor.

An attempt by Alfonso's men on St Peter's Day, 29 June, to
pay the census of 100 ducats fixed by Alexander VI, was rejected.
Even if 10,000 ducats had been offered, Julius said, it would not
have been accepted. Several years of arrears of the 'correct' census
of 4,000 ducats were owed, and he wanted Cento and La Pieve, as
well as compensation of 100,000 ducats because Alfonso had put
himself under the protection of France.[43] By late June there were
reports that bulls condemning Alfonso, as fierce as those issued
against Venice the previous year, were being prepared.

The campaign against Ferrara began in early July, with
Cardinal Alidosi directing operations as legate. Cento and La
Pieve were among the first places to fall; by the end of the month,
the papal troops had made substantial inroads on Alfonso's lands
east of Bologna towards Ravenna. The duke sent an offer to Rome
to relinquish his claim to Cento and La Pieve, to hand over all the
lands that he held in the Romagna, and to pay the expenses
incurred by the pope in the campaign, provided that he did not
try to take Ferrara. But Julius wanted Ferrara, and on 9 August
published a severe bull against Alfonso, excommunicating him as
a rebel against the Church, declaring all his dignities and fiefs to

be confiscate. His association with France figured largely among the indictments against him in the bull. He was blamed for adhering to Cardinal Rouen, who was said to be plotting to become pope during Julius's lifetime. If the French helped Alfonso, Julius threatened, he would excommunicate them too.[44]

French troops were assisting Alfonso, and, more than ever, Julius saw the campaign as really being a campaign against France. The acquisition of Modena, Alfonso's second city, by the papal forces, after some successful intrigue between Alidosi and the Rangoni, the leading family in the city, was greeted by the pope as a weakening of the position of the French. Hearing that Alfonso had managed to reach Ferrara with some troops, just when Julius believed that the city was ready to fall to him, he said he would rather that Ferrara were ruined than that it should fall into their hands.[45]

So important was the campaign to Julius that he could not bear to sit in Rome, away from the field of action. He decided to go to Bologna to supervise operations, perhaps to lead the campaign against Ferrara personally. In optimistic moments, he saw himself capturing Ferrara, and then taking his troops to drive the French out of Parma. (He now included Parma and Piacenza, held by Louis as part of the duchy of Milan, on his list of lands to be recovered for the Church, on the grounds that they had belonged to the exarchate of Ravenna.)[46] His decision to leave seems to have been taken quite suddenly: Paride de' Grassi said that he made his mind up on 1 September 1510 and left the same day.[47] But there had been talk in August that he might go – rumours had reached France before the end of that month. Perhaps he had been thinking about making the journey, and came to his decision when he was travelling through the Patrimony, as he often did in the heat of summer. He had left Rome for Ostia on 18 August and, from there, had had himself taken to Civitavecchia by the Venetian galleys being used in the expedition against Genoa. At Civitavecchia he gave orders for the second attempt on Genoa, and received the news of the fall of Modena. Was it this good news and the optimism it gave him that made him determined to go north? Within a few days of the news of the fall of Modena, the datary had been sent to Rome to summon all the cardinals, except the aged Caraffa, to join the pope on the way to Bologna.

Julius travelled quickly this time; he was unimpeded by the huge train that he had had with him in 1506, and there were none of the formal entries to cities and ceremonies of welcome to be gone through, and no Venetian-held territory to avoid. He reached Ancona on 9 September, and then went up the coast by sea to Senigallia, where he was met by ambassadors of all the cities of the Marche and Romagna. Then he took the most direct route to Bologna along the Via Emilia; passing rapidly, despite pouring rain, through Cesena, Forlì, Faenza and Imola. He entered Bologna, in magnificent style, on 22 September, with a procession modelled on the formal entry of 1506.

But this was not the triumphal return for which he must have hoped. He had been ill and discouraged when he reached the city. News had come of the failure of the second attempt on Genoa. The Bolognese were discontented, alienated from the papal administration by the abuses of its officials. Cardinal Alidosi, the legate, was deeply unpopular. Julius took to his bed, suffering from tertian fever, and though any good news, such as the advance of Venetian forces coming to support the attack on Ferrara, would cheer him up, his illness was causing concern.

Despite his illness, Julius attended to raising several thousand infantry for the campaign, and sending men and money to the papal camp at Modena. Those who should have been attending to such matters were doing little to further the progress of the campaign.

The nominal commander of the papal troops was Francesco Gonzaga, Marquis of Mantua and father-in-law of Francesco Maria della Rovere, who had been appointed in late September. He would not be much use. After a moment of glory at the Battle of Fornovo in 1495, he had accomplished little to sustain the military reputation that he had won that day. He was indecisive and untrustworthy, using pretended attacks of the gout and syphilis, from which he did actually suffer, as excuses for inaction. With no sense of loyalty to the pope, he was more concerned to maintain good relations with the French, being encouraged in this by his wife, Isabella d'Este. If it had not been for his relationship with Francesco Maria, and the strategic importance of his duchy of Mantua, it is doubtful whether Julius would have chosen him for his military abilities alone. So unreliable was he considered to be, that his elder son Federico was held as a hostage in Rome. The boy had been sent there in August 1510 when the pope had secured Francesco's release from imprisonment in Venice, where he had been held since being captured while fighting for the French in 1509. A more tangible pledge than the word of the Marquis had been required by the Venetians to support his promise that he would not serve the French against them again.

Julius was not being much better served by Francesco Maria, who was in charge of the papal camp near Modena, or by Cardinal Alidosi. Their rivalry and mutual dislike had turned to bitter enmity, and neither could stomach the idea of carrying out a plan suggested by the other. Anxious about their disputes, Julius sent a brief to his nephew saying that he did not have to obey the cardinal's orders. When Alidosi, who had been avoiding going to the camp, finally went there in early October, Francesco Maria seized him and sent him to Bologna under guard.

As soon as the cardinal arrived and saw Julius, he apparently won him round and was released. He still enjoyed his customary freedom of access to the pope. But he had lost a lot of influence with him. The protests of the Bolognese against him, and his maladministration of the money sent for the campaign, had had an effect on his standing. More damaging still, he was 'a fanatical French partisan, and the pope knows it'.[48] Nevertheless, whether because of his long-standing affection for Alidosi, or because he did not want to let fall a conspiracy that the cardinal had started up in Ferrara, Julius did not disgrace him. He was confirmed in his legation, and even given the bishopric of Bologna when it fell vacant in mid-October, much to the disgust of the Bolognese.

The day after this appointment, on 19 October, a French army under the command of the viceroy of Milan, Chaumont, arrived at the gates of Bologna. With him, eager to return home, were the Bentivoglio.

For some months after the absolution of Venice, Louis had continued to be reluctant to break openly with the pope. Julius was insisting that the king should make two pledges: that he would withdraw his protection from Alfonso, and that French troops would not cross the Po. Unless he received assurances on these points, he said, there could not be any understanding between him and the king.[49] Louis and Rouen tried to find a formula that would satisfy him, but without success. It appears that the king was genuinely reluctant to find himself at war with the pope. God had been gracious to him, he told the Florentine ambassador in May 1510: he had better health than at any time in his life, he had the prospect of an heir, he was wealthier than any King of France had been before and he was loved and feared by his subjects. All he had left to desire was the salvation of his soul, and the preservation of his honour and glory in this world. He could not think of any better way of securing these than by coming to the defence of the Church.[50] After Cardinal Rouen died, later that month, Louis and his councillors hoped that Julius would become less suspicious and more amenable, but their hopes were in vain. Making no attempt to conceal his satisfaction and relief at Rouen's death, which he said was good news for the papacy and for all Italy, Julius did not want to hear of any agreement. Even if Louis were to agree to his two points, he said, he did not want to be friends with him. The French wanted to make him their chaplain, but he intended to be pope.[51]

Now Louis began to say that if Julius forced his hand, and he found himself at war with the pope, he was sure that he would be justified in the eyes of the other Christian princes. On hearing of the threat to Genoa, he ordered Chaumont to prepare to use the Bentivoglio against Julius, and asked him to suggest 'all the ways you could use to hinder him and trouble him in his states as he is doing in mine'.[52] Yet still, when the first attack on Genoa failed, there were hopes at the French court that a brake could be put on the slide to open warfare with the pope. 'Although it was a great injury that the pope wanted to inflict on this crown, nevertheless it failed, and on the other hand, it would be dangerous to seek for revenge, because there can be no more justified action against a prince than one in defence of the Church, so that if His Majesty wished openly to attack it, he would have to fear bringing the whole world down on him.'[53] In August, Louis was ready to consider making peace, but Julius was not. The king decided to recall his ambassador from Rome, and to set about recovering the towns that Alfonso d'Este had lost to the papal troops, and to restore the Bentivoglio to Bologna.

Yet, once his army approached Bologna, he was ready to suggest a three-month truce. Chaumont had believed that if he came to the defence of Alfonso, Julius would retire from Bologna, leaving the field free for the restoration of the Bentivoglio. Had the pope been well enough to travel, he might have done so. As it was, Chaumont apparently had instructions to negotiate, rather than besiege the city with the pope inside it. Julius, still bedridden with fever and sick with chagrin at the position in which he found himself, was under considerable pressure from the cardinals, especially Alidosi, to make peace with France. Negotiations were opened with Chaumont, but the pope could not bring himself to agree to the terms that were being put to him. The sticking-point was Ferrara. He was ready to agree to observe the provisions of the League of Cambrai, he said, but he must have Ferrara.[54]

His resistance was stiffened when the Bolognese, sweetened by cuts in taxes and other concessions, took up arms to defend the city against the French. Two cardinals, Isuagles and Aragona, were appointed to lead the Bolognese, and they paraded, with armour under their cardinals' robes, through the streets. (Alidosi, mortified at not being appointed himself, joined in uninvited.) Hearing the people calling his name, Julius, shaking with fever, appeared on a balcony, blessed them and then, crossing his arms on his breast, seemed to commend himself to them. Returning joyfully to his bed, he was heard to say that now he had beaten the French.[55]

The French army did, indeed, begin to withdraw after a few days, though it was less the piece of theatre in Bologna that caused them to do so than the heavy rain that turned their camp into a quagmire, the protests of the English ambassador that if Chaumont attacked the pope, King Henry would attack Louis, and the approach of Venetian and Spanish troops who had come to support the pope.

The arrival of Venetian forces to help the pope needs little explanation. Despite the fact that there was still no formal alliance between the papacy and Venice, the Venetians, as the expeditions against Genoa demonstrated, were eager to retain the pope's goodwill and ready to comply with his requests for military support. His call for help against Ferrara fell on willing ears: the Venetians still had their own scores to settle with Alfonso. In the campaign against Ferrara, their troops would be of more use to him than his own.

The presence of Spanish troops requires rather more explanation. How did the forces of another signatory of the Treaty of Cambrai come to be supporting the pope? What had happened was that Julius had finally agreed to grant Ferdinand formal investiture with the kingdom of Naples, insisting that, in return, Ferdinand should send several hundred men-at-arms to join in the attack on Ferrara.

Attacking the city of Venice itself, annihilating the power of the Venetians, had not been one of the aims set out in the treaty, but by November 1509 both Maximilian and Louis were considering this both desirable and feasible. Ferdinand did not agree. Furthermore, he feared that the destruction of Venice could be only the prelude to a French attempt to subdue the rest of Italy.

But he was not prepared to join Julius in going to war against the French. He did not trust the pope, considering him to have a 'mala natura',[56] and was watchful for attempts by the pope to set him and Louis at odds. Containing the French, circumscribing Louis's options, was the policy that he advocated. Persuade, or force, the Venetians to surrender to Maximilian all he claimed under the Treaty of Cambrai, and there would be no further justification for an attack on her. She could then be received into the league, and plans laid for war against the infidel.

In February 1510 Julius had suggested that Ferdinand should join him in one of three confederations: with Henry of England and Venice, with Henry alone, or on their own. Ferdinand, he said, because he held the kingdom of Naples, had a special obligation to defend the lands of the Church. If he would enter a league with the papacy, he would be given the investiture of Naples. Ferdinand replied to these suggestions in March, saying that he could not possibly have Venice for an ally while she still held lands belonging to the Empire – he must keep on good terms with Maximilian, with whom he shared responsibility for their common heir, the young Archduke Charles. Nor did he want Louis for an enemy. By suggesting the second combination, Julius was trying to separate Ferdinand and Henry from Louis and Maximilian, and this, he believed, was the real motive behind the third suggestion – a bilateral alliance between him and the pope – and not the mutual defence of their lands, as Julius was saying. The pope was merely trying to eliminate the necessity for Venice to restore lands to Maximilian, and Ferdinand had nothing to gain from this. He therefore instructed his ambassador in Rome, Jeronimo Vich, to tell the pope that he was ready to make a league for the defence of the Church, but that there must be an explicit obligation to see that the conditions of the Treaty of Cambrai were fulfilled. Julius must know that the French were sowing suspicions against him in Maximilian's mind, saying that he wanted the kingdom of Naples for himself, that he was intriguing to rouse all the Italians against Louis and Maximilian and Ferdinand, and that he had made a secret league with Venice. Maximilian would be still more suspicious if he heard that Ferdinand and the pope had made a league without mentioning Cambrai. The pope should hold Maximilian in more account than he did: it was he who held the key to whether or not Louis would return to Italy in person. If Julius helped Maximilian and tried to make the Venetians satisfy his demands, then Ferdinand would be ready to make a league with him, provided he received the bull investing him with Naples beforehand or at the same time. Maximilian, Louis, Henry and the King of Portugal should be named as confederates.[57]

So little did Julius share the king's estimation of Maximilian's importance that he thought that Vich, in saying that Maximilian's claims must be satisfied, was exceeding his instructions. It was frustrating, too, to be told that the king wanted to guard against the French exercising a tyranny over Italy, and then to be given the cautious advice that he should show confidence in them, but feel none, and guard his back by allying himself with other powers.[58] The attack on Genoa was condemned by Ferdinand as just encouraging Louis to return to Italy, and he offered the French help in their defence of the city. Julius regarded Ferdinand as duplicitous, but still wanted an alliance with him. If he couldn't get Spanish troops to be used against Genoa, he said, he was determined to have them with him against Ferrara, and he made this a condition of granting the investiture.[59]

In consistory on 5 July 1510 he proposed that Ferdinand be given the investiture of Naples on the same kind of terms as those on which Francesco Sforza had once held the Marche: that is, on condition that he provided military assistance to the Holy See. The earlier investiture that Louis had received was now void. Ferdinand accepted that if he wanted the investiture, he would have to provide the troops that the pope was demanding, but he did not want this to be made an explicit condition; at least, he said, it should be put in a separate document from the bull. Get the bulls issued, he ordered Vich, before the pope changes his mind again.[60]

As a consequence of these negotiations, 300 Spanish lances were sent from Naples under the command of Fabrizio Colonna to help Julius in the campaign against Ferrara. Only when they arrived, and Fabrizio had taken an oath that he and these troops would serve the pope, would the bulls of investiture be handed over to Vich.

At one moment, while Chaumont had been encamped beneath the walls of Bologna, and Julius had seemed to have no alternative but to come to terms with the French, the pope had been so sick with vexation that he could neither eat nor sleep and had said that he wanted to die rather than be 'a prisoner of the French'; he would take poison first.[61] After the immediate danger had passed, and the French had left, he recovered his spirits and appetite and could sleep again, but he was still quite ill with tertian fever and haemorrhoids. As usual, he was being an uncooperative patient, eating foods that had been forbidden to him and threatening to hang his servants if they told the doctors. But it was his temper that it was thought might finish him off, for he frequently fell into a rage, calling on the devil. He improved a little in early November, when he had himself carried, against medical advice, to the house of a friend, Giulio Malvezzi, where he stayed until the middle of December. The doctors said that they could cure him within a week if he would only follow their instructions, but the only one to whom he would listen was a Jewish doctor, who apparently believed in minimal intervention and letting Julius's own naturally strong constitution deal with the disease. 'His constitution is miraculous; if he'd only look after himself for four days, he'd jump out of bed', wrote a Venetian observer.[62]

But he did not look after himself. He fretted at the lack of progess against Ferrara. Hopes that it could be gained through a conspiracy were dashed when the plot inside the city was discovered. Another of Alfonso's strongholds, Sassuolo, fell in mid-November, but then there was some indecision about what to do next. A council of war held in Julius's bedchamber concluded that the best plan was to take Mirandola before moving on to Ferrara.

Mirandola was a strongly fortified little town to the west of Ferrara and north of Modena, which belonged, together with another, Concordia, to the Pico family. A series of inheritance disputes and family quarrels had divided the family for many years. At the time, it was held by the widow of Lodovico Pico, who had been killed while serving as a *condottiere* with the pope's forces in December 1509. Shortly after Lodovico's death, Julius had sent a brief to the widow, Francesca, assuring her of his protection for herself and her two young children.[63] Francesca, however, was the natural daughter of Giangiacomo Trivulzio, the senior Italian commander in the service of the French. Consequently, although she had promised not to receive troops hostile to the pope, with her father's help she had brought French soldiers to Mirandola; and she was taken under the protection of Louis in early October. Alfonso d'Este took refuge with her for a few days about that time. Held for the French, Mirandola could be a great hindrance to the campaign against Ferrara.

Concordia fell after a few days' siege, on 18 December, but the papal commanders delayed in moving on to Mirandola. They – Francesco Maria della Rovere included – lacked enthusiasm for the enterprise, and seem to have infected Fabrizio Colonna with their sluggishness. Ignoring Julius's orders to press on, when Francesca refused a summons to surrender they decided to call off the attack. They had some excuse in the unusually severe winter weather, with harsh cold and deep snow, but this was not an excuse that the pope was prepared to accept. When the legate in the camp, Cardinal Vigerio, sent to say that it was impossible to take Mirandola or accomplish anything else that winter, he was furious, and determined to go to supervise operations personally. Nobody could dissuade him, though many tried, 'describing to him the danger, and the dishonour to the Church, and to him'.[64]

On 2 January 1511, saying 'Let's see if I've got as much balls as the King of France',[65] he set out from Bologna, borne in a litter, to San Felice, a few miles from Mirandola. There he praised the Venetian troops and held talks with their commander, cursed his own, and gave orders for artillery to be brought up. When it stopped snowing, on 6 January, he set off for Mirandola with trumpets sounding, intent on seeing his troops being paid, because he was sure that he was being cheated. Once he arrived, he decided to stay, and sent for his beds and the unfortunate cardinals who had come with him. Something was sure to be accomplished now, wrote the Venetian envoy to his brother, because the pope made everybody tremble, roundly cursing his men in terms that the envoy could not bring himself to commit to paper.[66]

Nevertheless, no amount of swearing could galvanize the papal commanders into doing their job properly. They were conspicuously less active than the Venetians in digging a mine and placing their artillery, and once they had got the latter in position, decided that it had to be moved. In the end, Julius asked the Venetians to set it up for him. To escape being yelled at, Francesco Maria avoided coming to see Julius and spent much of his time gaming with Fabrizio Colonna. Francesco Maria was evidently identifying his interests with those of the network of families, the Gonzaga and the Este, into which he had married: his mother-in-law, Isabella, was Alfonso d'Este's sister. Julius took to making his plans without even bothering to consult his own commanders, talking only to the Venetian ones whom he trusted. In fact, he ignored most advice given to him, followed his own mind, which was unpredictable, and acted immediately. Annoyed by the resistance of Francesca Trivulzio, he spoke of putting Mirandola to the sack, so that the 'poor infantry' could have some reward.

If Mirandola paid a ransom, he said, Francesco Maria would get it – 'I know how these things are done' – and he did not want that.[67] But nor did he wish to appear cruel, or to be cruel. Thus to spare the town from a sack, he decided that the best solution would be to demand the payment of a ransom that he would then divide among the infantry.

Those who were with Julius at the siege of Mirandola and saw him undaunted by cold and wind and snow and artillery fire, knew that they were witnessing a legend in the making. 'This is something to put in all the histories of the world', the Venetian envoy exclaimed to Alidosi, 'that a pope should have come to a military camp, when he has just been ill, with so much snow and cold, in January! Historians will have something to write about.'[68] So close were his lodgings to the walls that a shot from an arquebus passed through the kitchen where he was sleeping, wounding two of his grooms with fragments of stone. He moved to the quarters of Cardinal Isuagles, but the defenders turned their artillery on that too. The Venetians believed that the pope's own men were signalling to those inside Mirandola, directing their aim, because they hoped he would be driven away. But he was not to be disturbed by coming under fire, and soon moved back to his original lodgings. He would rather be shot in the head than withdraw one pace, he declared.[69] Nor could he be persuaded to stay indoors. He would stand watching the siege operations, barely covered by a sheltering roof, with the snow drifting around his feet, careless of the winter wind. In the light of his remark as he was leaving Bologna, Julius might well have enjoyed the comparison that Guicciardini made between him and Louis, though he might well not have liked Guicciardini's final comment.

> And it was certainly a notable occurrence, and something not seen before, that the King of France, a secular prince, still young and then in good health, nurtured in arms from his youth, at that time taking his ease indoors, administered through captains a war made principally against himself; and on the other hand, to see that the supreme pontiff, the vicar of Christ on earth, old and ill and nurtured in comfort and pleasures, should have come in person to a war waged by him against Christians, encamped by an unimportant town, where, subjecting himself like the captain of an army to fatigue and dangers, he retained nothing of the pope about him but the robes and the name.[70]

After two days' bombardment, envoys from Mirandola came to ask for terms on 19 January, and the town surrendered the next day. A ransom of 6,000 ducats was imposed, and Francesca was forced to leave. Her exiled brother-in-law, Gianfrancesco, was put in her place. Impatient to enter the city, Julius was hauled up a ladder over a breach in the wall, because he did not want to wait for the earth that had been piled behind the gates to be removed. Once the infantry entered, ransom or no ransom, it was difficult even for Julius to stop their plundering. Hearing that they were heading for a convent where the townspeople's valuables had been put for safekeeping, he had himself carried there and berated everyone around, including Francesco Maria in the hearing of his own men, and Cardinal Alidosi. It seemed he had to do everything himself. He reviewed his own troops because he was sure that he was being cheated – and, indeed, he was being cheated, according to the Venetian envoy. He ordered the infantry to leave the town, and went from house to house, making his men batter on the doors and telling the soldiers to come out or be hanged.

When Julius had first arrived at Mirandola, he had made people around him laugh by constantly chanting 'Mirandola, Mirandola'. Once Mirandola had been taken, the chant changed to 'Ferrara'.[71] He had been considering leading his troops there in person, but changed his mind and returned to Bologna instead – some said because he was afraid that, if his men were defeated, he might be captured. He reached Bologna on 7 February, travelling on a sled drawn by oxen. But Bologna was none too safe for him either, at that time, for the French were approaching again, and four days later he left, still drawn on the sled, and travelled to Ravenna.

It made sense for him to avoid the possibility of falling into his enemy's hands, but it meant that the campaign against Ferrara was not prosecuted with much rigour. He raised infantry and made plans, but, with Francesco Maria and Fabrizio Colonna as dilatory as ever, little was accomplished. Their inactivity made the Venetian commissioner who had to try to coordinate his men's movements with theirs despair. He didn't see how anything honourable could be achieved, because the papal commanders 'don't want to do anything'. 'There is no control in the papal camp, there's no will, there's no one who commands or wants to command, there's no one to carry out orders', there were no auxiliaries, and there was no fodder. The only commodity in good supply was wine; all other victuals were scarce and expensive.[72]

This lack of progress did not enrage Julius as much as might have been expected. For one thing, he was enjoying himself in

Ravenna. As ever, he loved being in a port, and spent a lot of time
on the seashore and looking at ships. He went on pleasure trips in
the area, too, experiencing an earthquake while he was at Cesena,
but refusing to regard it as a bad omen. There was also serious
business to be dealt with. On 10 March he published the names
of eight new cardinals, including Christopher Bainbridge, Archbishop of York, the English ambassador, and a Swiss bishop,
Matthaeus Schiner, who earned his hat by his work recruiting
Swiss infantry for the pope. The other six were Italian, largely his
own men.[73] He also created a ninth – Matthaeus Lang, Bishop of
Gurk – but it was by no means sure that he would accept, and his
nomination was not published.

Two days later, Lang arrived in Mantua to begin a series of
peace talks, which became the most important diversion from the
prosecution of the campaign against Ferrara.

King James of Scotland had helped to initiate discussions
about peace by sending an envoy, Andrew Forman, Bishop of
Moray, to act as a mediator. (James said that he wanted to bring
about peace between the Christian powers to facilitate a crusade.)
Forman would spend many months shuttling between Louis and
Julius, with no great success. He was described as 'a good man,
and very well-disposed to the pope, but as it happens he doesn't
understand Italian affairs very well, and he could be more astute
and experienced than he is'.[74] At least he made it possible to keep
some communication open between the pope and the king. He
came to see Julius at Mirandola, and was in the papal camp at
the same time as envoys from Maximilian and Lang.

Forman's principal concern was to make peace between
France and the papacy; Lang and Maximilian were concerned
with pressing for a settlement of Maximilian's claims against
Venice. It was Julius who was the proposed mediator in that
dispute: the Venetians were ready to let him negotiate on their
behalf, but Maximilian could not make up his mind. He proposed
holding a peace conference at Mantua to discuss all the issues
dividing the powers, an idea that Ferdinand backed warmly.
Louis was not so keen, saying that it was unlikely that the pope
would send a representative. He believed that Julius wanted to
win Maximilian over and turn him against Louis, a suspicion
fuelled when the pope ordered Modena to be handed over to the
charge of the Imperial envoy, Vert von Furst, in late January, and
sent Marcantonio Colonna to hold it for him. A brief to the
Modenese ordered them to swear homage to Maximilian, in order

to avoid the disorders of war:[75] patently the pope was reckoning that the French would not attack Modena if it was held for their ally, and presumably was not confident that his own forces could defend it successfully against them. This device also served to make Louis more anxious to emphasize his alliance with Maximilian; and, in the circumstances, he could not refuse to send an envoy to the diet.

Louis was quite right to suspect that Julius did not want to send a representative to Mantua. The pope wanted any peace talks to take place at his court, and wrote on 11 February 1511 urging Lang to come to Bologna. When Lang, and Louis's envoy, Etienne Poncher, Bishop of Paris, and Ferdinand's envoys assembled in Mantua in mid-March, Julius sent a trusted chamberlain – but only with the message that Lang would be wasting his time trying to conduct negotiations involving papal interests anywhere but at the papal court. The Spanish ambassadors urged him to go, assuring him that if the peace talks foundered because of Julius, their king would increase his support for Maximilian. One of them, Vich, who was usually resident at the papal court, left Mantua on 24 March to elicit confirmation from Julius that he was interested in a general peace. He was also to obtain a safe-conduct for Lang, who would wait at Modena for the pope's response. If it were favourable, he would go to Ravenna, but he would stay there only a few days if he felt that Julius was not being sincere. If he thought that there was a good chance of peace, he would summon the Bishop of Paris to join in the discussions.

The pope sent to say that he was pleased to hear of Lang's decision, but wanted to meet him in Bologna, where he said that he could pay him greater honour, and asked him to wait in Modena until the preparations to receive him were completed. Leaving Ravenna on 3 April, Julius intended to send his army from its winter quarters and direct it – under his personal supervision – against Bastia, a strategically important fortification on the Po that was held for Alfonso. Francesco Maria and the cardinals tried to dissuade him without success, but heavy rains, which filled all rivers and ponds to bursting point, did make him change his mind. He entered Bologna on 6 April, mounted on a fine horse, rather than the usual papal mule. The horse was frightened by the firing of artillery to welcome the pope and nearly threw him in the main square; Julius, bringing it back under control, looked more like a soldier putting his mount through its paces, it was said, than an aged pope with the cares of the world on his shoulders.[76]

Whether Julius did want peace is rather doubtful. What he seems to have been trying to do was to win Lang over, an important step in weaning Maximilian away from the French. He insisted that Lang should make a formal entry on 10 April, and during this he was paid great honour, passing through the streets accompanied by Francesco Maria, the papal guard, the households of the pope and the cardinals, and many Bolognese nobles. Lang had tried to avoid involvement in such a ceremony, quite possibly because he wanted to avoid the expense of ensuring that he and his entourage of 200 horse could cut sufficiently impressive figures: he had to borrow to pay his expenses. The following day, he was received in a public consistory, and then Julius sent him a present of dozens of cartloads of food and wine. More provisions were sent every day. Short of money as he was, Lang no doubt found these presents very welcome, but there was one thing Julius wanted to give him that he refused to accept – a cardinal's hat. The pope had the robes and a fine mule ready to send to him, but Lang said that he did not want even to consider accepting nomination as a cardinal until peace was made.

The peace talks were not going well. Lang gave offence by refusing to wear ecclesiastical dress, and by insisting on his dignity as a representative of the Emperor. It was said that he broke all the rules of protocol, by sitting down during his audiences with the pope. He pitched his demands high – first, that the Venetians should cede all territories to which the Emperor or the Habsburgs had a claim; then, that they might keep Padua and Treviso and the Balkan territories they held, in return for an immediate payment of 200,000 ducats and the census of 100,000 ducats a year. Lang's own comments on the negotiations speak of the difficulties of making any progress when the pope was laid up in bed with the gout, and of Julius's lack of real interest in a peace. The pope seemed to be spoiling for a fight, he wrote, 'but many believe that the pope longs for battle rather out of his anger and bad temper, than for any better or more well-founded reason.' He himself, he insisted, was sincerely trying for peace, and if Poncher heard any reports to the contrary, he was not to believe them.[77]

According to Guicciardini, when Julius deputed three cardinals, Riario, Isuagles and Medici, to negotiate with him, Lang refused to meet them in person, and sent three of his men in his place, 'as if it was beneath him to treat with anyone other than the pope';[78] but Lang's own account does not reflect such an attitude. He wrote that Julius deputed the three cardinals simply to report on the state of negotiations, together with the Spanish ambassadors, and did not mention any deliberate refusal on his own part to talk to them.[79] The day before the appointment of the cardinals, he had already decided to leave in three days unless the Spanish ambassadors could make a breakthrough, and it was only with difficulty that they persuaded him to stay a little longer. But soon he broke off negotiations, took leave of the pope and departed from Bologna on 25 April.

It may be that Lang was not aware of how much offence his behaviour was causing. It may be that he had come to Bologna sincerely ready to make peace. He moved away fairly slowly, waiting for news of the progress of Forman's shuttle diplomacy. Poncher thought that he might return to Bologna if those negotiations looked hopeful. But he also suspected that Lang might not want anyone but himself to have the credit for bringing peace.

Whatever Lang's motives, his presence in Bologna had at least brought a halt to hostilities between the two armies. Once he had left, the French were soon menacingly close to Bologna again. And, once again, Julius had to flee from the danger of being captured by them. A week after his departure, Bologna was lost, by the incompetence, and perhaps the treachery, of his nephew, Francesco Maria della Rovere, and of his favourite, Cardinal Alidosi.

When Julius left the city on 14 May, the Bolognese had seemed ready to fight for him. They sent letters after him, 'declaring as much devotion and loyalty to His Holiness as one could ever hope for'.[80] But on 16 May they refused to receive some troops of Francesco Maria that Francesco wanted to bring into the city, and increased their own guards at the gate to prevent them from forcing their way in. All winter, the papal, Spanish and Venetian troops had inflicted great damage on the Bolognese district, and they had caused acute shortages. The Bolognese had scant reason to see the papal troops as welcome defenders, and their refusal to accept them may have been the result of a fear of being plundered, rather than a manifestation of disloyalty. Using powers conferred on him by Julius, Alidosi raised a force of 2,000 Bolognese infantry under fifteen captains. On the morning of 20 May he put himself at the head of these men to lead them to join the papal army, but they refused to leave the city, saying that they wanted to defend their houses and families. The following day, Alidosi got the consent of the Forty (which he did not usually bother to ask for) to bring in 1,000 infantry and some light horse commanded by Ramazzotto, who had been particularly brutal in his depredations in the *contado*.

On hearing of this, the Bolognese people erupted. The supporters of the Bentivoglio spread rumours that all the papal troops were coming, and then put it about that Ramazzotto and his men were already in the city. The church bells rang out, and the Bolognese, crying 'Popolo, popolo', seized their arms and prepared to fight. Bentivoglio partisans captured one of the city gates, and sent to summon the Bentivoglio, who were waiting not far off. Papal partisans were armed too. Cornelio Pepoli rode through the crowd exhorting them to cry 'Giulio' and 'Chiesa'. A messenger whom Alidosi sent to inform Francesco Maria of what was happening was killed, and a group of soldiers that he sent was beaten back. Losing heart, he took refuge in the castle, and then fled the city. A signal-fire brought the Bentivoglio hurrying to Bologna, which they entered around midnight with many other exiles, to a delirious reception. The papal army slunk away, leaving their artillery and baggage trains behind them. The Venetian troops, endangered by this retreat – of which they were not informed by Francesco Maria until after it had taken place – were forced to leave theirs too, to facilitate their escape. On 26 May the governor of the new papal fortress at the Porta Galliera surrendered, and the people used the mines and ammunition that they found there to raze it to the ground.

No reprisals were taken against papal partisans. Two young men who had thrown down and burned a painted wooden statue of Julius from the façade of the Palazzo Comunale were sentenced to death (later commuted to banishment), and the statue itself was replaced by a painting of the pope. The legate's lieutenant, who had feared for his life, was treated with respect. Letters were sent to Julius and to the College of Cardinals, speaking of the devotion of the Bentivoglio to the Holy See. All that they wanted was to re-establish the government as it had been during their father's lifetime. (This they proceeded to do, abolishing the Forty and restoring the Sixteen.) But they also sent ambassadors, including Alessandro Bentivoglio, to Louis, to thank him for his help and ask for his protection. This he was pleased to grant, writing on 30 June to promise perpetual protection for the four brothers Annibale, Anton Galeazzo, Alessandro and Ermete Bentivoglio, and their descendants, and for the city and government of Bologna, against anyone who attacked their security or their privileges (saving the legitimate rights of the Church). In return for this protection, they were to help him in every enterprise, especially those undertaken to conserve his dominions in Italy, to grant transit and lodgings to French troops, and not to make an alliance with anyone without the consent of the King of France.[81]

In their letters written earlier in June to a number of cardinals who they hoped would be friendly, the Sixteen had asked them to try to mitigate any anger that Julius might be feeling.[82] Unless they were supreme optimists, they can hardly have expected him to be anything but furious, and bent on revenge. As soon as he heard the news from Bologna, he was planning to regroup his forces. He knew well where the blame lay. Francesco Maria was summoned to Ravenna, where Julius was staying, and roundly abused. Alidosi was ordered not to come to Ravenna, but, hearing that Julius was angry with Francesco Maria as well as himself, and afraid that he would lose his legation, came nonetheless, hoping that he could use his practised skill in manipulating the pope to shift the burden of blame on to his rival.

He reached Ravenna on 23 May. That morning, a consistory had been held in which Julius had appointed Cardinal Isuagles to replace him in his legation. He may have already heard the news as he rode through the streets, accompanied by dozens of armed men, on his way to seek an audience with the pope. Francesco Maria, who had just been with the pope, and, no doubt, had had a thoroughly uncomfortable time of it, met him and was greeted with a smile. Well aware what lay behind that smile, Francesco Maria, who had only three attendants, fell upon him and dragged him from his mule. The cardinal's escort was not prepared to attack the pope's nephew, and stood by while Francesco Maria and his men stabbed Alidosi, mortally wounding him.

So brutal an end evoked little sympathy. Even Julius, grieved though he was, and mortified that a cardinal should have been cut down in the street by his own nephew, would, it was thought, recognize that Francesco Maria had had good reason for what he had done. In Venice, according to a Mantuan agent, they blamed him only for having waited so long to do it.

Francesco Maria, who had hurried to Urbino, justified the murder in a letter to his father-in-law by saying that Alidosi's treacheries had put Julius, the cardinals, the whole of Italy in danger. He wanted there to be a full investigation, so that all

Alidosi's treacherous proceedings and his ingratitude to the pope could be brought to light. 'The affairs of His Holiness and of Holy Church had been brought to such a pass by his misdeeds, that I couldn't stand it any more.' Although the pope was thinking of taking action against him, 'I hope His Holiness will come to recognize what he perhaps does not recognize at the moment.'[83]

But, for the moment, Julius was too shocked and grieved to be prepared to consider any justification for the murder. And now, to add to this personal blow, and the political blow of the loss of Bologna, he was to be faced with the severest test of his spiritual authority that a pope could face. A group of dissident cardinals, acting in concert with the French, had announced that they were summoning a general council of the Church. Citations to the council were put up even in Rimini, where Julius had gone when he was told of Alidosi's death. No one dared to tell him.

10

Il Papa Terribile

The news of the summoning of a general council of the Church could not be kept from the pope for long. In any case, the summons did not come as a bolt from the blue. Ominous signs of preparations for it had been manifest in France for several months, and it had also become evident that a group of cardinals would be ready to defy Julius and take up the scheme. With hindsight, the first signs of impending trouble could be seen in the aftermath of Cardinal Rouen's death in late May 1510. Not only had his demise not brought about the improvement in Julius's attitude towards the French that Louis had hoped for, it had, directly or indirectly, given rise to growing ill-feeling and distrust between Julius and the French cardinals in Rome.

Even before Rouen had died, Cardinal de Clermont, one of his *nipoti*, had wanted to leave Rome for France; Louis had given permission, but Julius had not. He had not refused permission, the pope claimed, just issued instructions that if de Clermont did try to go, he should be arrested on the road. All the French cardinals wanted to return home once news of Rouen's death arrived, but Julius refused to let any of them leave. Other cardinals were being summoned back to Rome, he said, because there was important business to be dealt with, so he would not give leave to go to those already there. It was sensed that there was more to the matter than that: perhaps, thought the Florentine ambassador, the pope was afraid that if there was a breach with Louis, and the French cardinals were away from the papal court, they 'might stir up some trouble'.[1]

Probably one reason why the cardinals, and especially Rouen's three *nipoti*, de Prie, de Clermont and Alby, wanted to go was to ensure their share of the pickings from the rich estate that Rouen had left – 200,000 scudi in gold and silver alone, according to Alby,[2] and a rich collection of benefices and offices. But Julius wanted it too. Unless special permission had been given, a cardinal's estate went to the pope, not the cardinal's family. Rouen had obtained a brief conferring the right to dispose freely of his property, but Julius claimed that this had been given to him while he was in Rome in 1503 and related only to what he had accumulated up till then, not to what he had garnered from his benefices and the profits of his legations since. He wanted this treasure for use against the infidel, he said.[3]

Since the treasure was in France, there was small chance of the pope's getting his hands on it. He had more say over the disposal of other parts of Rouen's 'inheritance', and the attitude that he adopted annoyed the French cardinals still more. De Clermont asked for the legation of Avignon, and was refused; Alby asked for the legation of France, and was refused. Julius also avoided complying with Louis's request that the archbishopric of Rouen should be given to one of the late cardinal's *nipoti* by leaving it vacant, until, he said, he could find someone who would accept it against Louis's will. Other benefices were given to people calculated to annoy the king.[4]

All this was part of the pope's ever more manifest hostility to the French in the summer of 1510. Alby soon began to fear that if there was an open breach between the pope and the king, he and de Clermont, and possibly the other French cardinals too, would be arrested. At the end of June, de Clermont was arrested, as he was preparing to go hunting outside Rome; Julius evidently considered the hunting expedition to be a cover for flight.

Incarcerated in the Castel Sant' Angelo, de Clermont was questioned about allegations that he had conspired to make Rouen pope while Julius was still alive. Julius must have believed that there was something to these accusations, because his anger did not cool quickly, as it usually did. He refused to release him, saying his misdeeds merited a death sentence; and though he promised the cardinals he would spare his life, he threatened that he would be imprisoned for a long time.[5] The other French cardinals were also threatened with being sent to the Castel Sant' Angelo: as a body, when they brought letters from Louis asking for de Clermont's release; de Prie as an individual, when he asked permission to leave Rome; and Alby with Cardinal Cosenza, when letters critical of the pope that they had written were intercepted by the Venetians and sent back to Rome. Confronted with these letters after a meeting of consistory, they knelt before Julius to beg his pardon, which the intercession of the other cardinals obtained for them.

By mid-July, as Julius's hostility to Louis, and his estrangement from the French cardinals, became more open, there were no more Frenchmen in his household, and the French were going about Rome 'like dead men'.[6] At the French court, anger against the pope had reached such a pitch that 'withdrawing obedience from him, raising a council against him, bringing ruin on his temporal and spiritual power is the least they are threatening to do to him.'[7] The first step towards the summons of a general council of the Church was already being taken, with the calling of a council of the French clergy. Questions to be brought before it included whether the pope could legitimately make war on the King of France, and whether a pope who had bought the papacy and sold benefices, and was guilty of infamous conduct, could be considered a pope at all.[8] On 17 September the Chancellor of France gave a long discourse to the prelates assembled at Tours, recounting all the benefits that Louis had conferred on Julius, before and after he became pope. In it, he spoke of Julius's ingratitude: how he had broken the alliance made at Cambrai, without any justification, how he had roused the Swiss against the French, and tried to take Genoa, and made a league with Venice, and was attacking Alfonso d'Este, the king's ally.[9] This speech, delivered in the presence of the king, made clear what were Julius's real crimes in Louis's eyes. Apart from asking that representations should be made to the pope before the obedience of the French clergy was formally withdrawn from him, the prelates loyally gave Louis the response that he wanted. Julius was to be asked to put an end to the current wars and conflicts, and to summon a general council of the Church. If he did not, they asked Louis to call on Maximilian and other princes to join him in summoning one. The prelates were to reassemble in March at Lyons to hear the pope's reply.

Meanwhile, Louis was making other preparations for a general council, ensuring that he would have some cardinals on hand to lend legitimacy and weight to its summons. Among the cardinals heading north after Julius had ordered them all to join him on his journey to Bologna, was a group that had no intention of obeying him and was working in concert with Louis. On 27 September the king wrote to Florence asking that these cardinals should be made welcome there as they passed through on their way to Milan, where they were going for the 'welfare, union and repose of Christendom, the service of God and the restoration of the Church'.[10]

Not all the French cardinals were taking this route. De Clermont was still in prison; d'Albret was estranged from Louis, who disputed his family's claims to the kingdom of Navarre; and Alby did not join them either. Why he did not do so is not clear. In any case, he died in Ancona on 17 September – of poison, said the French, including his brother Chaumont, the viceroy; of drink, said others, for 'he drank for ten' and was finished off by the 'bad air' of the Marche.[11] His death provided an excuse for the actions of the two Spanish cardinals who were in the group of five heading for Florence rather than Bologna. Cardinals Carvajal and Cosenza wrote to Ferdinand that they were afraid of Julius, and that he was planning to kill all the ultramontane cardinals because he only wanted to have Italian ones. This likely story was confirmed, they claimed, by the deaths of Alby and of d'Albret – who was not in fact dead. It did not win them any sympathy from Ferdinand, who told them that they should rejoin the pope.[12] Of the remaining three, two were French, de Prie and Briçonnet, and the third, Sanseverino, had represented French interests at the papal court for several years.

Why were there men prepared to join with Louis in launching this most serious of challenges to the authority of the pope? For Briçonnet, the former chief advisor of Charles VIII, and de Prie, nephew of Cardinal Rouen, the reason was probably a feeling that their chief loyalty was to the crown of France rather than the papacy. Briçonnet had been one of the more outspoken cardinals in consistory, not afraid to defend French interests, or to challenge the pope on other matters either.[13] Sanseverino had identified his interests with France for many years – he had been one of the cardinals who accompanied Charles VIII to Italy in 1494. He had handled the business relating to benefices for France at the papal court, although he was not always on the best of terms with Louis. A somewhat abrasive character, he had crossed swords with Julius on a number of occasions: laying claim to an important abbey, Chiaravalle, that Julius wanted for his *nipote* Sisto, Cardinal San Pietro ad Vincula; and opposing the grant of lands to Niccolò della Rovere.[14] A secular-minded man, he will not have worried unduly about the implications for the welfare of the Church of what he was doing. Of the two Spanish cardinals,

Cosenza, Francisco Borgia, may have been genuinely concerned for his personal safety. He had, after all, been detected writing defamatory letters about the pope to Maximilian only two months before, and been threatened with imprisonment. Disappointed ambitions may have been the motive for the participation of the second Spanish cardinal, Bernardino Carvajal, in the cabal. A learned and capable man, he had a taste for politics and had represented the interests first of Spain and then, after he had fallen out with Ferdinand in 1504, of the Empire, at the papal court. He had been sent as legate to Germany in July 1507, but was recalled a year later, in semi-disgrace, suspected of being too keen to win Maximilian's favour to be a reliable agent of the pope.[15] He was known as an ambitious man who aspired to be pope, but his career seemed to be running into the sand, and he may have reckoned that associating himself with the call for a council was the best way to achieve the prominence that he craved. Of the five cardinals, Carvajal was the one who most obviously hoped to be elected pope by the council.

While the five cardinals were in Florence, Julius sent the datary, Francesco Argentino, to them, with briefs ordering them to go to Bologna. Although the replies that they gave apparently satisfied the datary, they immediately set off, not for Bologna, but for Pisa, and from there made their way to the duchy of Milan. They were still being cautious in revealing their plans, but the Florentines at least were able to make an educated guess that they might include a council. From Pavia, Carvajal secretly sent an envoy to Bologna to suborn other cardinals into joining them, but the man was captured and interrogated, and the documents he was carrying were seized. Thus Julius was given positive proof that the dissident cardinals were hoping to depose him and summon a council; they had already sent messages to Maximilian and to Henry VIII of England asking for their support. Negotiations were reported between Julius and the disaffected cardinals in Lombardy, but while in early January it was said in Bologna that they were seeking to be reconciled with the pope, in France later that month the story was that he had sent to ask them to return to Rome, promising that they would be well treated and given every guarantee they could wish. Their reply, the report ran, had been that they had left because they did not wish to be caught up in actions directed against Louis, and that when the pope was reconciled with the king, they would be ready to obey his commands.[16] A little later, the word in France was that Julius had even asked the cardinals to mediate for him with Louis, promising honours and benefices if they could secure a good peace for him, but claiming that he could make peace without them anyway, and could induce Louis to hand them over to him in fetters. The cardinals' response had been to urge Louis to make war on Julius, and then summon him to a council.[17]

The decision to convoke a council was not formally taken until 16 May, in Milan. Three of the cardinals, Carvajal, Briçonnet and Cosenza, with the proctors of Louis and Maximilian, declared that the council would open on 1 September in Pisa. General councils had always been recognized as the best remedy for the kind of ills that cried out for reformation in the Church, they said, but Pope Julius had neglected his duty to call one. Besides, the papacy itself was in need of emendation, and the responsibility for summoning the council therefore devolved upon the cardinals. Julius was asked to accept and confirm the convocation, and he and the other cardinals were urged not to obstruct the council. Because he had imprisoned one cardinal and threatened others, they could not tell him personally of the convocation, so the citation was to be fixed on the doors of churches in Parma, Reggio and Modena, to ensure that it came to his attention.[18]

The three cardinals present at the meeting claimed to have the support of six of their colleagues. Apart from Sanseverino and de Prie, they listed Philippe de Luxembourg, Adriano Castellesi, Carlo del Carretto and Ippolito d'Este. Three of these, however, Luxembourg, Castellesi and del Carretto, dissociated themselves from what had been done in their name. Even Ippolito d'Este, dependent as his brother Alfonso was on the support of France, did not declare his adherence, and kept his distance from the council. Only the original group of five cardinals were ready to proceed with preparations for it.

Nor did the presence of Maximilian's proctor at the meeting in Milan portend a broadening of effective secular support for the council. The announcement would have been made sooner, but for the hesitation of Maximilian. He needed French support and French subsidies if he was to make any headway in the war against Venice, but he also hoped that Julius might pressure the Venetians into giving him what he wanted in return for peace. Once he had associated himself with the convocation of the council, he pressed for it to be held somewhere under his jurisdiction, as he wished to attend it in person. In a letter to the Florentines in late September urging them to send representatives to the council, he said that he had summoned it, in his capacity as 'advocate of the Church', with the help of Louis and some cardinals.[19] But not until October did he actually appoint five prelates to represent him, and he was in no hurry to send them. Cardinal Sanseverino, who had gone to Germany to stimulate him into more active support, was sent away discontented in early November, with only fine words. Even if Maximilian had been more determined in his support, he had no power to command the clergy of the Empire to recognize the council, let alone attend it, and they showed no enthusiasm for it at all.

Ferdinand's opposition to the whole idea was unequivocal from the start. When Louis asked him to summon a council of the Spanish clergy, renounce obedience to the pope and join in the calling of a general council, he refused outright, and told Julius that he was ready to come to his defence.[20] He tried to protect Cosenza and Carvajal from the consequences of their actions, interceding for them with Julius; but once they had joined in the summons of the council, he considered that they should be demoted – they had offended God, the Church and the pope and were working for a schism.[21] This was genuinely abhorrent to Ferdinand, and he never wavered in his opposition, whatever his political differences with the pope.

No other monarchs backed the council. Henry VIII of England followed his father-in-law Ferdinand in rejecting Louis's overtures. The King of Poland, after consulting his clergy, decided that it would be dangerous for Christianity. But it was some months before it was clear that Louis would have so little success in attracting support for it, and the initial news of its convocation caused great consternation at the papal court. Some response had to be made.

Julius was not a man to dither in such circumstances. The threat had been discussed in consistory in late April, and there had been rumours in Venice in early May that he was considering calling a council himself. Once news reached him of the declaration in Milan, he announced that this was indeed what he intended to do. He would hold a general council to reform the Church. No time was lost: the matter was decided in consistory in early June, and even before he returned to Rome in late June briefs were prepared summoning a council to meet in the Lateran palace at Rome the following Easter. Julius may have been keener on the idea than some of his cardinals. They objected to his saying that he wanted reform to begin at the top with himself,[22] and rather hoped that the problem could be settled as part of a general peace.

The bull announcing the summons of the Lateran Council, dated 18 July, explicitly linked it to the convocation of the council to be held at Pisa. Only the pope could lawfully summon a council, and the convocation of 16 May was declared illegal; all who adhered to the Pisan council would fall under the interdict. The pope was summoning the Lateran Council to put an end to the danger of schism, to promote peace among Christians and to prepare for an expedition against the infidel.[23] Julius also wanted to begin proceedings for the demotion of the cardinals supporting the Pisan council, particularly Briçonnet, Carvajal and Cosenza, but the cardinals in Rome, wary of precedents, were not so keen. In consistory on 28 July it was decided that the College would send an envoy to them, saying that if they returned to Rome within sixty-five days and asked for pardon, they would be granted it, but if they did not come, they would be declared heretics and schismatics, and would lose their cardinals' hats and all their benefices.[24]

Soon all thoughts of the council were pushed aside, as a grave illness struck Julius, bringing him very near to death and making the prospect of a conclave seem imminent. He fell ill on 18 August with fever, a headache and vomiting. Within two days, he was so sick that he was believed to be dying. He was eating very little, and became extremely weak, barely breathing, unable to hear or speak. The food that he did ask for when he was conscious – sardines, salted meat, olives and wine – was thoroughly disapproved of by his doctors. When he was thought to be dying, they agreed that he could eat whatever he wanted, because they considered that it would make little difference anyway. He called for fruit – plums and strawberries and grapes – which he chewed avidly, without swallowing the flesh. Federico Gonzaga helped by pleading with Julius to take food from his hands, for his sake and for love of the Madonna of Loreto, and Julius's affection for the boy encouraged him to accept the broth that he offered him. This illness made him melancholy – at one point, he told Cardinal Riario that he wanted to die[25] – and one of his household prelates, Girolamo Arsago, Bishop of Ivrea, helped to raise his spirits by goading him, telling him that he was a coward, that he wanted to die for fear of the council, and remarking to Francesco Maria, in a voice meant to carry to Julius's ears, 'Since he wants to die, let's cut him to pieces quickly and plunder the palace.' He succeeded in rousing Julius to anger: he threatened to have Arsago thrown from the window.[26] When the pope felt stronger, his doctors were menaced with the same fate if they did not allow him what he wanted. One thing he wanted was wine. To have some, he played a trick on them, asking to be allowed bread soaked in wine; when this was brought, he drank the wine and told his attendant that he could have the bread.[27] By the end of the month, the speed of his recovery on his chosen diet of fruit and wine was causing astonishment. He was calling for instrumental music to be played to him every day, something it was said that he did not usually enjoy. Those around him were beginning to have to be careful what they said to him, because, as Julius began to feel more like himself again, they were in danger of provoking his characteristic thundering responses.[28]

The crisis of Julius's illness was an anxious time for his relatives. How far they were moved by genuine concern for his life, and how far by concern for the consequences for their own fortunes that his death would entail, is not clear. There were suggestions that he was being shamefully neglected by his family and servants, but the Mantuan agent who reported this also reckoned that Francesco Maria had helped to save the pope by keeping everyone up to the mark.[29] Julius's sister-in-law, Giovanna da Montefeltro, spent much time at the palace while Julius was sick, largely to intercede for Francesco Maria, whom he had not forgiven for the murder of Alidosi. Niccolò della Rovere also waited near the pope's sickbed. He, Francesco Maria and Felice were beneficiaries under a will that Julius made on 24 August; he was to have 10,000 ducats and the other two 12,000 each.[30]

Perhaps of more importance to Francesco Maria than the money, was the absolution that he was given by the pope. The cardinals were a great deal more sympathetic to him after he killed Alidosi than Julius was. Julius had refused to see him, and spoke of confiscating his lands. In mid-July Francesco Maria was summoned to Rome to answer before a tribunal of cardinals. He arrived the day before Julius fell ill, but the pope refused to see him. His defence for the murder was that Alidosi had been a traitor: a point of law had been found that declared that anyone who killed a traitor to the Emperor or the pope should have his or her freedom, indeed be rewarded, rather than punished.[31] A finding in his favour seemed very likely, but when Julius fell ill, Giovanna urged the pope to absolve her son, and on 20 August he agreed. A few days later, he finally agreed to see Francesco Maria and received him quite well, but he still had not truly forgiven him. Francesco came to lodge in the papal palace, but Julius did not want to see him much, or even hear about him, and said that he had no further use for his services.[32] The judges were more sympathetic, accepted the arguments and witnesses to Alidosi's treacheries brought forward in his favour, and acquitted him in mid-September.

The belief that Julius was dying brought about not only the usual flurry of negotiations among the cardinals in anticipation of a conclave, but also another customary accompaniment to the death of a pope, the fear of disorder in Rome. This time, however, instead of the Colonna and Orsini squaring up to each other as usual, they and other baronial families swore to put aside all disputes, ill-will, and 'the pernicious names of Guelfs and Ghibellines', to defend the 'Roman republic'. Fabrizio Colonna took the oath on behalf of the Colonna, and Giulio Orsini for Giangiordano and the other Orsini, at a meeting held on the Capitol, which they attended along with many leading Roman citizens and the officials of the commune of Rome. Four men from each district (*rione*) of Rome were to accompany the barons, at their request, to make representations to the pope and cardinals concerning the welfare of the city and people of Rome.[33]

Julius had made a policy of keeping his distance from the Roman barons. He was not hostile to them, but did not want to be dependent on either faction, the Colonna any more than the Orsini. Very few barons had been given *condotte*, and only Marcantonio Colonna had been given a command of any consequence. Not one Orsini *condottiere* had been taken into papal service, and Julius had adamantly refused members of the family permission to take up *condotte* that they had arranged with Venice, only relenting about May 1510. He had not appointed any cardinals from the four major baronial families either – the death of Cardinal Giovanni Colonna in 1506 meant that neither the Colonna, the Orsini, the Conti nor the Savelli had a representative in the College – nor had he appointed any from Roman citizen families. The only specific request that the barons meeting in Rome during his illness were known to have in mind was to ask for 'a cardinal each', which others considered reasonable, so strong was the tradition that the major Roman families should have members in the College.[34]

The discontent of the Roman citizens was of much longer

standing than that of the barons. Since the return of the papacy to Rome in the early fifteenth century, after the Schism, the powers of the communal government had been eroded by the papal government, and little of significance remained of its powers of raising revenue or administering justice. The prosperity of Rome may have been dependent on the crowds of outsiders who came to work in or around the papal court and administration, or came to transact business with them, but this made it no less galling for prominent citizen families to have so little effective part in the running of their own city. Julius had done nothing to appease these grievances. He wanted good order kept in Rome, and he took steps to ensure that grain was provided in times of shortage; but, in general, he did not pay the Romans much attention.

The documents recording the oaths taken by the barons and the citizens on 27 and 28 August made careful mention of the honour and glory of the pope and the Apostolic See, but there was little doubt in anyone's mind that Julius would not look upon these gatherings with favour, if he came to hear of them. His unexpected recovery brought swift denials by the Romans of any intention to attack the authority of the papal government. The barons kept their nerve, maintained their united front, and left the city. Their unity and their estrangement from the pope was perceived as a problem: one that became more serious in the winter, as Louis began to think of using disaffected barons to attack Rome.

Louis was still Julius's major problem. After the loss of Bologna, he had picked up negotiations with the king again. Proposals and counter-proposals passed backwards and forwards all summer and into the autumn. Much of the work was done by the Scots bishop Andrew Forman, but other agents were used as well, including Angelo Leonino, by this time governing Avignon, who was sent on missions to the French court, and Giangiordano Orsini, who returned from a visit to France in July 1511 with proposals that his wife Felice helped him to put before her father.

None of this diplomatic activity was very fruitful. Louis perhaps wanted peace more than Julius did, but peace on his terms, and the pope did not like his terms, any more than the king liked those sent by the pope. Bologna was the principal sticking-point. Julius wanted it back, under a form of government of his choosing, and he wanted the Bentivoglio out. Louis took the city and the Bentivoglio into his protection, and swore that he could not allow them to return to the oppressive regime of recent years.

His devotion to the liberties of the Bolognese was motivated by a
fear that if Bologna was once again under papal control, it would
be used as a base for an attack on Lombardy. For similar reasons,
he would not abandon Alfonso d'Este and Ferrara to their fate.
To please the king, Julius said that he would renew Alfonso's
investiture with Ferrara, but that all his lands south of the Po
were to go to the papacy, he was to pay the census at the rate due
before Alexander VI reduced it, and the pope was to have a
visdomino in Ferrara. None of these conditions, or any others that
Julius was asking for, was acceptable to the king. He would see
that Alfonso asked for pardon, but he should keep all his lands, on
the same conditions as before the war, as Julius had promised
under the terms of the Treaty of Cambrai.[35]

Louis also referred back to the Treaty of Cambrai in his
insistence that, as part of any peace settlement, Maximilian
should receive all the lands that he claimed from Venice under its
terms. He protested that Julius made no mention of Maximilian's
claims in the proposals that he sent. But the pope was still hoping
to bring about an agreement between Maximilian and Venice, so
that they could be brought into a league against France. The
difficulties in bringing about such an agreement were immense –
the two sides were as far apart in their demands as Louis and
Julius were – but his efforts continued, and he was not prepared
to bring the problem within the scope of his negotiations with
France.

Ferdinand, too, favoured a separate peace between
Maximilian and Venice. This he saw as one device to counter the
plans for the conquest of Italy that he believed Louis to nurture.
Another would be for Julius to pay for a large contingent of
Spanish troops to defend the lands of the Church and the authority
of the pope, and recover what the Church had lost. Before the
Spanish troops came to the pope's aid, he wanted an alliance with
Julius and Venice, which must, he insisted, be clearly in favour of
the Church, and not *against* anyone.[36] Ferdinand's son-in-law,
Henry VIII, was to be invited into the league too.

Negotiations for this league were soon under way and, despite
being held up by Julius's illness, were concluded quite quickly.
On 4 October 1511 the league between Ferdinand, Venice
and the pope was formally concluded. Julius wanted it called
'Sanctissima', 'Most Holy', because it was for the benefit of the
Church,[37] and, on the following day, held an impressive ceremony
at Santa Maria del Popolo to publish its terms. The league was

said to be for the recovery of Bologna and all other lands of the Church that were being occupied by others. Ferdinand was to send the viceroy of Naples, Ramón Cardona, or another suitable captain, to command the forces of the league, with 1,200 men-at-arms, 1,000 light horse and 10,000 Spanish infantry. Julius was to supply 600 men-at-arms, under the command of the Duke of Termini, while the Venetians were to provide as many troops as they could (no number was specified), and to make available their fleet, which would work in conjunction with eleven Spanish galleys. Julius and Venice were to pay the Spanish commander 40,000 ducats a month towards the expense of the troops. Maximilian could join the league within forty days if he chose; Henry, it was noted, had participated in the negotiations and was expected to join in the league, but the mandate from England had not yet arrived.[38] Henry did indeed ratify the league, on 13 November.

Louis had wanted to avoid war. The French were not wholly comfortable with the idea of using military force against the Church. After the capture of Bologna, Louis's chosen instrument to bring Julius to make peace was the council. At first, his enthusiasm for that seemed to be waning too. In late May one of his ministers, Robertet, remarked that he did not think that the council would ever meet; the dissident cardinals had their minds on bishoprics rather than the reform of the Church.[39] They also wanted the French king to take the Romagna, and hand it over to them; Louis refused to agree. But once he realized that Julius was ready for war, rather than peace, he ordered twenty-four French bishops to attend the council in person, and all other French prelates to send proctors or to go themselves. He wrote to Florence to ask that Pisa should be made ready to receive it.

Louis was quite explicit about his motives for supporting the council – 'he would not have embarked on this council, except to bring the pope to an agreement; and so he said "If we give up on the council, the pope won't want anything to do with a peace." '[40] Few can have been deceived into thinking that reform of the Church came very high on the true agenda of the council, and it was attracting very little support. Only the French clergy went through the motions, as slowly as they dared, to appease the king. The Florentines tried hard to escape having to play hosts to it in Pisa, arguing, with some truth, that Pisa was in no fit state to receive a large assembly of outsiders. They were in a very difficult position. Refusing to accept the council in Pisa would have offended the French, on whose alliance the regime in Florence was dependent; accepting the council in their territory brought them under papal interdict, and the goods of their merchants, particularly in the Papal States, in peril of confiscation. Louis's seizure of the property of Julius's relatives in Genoa and Savona in retaliation was small compensation. The Florentines did, however, refuse to compel their clergy to attend the council, and they refused to accept in their territory the large contingent of French troops that the dissident cardinals insisted they needed for their own protection. Those who came for the council were met with hostility and resentment by the Pisans; at first, they were even locked out of the cathedral.

Four cardinals had reached Pisa at the end of October – Carvajal, Briçonnet, de Prie and d'Albret (who had been forced to participate by Louis and sent a message to Julius to say that he would try to get away and come to Rome). They had proxies from Sanseverino, Cosenza (who died on 4 November at Reggio), and, they claimed, from Luxembourg, but he denied this. Apart from the four cardinals, there were only two archbishops, fourteen bishops and five abbots, all French except for one Italian abbot. In addition, there were a few theologians and jurists, some of whom came from Milan. The council was formally declared open on 5 November, with Carvajal presiding. But so miserable was the attendance at the first two sessions, so small the prospect of more prelates joining them, so hostile the reception from the Pisans, that the third session was hastily brought forward to 12 November and it was decided to transfer the council to Milan. Reassembling there in December, the council felt a little safer, but was no more welcome to the people, who fell under papal interdict because of its presence. Most of the clergy observed the interdict, defying the French governor, who insisted that they should continue to hold the usual services.

Even before it had become obvious that the council was a fiasco, Julius's confidence had been buoyed up by the Holy League. Now he was stronger than the French, he said, and again he spoke of driving them back over the Alps.[41] Louis, meanwhile, was threatening to take the war to the pope and drive him from Rome.[42] Ultimately, Julius proved the better prophet – but not before it looked as though Louis's predictions would come true.

When Ferdinand had first proposed that Julius should pay for Spanish troops to help defend the lands of the Church, he had told his ambassador in Rome, Vich, that they should be kept firmly under Spanish command. Up until then, he said, Julius had governed military matters so poorly that he had lost more through the bad order of his men than through the action of the enemy.[43] Ferdinand was probably referring only to the wars since the Treaty of Cambrai, but his comment was all too apt for most of Julius's military efforts, as cardinal and as pope. The campaign against the French in the winter of 1511–12 was no exception. Cardinal Giovanni Medici was sent to the Romagna as legate in early October 1511. He was to have overall charge of the papal troops there, while the Neapolitan Duke of Termini, whom Julius appointed as his lieutenant-general that month, was to have the military command. But the duke never arrived in the Romagna, dying at Civita Castellana in December on his way north. Once again, Julius could not find an effective commander for his troops. He was still not sure that he wanted the Duke of Urbino to take part in the campaign, and besides, Francesco Maria had an uncomfortable habit of requesting more money and men as soon as he was asked to do anything. Faced with paying a monthly subvention of 20,000 ducats to the Spanish troops, and with helping the Venetians to find the cash to pay their share, the pope did not like to hear requests for money from his own men. He was convinced that he was being cheated, and that his soldiers were selling off their supplies for their own profit. He kept on urging Cardinal Medici to *do* something – above all, to go and take Bologna back. Convinced that Bologna was ripe for the taking, he was impatient with the cardinal's argument that it would be better to wait for the Spanish troops to come from Naples, but at last he accepted it, and told him to concentrate on keeping the Romagna safe until the reinforcements arrived.

The Spanish troops, however, were slow in coming, and when they at last did arrive in the Romagna were not much more active. In late January 1512 the papal and Spanish forces, commanded by the viceroy, Cardona, began to besiege Bologna, but a lightning manoeuvre by the young French commander, Gaston de Foix, who contrived to enter Bologna with his men undetected by the besiegers in early February, relieved the city. Soon Julius was complaining that the Spanish were wasting his money; he grumbled that the viceroy lacked experience and understanding, and accused him of intriguing with de Foix.[44]

His anger increased when he heard that no effective attempt had been made to block the return to Bologna of Gaston de Foix on 21 March, this time with Cardinal Sanseverino, who had been appointed 'legate' of Bologna, at Louis's demand, by the council in Milan. Louis wanted the council itself to transfer there. More ominously, he had sent orders to de Foix to invade the Romagna, and to hand over to Sanseverino any lands that he captured there. Cardona was no match for de Foix as a general, and was forced to confront the French in a battle before the walls of Ravenna on 11 April, Easter Sunday. This, one of the bloodiest battles of the Italian wars, ended in crushing defeat for the papal and Spanish troops, with the capture of the legate, Cardinal Medici, and of two Spanish commanders, Fabrizio Colonna and the Marchese di Pescara. French jubilation at the victory was stilled by the news that Gaston de Foix was among the dead, but the army easily took Ravenna, and the rest of the Romagna was conquered within a matter of days.

Panic was the natural reaction in Rome to this news. It was known that the French had been threatening to march on Rome, and now it seemed that nothing could stop them. At first, Julius thought of flight from Rome, and galleys were being prepared, but on the following day, 15 April, Giulio de' Medici arrived, sent by his cousin the legate. He told of the heavy losses that the French had suffered, of the demoralization of the army at the loss of de Foix, and of the discord between the new commander, La Palice, and Cardinal Sanseverino. These reports rallied Julius's spirits, and he began to discuss with the Spanish ambassador, Vich, how to regroup and increase the forces of the league. Faced with the necessity of explaining to himself how God could let the Spanish suffer such a defeat, Vich had decided it was the pope's sins that had prompted God to give the French victory in an unjust cause.[45] But, whatever his personal views on Julius, he did provide much-needed support in the difficult weeks ahead. Apart from a moment of discouragement in early May, when news came of the fall of the fortress of Ravenna to the French, Julius's nerve held, despite great pressure from the cardinals to seek for peace. He agreed to send peace proposals to France, but they were little different from the ones that he had made the year before, and could not be acceptable to Louis now; indeed, he sent for the ambassadors of the league to tell them that he was merely playing for time.[46]

He did not have to stall for very long. By the middle of May both Ferdinand and Henry had declared their intention of continuing the fight against the French. And, at the end of the month, an investment that Julius had been making for years finally paid

off, as a large force of Swiss mercenaries, under the command of
Cardinal Schiner, advanced into the Milanese.

Extracting money from Julius to pay for troops was often as
arduous, and provoked as many cries of anguish, as pulling teeth.
He was always ready to suspect that he was being cheated, and
was especially reluctant to pay for troops that would not be under
his own control. And yet he never seemed to grudge paying out
large sums for Swiss mercenary infantry, and submitted to the
blackmail to which they subjected all their employers with comparatively good grace. He had entrusted his personal security to a
corps of Swiss since 1506 – the foundation of the famous papal
Swiss Guard. Up to the summer of 1511, however, he had had
very little return on the investment.

The 6,000 Swiss that he had recruited for the campaign
against Genoa in 1510 had gone home without having done anything.[47] They had claimed that they had not been paid, but other
reports indicate that Julius had paid out at least 36,000 ducats
and had had 50,000 ducats more ready to send to them. There
were also political problems: not all the Swiss were agreed that
they should be fighting for the pope against the King of France,
who had been their traditional employer for decades. The combination of political ambiguity and difficulties in getting payment
to them, despite the large sums of money that Julius made available, brought an attack on the duchy of Milan to an end within
six weeks in late 1511.

Nevertheless, Julius was still very keen to have their services.
In January 1512 he appointed Cardinal Schiner as papal legate to
the Swiss. Then, in March, to help resolve the conflicts over
whom the Swiss should be serving, and at the request of those
who were advocating serving the Church, he sent a bull excommunicating those Swiss who went to serve France. The following
month, the cantons formally wrote to Cardinal Schiner, who had
gone to Venice to negotiate a contract with the Holy League, to
say that they had decided to invade Milan again, to support
Julius and the papacy against the French.[48]

On 28 May the Swiss, 18,000 men in all, met in Verona,
where Schiner was waiting with a bejewelled ceremonial cap and
sword sent to them by the pope as symbols of their role as
protectors of the Church. By 2 June they had reached Valleggio,
where they joined up with the Venetian forces, and on 6 June they
met up with the papal troops at Cremona. The French were
already in retreat. Just as the Swiss were heading for Verona,

Maximilian withdrew the German troops who were with the French, and the disorganized and demoralized French army left the Romagna. They were in no condition or mood to stand up to the combined forces of the league and the Swiss, and, apart from leaving behind the garrisons of a handful of fortresses, they evacuated the duchy of Milan virtually without a fight by the end of the month.

Now there was no further need to pray to God for victory, declared Julius: now he had granted everything that had been asked.[49] On the pope's orders, celebrations in Rome lasted for several days, with bonfires throughout the city and a night-time procession to the Vatican from San Pietro in Vincoli, where he had been staying for a few days. He was accompanied by all the cardinals, each of whom was preceded by forty torches carried by his servants. 'It was a superb sight, all the more as there wasn't a house which didn't have torches and candles at the windows, and so many bonfires in the streets, especially in those through which the pope passed, that there'd never been so many seen at one time in Rome. It was estimated that there were three thousand blazing torches behind the pope.'[50] The news that the French had lost Genoa was greeted by Julius with particular delight, and cries of 'Fregoso! Fregoso!'[51] On St Peter's Day, 29 June, he presented the basilica of the apostle with a golden altar cloth with the inscription 'Julius Papa Secundus Italia Liberata'.[52] Two great banners were sent to the Swiss, one decorated with the papal tiara and keys and the inscription 'Pope Julius II, nephew of Sixtus IV of Savona', the other with the arms of the della Rovere and a religious text, declaring 'The Lord is my helper, I will not fear what any man can do to me.'[53] Every Swiss town that had sent a contingent of men received a standard painted or embroidered with a religious image of its choice.

As the rejoicings in Rome were in full swing, envoys from Bologna arrived to seek the pope's pardon. However elated he was feeling, he was in no mood to forgive the Bolognese lightly. Necessity had brought their submission, as he well knew. Only when there was no hope of further help from the French and the Bentivoglio recognized that they could not stay in the city without them, did the Bolognese turn their minds to making their peace with the pope. The Bentivoglio left on 10 June, and the governing council wrote the same day to the legate of the Romagna, Cardinal Gonzaga, asking him to come.[54] It still had spirit enough to refuse to give the hostages that the legate demanded, and to face down

Francesco Maria della Rovere when he said that he would enter the city with all his troops; it warned him that the Bolognese would take up arms to repel them, and of the danger that the Bentivoglio might take the opportunity to return from their refuge in Ferrara.[55]

On 13 June, the day on which Francesco Maria and only some of his troops entered Bologna with the legate, the governing councils of the city wrote to Julius telling him that they had asked them to come. Now that the Bentivoglio had gone, there was nothing to prevent the Bolognese from giving true obedience to the Church and the pope. The Bolognese understood that he might be somewhat annoyed, they said, but Bologna had had an appalling year, and would he please be merciful.[56] The ambassadors whom they sent were instructed to ask for pardon and absolution, but also for the restoration of the city's former privileges: all the troubles of recent years stemmed from failure to observe these.[57] Either the Bolognese did not realize how annoyed Julius was, how much he had felt the loss of the city – not to mention incidents such as the destruction of Michelangelo's statue of him[58] – as a personal blow, or they were hoping to brazen it out. Perhaps they had yet to appreciate fully the extent of the rout of the French, and the consequent weakness of their own position.

Julius's reception of the ambassadors should have left them in little doubt about his attitude. He received them formally on 27 June in the church of San Pietro in Vincoli, which was packed by prelates and *curiali*, seated with his back to the altar and flanked by eight cardinals. After the envoys had presented their letters of credence, asking for pardon and promising 'perpetual and inviolable loyalty' in future, Julius replied, at length. He spoke of all the effort and expense that he had endured to wrest the city from servitude to the tyranny of the Bentivoglio; he emphasized how, moved by his love for Bologna, he had gone there twice, with all his court, which had left the city 400,000 ducats the richer; and he recalled the other benefits, private and public, that he had bestowed on the Bolognese. And yet, in a moment, he had seen the city turn her back on her benefactor and forswear what had been promised many times, leaving her true lord for the enemies of the pope and Holy Church. Here he recalled the persecution of his soldiers, the dismantling of the fortress, and the destruction of his statue – which he had had made at his own expense, when the Bolognese should have been the ones to raise it up, at their expense, to commemorate him. To make their rebellion all the more open, they had obeyed schismatics, and committed a thousand other faults to the dishonour of the pope and the Apostolic See, so that they might have brought about his total ruin. Ungrateful, they were, disloyal, men of ill will – not one had given the slightest sign of being his servant or his friend: at least they might have seized the Bentivoglio when they fled. And so he went on, showing a more detailed knowledge of what had happened in Bologna (the envoys thought) than they themselves had. But he would punish them, and give them such a government, and impose such order, that he would make them obey: if they wouldn't do it for love, he would force them to it.[59]

Refusing all petitions to restore their former privileges, Julius would not even reinstate the office of the Forty, saying that they had behaved like tyrants. He appointed one of his *nipoti*, Orlando del Carretto, his treasurer, as vice-legate to govern the city. The pope thought highly of him, and the Bolognese professed themselves pleased by him; but, unfortunately, his lieutenant, Francesco Frescobaldi, followed the pattern of preceding papal governors in the city by behaving despotically, enriching himself by extortion. Julius refused to settle on any other form of government, and it was not until after his death that the new pope, Leo X – Giovanni de' Medici, who had been legate of Bologna – restored the Forty, and later confirmed all the city's privileges.

One thing that had particularly annoyed Julius about the events at Bologna was that Cardinal Sanseverino, who had been appointed 'legate' by the schismatic council, had been accepted in the city. In March 1512 Louis had given orders that the council should be transferred to Bologna. But soon, as the French army fell apart, the cardinals and prelates in Milan did not feel safe even there, and instead of heading south, decided on 4 June to move north to Asti. Still they felt insecure, and soon took refuge over the Alps in Lyons. There the tenth and final session of the council was held on 6 July. The dissident cardinals were still unwilling to admit defeat, but soon even Louis began to tire of what had become a useless diplomatic inconvenience. This was another hangover of Julius's pontificate that it fell to Leo to tidy up.[60]

The demise of the Pisan council did not lead to the abandonment of the council that Julius had summoned. Plans for it were too far advanced, and to drop the scheme would have made all too blatant the political motive behind it. Although it would probably not have occurred to Julius to summon a council had he not been pushed into it by the need to respond to the challenge of Louis and the dissident cardinals, he seems to have decided to make the best of it. The signs were that it would attract much wider support than the Pisan council, and it provided a perfect opportunity for a display of the majesty of the papacy. Recognition of what, for many, should have been its real purpose, provision for the reform of the Church, had been given too, even before it opened. At the consistory in March at which it was decided to open the council at the Lateran after Easter, a commission of eight cardinals was appointed to examine the complaints of the intolerable expense of doing business at the curia. Julius wanted some sign that reform was beginning at the head of the Church, and he wanted all the clerics in Rome to behave more decorously than they usually did. His mark of reformation in his own behaviour was to have his beard shaved off.[61]

The council opened on 3 May. The day before, Julius had made his way to the Lateran, accompanied by sixteen cardinals, ambassadors and many prelates (of whom there was no shortage in Rome), and a strong military escort, including Costantino Arniti, Giulio Orsini, Marcantonio Colonna and Niccolò della Rovere.

The impressive opening ceremony the following day lasted six hours and included a Mass of the Holy Spirit, and a sermon from Egidio da Viterbo, invoking the aid of St Peter for the council. After this, the pope and prelates entered a special enclosure that had been constructed in the basilica for the participants in the council, the entrance to which was guarded by a splendidly dressed contingent of Knights of Rhodes. Julius's address was read out for him by Cardinal Farnese. It declared that he had long wanted to hold a council, but had deferred it because of the wars between Christian princes; now, the threat of division in the Church made it urgent.[62] The first session was held on 10 May, with Julius presiding. Here he described the task of the council to be threefold: rooting out schism, the reform of the Church, and a crusade. If he had not governed his flock as he should have, he apologized, but he had meant well, and he was ready to do anything for the Christian faith.[63] At the second session, a week later, the proceedings of the council of Pisa were declared null and void. A letter from Henry VIII announcing his accession to the Holy League was read out, and then another from Ferdinand, accrediting Vich to represent him and his daughter, Queen Joanna, at the council. Although virtually all the prelates who attended were Italian, it was already clear from these letters, and the presence of the Venetian ambassador too, that the Lateran Council would enjoy general recognition. To gain time for the representatives of other nations to appear, and to avoid holding sessions in the heat of summer, the council was adjourned until November. Julius was well satisfied with what had been accomplished so far.

With the Lateran Council set to triumph over the Pisan, the French on the run from Italy, and Bologna back in the fold, by the end of June three of the pope's major preoccupations were on the way to being resolved. Still another persisted, however – Ferrara.

Alfonso d'Este had remained an ally of France through good times and bad. His artillery, his pride and joy, had done much to secure victory for the French at the Battle of Ravenna. By casting an artillery piece using the bronze from the head of Michelangelo's statue of the pope after its destruction in Bologna, and calling it 'La Giulia', he had struck a more personal blow against Julius, one that went home. But the rout of the French meant that Alfonso, like the Bolognese, had to think of coming to terms with Julius. The ground was prepared by the Gonzaga, who helped to arrange a safe-conduct for Alfonso to go to Rome. He also obtained guarantees from Fabrizio Colonna, who had been his prisoner since the Battle of Ravenna, and the Spanish ambassador in Rome; his honourable treatment of Fabrizio and the Spanish prisoners that he held had earned him their goodwill. After recalling at length Alfonso's offences against the papacy, including his treatment of the statue's head, the safe-conduct, dated 11 June, stipulated that he could come safely to Rome, and leave again freely even if he had not reached any agreement with the pope.[64]

Alfonso arrived in Rome on 4 July, accompanied by an escort of gentlemen and a few troops. Julius sent Federico Gonzaga to greet his uncle, who rode through the streets with Fabrizio Colonna on one side and Giangiordano Orsini (whom he had met by chance) on the other. Alfonso stayed quietly in Cardinal Gonzaga's palace for the first few days, receiving visits made on behalf of the ambassadors and cardinals. His cause had much sympathy in Rome, but he also had enemies near the pope, including Alberto da Carpi, now Imperial ambassador in Rome.[65] After some debate over the form of words to be used in his formal request for pardon – like the Venetians in 1509–10, he kicked against the degree of submissiveness and self-reproach that the pope and his officials wanted him to display – Alfonso was absolved by Julius in consistory on 9 July. He was not badly treated during the ceremony. While he was waiting to enter consistory, he was entertained by a sumptuous collation of fruit, confectionery and wine, and the music of violins. Naturally, Julius did not let slip the opportunity to expatiate on Alfonso's errors in reply to the duke's words of penitence, but he embraced him warmly and seemed friendly enough.[66]

Then, however, the hard bargaining began, and it became evident that Julius was in no mood to be indulgent. A commission of six cardinals – Ciocchi, Fieschi, Vigerio, Aragona, Bainbridge and Leonardo della Rovere – was appointed to examine Alfonso's case. Most of these were Julius's men, though Aragona, boon companion of Julius as he was, was also related to Alfonso, whose mother had been a daughter of Ferrante, and was highly sympathetic to the duke. In fact, all the commission, except for Leonardo della Rovere, were sympathetic to him, but the final decision did not rest with them, but with the pope. He was putting forward two demands that Alfonso firmly rejected. One was that he should release two of his brothers, Giulio and Ferrante, who were languishing in prison in Ferrara, after conspiring against Alfonso in 1506. Julius had a private interest in the fate of Ferrante, who was his godson and had recently smuggled out a letter to the pope, pleading for his help. Julius argued that Alfonso's brothers were included among the prisoners whose release was stipulated as a condition of his safe-conduct – Alfonso replied, with justification, that the prisoners referred to in that document were the prisoners of war, Fabrizio Colonna and the subjects of Ferdinand and of Venice. The second demand that the pope was making was even more unacceptable to Alfonso. Julius wanted Ferrara.

Before Alfonso had come to Rome, Julius had said that if he proved compliant, he planned to send him back to Ferrara with an envoy who would take possession of it; subsequently, the duke would be reinvested with it, on terms that would prevent any further recalcitance against the papacy.[67] Now Julius did not want Alfonso to have Ferrara on any terms. He offered to let him choose another city, worth up to 25,000 or 30,000 ducats. Asti would be suitable, Julius suggested, claiming that it was his to dispose of. Rimini was another suggestion; and even Urbino was mentioned, with the proposal that Francesco Maria should exchange his duchy for that of Alfonso.

But the duke would not hear of such terms, claiming that he

had been promised that if he came to Rome, there would be
no question of his being asked to yield Ferrara. He left – virtually
fled – Rome on 19 July, escorted by Fabrizio Colonna, and went
to Fabrizio's fortress of Marino. Julius protested that he had had
no intention of breaching the safe-conduct that he had given to
the duke, who had been free to go. He blamed Fabrizio Colonna,
rather than Alfonso, for the manner of their departure, which
involved forcing their way out of the Porta San Giovanni. Alfonso
himself wrote that he had left Rome because Julius had asked him
to surrender Ferrara, and did not mention any fear that the safe-
conduct would not be honoured; indeed, he said that the pope had
given him permission to leave.[68] Obviously, however, he considered the demand for Ferrara to be in itself a breach of the
spirit, if not the letter, of the terms on which he had agreed to
come to Rome, and felt sufficently insecure to let Fabrizio talk
him into making a hasty and unannounced departure.

With Alfonso and his men around the Vatican, Julius had felt
insecure too. He had been persuaded that the duke was the most
vindictive of men – his treatment of his brothers lent colour to
that contention – and maintained that he had asked for Ferrara
because he did not see how he could trust him.[69] Only a few days
before Alfonso arrived in Rome, Julius spoke of an exchange that
he had been told had taken place between Alfonso and Louis.
Asking for the king's advice, Alfonso had told him the pope
wanted Ferrara, and that he would have to play for time; Louis
had responded that he couldn't help him this year, and he should
make what arrangements he could, but that he would help him
another year. Commenting on this information, Julius told the
Venetian ambassador that he wanted to take Ferrara from
Alfonso, and that the safe-conduct that he had given him had
been for his person, not his lands.[70] To leave Ferrara in the hands
of Alfonso would be to leave a way open for the King of France to
trouble the Papal States once again, and plainly Julius considered
his work incomplete unless Alfonso was driven out. The idea that
he must have Ferrara would obsess him until he died.

The help and support that the Colonna had given Alfonso
during his time in Rome (they had made great efforts to honour
and entertain him, as well as pleading his cause at court) marked
the degree of estrangement that had developed between them
and the pope. Relations between them had never recovered after
the Colonna involvement in the meetings held in Rome during
Julius's illness in August 1511. Even Marcantonio Colonna had

lost favour; he had wanted to leave papal service, because he did not want to serve under the Duke of Termini. Julius became alarmed by this estrangement from the Colonna and the continuing discontent in Rome, and there was an unconfirmed report that he had turned to the Orsini, summoning Giangiordano and Giulio to Rome, so as to have some assistance if the Colonna party caused trouble.[71] As the French advanced south in the spring of 1512, he became even more alarmed, because some of the disaffected barons, including Roberto Orsini and Pompeo Colonna, and their Roman allies were in touch with the French army.

At the time of crisis after the Battle of Ravenna, however, the barons stayed loyal to the pope. Giulio Orsini brought Roberto back into line, and, for the first time, Julius gave *condotte* to members of the Orsini family: accepting a *condotta* for himself, Giulio appointed three younger Orsini, Franciotto, Orsino and Giancorrado, to be his subordinate commanders. (Giangiordano, as ever going his own way according to his own sense of honour, refused a *condotta* from his father-in-law, saying that he could not oppose Louis because he was a member of the Order of Saint-Michel, but promised that he would put his estates at the disposal of the papal troops.)[72] Muzio Colonna finally accepted the *condotta* that the pope had been offering to him for several months, and Marcantonio, who had been in the fortress of Ravenna when it fell to the French and had given them an undertaking not to oppose them for three months, said that he would find a way out of this obligation.[73]

No agreement was reached with Prospero Colonna, who pitched his demands too high. Just before news of the battle arrived, he had refused to come to Rome, insisting that Julius must 'make up his mind to treat the Roman barons differently from in the past, and should be prepared to make four cardinals, suggesting Bishop [Pompeo] Colonna, Roberto Orsini, a Conti and a Savelli, and two Roman gentlemen as well'.[74] After the battle, he did come to Rome, but insisted that he must have the title either of Captain of the Church (which Francesco Maria held) or of Gonfaloniere of the Church (which was held by Francesco Gonzaga). Told by Julius that these titles were not available, and by the Spanish ambassador that he had no mandate to agree to his being captain of the league, a position that Julius was ready to concede, he left again.

Prospero's demands for titles and cardinals had lost him the trust of the pope; the assistance that Fabrizio and Marcantonio gave to Alfonso made him distrust them too. Pompeo he had never trusted, and he took away his bishopric of Rieti for his part in helping Alfonso to escape. It was reported that, in a secret consistory in early September, he had confiscated not only the bishopric but Pompeo's other benefices and the lands that he and his brothers held, but this sentence does not seem to have been executed.[75] Julius was not reconciled to the Colonna, his friends of so many years' standing, before his death.

Another important connection was severely damaged by the outcome of Alfonso's visit to Rome – that between Julius and Ferdinand. Dissatisfaction with the performance of the Spanish troops in the Romagna had already brought a stream of complaints from Julius, and grumbles that the money that he was spending on them was being wasted, while that spent on the Swiss was like money in the bank, because of the results it produced.[76] One reason why he had been so keen to recruit Swiss troops in the winter of 1511–12 was because 'he fears, now that he has escaped from servitude to the French to fall into a worse one, which is to the Spanish.'[77] His suspicions exasperated Vich, who found him very difficult to deal with. 'In the hospital in Valencia there are a hundred people chained up who are less mad than His Holiness', he told Dovizi.[78]

Vich had been instructed, when he was negotiating the release of the Spanish prisoners held in Ferrara, to try discreetly to reconcile Alfonso and the pope. A guarantee from Vich that he would be safe was one of the inducements that brought Alfonso to Rome, and the ambassador protested to Julius when he demanded the duke should relinquish Ferrara. After Alfonso fled, Julius suspected, with reason, that he would be smuggled out of his reach among the Spanish troops that Prospero Colonna was leading north from Naples to Lombardy. He had already been baulking at continuing to pay for Spanish troops, or letting them go to the Romagna: they hadn't come when he needed them, he said, and now they were coming when he didn't.[79]

Vich did not mince his words to Julius when he protested about his refusal to allow Prospero through. After all that Ferdinand had done 'to lift the feet of the King of France from Your Holiness' throat', and when the troops were to be sent against the common enemy, was Julius refusing to let them through? He was wrong to think that Alfonso would be with them – he had already gone. Julius was incensed, and they had a furious row. The pope shouted, 'Go and do the worst you can because I'll do the same to you', but when Vich replied, 'It's a bargain, Holy Father',[80] Julius walked up and down the room three times to recover his self-control, and then said, 'Listen. You have the duke detained – I don't want you to hand him over to me, just hold on to him until those troops have passed.' Vich replied that Alfonso was no longer on Spanish territory.[81] Not until September, when Julius began to feel that things were not going so well for him as he had hoped, did the pope agree to allow the troops to pass through, and he was still worried that Alfonso would go with them.

By then, there were already rumours that Julius wanted the Spanish out of Italy. Ferdinand thought that he did and that he was trying to break up the Spanish army there.[82] As a long-term aim, Julius did want Italy free of foreign powers, but he does not seem to have thought that this was yet in the realm of practical politics. Sketching out his political programme to a Mantuan envoy – the independence of the Church and the maintenance of its prestige, the achievement of a balance of forces in Italy, the expulsion of foreigners and a war on the Turks – he spoke of 'rooting out' the French partisans in Ferrara and Florence, but to the suggestion that it would be good to be rid of the Spanish as well, replied that they had to be put up with. At present, Naples was well off in the hands of the King of Spain.[83]

There was still work for the 'foreigners' to do in Italy. Julius was a little ambiguous in his concurrence with the decision taken by the representatives of the league in Lombardy, that Spanish troops should go to restore the Medici to Florence in August 1512. Overturning the pro-French regime in Florence had been on his personal agenda since the summer of 1510, and he was happy for the Spanish troops to earn themselves some money by plunder, hoping that this would relieve him of some pressure to make payments to them. The increase in Spanish influence in Tuscany that would result from their restoring the Medici was less welcome to him. But he would be pleased to have support from Ferdinand, or Maximilian, for his campaign against Ferrara. Until that was accomplished, any thought of ridding Italy of all outside interference was as distant a prospect as the crusade against the Turks – a pleasant fancy, not a serious aim.

The expedition against Florence was about the only policy on which the league could agree, for the sudden collapse of French power in Italy had removed its *raison d'être*. The most serious dispute was over the fate of the duchy of Milan. Who should be the duke was the least controversial problem. It was agreed that Lodovico Sforza's son, Maximilian, who had been brought up at his namesake's court, should be invested with the duchy, though Ferdinand canvassed the idea that his grandson and namesake, the younger son of Philip of Burgundy, should be given the duchy and married to a Sforza girl. Who should prepare the duchy to receive him was a matter of dispute. The Swiss were reluctant to leave the prize that they had won, and Cardinal Schiner had notions of governing it himself, at least until the boy should arrive, while Cardinal Lang thought that he should be the one to prepare for and guide the young duke. Which lands the duchy should comprise was the most difficult problem to resolve. The Swiss took their reward in the form of places that they had long coveted at the foot of the Alps, such as Bellinzona, Lugano and Locarno; Maximilian and Venice both claimed Verona, Brescia and Bergamo; Julius took Parma and Piacenza, claiming them for the Church on the grounds they had been part of the lands left to the papacy in the twelfth century by the Countess Matilda of Canossa.[84]

Neither Maximilian nor Ferdinand nor the Swiss approved of Julius's appropriation of Parma and Piacenza. Schiner resisted the pope's orders to hand the towns over to papal officials in June, but then reluctantly obeyed. Julius wanted other territories too – he accepted the submission of Reggio and claimed Modena (both Imperial fiefs), and still had his heart set on taking Ferrara. The question was did he want these lands for the Church, or did he want them for Francesco Maria? It was suggested to him in July that he might give them to his nephew – it is not known who made the suggestion – and Bartolomeo della Rovere said in August that Julius wanted Francesco Maria to have Ferrara at least.[85] There was also a scheme about that time to use Parma and Piacenza as a dowry for Francesco Maria's sister, who would be married to Maximilian Sforza.

It is unlikely that the pope ever seriously intended to give his nephew all this. To do so would be to invite his successor to take the lands away as soon as he could: no pope could tolerate so much territory being in the hands of one subject. It took several months to persuade Julius to give Francesco Maria the less important town of Pesaro, after the young Sforza lord died in August 1512. This was a much more easily justifiable addition to Francesco Maria's lands: a papal vicariate, near to Urbino, and with no heir with a strong claim who needed to be dispossessed.[86] Yet it was only on his deathbed that Julius invested his nephew with the town.

Francesco Maria was still giving the pope little incentive to bestow excessive favours upon him. In early March 1512 he even sent his secretary, Baldassare Castiglione, to France to offer his services to Louis. Among the services that he offered was to cause Cesena, Rimini and Fano to revolt against the pope. Julius had wronged him and shamed him ever since the beginning of the war against Ferrara, he claimed, calling him a traitor, saying that he was intriguing with the French. He had promoted the Duke of Termini over his head, and taken almost half his troops away. His pension had not been paid for eight months; the pope never mentioned him when he was negotiating with Louis or Maximilian or Ferdinand. He had asked leave of the pope and had decided never to serve him again. Whatever the future author of the *Book of the Courtier*, who drafted this catalogue of grievances, thought of his master's treachery, the French themselves were highly critical. Francesco Maria felt that they were insufficiently appreciative, and after the Battle of Ravenna and the death of de Foix, feared that they would hold him in even less account. Besides, he told his father-in-law, explaining his decision to switch his allegiance back to Julius a few weeks later, the pope had softened towards him and admitted that he had been in the wrong. He might incur blame if he refused to hear his uncle's appeal, when the pope was in so much trouble.[87]

The return of his nephew to the fold was certainly very welcome to the pope, but Francesco Maria had not changed his ways. Ordered to attack Ferrara, Francesco Maria still hung back. Castiglione assured Isabella d'Este that her son-in-law was determined to show his sympathy for her brother, and that he was constantly telling the pope how difficult an enterprise it was.[88] Julius can have had few illusions about him. It is possible that he tried to spur him on by promising that Ferrara would be his,[89] but it is unlikely that he meant it.

Ferrara was an obsession for Julius, and he was prepared to pay a high price for support for his campaign, or even for a promise not to oppose it. This, and his desire to have Maximilian publicly accede to the Lateran Council, brought him, in November 1512, to agree to help Maximilian against Venice. Driving the barbarians from Italy was still a distant dream.

Julius had been trying to promote peace between Venice and

Maximilian, on and off, since the Venetian ambassadors had come to Rome to seek pardon after the Battle of Agnadello. His fluctuations of interest in working to this end were chiefly caused by his low opinion of the utility of Maximilian as an ally. With the advent of the Pisan council, the pope became more interested in winning over Maximilian, and more ready to press the Venetians to make concessions to him. When Lang, as Maximilian's representative, opposed Julius's attempts to take Ferrara in the summer of 1512 and made it known that he did not want the papacy to have it, the idea of coming to terms with Maximilian, winning him over to the Lateran Council, and gaining his approval, or at least his forbearance, for Julius's acquisition of Ferrara, seemed still more worthwhile.

Maximilian's opinion of the pope was no higher than the one that Julius held of him. The apparently mortal illness that Julius suffered in August 1511 revived Maximilian's extraordinary ambition, first manifest in 1506, to become pope himself. He wrote in September 1511 to one of his ministers, Paul von Liechtenstein, asking him to approach the Fugger banking house to provide 400,000 ducats to finance this scheme,[90] and two days later, wrote to his daughter Margaret a bizarre letter that would read like a curious joke were it not for the business letter to Liechtenstein. He would be sending Lang to Rome, he said, to induce Julius to take Maximilian as a coadjutor in the papacy, so that after Julius's death, he would be assured of becoming pope. Then he would become a priest, and afterwards a saint, so that after his death, she would have to adore him. He was asking Ferdinand for his support, which would be given if he renounced the Empire to their grandson, Charles. The people of Rome, he claimed, had sent to say that they were ready to create a pope of his choosing, and he was beginning to lobby the cardinals – two or three hundred thousand ducats would be very useful here. He asked her to keep this secret, although he knew that it would be difficult to keep such a matter, involving so many people and so much money, quiet for long.[91]

At the time Maximilian wrote this letter, he was sure that Julius would die soon. News of the pope's recovery brought a more sober approach to relations with the papacy, and Maximilian began to signal an interest in joining the Holy League. The French became seriously concerned that they would lose their ally, and the truce agreed between Maximilian and Venice in early April 1512 would do little to reassure them, nor the fact that he gave the Swiss permission to march through his lands on their way to the Milanese. Later that month he set out the terms that he wanted if he were to join the league against France. These included an undertaking by Julius and Ferdinand to help him against the Venetians if he could not make an agreement with them; the grant of a *decima*, a tax on the German clergy; and permission for a levy for a 'crusade' against the schismatics. While the levy was being collected, he wanted a loan of 100,000 ducats from Julius to help pay his troops.[92]

Julius granted the *decima* on the German clergy – much though he wanted not to displease them, for a council of German prelates had decided in February 1512 that the Pisan council was schismatic. Lang was supposed to come to Rome to negotiate, but the differences that arose over the disposal of the lands of the duchy of Milan, Maximilian's discontent that the pope should have Parma, Piacenza and Reggio, and Lang's efforts to obstruct his taking Ferrara, made him linger in northern Italy. The pope did not relax his territorial claims, insisted that Lang must come to Rome, and declared he did not want to see Venice ruined and deprived of her lands by Maximilian. By late August he was ready to compromise, however. He would agree to Maximilian having some of the towns that he claimed from Venice, if Maximilian would agree to his having Ferrara. In the light of this response, Lang decided to go to Rome – but only after the Spanish troops had returned to Lombardy from their campaign against Florence, and he himself had been to consult Maximilian.[93]

He eventually reached Rome in November 1512. He went privately to the Vatican on 3 November, and dined and slept there without seeing the pope, but they spent the whole of the following day together in the Belvedere. Then Lang left, to make his public entry to Rome, and to be received formally by the pope. During this reception, all the ambassadors in Rome petitioned the pope one by one 'for a general peace in Italy, in the name of their kings and lords'.[94] But the agreement signed on 19 November pleased few. The Venetian ambassadors, backed into a corner, declared early on in the talks that they could not accept the terms that Julius wished to impose on them, and he therefore declared them excluded from the league. The Spanish ambassadors tried to prevent the agreement from being concluded at all: Ferdinand considered the prospect of driving the Venetians into the arms of the French as politically disastrous. But with both the main parties to the negotiations ready to cede what the other wanted to gain their own ends – Lang to gain the prospect of military help and the grant of spiritual censures for Maximilian against Venice; Julius to gain acquiescence in his tenure of Modena, Reggio, Parma and Piacenza, and a promise that Maximilian would not help Alfonso d'Este – terms were agreed and signed with little difficulty.

The league was formally announced on 25 November at a ceremony in the church of Santa Maria del Popolo, with all the cardinals present. Among them sat Lang, who had been published a cardinal in consistory the day before, but was still refusing to accept the insignia of his status. He was, with difficulty, prevailed on to wear at least episcopal robes. To honour him, after a Mass of the Holy Spirit, Egidio da Viterbo preached in praise of Julius and Maximilian, and then the terms of the league were read out, in Italian so that everyone could understand them. The pope then dined in the cloisters, with Lang, who had already put off his clerical dress, at his table.[95] His mission accomplished, Lang was ready to leave Rome, but Julius persuaded him to come on a hunting trip to Ostia, and to appear at the next session of the Lateran Council in early December.

Initially, he had not wanted to attend it, but one of the purposes of his visit, for Julius, was to make manifest Maximilian's adherence to the council, and the re-convening of the council had been held over from November because of his arrival. He did come to the session on 4 December, but behaved with his customary lack of grace and was, as usual, dressed 'in the German style', not even in bishop's robes, let alone in those of a cardinal. During an oration in praise of the council, he passed the time drafting the speech that he would make acknowledging the Lateran Council as the true one; he had refused to accept the statement that had been prepared for him. After his mandate from Maximilian had been read out – giving him powers to annul the Pisan council and not only ratify the Lateran one, but also defer it, transfer it to another place or wind it up – Lang rose and read out the statement that he had drafted, confirming the Lateran Council in Maximilian's name.[96] When the session was ended, he left immediately for Lombardy, without even returning to his lodgings.

It is not surprising that Julius was not satisfied by his behaviour, complaining that he had not repudiated the acts of the Pisan council, just recalled from it any prelates who were subjects of the Empire. He also complained that Lang had not kept his

promises, notably to withdraw German troops from the defence of
Ferrara.[97] He issued formal warnings to the Venetians that they
would be excommunicated if they did not give Maximilian the
lands that he claimed, but he made no preparation for war against
Venice. Instead, he began once more to try to promote an agreement between Venice and Maximilian. Had he wanted to make
war on Venice, it is difficult to see how he could have done so.
The Swiss did not want to attack her, and nor did Ferdinand, who
thought that nothing could be more favourable to France than
the exclusion of Venice from the league between the pope and
Maximilian. Venice would go to the defence of Ferrara, he
thought, and would be drawn into an alliance with France.[98] This
was a prospect that began to worry Julius too. The treaty with
Maximilian was beginning to look like a mistake.

Before it became clear how he proposed to resolve this
dilemma, his health began to give way again. According to the
Venetian ambassador, it was anxiety about the possibility that
Venice and France would form an alliance that first made him
ill.[99] He took to his bed about 8 January, weak but not feverish,
eating little. By the beginning of February there were doubts
whether he would survive. He began to suffer attacks of fever –
one followed a day when he had felt a little better and insisted on
tasting eight types of wine, to discover which would do him good
– and he no longer wished to discuss affairs of state.

But he was anxious that the council should continue its work.
At its last session, on 10 December, it had been decided that
proceedings should be begun against the Pragmatic Sanction, the
law introduced in 1438, abrogated in 1461, and revived by Louis
XII, bestowing on the crown wide powers over the Church in
France. At the next session, planned for 16 February, this matter
was to be dealt with further, and Julius wanted it to go ahead.
Cardinal Riario stood in for him as president of the council. Apart
from the Pragmatic Sanction, the most important business of the
session was a reading of Julius's bull against simony in papal
elections first promulgated in 1505. There had been strong opposition to this from some of the cardinals, and it had taken three
sessions of consistory to win their consent. The renewal of the bull
was on the insistence of the pope, for as he realized that he was
dying, it was on the welfare of the Church that his mind ran.

This was not because he was afraid of death, or was troubled
by a guilty conscience. He met death calmly, with a clear mind.
On 20 February, after receiving the sacrament with great devotion

from Cardinal Riario, he summoned the whole College to his bedside. He exhorted them to unite in the election of a good pope: the election was their prerogative, and the council should not become involved, nor should the 'schismatic' cardinals be allowed to take part. These admonitions he made in Latin; when he turned to the affairs of his family he spoke in Italian. They knew how much he had done to recover the property of the Church, he said, and now he asked them to agree to the grant of Pesaro to the Duke of Urbino. The cardinals agreed. He asked them for nothing more for his family, for 'his mind was on the welfare of the Church, and not the ties of blood.'[100] His daughter, Felice, asked him to promote her half-brother, Giandomenico de' Cupis, to the College, but although the bull had already been drawn up, he refused, saying that he did not want to do something displeasing to the cardinals. Felice herself had already been given back 12,000 ducats that she had first been granted when he was gravely ill in 1511, and that she had returned to him during the crisis following the Battle of Ravenna, receiving Nepi in exchange.

The pope also spoke of his enemies, especially the dissident cardinals – he pardoned them all, he said, but as an individual, not as pope. He thought it fitting that the pardon and absolution of those who had injured the papacy should be left to his successor.[101] Only to his successor, properly elected, should the castellan of the Castel Sant' Angelo surrender the fortress and the treasure in it.

As the cardinals took leave of him, kissing his hand and receiving his blessing one by one, many were weeping. What moved Cardinal Gonzaga, was 'seeing him near to death, but by no means afraid of death', turning towards God

> and in the greatness of his spirit taking care for all those things which in such circumstances are generally neglected or forgotten by those who find themselves at the very end of their life. His Beatitude sees, hears, understands, speaks, gives orders, makes dispositions and provisions as though he were in the greatest bodily vigour and health he had ever been: he is not disturbed at all, although he recognizes he is dying.

The orders that he had given and continued to give, showed 'the integrity of his mind and the deep love he has felt for the Catholic Church, and all that he has done, was done for a good end, and so may God our Redeemer grant him eternal life'.[102]

Conscious and unafraid to the last, Julius died that night. His own tomb unfinished, he was buried in St Peter's beside his uncle Sixtus IV. As he lay in state in the church before his burial, the people of Rome flocked to see him, showing him an affection and respect that they had rarely accorded him in his lifetime. 'In the forty years I have been in Rome', wrote Paride de' Grassi, 'I have never seen, nor indeed has ever been seen, such a huge crowd of people flocking to the body of any pope.' The guards could not control those who pressed forward insisting on kissing his feet and who, as they did so, 'prayed aloud, through their tears, for the salvation of his soul, who had been a true Roman pope and Vicar of Christ, upholding justice, extending the Apostolic Church, punishing and conquering tyrants and powerful enemies'. Even many of those to whom the death of Julius might have been supposed to be welcome, for one reason or another, wept, 'because, they said, this pope rescued all of us, all Italy and all Christendom from the hands of the barbarians and the French'.[103]

Not all Italians agreed with this assessment. 'This pope . . . was the cause of Italy's ruin', wrote the Venetian diarist Sanuto, 'Would to God he had died five years ago, for the good of Christianity, and of this republic and of poor Italy.'[104] It was hard for the Venetians, against whom he had sought to rouse the most powerful states in Europe, to see him as a man devoted to the liberation of Italy. Julius did think and speak of Italy, and of his wish to see her free from foreign interference. 'We want to bring it about that the Italians should be neither French nor Spanish, and that we should all be Italians, and they should stay in their home, and we in ours.'[105] He wanted to 'bend all my thoughts to the liberation of Italy', he said, 'which I very much hope to see, and I am certain that this is God's will'.[106]

For Julius, freeing Italy from subordination to foreign powers was a cherished ambition, but it was a long-term one. It was not quite such a castle in the air as his visions of personally going on crusade were, but there was always something else to be done first – something for which the assistance of those foreign powers might be useful. As a cardinal, he had been prepared to bring the Duke of Lorraine to Naples to oppose Ferrante, to encourage the French to come to Italy in the hope that they would depose Alexander VI, to conquer his own home town of Savona for the French, to argue that he could not behave as a good Italian until his brother had been assured that he could keep all his lands. Throughout his pontificate, he was ready to use 'barbarians' to further his aims in Italy – without the help of French troops, and then of the Spanish and the Swiss, the 'warrior pope' would have had little military success to boast of.

There were many who would not have agreed with the mourners that Julius had been a 'true pope and Vicar of Christ' either. Guicciardini described him at the siege of Mirandola as preserving 'nothing of the pope about him but the robes and the name'.[107] It was Guicciardini who put his finger on the central problem in assessing Julius II as pope. He would, he wrote, be much honoured by those who 'judge that it is more the office of the popes to increase, with arms and the blood of Christians, the dominions of the Apostolic See than to labour, with the good example of their own lives and by correcting and caring for those fallen by the wayside, for the salvation of those souls, for which they boast that Christ appointed them his vicars on earth'.[108]

Julius was undoubtedly sincere in his conviction that he would strengthen the Church by securing the independence of the Papal States. On occasion, he expressed reluctance to spill Christian blood, but he never seems to have doubted that the use of force to attain his ends was justified. He was sincere in his desire to defend and promote the authority of the Church and of the papacy. To some extent he confused his own personal status and honour with those of the Church, and he did become distracted by fixations, such as taking Ferrara. But he did not confuse the interests of his family with the interests of the papacy, as his own uncle had done, and as Alexander VI had done.

He was also sincere in his faith, and had a sense of clerical decorum. He insisted, for example, that those who held the title of cardinal-priest should have been ordained as priests. Early in his pontificate he had supervised the ordination of Cardinals Riario and Sisto della Rovere, of Francesco Alidosi and Antonio Ferreri, and personally consecrated a number of his household prelates and cardinals as bishops.[109] He disliked long rituals, and was often impatient of the details of the ceremonial tradition guarded by the papal masters of ceremonies. Sometimes he would challenge their rulings, based on their cherished books, and would insist on doing things his way: simply.[110] But he was conscientious in his attendance at mass, and if he was too unwell to take part in the ceremonies of the papal liturgy, he would celebrate or hear mass privately. He was angry when he heard that the cardinals were rushing through the ceremonies for Holy Week in 1508, which he was too unwell to attend himself, and vexed that none of them came to his private chapel to take communion.[111] As the convocation of the Pisan council brought the need to respond to calls for the reform of the Church, he was readier than most of the cardinals and many of the *curiali* to contemplate beginning at the head, with himself and his court.

Julius did try to fulfil the duties and responsibilities of his office as he saw them, but he was really not cut out to be a pope. He was the type of the plain-spoken, short-tempered, vigorous, impetuous, big-hearted man of action, of uncomplicated, genuine faith. A Franciscan he may have been, but he was never made for the religious life: he said of himself that he would have made a bad monk, because he could not stay still.[112] He should have been a soldier: with some training he might even have been a successful one.

'Certainly worthy of great glory, if he had been a secular prince'[113] – an ironic comment from Guicciardini, and a strange epitaph for a pope, but perhaps the most fitting for the 'warrior pope', Julius II.

Notes

— • —

1 THE PAPAL NEPHEW

1 Giovanni Mercati, *Niccolò Perotti*, pp. 161–3.
2 Pastor, *History of the Popes*, vol. IV, pp. 237, 257–8, quoting A. Schmarsow, *Melozzo da Forlì* (Berlin, 1886), p. 18.
3 Ibid., pp. 236–7, quoting A. von Reumont, *Geschichte der Stadt Rom*, vol. III (Berlin, 1870), p. 165.
4 From F. Gregorovius, *Geschichte der Stadt Rom im Mittelalter*, 3rd edn, vol. VII (Stuttgart, 1880), p. 231.
5 Pastor, vol. IV, pp. 238–9. Platina (Bartolomeo dei Sacchi) was Vatican librarian under Sixtus IV; he wrote brief lives of the popes. Jacopo Ammannati was a learned cardinal.
6 ASforzesco, b. 68: Gianantonio Ferrofin(?), 6. Aug. 1471; ibid.: Nicodemo da Pontremoli to Cecco Simonetta, 20 Nov. 1471; ibid.: Nicodemo, 15 Sept. 1471; b. 69: Giovanni Arcimboldi et al., 12 Jan. 1472.
7 Ibid., b. 69: Archbishop of Novara, 25 Apr. 1472; Nicodemo, 26 Apr. 1472; b. 70, c. 33: Sixtus IV to Galeazzo Maria Sforza, 6 May 1472.
8 Ibid., b. 70, c. 132: Giovanni Arcimboldi, 29 May 1472.
9 Ibid., b. 69: Arcimboldi, 22 Apr. 1472.
10 Ibid., b. 71, c. 236: Archbishop of Novara and Gianandrea, 19 Nov. 1472.
11 He was promoted by the pope from count to duke in 1474 – see below, p. 22.
12 AGonzaga, b. 845, c. 122: Gianpietro Arrivabene, 16 Jan. 1474.
13 Ibid., c. 121: Gianpietro to Barbara Gonzaga, 16 Jan. 1474.
14 ASforzesco, b. 73: Galeazzo Maria Sforza to Sacromoro, 27 Oct. 1473; b. 74: Sacromoro, 13 Jan. 1474.
15 AGonzaga, b. 845, c. 149: Gianpietro Arrivabene, 15 June 1474.

16 ASforzesco, b. 76: 'Iuntinus de Pistoris(?)' to Sacromoro, 11 June 1474, Todi.
17 Ibid.: Sacromoro, 21(?) June 1474.
18 Flavio di Bernardo, *Gianantonio Campano*, pp. 363–74.
19 AGonzaga, b. 845, c. 231: Cardinal Francesco Gonzaga, 9 July 1474.
20 ASforzesco, b. 77: Vincula to Sixtus, 31 Aug. 1474, Città di Castello.
21 AGonzaga, b. 845, c. 167: Gianpietro Arrivabene, 9 Sept. 1474; c. 169: Arrivabene, 16 Sept. 1474.
22 ASforzesco, b. 77: Sacromoro, 2 Sept. 1474.
23 Bibl. Marc. 3622, c. 2: Vincula to Sixtus, 3 Aug. 1474, from camp at Città di Castello.
24 ASforzesco, b. 70, cc. 104–6: Giovanni Arcimboldi, 14 July 1472.
25 I.e. he could draw the income as abbot, but was not obliged to reside with the monks there.
26 AGonzaga, b. 845, c. 506: Gianpietro Arrivabene, 16 Nov. 1475; c. 510: Arrivabene, 29 Nov. 1475.
27 The Angevin claim to Naples dated from 1263, when Charles of Anjou accepted the investiture of the kingdom of the Two Sicilies from Urban IV, who wanted his help against the Hohenstaufen and their Ghibelline allies. The Orléans claims to Milan derived from the marriage of Valentina Visconti, half-sister of Filippo Maria, the last Visconti Duke of Milan, to Louis d'Orléans; Francesco Sforza, father of Galeazzo Maria, had married Filippo Maria's illegitimate daughter, Bianca Maria.
28 ASforzesco, b. 963: Guido Visconti, 29 Feb. 1476, Genoa.
29 AS Milano, Autografi, Ecclesiastici, b. 32, f. 255: Vincula, 4 Mar. 1476, Savona.
30 AGonzaga, b. 845, c. 609: Gianpietro Arrivabene, 2 Apr. 1476.
31 L.-H. Labande, *Avignon*, pp. 197–8.
32 Paul Ourliac, 'Le Concordat de 1472' (1941), p. 209.
33 AGonzaga, b. 845, cc. 619–20: Gianpietro Arrivabene, 20 May 1476.
34 Labande, *Avignon*, p. 211.
35 ASforzesco, b. 963: Guido Visconti, 2 June 1476, Genoa.
36 ASforzesco, b. 542: Giovanni Biamo(?), 6 May 1476, Lyons.
37 Labande, *Avignon*, pp. 216–17.
38 Ibid., pp. 218–19.
39 ASforzesco, b. 964: Daniele de' Rossi, 24 June 1476, Savona.
40 Ibid., b. 80: Sacromoro, 18 Feb. 1476.
41 AGonzaga, b. 845, c. 604: Gianpietro Arrivabene to Barbara Gonzaga, 9 Mar. 1476.
42 ASforzesco, b. 81: Sacromoro, 24 May 1476; Sacromoro, 30 May 1476.
43 Ibid.: Sacromoro, 17 May 1476.

44 ASforzesco, b. 80: Sacromoro, 27 Feb. 1476; b. 81: Sacromoro, 21 June 1476, Vetralla; b. 82: Sacromoro, 29 July 1476, Narni – 'esso cardinale non e cosi sempio, ch'el non habia gustato la natura de quello Re'; AGonzaga, b. 845, c. 676: Gianpietro Arrivabene, 15 Sept. 1476, Foligno.
45 ASforzesco, b. 82: Sacromoro, 31 Oct. 1476; Sacromoro, 13 Nov. 1476.
46 Ibid.: Sacromoro, 20 Dec. 1476.
47 See above, p. 10.
48 AGonzaga, b. 846, c. 20: Gianpietro Arrivabene, 16 Mar. 1477 – 'e in rotta col papa piu che mai'.
49 Ibid., c. 158: Gianfrancesco Gonzaga to Barbara Gonzaga, 22 Mar. 1477; ASforzesco, b. 83: Duchi to Sacromoro, 20 Apr. 1477, Milan.
50 ASforzesco, b. 83: Sacromoro, 14 May 1477.
51 Lorenzo de' Medici, *Lettere*, vol. III, pp. 370–1.
52 Bibl. Marc. 3622, c. 1: Vincula to Sixtus, 4 Aug. 1480, Lyons.
53 ASforzesco, b. 87: copy Vincula to Sixtus, 24 Aug. 1480, Vendôme.
54 *Lettres de Louis XI*, vol. VIII, pp. 285–8: Louis to Vincula, 25 Oct. 1480, Plessis-du-Parc.
55 Ibid., pp. 363–6: Vincula to Louis, 29 Oct. 1480, Péronne.
56 Bibl. Marc. 3622, c. 18: Vincula to Sixtus, 10 Feb. 1481, Tours.
57 Labande, *Avignon*, pp. 317–18.
58 Ourliac, 'Le Concordat de 1472' (1942), p. 123.
59 *Lettres de Louis XI*, vol. IX, pp. 72–3: Louis to Consuls of Avignon, 4 Sept. 1481, Plessis-du-Parc.
60 AS Florence, Otto, b. 2, c. 228: Tomasso Ridolfi, 5 Feb. 1482, Milan.
61 ASforzesco, b. 91: Branda da Castiglione et al., 14 Jan. 1482.
62 Ibid., b. 90: Branda da Castiglione and Antonio Trivulzio, 5 Sept. 1481.
63 Ibid., b. 91: ambassadors of league, 12 Mar. 1482.
64 Ibid., b. 88: Bishop of Como and Antonio Trivulzio, 18 Mar. 1482 [misfiled].
65 AS Modena, Roma, b. 8, 34/2: Niccolò Sadoleto, 28 Apr. 1484.
66 Nothing can be found out about it, as the archives of the Penitentiary are still closed to researchers.

2 THE POWER BESIDE THE THRONE

1 ASforzesco, b. 83: Sacromoro, 6 May 1477.
2 Ibid., b. 94: Antonio Trivulzio and Branda da Castiglione, 4 Dec. 1483.
3 Infessura, *Diario*, p. 129.
4 Ibid., pp. 170–1.
5 Burckhardt, *Diarium*, ed. Thuasne, vol. I, pp. 515–18: Guidantonio

Vespucci, 29 Aug. 1484; ? to Lorenzo de' Medici, 29 Aug. 1484; see below, p. 119.

6 ASV, Arm. XXIX, vol. 44, ff. 83v–84r.
7 AS Florence, X, b. 32, c. 103: Guidantonio Vespucci, 31 Aug. 1484.
8 AS Modena, Roma, b. 8, 35/2: Cristoforo de' Bianchi, 13 Oct. 1484; ? to Lorenzo de' Medici (see note 5 for reference).
9 AOrsini, b. 102, c. 10: Franceschetto Cibò to Virginio Orsini, 27 July 1485.
10 E.g. Pastor, vol. V, p. 242.
11 ASV, Arm. XXIX, vol. 44, ff. 32r–33r, 150r–v, 190v–191v.
12 AS Florence, X, b. 32, c. 213: Guidantonio Vespucci, 25 Sept. 1484.
13 AS Modena, Roma, b. 8, 35/15: Cristoforo de' Bianchi, 13 Oct. 1484; A. Fabroni, *Laurentii Medicis Magnifici Vita*, vol. II, p. 316: Guidantonio Vespucci to Lorenzo de' Medici, 25 Sept. 1484.
14 ASV, Arm. XXIX, vol. 49, ff. 31r–35r.
15 See below, pp. 66–7.
16 ASV, Arm. XXIX, v. 49, *passim*.
17 di Vascho, 'Diario', p. 521.
18 AOrsini, b. 142, c. 20: Obietto Fieschi to Virginio Orsini, 15 Jan. 1485.
19 AS Florence, X, b. 34, c. 220: Guidantonio Vespucci, 3 July 1485.
20 AGonzaga, b. 847, c. 301: Gianpietro Arrivabene, 6 July 1485.
21 AS Florence, X di Balìa, b. 34, c. 274: Guidantonio Vespucci, 23 July 1485; AGonzaga, b. 847, c. 320: Gianpietro Arrivabene, 21 July 1485.
22 E.g. E. Pontieri, *Ferrante d'Aragona*, pp. 450–1.
23 Pontieri, 'La "Guerra dei Baroni" napoletani' (1970), pp. 246–7: Jacopazzo d'Alesandro, 5 Sept. 1485, Naples.
24 E.g. ASforzesco, b. 98: Gianfrancesco Oliva, 5 Oct. 1485.
25 E.g. ASV, Arm. XXXIX, v. 19, ff. 32r, 51r, 58v–59r.
26 Infessura, *Diario*, pp. 192–3.
27 A. Cappelli, 'Lettere di Lorenzo de' Medici', pp. 280–1: Aldrovandino Guidoni to Ercole d'Este, 22 Mar. 1486.
28 ASV, Arm. XXXIX, v. 19, ff. 285v–286r.
29 AGonzaga, b. 847, c. 534: Gianpietro Arrivabene, 18 Apr. 1486; Cappelli, 'Lettere di Lorenzo de' Medici', p. 282; ASV, Arm. XXIX, v. 46, ff. 264r–266r.
30 ASV, Arm. XXXIX, v. 19, ff. 373v–374r.
31 Ibid., f. 423v; Paladino, 'Per la storia della Congiura dei Baroni', pp. 225–6: Battista Bendedei, 11 June 1486, Naples.
32 Infessura, *Diario*, pp. 201–2.
33 Pontieri, 'La "Guerra dei Baroni" napoletani' (1972), pp. 206–7: Bernardo Rucellai to Lorenzo de' Medici, 26 Oct. 1486, Naples.
34 Ibid., pp. 218–9: Pierfilippo Pandolfini to Lorenzo de' Medici, 30 Nov. 1486.

35 Volpicella (ed.), *Regis Ferdinandi Primi Instructionum Liber*, pp. 36–9: Ferrante's instructions to Luigi, 24 Sept. 1486, Naples.
36 Pontieri, 'La "Guerra dei Baroni" napoletani' (1972), p. 246: Pierfilippo Pandolfini to Lorenzo de' Medici, 1 Feb. 1487.
37 Bibl. Marc. 3622, cc. 13–14, 16, 20–43, 46–7.
38 'Dignitate status ecclesiastici'.
39 AOrsini, b. 101, c. 199: copy Albino to Ferrante, [? June 1487].
40 Pontieri, 'La "Guerra dei Baroni" napoletani' (1973), pp. 212–13: Pierfilippo Pandolfini to Lorenzo de' Medici, 11 Apr. 1487; ASforzesco, b. 100: Bishop of Como, 22 Apr. 1487.
41 ASforzesco, b. 100: Bishop of Como, 16 May 1487.
42 Ibid.: Bishop of Como, 20(?) Mar. 1487. Florence and Genoa were disputing the possession of Sarzana.
43 Bibl. Marc. 3622, c. 31: Vincula to Innocent, 17 Apr. 1487, Montefano.
44 Infessura, *Diario*, p. 228.
45 *Lettere, Istruzioni ed Altre Memorie de' Re Aragonesi*, p. 118: Ferrante to Giovanni Albino, 30 June 1487, Naples.
46 Ibid., pp. 140–1: Ferrante to Albino, 23 July 1487, Naples.
47 ASforzesco, b. 100: copy [Giangiacomo Trivulzio to Innocent] – for identification see Ibid.: Bishop of Como, 24 May 1487.
48 Infessura, *Diario*, p. 228.
49 ASforzesco, b. 100: Bishop of Tortona, 5 Sept. 1487.
50 AGonzaga, b. 847, cc. 786–7: copy Sigismondo Rocca, 9 Apr. 1488.
51 Ibid., b. 848, c. 461: Gianlucido Cataneo, 15 Oct. 1491.
52 Ibid., cc. 3–5: Cataneo, 18 Jan. 1489.
53 Ibid., c. 93: Cataneo, 17 Nov. 1489. For the building of the fortress at Ostia, see below, pp. 192–3.
54 ASforzesco, b. 105: Stefano Taberna to Lodovico Sforza, 22 Feb. 1492.

3 EXILE

1 See above, pp. 25–6, 27, 40.
2 AGonzaga, b. 849, c. 55: Fioramonte Brognolo to Isabella d'Este, 18 July 1492; cc. 223–4: Antonello Salerno, 21 July 1492, Rimini.
3 'Inimico capitale' – AOrsini, b. 101, c. 236: copy Virginio Orsini to Santi, 7 Apr. 1488.
4 Sigismondo de' Conti, *Le Storie de' Suoi Tempi*, vol. II, p. 56.
5 ASforzesco, b. 106: Stefano Taberna, 4 Aug. 1492.
6 G. B. Picotti, 'Giovanni de' Medici nel Conclave', pp. 159–61: Niccolò Michelozzi to Piero de' Medici, 12 Aug. 1492.
7 Ibid., pp. 136–7: Gianandrea Boccaccio, 20 Jan. 1493.
8 AGonzaga, b. 849, c. 156: Antonio Magistrello, 11 Aug. 1492; c. 195: Silvestro Calandra, 24 July 1492, Urbino.

9 Ibid., c. 325: Gianlucido Cataneo, 3 Aug. 1493.

10 AS Roma, Archivio del Collegio de' Notari Capitolini, vol. 176, ff. 706r–707v.

11 de' Conti, *Storie*, vol. II, pp. 55–6.

12 AGonzaga, b. 849, c. 361: Giacomo Scotto to Gianlucido Cataneo, 24 Jan. 1493.

13 Ibid., cc. 89–90: Fioramonte Brognolo, 9 Dec. 1492.

14 E.g. the status of Ferrante's daughter Beatrice, Queen of Hungary, who was resisting divorce; and the possession of Benevento.

15 Burckhardt, *Diarium*, ed. Thuasne, vol. II, pp. 622–4: Filippo Valori, 20 Jan. 1492(3).

16 See note 12.

17 Burckhardt, *Diarium*, ed. Thuasne, vol. II, pp. 630–1: Valori, 9 Feb. 1492(3); pp. 626–8: Valori, 26 Jan. 1492(3).

18 Pontieri, *Ferrante d'Aragona*, pp. 575–6: Vincula to Virginio Orsini, 26 Apr. 1493, Ostia.

19 AGonzaga, b. 849, c. 327: Gianlucido Cataneo, 23 Aug. 1493.

20 ASforzesco, b. 107: Stefano Taberna, 24 Sept. 1493.

21 AGonzaga, b. 849, c. 327: Gianlucido Cataneo, 23 Sept. 1493.

22 Ibid., b. 850: Cataneo, 14 Jan. 1493(4).

23 ASforzesco, b. 109: Ascanio Sforza to Lodovico Sforza, 23 Apr. 1494.

24 *Lettres de Charles VIII*, vol. IV, p. 15: Charles to Lodovico Sforza, 10 Feb. 1494, Amboise.

25 ASforzesco, b. 552: Carlo Barbiano to Lodovico Sforza, 6 Mar. 1494, Lyons – 'batterlo'.

26 See below, pp. 104, 105.

27 P. Negri, 'Studi sulla crisi italiana' (1923), p. 131: Lodovico Sforza to Ercole d'Este, 27 Dec. 1494.

28 ASforzesco, b. 110: copy Bartolomeo Zambeccari to Nestore Palliotti, 18 June 1494.

29 ASforzesco, b. 554: Vincula to Lodovico Sforza, 28 Sept. and 1 Oct. 1494, Genoa; b. 111: Lodovico Sforza to Vincula, 6 and 9 Oct. 1494, Vigevano; AS Milan, Autografi, Ecclesiastici, b. 32: Vincula to Lodovico Sforza, 9 Oct. 1494, Genoa.

30 Originally in the service of the Duke of Burgundy, Commynes had gone over to Louis XI, and was then a councillor of Louis's son, Charles VIII. His practical experience and knowledge of men make his memoirs a fascinating record of the politics of his day.

31 See below, p. 107.

32 Burckhardt, *Diarium*, ed. Thuasne, vol. II, pp. 661–6: French version of the articles between Charles and Alexander.

33 Ibid., p. 659.

34 ASforzesco, b. 114: summary of letters from Rome and elsewhere, Feb. 1495.

35 Philippe de Commynes, *Mémoires*, vol. II, pp. 248–50.

36 Labande, *Avignon*, pp. 477–98.
37 Desjardins and Canestrini, *Négociations*, vol. I, pp. 662–3: Francesco Soderini et al., 10 May 1496, Lyons.
38 Commynes, vol. II, pp. 358–60.
39 Commynes, vol. II, p. 359; ASforzesco, b. 506: Mafeo Pirovano, 9 Jan. 1497, Turin.
40 ASforzesco, b. 506: Pirovano, 8 Jan. 1497, Turin.
41 Ibid., b. 1223: Lucio Malvezzi, 9 Mar. 1497, Savona.
42 Ibid., b. 506: Pirovano, 7 Jan 1497, Turin.
43 Ibid., b. 558: summary of intercepted letters from Lyons to Rome.
44 Ibid., b. 153: Giovanna da Montefeltro to Pierpaolo da Cagli, 9 Jan. 1497, Senigallia.
45 Ibid., b. 506: Pirovano, 9 Jan. 1497, Turin.
46 AGonzaga, b. 850: Sigismondo Golfo, 22 Jan. 1494, Urbino.
47 Djem had been held in the Vatican since 1489.
48 ASforzesco, b. 120: 'Petitione facte per Fran.co Confalonero ad nome del R.mo Car.le S. P. in Vin.la', 28 Mar. 1497, Turin.
49 Ibid., b. 389: Battista Sfondrato, 14 Jan. 1497, Venice.
50 Ibid., b. 119: Lodovico Sforza to Ascanio Sforza, 13 Jan. 1497, Milan.
51 The former Principe d'Altamura, who had succeeded his nephew Ferrantino in October 1496.
52 ASforzesco, b. 507: Mafeo Pirovano, 21 Apr. 1497, Turin.
53 Ibid., b. 121: Ascanio Sforza, 7 June 1497.
54 Ibid., b. 510: Pirovano, 28 Feb. 1498, Turin.
55 Ibid.: Pirovano, 1 May 1498, Turin.
56 See above, p. 318 n. 27.
57 ASforzesco, b. 558: summary of letters from Pierpaolo da Cagli, 15 May 1498, Paris.
58 Ibid.: summary of news from France written from Paris, 26 July 1498.
59 Bibl. Marc. 3622, c. 45: Vincula to Alexander, 10 July 1497, Carpentras.
60 E.g. L.-G. Pélissier, 'Sopra alcuni documenti' (1894), pp. 339–40: Vincula to Alexander, 11 Sept 1498, Chieri; ASforzesco, b. 559: Ascanio Sforza, 20 Mar. 1499.
61 See below, p. 124.
62 Giustinian, *Dispacci*, vol. I, p. 274: 17 Dec. 1502.
63 See below, chapter 4, note 2.

4 THE ELECTION

1 Giustinian, *Dispacci*, vol. II, p. 181: 4 Sept. 1503.
2 Spanish troops had originally been sent to help King Ferrantino to recover the kingdom of Naples, but in the Treaty of Granada in

1500, France and Spain agreed to partition the kingdom of Naples between them. In 1501 King Federico had been forced to surrender to a second French invasion, and had gone into exile in France. Thereafter, the Spanish in Naples were fighting to take the kingdom for themselves.

3　AS Modena, Roma, b. 14, 98-VII/11: Beltrando Costabili, 5 Sept. 1503.
4　Giustinian, *Dispacci*, vol. II, pp. 181–2: 5 Sept. 1503.
5　AS Modena, Roma, b. 14, 98-VII/20: Costabili, 10 Sept. 1503.
6　Giustinian, *Dispacci*, vol. II, pp. 195–6: 14 Sept. 1503.
7　Burckhardt, *Liber Notarum*, p. 370.
8　Giustinian, *Dispacci*, vol. II, pp. 199–202: 22 Sept. 1503; Burckhardt, *Liber Notarum*, pp. 372–87; AS Modena, Roma, b. 14, 98-VII/29: Beltrando Costabili, 23 Sept. 1503; b. 19, 121–5/25: copy Lodovico Fabriano to Cardinal Ippolito d'Este, 4 Oct. 1503.
9　AS Modena, Roma, b. 14, 98-VII/81: Costabili, 8 Nov. 1503.
10　Burckhardt, *Liber Notarum*, p. 399.
11　AS Modena, Roma, b. 14, 98-VII/86: Costabili, 14 Nov. 1503.
12　Burckhardt, *Liber Notarum*, p. 399.
13　Giustinian, *Dispacci*, vol. II, pp. 272–3: 30 Oct. 1503.
14　Machiavelli, *Legazioni*, vol. II, p. 590: 31 Oct. 1503.
15　Guicciardini, *Storia d'Italia*, book VI, chapter 5.

5 THE PATRIMONY OF THE CHURCH

1　Sanuto, *I Diarii*, vol. V, col. 81.
2　Ibid., cols 383–4.
3　Ibid., col. 361.
4　Machiavelli, *Legazioni*, vol. II, p. 619: 11 Nov. 1503, Rome.
5　Giustinian, *Dispacci*, vol. II, p. 277: 1 Nov. 1503.
6　Ibid., p. 285: 8 Nov. 1503.
7　Ibid., pp. 414–18: 31 Jan. 1504.
8　Sanuto, vol. V, cols 480–1.
9　Giustinian, *Dispacci*, vol. II, pp. 418–20: 31 Jan. 1504.
10　Ibid., pp. 315–16: 28 Nov. 1503.
11　ASV, Arm. XXXIX, vol. 22, f. 4r.
12　CUL, Add. 4760, f. 16: copy Beltrando Costabili to Ercole d'Este, 9 Apr. 1504.
13　Giustinian, *Dispacci*, vol. II, pp. 78–80: 26 Apr. 1504.
14　Imprisoned in Spain, he escaped in 1506, but was killed the following year helping his brother-in-law, the King of Navarre, in an attack on a minor fortress.
15　Romeo Galli, 'Imola', pp. 431–2: Gianbattista Tonello to Caterina Sforza, 24 Mar. 1504.

16 Giustinian, *Dispacci*, vol. III, p. 155: 21 June 1504.
17 Le Glay, *Négociations*, LXII–LXIII.
18 Machiavelli, *Legazioni*, vol. II, p. 614: 10 Nov. 1503.
19 ASV, Arm. XXXIX, vol. 22, ff. 19r–20r: brief to Carlo del Carretto (nuncio in France), 7 Feb. 1504.
20 Venice still held ports in Puglia, taken as pledges for loans to Ferrantino.
21 AGonzaga, b. 856, cc. 28–9: Gianlucido Cataneo, 7 Feb. 1504.
22 CUL, Add. 4759, f. 229: Beltrando Costabili to Ercole d'Este, 20 Dec. 1503.
23 Giustinian, *Dispacci*, vol. III, pp. 65–7: 19 Apr. 1504.
24 ASV, Arm. XXXIX, vol. 22, ff. 57r–58r: brief to Maximilian, 14 May 1504.
25 Giustinian, *Dispacci*, vol. III, pp. 351–3: 31 Dec. 1504.
26 Ibid., p. 542: extract Giovanni Acciauoli, 5 May 1505.
27 AGonzaga, b. 856, cc. 28–9: Gianlucido Cataneo, 7 Feb. 1504.
28 Giustinian, *Dispacci*, vol. III, p. 167: 2 July 1504.
29 Ibid., p. 220: 2 Sept. 1504.
30 Cessi, *Dispacci*, p. XXII: Domenico Pisano, 15 Jan. 1505.
31 Sanuto, vol. V, col. 294.
32 M. Michaeli, *Memorie storiche della Città di Rieti*, pp. 40–3.
33 S. Marchesi, *Supplemento istorico dell'antica Città di Forlì*, pp. 609–25.
34 They had obtained a grant from Sixtus IV in 1482 of powers that they had in fact already taken for themselves.
35 Secondo Balena, *Ascoli nel Piceno*, pp. 431–5; Giuseppe Fabiani, *Ascoli nel Quattrocento*, vol. I, pp. 146–8.
36 Giustinian, *Dispacci*, pp. 196–7: 10 Aug. 1504.
37 AS Modena, Roma, b. 15, 98-IX/49: Beltrando Costabili, 17 Aug. 1504.
38 AS Florence, X, b. 73, c. 373: Giovanni Acciaroli, 14 Sept. 1504.
39 The following account of Julius's policies to bring order to the Papal States is largely based on the volume of papal briefs, ASV, Arm. XXXIX, vol. 22, *passim*.
40 Ibid., ff. 328r–v.
41 Ibid., Arm. XXIX, vol. 57, f. 124v.
42 See e.g. Guicciardini, *Storia d'Italia*, book VII, chapter XI.
43 D. Erasmus, *The "Julius Exclusus"* (trans. P. Pascal).
44 Giustinian, *Dispacci*, vol. III, pp. 411–12: 12 Feb. 1505.
45 Sanuto, vol. III, cols 1257, 1295; Guicciardini, *Storia d'Italia*, book VII, chapter III.
46 AS Bologna, Comune, Registrum Litterarum, b. 6, ff. 233v–234r: 4 Nov. 1503.
47 Giustinian, *Dispacci*, vol. III, pp. 149, 192–3: 17 June, 4 Aug. 1504.
48 AGonzaga, b. 857, cc. 130–1: Antonio Magistrello, 1 Aug. 1506.
49 Sanuto, vol. VI, col. 408.

50 de' Grassi, *Le Due Spedizioni Militari di Giulio II*, ed. Frati, p. 4.
51 Machiavelli joined him as a Florentine envoy just after he had set off from Rome, and stayed with him for nearly two months.
52 Machiavelli, *Legazioni*, vol. II, p. 954: 28 Aug. 1506, Civita Castellana.
53 de' Grassi, ed. Frati, is the main source for these and other details of the expedition.
54 Ibid., p. 26.
55 C. Pinzi, *Storia di Viterbo*, vol. IV, pp. 404–7.
56 Ibid., pp. 408–11.
57 Machiavelli, *Legazioni*, vol. II, p. 965: 5 Sept. 1506.
58 Machiavelli, *Discorsi*, book I, chapter XXVII.
59 Machiavelli, *Legazioni*, vol. II, p. 980: 13 Sept. 1506, Perugia.
60 AGonzaga, b. 857, cc. 195–6: Federico Cribello, 14 Sept. 1506, Perugia.
61 de' Grassi, ed. Frati, p. 42.
62 Machiavelli, *Legazioni*, vol. II, pp. 977–8: 12 Sept. 1506, Corciano.
63 Ibid., pp. 982, 988–9: 14 and 19 Sept. 1506.
64 de' Grassi, ed. Frati, pp. 46–7.
65 Ibid., pp. 49–50.
66 Sanuto, vol. VI, cols 421–2; Machiavelli, *Legazioni*, vol. II, p. 997: 26 Sept. 1506, Urbino.
67 Ibid.
68 A 'lance' was a unit of six mounted men, carrying a variety of weapons.
69 de' Grassi, ed. Frati, pp. 54–5.
70 Machiavelli, *Legazioni*, vol. II, pp. 1007–8: 3 Oct. 1506, Cesena.
71 Ibid., p. 1017: 10 Oct. 1506, Forlì.
72 AS Bologna, Comune, Lettere al Comune, b. 7, 41: Louis XII to Sixteen, 11 Sept. [1506], Chambéry.
73 Machiavelli, *Legazioni*, vol. II, pp. 1024–5: 16 Oct. 1506, Castrocaro.
74 de' Grassi, ed. Frati, pp. 65–6.
75 Ibid., p. 65.
76 Ibid., pp. 69–70.
77 Ibid., pp. 79–80.

6 THE PAPAL COURT

1 Partner, *The Pope's Men*, pp. 208–9.
2 See below, p. 202.
3 C. L. Stinger, *The Renaissance in Rome*, p. 127.
4 Sanuto, vol. XIII, col. 349.
5 Giustinian, *Dispacci*, vol. III, pp. 188–9: 29 July 1504.

6 AS Bologna, Comune, Lettere al Comune, b. 8, 90: Carlo Grato to Forty, 11 Mar. 1511, Ravenna.
7 Terrateig, *Politica en Italia*, vol. II, p. 139: Ferdinand to Jeronimo Vich, 17 Sept. 1510, Hita.
8 Cessi, *Dispacci*, p. 132: 12 Oct. 1509.
9 Ibid., p. 207: 23 Dec. 1509.
10 AS Modena, Roma, b. 19, 121-III/9: Lodovico Fabriano to Cardinal d'Este, 12 May 1505.
11 AS Bologna, Senato, Lettere, Ser. XIII, vol. 1, cc. 2, 44: Thomasino 'Barbiero' to Forty, 4 May 1507, 15 July 1508.
12 Rodriguez Villa, 'Francisco de Rojas' (1896), p. 391: Gonsalvo to Rojas, 17 May 1504, Naples.
13 AGonzaga, b. 856, 81: Gianlucido Cataneo, 23 Mar. 1504.
14 Ibid., b. 859, cc. 477–8: Stazio Gadio, 16 Aug. 1511.
15 Moncallero, *Epistolario di Bernardo Dovizi*, p. 326: 23 Oct. 1511.
16 Ibid., p. 348: 20 Nov. 1511, Civitavecchia.
17 AGonzaga, b. 860, cc. 342–5: Stazio Gadio, 18 Dec. 1512.
18 Ibid., cc. 19–21: Folenghino, 14 June 1512.
19 Moncallero, *Epistolario di Bernardo Dovizi*, p. 348: 20 Nov. 1511, Civitavecchia.
20 Luzio, *Isabella d'Este negli ultimi tre anni*, p. 74: Alessandro Gabbioneta, 11 Apr. 1511.
21 AGonzaga, b. 859, cc. 481–2: Stazio Gadio, 22 Aug. 1511.
22 Luzio, *op. cit.*, p. 87: Grossino, 11 Nov. 1511.
23 He recounted his connection with the della Rovere in AGonzaga, b. 856, c. 572: Marco Vigerio, 3 Mar. 1505.
24 Sanuto, vol. VI, col. 269.
25 See above, p. 165.
26 BL, Add. 8441, f. 224v.
27 AS Venice, X, Roma, b. 20, cc. 102–3: Girolamo Donà, 1 Mar. 1511, Ravenna.
28 See below, pp. 248, 250.
29 Terrateig, vol. II, p. 164: Ferdinand to Vich, 28 Jan. 1511, Guadalcanal.
30 The Sienese had 'discovered' that the della Rovere were originally from Siena.
31 AS Venice, X, Roma, b. 20, cc. 102–3: Girolamo Donà, 1 Mar. 1511, Ravenna.
32 See above, and p. 173.
33 Moncallero, *Epistolario di Bernardo Dovizi*, pp. 447, 449: 2, 3 Mar. 1512.
34 Luzio, *Isabella d'Este negli ultimi tre anni*, p. 208: Gabbioneta, 20 Feb. 1513.
35 AS Modena, Roma, b. 17, 98-XX/17: Beltrando Costabili to Cardinal d'Este, 26 Sept. 1508.

36 See below, p. 277.
37 See below, pp. 235–6, 294.
38 See below, p. 286.
39 Giustinian, *Dispacci*, vol. III, p. 443: 6 Mar. 1505.
40 AS Modena, Roma, b. 17, 98-XX/39: Beltrando Costabili, 10 Nov. 1508.
41 Sanuto, vol. VIII, cols 37, 169.
42 AS Modena, Roma, b. 14, 98-VII/103: 29 Nov. 1503.
43 Ibid., b. 19, 121-III/36: Lodovico Fabriano to Cardinal d'Este, 2 Dec. 1505; Burckhardt, *Liber Notarum*, pp. 498–9.
44 AGonzaga, b. 856, cc. 449–50: Lodovico Brognolo, 1 Dec. 1505.
45 Moncallero, *Epistolario di Bernardo Dovizi*, p. 320: 22 Oct. 1511.
46 Some historians mention two other daughters, Giulia and Clarice, but there is no reference to them in contemporary sources. If Felice had sisters, presumably they were dead by the time that Julius became pope. It is possible that Felice's stepdaughters, Giulia and Clarice Orsini, have been taken for her sisters.
47 The son of Antonello da Sanseverino.
48 Luzio, *Isabella d'Este negli ultimi tre anni*, p. 60: P. Barignano to Isabella d'Este, 19 Apr. 1511, Milan.
49 Laura's grandfather, Lodovico Migliorati, had taken the surname of his Orsini mother Elena, sister of the *condottiere* Napoleone Orsini.
50 See above, p. 180.
51 See above, p. 63.
52 See below, p. 307.
53 E.g. see above, pp. 20–1.
54 See below, p. 211.
55 Guicciardini, *Storia d'Italia*, book IX, chapter XVIII.
56 See below, pp. 287–8.
57 Luzio, 'La reggenza d'Isabella d'Este', p. 78: Cassola to Isabella d'Este, 21 Aug. 1510, Augsberg; id., *Isabella d'Este negli ultimi tre anni*, pp. 39–40.
58 Klaczko, *Jules II*, pp. 290, 293.

7 'JULIUS CAESAR PONTIFEX II'?

1 H. Hibberd, *Michelangelo*, p. 86.
2 AGonzaga, b. 860, c. 31: Folenghino, 26 June 1512.
3 D. Brown, 'The Apollo Belvedere', pp. 235–8.
4 AS Rome, Archivio del Collegio de' Notai Capitolini, vol. 176, ff. 706–707v.
5 P. Verdier, 'La Rocca d'Ostia', p. 303.
6 *Il Borgo di Ostia*, p. 72.
7 J. Hale, 'The Early Development of the Bastion', pp. 481–2.
8 ASforzesco, b. 109: Stefano Taberna to Lodovico Sforza, ? May

1494; ibid.: Taberna to Lodovico, 3 May 1494; ibid., b. 119: Taberna to Lodovico, 8 Feb. 1497.

9 Labande, *Avignon*, pp. 334–5.
10 ASforzesco, b. 510: Vincula to Mafeo Pirovano, 20 Mar. 1498, Chieri.
11 Ibid.: Vincula to Pirovano, 20 Mar., 20 Apr. 1498, Chieri.
12 Giustinian, *Dispacci*, vol. III, pp. 30–1: 22 Mar. 1504.
13 Luzio, *Isabella d'Este negli ultimi tre anni*, pp. 163–4: Crossino, 26 Sept. 1512.
14 AS Modena, Roma, b. 17, 98-XXI/4: Beltrando Costabili to Cardinal Ippolito d'Este, 21 Feb. 1509.
15 E.g. Stinger, *The Renaissance in Rome*, pp. 270–6; A. Bruschi, *Bramante*, pp. 160ff.
16 J. S. Ackerman, *The Cortile of the Belvedere*, p. 43; Weiss, 'The Medals of Julius II', p. 181.
17 The sixteenth-century artist who wrote invaluable lives of the Italian artists who had preceded him.
18 Vasari, *Le Vite*, vol. IV, pp. 79–80.
19 AS Modena, Roma, b. 16, 98-XIX/33: Beltrando Costabili, 20 Aug. 1508.
20 Stinger, *The Renaissance in Rome*, p. 269.
21 Bramante died in 1514.
22 BL, Add. 8441, ff. 107r–v.
23 Stinger, *The Renaissance in Rome*, pp. 199–200.
24 C. Hope, 'Artists, Patrons and Advisers', pp. 315–6.
25 R. J. Clements (ed.), *Michelangelo: A Self-Portrait*, p. 50.
26 E.g. Hibberd, *Michelangelo*, p. 105.
27 Seminar paper given by Richard Cocke to the seminar on Italian history from *c.*1500 at the Institute of Historical Research, University of London, December 1991.
28 A. Condivi, *Vita di Michelangelo Buonarroti*, p. 76.
29 Hibberd, *Michelangelo*, p. 95.
30 Condivi, *Vita*, pp. 61–2.
31 Hibberd, *Michelangelo*, pp. 149, 151.
32 C. L. Frommel, 'Die Peterskirche', p. 88.
33 Id., ' "Capella Iulia" ', pp. 29–30.
34 AS Modena, Roma, b. 16, 98-XV/72: Beltrando Costabili, 12 Apr. 1507.
35 Frommel, ' "Capella Iulia" ', p. 34.
36 de' Grassi, ed. Frati, p. 26.
37 Sanuto, vol. VIII, col. 23.
38 de' Grassi, ed. Frati, pp. 107–8.
39 Ibid., p. 225.
40 Condivi, *Vita*, p. 63.
41 de' Grassi, ed. Frati, pp. 286–7.
42 Bruschi, *Bramante*, p. 203.

43 E.g. C. L. Stinger, 'Roma Triumphans', pp. 190–1, 196.
44 *Lettres du Roy Louis XII*, vol. I, p. 261: Andrea de Borgo and Motta to Margaret, 21 July 1510, Blois.
45 See below, p. 213.
46 de' Grassi, ed. Frati, pp. 172–4.
47 Sanuto, vol. VII, col. 64.
48 A. Denis, *Charles VIII et les Italiens*, p. 69.
49 AGonzaga, b. 860, c. 4: Folenghino, 11 May 1512.
50 E.g. Bruschi, *Bramante*, p. 12; S. von Moos, 'The Palace as a Fortress', p. 47.
51 See below, chapters 9 and 10.
52 See below, pp. 212–13.
53 AS Modena, Roma, b. 16, 98-XV/74: Beltrando Costabili, 16 Apr. 1507; b. 19, 121-V/15: Lodovico Fabriano to Cardinal Ippolito d'Este, 22 Apr. 1507.
54 G. De Fiore, *Baccio Pontelli*, pp. 70, 81.
55 Weiss, 'The Medals of Julius II', pp. 181–2.
56 E.g. ibid., pp. 170, 171, 172, 174, 176, 178, 179.
57 See below, p. 252.

8 THE LEAGUE OF CAMBRAI

1   Sanuto, vol. VI, cols 499, 501–2; de' Grassi, ed. Frati, pp. 99–101.
2   AS Bologna, Comune, Liber Partitorum, reg. 13, ff. 4r–5r.
3   Sanuto, vol. VI, col. 497.
4   AS Modena, Roma, b. 16, 98-XV/21: Beltrando Costabili, 1 Feb. 1507, Bologna.
5   Ibid., 98-XV/18: Costabili, 25 Jan. 1507, Bologna.
6   AS Bologna, Comune, Liber Partitorum, reg. 13, ff. 15v–16r.
7   Sanuto, vol. VI, col. 547.
8   AS Modena, Roma, b. 16, 98-XV/21: Beltrando Costabili, 1 Feb. 1507, Bologna.
9   Desjardins and Canestrini, vol. II, p. 191: Francesco Pandolfini, 24–8 Nov. 1506, Blois.
10 Ibid., p. 220: Pandolfini, 16 Feb. 1507, Bourges.
11 AS Modena, Roma, b. 16, 98-XVI/37: Beltrando Costabili, 16 June 1507.
12 Ibid., 98-XV/18: Costabili, 25 Jan. 1507, Bologna.
13 CUL, Add. 4761, f. 43: Costabili, 6 Feb. 1507, Bologna.
14 de' Grassi, ed. Frati, p. 165.
15 Ibid., p. 169.
16 Ibid., pp. 172–6.
17 See below, pp. 288–9 for a later attempt by the Romans to recover some of their lost powers.

18   Pastor, vol. VI, pp. 288–9.
19   AS Modena, Roma, b. 16, 98-XV/74: Beltrando Costabili, 16 Apr. 1507.
20   Giustinian, *Dispacci*, vol. III, pp. 136–7: 6 June 1504.
21   ASV, Arm. XXXIX, vol. 22, ff. 80v–81r: Julius to Cardinal Rouen, 8 June 1504.
22   AS Modena, Roma, b. 17, 98-XX/28: Beltrando Costabili, 23 Oct. 1508.
23   Terrateig, vol. II, p. 46: Jeronimo Vich to Ferdinand, 28 Feb. 1508, Rome.
24   Federico Seneca, *Venezia e Giulio II*, pp. 185–6: Manfredo de' Manfredi to Alfonso d'Este, 2 Mar. 1507, Bourges.
25   Desjardins and Canestrini, vol. II, p. 220: Francesco Pandolfini, 16 Feb. 1507, Bourges.
26   Giustinian, *Dispacci*, vol. II, pp. 444–5: 21 Feb. 1504.
27   A. Rodriguez Villa, 'Francisco de Rojas' (1896), pp. 380–1: Ferdinand and Isabella to Rojas, 25 Apr. 1504, Medina del Campo. See also, J. Fernandez Alonso, 'La legación frustrada de Cosimo dei Pazzi'.
28   Terrateig, vol. II, pp. 45–6: Jeronimo Vich, 28 Feb. 1508.
29   *Lettres du Roy Louis XII*, vol. I, p. 110: Ferdinand to Viceroy of Naples, 22 May 1508, Burgos.
30   Seneca, *Venezia e Giulio II*, p. 197: Roberto Acciaiuoli to X di Balìa, 5 Aug. 1508.
31   M. Brunetti, 'Alla vigilia di Cambrai', p. 18.
32   Wiesflecker, *Kaiser Maximilian I*, vol. III, p. 370, vol. IV, pp. 91–5.
33   E.g. Luzio, 'La reggenza d'Isabella d'Este', p. 40: Brognolo to Isabella, 18 Feb. 1510.
34   Burckhardt, *Liber Notarum*, p. 456.
35   See above, p. 165.
36   Rodriguez Villa, 'Francisco de Rojas' (1896), pp. 387–8.
37   I.e. those benefices held by clerics resident in Rome, working in the curia or transacting business there.
38   Le Glay, *Négociations*, pp. 115–16: Philibert Naturelli, 18 Apr. 1506.
39   See above, pp. 160–1 and below, pp. 262–3.
40   Seneca, *Venezia e Giulio II*, p. 182: Manfredo de' Manfredi to Alfonso d'Este, 24 Feb. 1507, Bourges.
41   Guicciardini, *Storia d'Italia*, book IX, chapter IX.
42   AS Venice, X, Roma, b. 20, c. 62: Domenico Pisano, 6 Jan. 1506(7), Bologna.
43   Sanuto, vol. VI, col. 177.
44   See note 42.
45   Ibid., c. 64: Pisano, 11 Jan. 1506(7), Bologna.
46   Cessi, *Dispacci*, p. xxxvii.
47   CUL, Add. 4761, ff. 43–4: Beltrando Costabili, 6 Feb. 1507, Bologna.

48 Seneca, *Venezia e Giulio II*, pp. 190–1: Roberto Acciaiuoli to X di Balìa, 7 Nov. 1507.
49 AGonzaga, b. 858: Lodovico di Camposampiero, 8 Apr. 1508.
50 CUL, Add. 4761, f. 173: Beltrando Costabili, 17 Apr. 1508.
51 Sanuto, vol. VII, col. 591.
52 Seneca, *Venezia e Giulio II*, p. 198: Roberto Acciaiuoli to X di Balìa, 23 Sept. 1508.
53 Terrateig, vol. II, p. 43: Jeronimo Vich to ?, 28 Feb. 1508.
54 Ibid., p. 47: Vich to Ferdinand, 28 Feb. 1508.
55 CUL, Add. 4761, ff. 257–8: Beltrando Costabili, 24 Oct. 1508.
56 Le Glay, *Correspondance de Maximilien*, vol. I, pp. 99–102: Maximilian to Margaret, 27 Oct. 1508, Breda.
57 Terrateig, vol. II, p. 63: Vich, 16 Dec. 1508.
58 Le Glay, *Négociations*, p. 238: terms of Treaty of Cambrai, 10 Dec. 1508.
59 Seneca, *Venezia e Giulio II*, p. 193: Roberto Acciaiuoli to X di Balìa, 15 July 1508.
60 CUL, Add. 4761, ff. 241–2: Beltrando Costabili, 5 Oct. 1508.
61 Ibid., ff. 251–2: Costabili, 23 Oct. 1508.
62 Seneca, *Venezia e Giulio II*, pp. 206–7: Acciaiuoli to X di Balìa, 24 Oct. 1508.
63 Le Glay, *Négociations*, pp. 237–43: terms of Treaty of Cambrai, 10 Dec. 1508.
64 Terrateig, vol. II, pp. 67–9: Ferdinand to Jeronimo Vich, 17 and 20 Feb. 1509, Villa Hoza and Castro Verde.
65 Sanuto, vol. VII, col. 760.
66 Ibid., vol. VIII, col. 30.
67 Ibid., col. 37.
68 Ibid., col. 35.
69 Ibid., col. 80.
70 Ibid., cols 133–4.
71 Ibid., col. 252.
72 Ibid., cols 321, 326, 329–30.
73 Luzio, 'La reggenza d'Isabella d'Este', pp. 40–1: Cardinal Sigismondo Gonzaga to Isabella, 10 June 1509, Ancona.
74 Seneca, *Venezia e Giulio II*, p. 133.
75 Cessi, *Dispacci*, pp. 36–7: 9 July 1509.
76 Ibid., p. 73: 15 Aug. 1509.
77 Ibid., pp. 149–50: 3 Nov. 1509.
78 Ibid., pp. 155–6, 165: 5 and 16 Nov. 1509.
79 Ibid., p. 178: 26 Nov. 1509.
80 Ibid., pp. 213–14: 1 Jan. 1509(10).
81 Sanuto, vol. IX, cols 579–92.
82 Ibid., col. 535.
83 Cessi, *Dispacci*, p. 223: 9 Jan. 1509.

84 Sanuto, vol. X, col. 10.
85 Ibid., cols 9–13.

9 'FUORI I BARBARI'

1   Cessi, *Dispacci*, pp. 33–4: 8 July 1509.
2   Ibid., p. 44: 18 July 1509.
3   Desjardins and Canestrini, vol. II, p. 389: Alessandro Nasi and Francesco Pandolfini, 3–4 July 1509, Milan.
4   Cessi, *Dispacci*, pp. 22–3: 5 July 1509.
5   Ibid., pp. 63–4, 76: 4 and 17 Aug. 1509.
6   Desjardins and Canestrini, vol. II, pp. 396–7: Nasi and Pandolfini, 20–1 July 1509, Milan.
7   Cessi, *Dispacci*, pp. 49, 53: 21 and 23 July 1509.
8   Desjardins and Canestrini, vol. II, pp. 405–6: Pandolfini, 12–15 Aug. 1509, Milan.
9   Ibid., pp. 411–12: Nasi, 11 Aug. 1509, Mortara.
10 Cessi, *Dispacci*, p. 79: 23 Aug. 1509.
11 He had originally been elected in 1506 – see above, p. 175.
12 Desjardins and Canestrini, vol. II, p. 421: Nasi, 22–3 Sept. 1509, Blois.
13 Ibid., p. 422: Nasi, 22–3 Sept. 1509, Blois.
14 Cessi, *Dispacci*, pp. 132–3: 12 Oct. 1509.
15 Ibid., p. 137: 25 Oct. 1509.
16 He was the son of Madeleine d'Amboise.
17 Cessi, *Dispacci*, p. 137: 25 Oct. 1509.
18 Ibid., pp. 156, 168, 169, 214, 226: 5 and 18 Nov. 1509, 1 and 9 Jan. 1509(10).
19 Desjardins and Canestrini, vol. II, p. 459: Nasi, 17 Jan. 1510, Blois.
20 Ibid., pp. 462–4, 461: Nasi, 28 and 23 Jan. 1510, Blois.
21 Ibid., pp. 471, 475: Nasi, 9 and 17 Feb. 1510, Blois.
22 AS Venice, Archivio Proprio, Roma, Reg. 3, n. 21, 28: 2(?) and 10 Mar. 1510.
23 Ibid., n. 31: 15 Mar. 1510, Civitavecchia.
24 Ibid., n. 2: 21 Jan. 1509(10).
25 Ibid., n. 38: 26 Mar. 1510.
26 Ibid., n. 61: 15 May 1510.
27 Sanuto, vol. X, cols 747 ff. and vol. XI, *passim* to col. 440, has much information about these expeditions.
28 Ibid., vol. VI, col. 490.
29 AS Modena, Roma, b. 16, 98-XV/57: Beltrando Costabili, 15 Mar. 1507, Viterbo.
30 CUL, Add. 4760, f. 137: Beltrando Costabili, 6 May 1505; AS Modena, Roma, b. 16, 98-XII/16: Costabili, 23 May 1505.

31 CUL, Add. 4761, ff. 99–100: Costabili, 27 Apr. 1507.
32 Sanuto, vol. VIII, col. 283.
33 Cessi, *Dispacci*, pp. 47, 55: 21 and 24 July 1509.
34 Ibid., pp. 204, 206: 13 and 23 Dec. 1509.
35 Ibid., pp. 59, 169: 29 July, 18–19 Nov. 1509.
36 AGonzaga, b. 858: Lodovico Brognolo to Isabella d'Este, 20 Mar. 1510, Rome.
37 AS Venice, Archivio Proprio, Roma, Reg. 3, n. 45: 10 Apr. 1510.
38 Ibid., n. 50: 24 Apr. 1510.
39 Ibid., n. 56: 6 May 1510.
40 Sanuto, vol. X, col. 369.
41 CUL, Add. 4762, f. 27: Beltrando Costabili, [30] May 1504.
42 Ibid., f. 49: Alfonso to Beltrando Costabili, 15 June 1510, Montagniana.
43 AS Venice, Archivio Proprio, Roma, Reg. 3, n. 101: 29 June 1510.
44 Sanuto, vol. XI, col. 108.
45 Sanuto, vol. XI, cols 213, 279.
46 I.e. lands that had been held until the middle of the eighth century by the representatives in Italy of the Emperor in Constantinople; the eighth-century popes claimed to have succeeded to this position.
47 de' Grassi, ed. Frati, p. 189.
48 AS Venice, X, Roma, b. 20, 93: Girolamo Donà, 10 Oct. 1510, Bologna.
49 Ibid., Archivio Proprio, Roma, Reg. 3, n. 57: 7 May 1510.
50 Desjardins and Canestrini, vol. II, p. 501: Alessandro Nasi, 18 May 1510, Lyons.
51 Sanuto, vol. X, col. 631.
52 Le Glay, *Négociations*, p. 355: Louis XII to Chaumont, 21 July 1510, Blois.
53 Machiavelli, *Legazioni*, vol. III, pp. 1257–8: 26 July 1510, Blois.
54 Sanuto, vol. XI, col. 551.
55 de' Grassi, ed. Frati, p. 203.
56 Terrateig, vol. II, pp. 92–3: Ferdinand to Jeronimo Vich, 5 Dec. 1509, Leon.
57 Ibid., pp. 104–10: Ferdinand to Vich, 18 Mar. 1510, Madrid.
58 Ibid., pp. 116–18: Ferdinand to Vich, 13 May 1510, Monzón.
59 Sanuto, vol. X, col. 829; Terrateig, vol. II, pp. 132–3: Ferdinand to Vich, 5 Aug. 1510, Monzón.
60 Ibid., pp. 132–3: Ferdinand to Vich, 5 Aug. 1510, Monzón.
61 Sanuto, vol. XI, col. 550.
62 Ibid., col. 634.
63 Ceretti, 'Francesca Trivulzio', p. 105.
64 AGonzaga, b. 859, cc. 543–4: Stazio Gadio, 29 Dec. 1511(10), Bologna.
65 Sanuto, vol. XI, col. 721 – 'Vederò, si averò si grossi li coglioni, come ha il re di Franza.'

66 Ibid., cols 721–2.
67 Ibid., cols 743–4.
68 Ibid., col. 745.
69 Luzio, *Isabella d'Este negli ultimi tre anni*, p. 44.
70 Guicciardini, *Storia d'Italia*, book IX, chapter XIII.
71 Sanuto, vol. XI, cols 723, 779.
72 Ibid., vol. XII, cols 97–8.
73 See above, pp. 173, 176.
74 Luzio, *Isabella d'Este negli ultimi tre anni*, p. 74.
75 *Lettres du Roy Louis XII*, vol. II, pp. 98–9: Julius to Conservatori and Community of Modena, 29 Jan. 1511, Mirandola.
76 de' Grassi, ed. Frati, pp. 261–2.
77 *Lettres du Roy Louis XII*, vol. II, pp. 160–3: Matthaeus Lang to Etienne Poncher, 16 Apr. 1511, Bologna.
78 Guicciardini, *Storia d'Italia*, book IX, chapter XVI.
79 *Lettres du Roy Louis XII*, vol. II, pp. 163–4: Lang to Poncher, 17 Apr. 1511, Bologna.
80 AGonzaga, b. 859, c. 245: Alessandro Gabbionetta, 17 May 1511, Ravenna.
81 R. Honig, *Bologna e Giulio II*, p. 42.
82 AS Bologna, Comune, Registrum Litterarum, b. 8, ff. 121r–v.
83 AGonzaga, b. 1069, cc. 227–8: Francesco Maria della Rovere, 31 May 1511, Urbino.

10 IL PAPA TERRIBILE

1 A. Renaudet, *Le Concile Gallican*, p. 2: Matteo Nicolini, 28 June 1510.
2 CUL, Add. 4762, ff. 39–40: Beltrando Costabili, 7 June 1510.
3 Sanuto, vol. X, cols 564–5.
4 Ibid., cols 803–4, 829.
5 AS Modena, Roma, b. 17, 98-XXII/29: Beltrando Costabili to ?, 2 July 1510; Sanuto, vol. X, cols 747–8.
6 Ibid., col. 829.
7 Machiavelli, *Legazioni*, vol. III, p. 1249: 21 July 1510, Blois.
8 Ibid., p. 1347: 10 Sept. 1510, Tours.
9 *Lettres du Roy Louis XII*, vol. II, p. 32: Andrea del Borgo and Mota to Margaret, 19 Sept. 1510, Tours.
10 Renaudet, *Le Concile Gallican*, pp. 9–10: Louis to Piero Soderini and Signoria of Florence, 27 Sept. 1510, Plessis-lès-Tours.
11 Sanuto, vol. XI, col. 534.
12 Terrateig, vol. II, pp. 144–5: Ferdinand to Vich, 23 Oct. 1510, Madrid.
13 E.g. see above, pp. 165–6.
14 See above, p. 180.

15 See above, p. 229.

16 Moncallero, *Epistolario di Bernardo Dovizi*, p. 250: Dovizi to Isabella d'Este, 3 Jan 1511, Bologna; Luzio, *Isabella d'Este negli ultimi tre anni*, pp. 48–9: Jacopo d'Atri, 22 Jan. 1511 [Blois?].

17 Ibid., p. 50: d'Atri, 14 Feb. 1511 [Blois?].

18 Sanuto, vol. XII, cols 250–4.

19 Renaudet, *Le Concile Gallican*, p. 280: Maximilian to Piero Soderini and X di Balìa, 27 Sept. 1511, 'Hamfels'.

20 Terrateig, vol. II, pp. 148–9: Ferdinand to Vich, 2 Nov. 1510, Madrid.

21 Ibid., p. 166: Ferdinand to Vich, 16 June 1511, Seville.

22 Sanuto, vol. XII, col. 243.

23 *Letters and Papers of Henry VIII*, vol. I, pp. 437–8.

24 Renaudet, *Le Concile Gallican*, p. 82: Pierfrancesco Tosinghi, 30 July 1511.

25 Sanuto, vol. XII, col. 449.

26 AGonzaga, b. 859, c. 487: Stazio Gadio, 25 Aug 1511.

27 Sanuto, vol. XII, col. 449.

28 AGonzaga, b. 859, c. 497: Stazio Gadio, 31 Aug. 1511.

29 Ibid., cc. 481–2, c. 497: Gadio, 22 and 31 Aug. 1511.

30 Ibid., c. 488: Gadio, 25 Aug. 1511.

31 Ibid., cc. 475–6: Gadio to Isabella d'Este, 16(?) Aug. 1511.

32 Ibid., c. 504: Gadio, 8 Sept. 1511.

33 C. Gennaro, 'La "Pax Romana" ', pp. 53, 50.

34 AS Florence, X, b. 105, c. 379: Pierfrancesco Tosinghi, 27 Aug. 1511.

35 *Lettres du Roy Louis XII*, vol. III, pp. 43–4: instructions of Julius to Bishop Andrew Forman, 25 Sept. 1511; pp. 53–5, Louis's response to terms proposed by Julius (possibly not to those dated 25 Sept.).

36 Terrateig, vol. II, pp. 168–74: Ferdinand to Vich, 16 July 1511, Hontiveros (2 letters).

37 Moncallero, *Epistolario di Bernardo Dovizi*, p. 260: 4 Oct. 1511.

38 Sanuto, vol. XIII, cols 88–93.

39 Renaudet, *Le Concile Gallican*, pp. 43–4: Roberto Acciaiuoli, 1 June 1511, Grenoble.

40 Machiavelli, *Legazioni*, vol. III, p. 1420: Roberto Acciaiuoli, 24 Sept. 1511, Blois.

41 Renaudet, *Le Concile Gallican*, p. 367: Pierfrancesco Tosinghi, 13 Oct. 1511.

42 Machiavelli, *Legazioni*, vol. III, pp. 1434–5: Roberto Acciaiuoli, 2 Oct. 1511, Blois.

43 Terrateig, vol. II, p. 169: Ferdinand to Vich, 16 July 1511, Hontiveros.

44 Moncallero, *Epistolario di Bernardo Dovizi*, pp. 445, 455: 2 and 9 Mar. 1512.

45 Terrateig, vol. II, p. 189: Vich to Ferdinand, 15 Apr. 1512.

46 Sanuto, vol. XIV, col. 159.

47 See above, p. 254.

48 Sanuto, vol. XIV, col. 159.

49 Ibid., col. 458.

50 AGonzaga, b. 860, cc. 252–3: Stazio Gadio, 2 July 1512.

51 Sanuto, vol. XIV, col. 450.

52 Luzio, *Isabella d'Este negli ultimi tre anni*, p. 139: Grossino, 30 June 1512.

53 Pastor, vol. VI, p. 418.

54 AS Bologna, Comune, Registrum Litterarum, b. 8, f. 189r: Anziani et al. to Cardinal Sigismondo Gonzaga, 10 June 1512, Bologna.

55 Honig, *Bologna*, pp. 66–7.

56 AS Bologna, Comune, Registrum Litterarum, b. 8, ff. 191v–192r: Anziani et al. to Julius, 13 June 1512, Bologna.

57 Ibid., ff. 192v–194v.

58 See above, p. 203.

59 AS Bologna, Senato, Carteggio, Serie VII, vol. 1: Bolognese ambassadors to Anziani et al., 27 June 1512.

60 N. Minnich, 'The Healing of the Pisan Schism', pp. 96ff.

61 AGonzaga, b. 860, c. 188: Stazio Gadio, 16 Mar. 1512.

62 Pastor, vol. VI, pp. 408–9.

63 Sanuto, vol. XIV, cols 229–30.

64 Luzio, *Isabella d'Este negli ultimi tre anni*, pp. 219–20.

65 Alberto had a personal grudge against Alfonso, because of the execution of some relatives found guilty of conspiracy against the Este.

66 AGonzaga, b. 860, c. 162: Mario Equicola to Isabella d'Este, 9 July 1512; Luzio, *Isabella d'Este negli ultimi tre anni*, p. 141.

67 A. Gonzaga, b. 860, cc. 20–1: Folenghino, 14 June 1512.

68 Ibid., cc. 43–4: Folenghino, 29 July 1512; Luzio, *Isabella d'Este negli ultimi tre anni*, pp. 142–3: Alfonso to Folenghino, 19 July 1512, Marino.

69 Ibid., p. 223: Isabella to Cardinal Ippolito d'Este, 21 July 1512, Mantua; p. 144: Folenghino, 25 July 1512.

70 Sanuto, vol. XIV, cols 454–5.

71 AS Florence, X, b. 103, c. 114: Antonio Strozzi, 9 Feb. 1511(2).

72 Sanuto, vol. XIV, col. 190.

73 Ibid., col. 185.

74 AS Florence, X, b. 109, c. 339: Antonio Strozzi, 18 Apr. 1512.

75 AGonzaga, b. 860, c. 298: Stazio Gadio, 3 Sept. 1512.

76 Ibid., c. 33: Folenghino, 26 June 1512.

77 Moncallero, *Epistolario di Bernardo Dovizi*, p. 394: 8 Dec. 1511.

78 Ibid., p. 466: 13 Mar. 1512.

79 AGonzaga, b. 860, c. 36: Folenghino, 6 July 1512.

80 'L'accepto'.

81 Ibid., c. 48: Folenghino, 14 Aug. 1512.

82 José Doussinague, *Fernando el Católico*, p. 550: instructions of Ferdinand to Juan de Lanuza, Oct. 1512.
83 AGonzaga, b. 860, cc. 61–2: Folenghino, 28 Aug. 1512.
84 C. Santoro, *Gli Sforza*, p. 350.
85 AGonzaga, b. 860, c. 61: Folenghino, 28 Aug. 1512.
86 The boy's uncle Galeazzo tried to become *signore* but did not have much support from the citizens.
87 Baldassare Castiglione, *Lettere*, vol. I, pp. 309–12: memorandum for Louis XII, Mar. 1512, Blois; pp. 313–4: Francesco Maria to Francesco Gonzaga, 17 Apr. 1512, Fossombrone.
88 Luzio, *Isabella d'Este negli ultimi tre anni*, p. 174: Isabella to Alfonso d'Este, 31 Oct. 1512.
89 AGonzaga, b. 860, c. 51: Folenghino, 15 Aug. 1512.
90 Wiesflecker, *Maximilian I.*, vol. IV, p. 92.
91 Le Glay, *Correspondance*, vol. II, pp. 37–9: Maximilian to Margaret, 18 Sept. [1512].
92 Terrateig, vol. II, pp. 218–19: Ferdinand to Vich, 8 June 1512.
93 *Lettres du Roy Louis XII*, vol. III, pp. 310–17: Jean le Veau to Margaret, 23 Aug. 1512, Trent.
94 AS Bologna, Comune, Lettere al Comune, b. 5: Bolognese ambassadors to Anziani et al., 5 Nov. 1512.
95 AGonzaga, b. 860, cc. 336–7: Stazio Gadio, 27 Nov. 1512.
96 Ibid., cc. 340–1: Gadio, 7 Dec. 1512.
97 Sanuto, vol. XV, col. 411.
98 Doussinague, *Fernando el Católico*, pp. 565–7: Ferdinand to Vich, 11 Jan. 1513.
99 Sanuto, vol. XV, col. 492.
100 Luzio, *Isabella d'Este negli ultimi tre anni*, pp. 207–8: Alessandro da Gabbionetta, 20 Feb. 1513.
101 AGonzaga, b. 861: Cardinal Sigismondo Gonzaga, 20 Feb. 1513.
102 Ibid.
103 BL, Add. 8442, f. 290r.
104 Sanuto, vol. XV, col. 561.
105 Giustinian, *Dispacci*, vol. III, p. 444: 6 Mar. 1505.
106 AS Venice, Archivio Proprio, Roma, Reg. 3, 87: 20(?) June 1510.
107 Guicciardini, *Storia d'Italia*, book IX, chapter XIII.
108 Ibid., book XI, chapter VIII.
109 Burckhardt, *Liber Notarum*, pp. 443, 446.
110 E.g. de' Grassi, ed. Frati, pp. 120–1.
111 BL, Add. 8441, ff. 197v–198r, 201r.
112 AS Modena, Roma, b. 15, 98-X/38: Beltrando Costabili, 18 Oct. 1504.
113 Guicciardini, *Storia d'Italia*, book XI, chapter VIII.

Sources and Select Bibliography

———— • ————

ARCHIVES

Bologna, Archivio di Stato: Senato, Carteggi and Lettere; Comune, Registra Litterarum, Libri Partitorum, Lettere al Comune and Bolle, Brevi e Diplomi.
Cambridge, University Library, Manuscripts, Add. 4757–62: transcriptions of despatches from Ferrarese ambassadors in Rome.
Florence, Archivio di Stato, Archivio della Repubblica: Carteggi, Responsive of the Otto di Pratica, X di Balìa and Signoria.
London, British Library, Manuscripts, Add. 8440–4: Diary of Paride de' Grassi.
Mantua, Archivio di Stato, Archivio Gonzaga, Serie E, XXV.
Milan, Archivio di Stato, Archivio Sforzesco, Potenze Esteri.
Modena, Archivio di Stato, Cancelleria Ducale, Carteggio Ambasciatori.
Rome, Archivio Capitolino, Archivio Orsini, Serie I.
—— Archivio di Stato, Archivio del Collegio de' Notari Capitolini.
Siena, Archivio di Stato: Concistoro and Balìa.
Vatican City, Archivio Segreto Vaticano, Armadii XXIX (Diversa Cameralia), XXXIX (Registra Brevium), Registri Vaticani, and Introitus and Exitus.
—— Biblioteca Vaticana, MSS. Chigiani L.I.18: Diary of Paride de' Grassi.
Venice, Archivio di Stato: Consiglio dei X, Dispacci degli ambasciatori da Roma, and Archivio Proprio, Roma, Reg. 3.
—— Biblioteca Marciana, Cod. Marc. Latino X, 175 (mss. 3622).

PRIMARY PRINTED SOURCES

L. de la Brière, 'Dépêches de Ferry Carondelet, Procureur en Cour de Rome (1510–1513)', *Bulletin Historique et Philologique du Comité de Travaux Historiques et Scientifiques* (1895), pp. 98–134.

Johannes Burckhardt, *Diarium sive Rerum Urbanarum Commentarii (1483–1506)*, ed. L. Thuasne, 3 vols (Paris, 1883–5).

—— *Liber Notarum*, ed. E. Celani, *Rerum Italicarum Scriptores*, XXXII (Città di Castello, 1906).

Calendar of Letters, Despatches and State Papers, Relating to the Negociations between England and Spain, vol. II *(1509–1529)*, ed. G. A. Bergenroth (London, 1866).

Calendar of State Papers and Manuscripts, Relating to English Affairs, Existing in the Archives and Collections of Venice and Other Libraries of Northern Italy, ed. Rawdon Brown, vol. I, *1202–1509* (London, 1864), vol. II, *1509–1519* (London, 1867).

Antonio Cappelli, 'Lettere di Lorenzo de' Medici detto il Magnifico, conservate nell' Archivio Palatino di Modena, con notizie tratte dai carteggi diplomatici degli oratori estensi a Firenze', *Atti e Memorie delle RR. Deputazioni di Storia Patria per le Provincie Modenesi e Parmensi*, i (1864), pp. 231–320.

Baldassare Castiglione, *Le Lettere*, ed. Guido La Rocca, vol. I (Verona, 1978).

Roberto Cessi, *Dispacci degli Ambasciatori Veneziani alla Corte di Roma presso Giulio II 25 giugno 1509–9 gennaio 1510* (*Monumenti Storici* published by R. Deputazione di Storia Patria per le Venezie, series I, *Documenti*, vol. XVIII) (Venice, 1932).

Philippe de Commynes, *Mémoires*, ed. B. de Mandrot, 2 vols (Paris, 1901–3).

Ascanio Condivi, *Vita di Michelangelo Buonarroti*, in Michelangelo Buonarroti, *Rime e Lettere* (Firenze, 1858).

Sigismondo de' Conti da Foligno, *Le Storie de' Suoi Tempi dal 1475 al 1510*, ed. D. Zanelli and F. Calabro, 2 vols (Rome, 1883).

A. Desjardins and G. Canestrini, *Négociations Diplomatiques de la France avec la Toscane*, vols I and II (Paris, 1859–60) (*Documents Inédits sur l'Histoire de France*).

Desiderius Erasmus, *The 'Julius Exclusus'*, trans. P. Pascal, ed. J. Kelly Soward (Bloomington, 1968).

Vincenzo Forcella, *Iscrizioni delle Chiese di Roma* (Rome, 1875).

Jacopo Gherardi da Volterra, *Il Diario Romano*, ed. E. Carusi, *Rerum Italicarum Scriptores*, XXIII, part iii (Città di Castello, 1904–6).

Antonio Giustinian, *Dispacci*, ed. Pasquale Villari, 3 vols (Florence, 1876).

Paride de' Grassi, *Le Due Spedizioni Militari di Giulio II*, ed. Luigi Frati, *Regia Deputazione di Storia Patria per le Provincie di Romagna: Documenti e Studi*, i (1886).

Francesco Guicciardini, *Storia d'Italia*, ed. E. Mazzali (Milan, 1988).

Stefano Infessura, *Diario della Città di Roma*, ed. O. Tommasini (Rome, 1890).

M. Le Glay, *Correspondance de l'Empereur Maximilien Ier et de Marguerite d'Autriche*, 2 vols (Paris, 1839).

—— *Négociations Diplomatiques entre la France et l'Autriche durant les Trente Premières Années du XVIe Siècle*, vol. I (Paris, 1845).

Lettere, Istruzioni ed Altre Memorie de' Re Aragonesi, supplement to Joannis Albini Lucani, *De Gestis Regum Neapolitanorum ab Aragonia*, in Giovanni Gravier (ed.), *Raccolta di Tutti i Più Rinomati Scrittori dell'Istoria Generale del Regno di Napoli*, vol. V (Naples, 1769).

Letters and Papers Foreign and Domestic of the Reign of Henry VIII, ed. J. S. Brewer; 2nd edition, revised by R. H. Brodie, vol. I (London, 1920).

Lettres de Charles VIII Roi de France, ed. P. Pélicier, 5 vols (Paris, 1898–1905).

Lettres de Louis XI Roi de France, ed. J. Vaesen, 11 vols (Paris, 1883–1909).

Lettres du Roy Louis XII et du Cardinal d'Amboise, 4 vols (Brussels, 1712).

Niccolò Machiavelli, *Legazioni e Commissarie*, ed. S. Bertelli, 3 vols (Milan, 1964).

—— *Discorsi sopra la Prima Deca di Tito Livio*, in S. Andretta (ed.), *Il Principe e Altre Opere Politiche* (Milan, 1976).

Lorenzo de' Medici, *Lettere*, ed. Nicolai Rubinstein and others (Florence, 1977–: in progress).

G. L. Moncallero, *Epistolario di Bernardo Dovizi da Bibbiena*, vol. I (Florence, 1955).

Emilio Nunziante, 'Alcune lettere di Joviano Pontano', *Archivio Storico per le Province Napoletane*, xi (1886), pp. 518–53.

R. Orsi, *De Obsidione Tiphernatum Liber*, ed. G. M. Graziani, *Rerum Italicarum Scriptores*, XXVII, part iii (Bologna, 1922).

Giuseppe Paladino, 'Per la storia della congiura dei baroni: documenti inediti dell' Archivio Estense, 1485–1487', *Archivio Storico per le Province Napoletane*, xliv (1919), pp. 336–67, xlv (1920), pp. 128–51, 325–51, xlvi (1921), pp. 221–65, xlviii (1923), pp. 219–90.

Gaspare Pontani, *Il Diario Romano*, ed. D. Toni, *Rerum Italicarum Scriptores*, III, part ii (Città di Castello, 1907–8).

Ernesto Pontieri, 'La "Guerra dei Baroni" napoletani e di Papa Innocenzo VIII contro Ferrante d'Aragona in dispacci della diplomazia fiorentina', *Archivio Storico per le Province Napoletane*, series III, ix (1970), pp. 197–347, x (1971), pp. 117–77, xi (1972), pp. 197–254, xii (1973), pp. 211–45.

A. Renaudet, *Le Concile Gallican de Pise–Milan: Documents Florentins (1510–1512)* (Paris, 1922).

A. Rodriguez Villa, 'Don Francisco de Rojas, Embajador de los Reyes Católicos', *Boletín de la Real Academia de la Historia*, xxviii (1896), pp. 180–202, 295–339, 364–400, 440–74, xxix (1896), pp. 5–69.

Marino Sanuto, *I Diarii*, ed. R. Ulin and others, vols I–XV (Venice, 1879–1886).

L. Ildefonso Serrano y Pineda (ed.), 'Correspondencia de los Reyes Católicos con el Gran Capitán durante las campañas de Italia', *Revista de Archivos, Bibliotecas y Museos*, xx (1909), pp. 453–62, xxi (1909), pp. 340–59, 558–66, xxii (1910), pp. 116–23, xxiii (1910), pp. 497–505, xxiv (1911), pp. 565–71, xxv (1911), pp. 124–33, 422–31, xxvi (1912), pp. 300–12, xxvii (1912), pp. 512–22, xxviii (1913), pp. 101–17, 371–89, xxix (1913), pp. 275–90, 456–72.

Ernesto Sestan (ed.), *Carteggi Diplomatici fra Milano Sforzesca e la Borgogna*, Istituto Storico Italiano per l'Età Moderna e Contemporanea, *Fonti per la Storia d'Italia*, vol. II (Rome, 1987).

F. Trinchera, *Codice Aragonese*, 2 vols (Naples, 1866–70).

Giorgio Vasari, *Le Vite de' Più Eccellenti Pittori, Sculturi e Architettori*, ed. R. Bettarini and P. Barocchi, vol. IV (Firenze, 1976).

Antonio di Vascho, *Il Diario della Città di Roma*, ed. G. Chiesa, *Rerum Italicarum Scriptores*, XXIII, part iii (Città di Castello, 1911).

Luigi Volpicella (ed.), *Regis Ferdinandi Primi Instructionum Liber* (Naples, 1916).

SECONDARY PRINTED SOURCES

J. S. Ackerman, *The Cortile of the Belvedere* (*Studi e Documenti per la Storia del Palazzo Apostolico Vaticano*, vol. III) (Vatican City, 1954).

Justo Fernandez Alonso, 'La legación frustrada de Cosimo dei Pazzi, Obispo de Arezzo (1504)', *Anthologica Annua*, xi (1963), pp. 55–90.

John F. d'Amico, *Renaissance Humanism in Papal Rome: Humanists and Churchmen on the Eve of the Reformation* (Baltimore, 1983).

Secondo Balena, *Ascoli nel Piceno* (Ascoli Piceno, 1979).

Giuseppe Benacci, *Compendio della Storia Civile, Ecclesiastica e Letteraria della Città d' Imola* (Imola, 1810).

Flavio di Bernardo, *Un Vescovo Umanista alla Corte Pontificia: Gianantonio Campano (1429–1477)*, *Miscellanea Historiae Pontificiae*, xxxix (1975).

C. F. Black, 'Politica e amministrazione a Perugia tra Quattrocento e Cinquecento', in *Storia e Cultura in Umbria nell' Età Moderna (Secoli XV–XVIII)* (Atti del VII Convegno di Studi Umbri, 1969) (Perugia, 1972).

—— 'The Baglioni as Tyrants of Perugia 1488–1540', *English Historical Review*, lxxxv (1970), pp. 245–81.

Il Borgo di Ostia da Sisto IV a Giulio II, ed. Silvia Danesi Squarzina and Gabriele Borghini (Rome, 1981).

Deborah Brown, 'The Apollo Belvedere and the Garden of Cardinal Giuliano della Rovere at SS. Apostoli', *Journal of the Warburg and Courtauld Institutes*, xlix (1986), pp. 235–8.

M. Brunetti, 'Alla vigilia di Cambrai: La legazione di Vincenzo Querini all'Imperatore Massimiliano (1507)', *Archivio Veneto-Tridentino*, x (1926), pp. 1–108.

Arnaldo Bruschi, *Bramante* (Rome, 1977).

Albert Buchi, *Kardinal Matthäus Schiner als Staatsman und Kirchenfurst*, 2 vols (Zurich, 1923).

Antonio Cappelli, 'Fra Girolamo Savonarola e notizie intorno il suo tempo', *Atti e Memorie delle RR. Deputazioni di Storia Patria per le Provincie Modenesi e Parmensi*, iv (1868), pp. 301–406.

Felice Ceretti, 'Francesca Trivulzio', *Atti e Memorie delle RR. Deputazioni di Storia Patria per le Provincie dell' Emilia*, n.s., v (1880), part ii, pp. 103–76.

Robert J. Clements (ed.), *Michelangelo: A Self-Portrait: Texts and Sources* (New York, 1968).

Gaspare De Fiore, *Baccio Pontelli, Architetto Fiorentino* (Rome, 1963).

Anne Denis, *Charles VIII et les Italiens: Histoire et Mythe* (Geneva, 1979).

José M. Doussinague, *Fernando el Católico y el cisma de Pisa* (Madrid, 1946).

Ariane Ducrot, 'Histoire de la Cappella Giulia au XVIe siècle depuis sa fondation par Jules II (1513) jusqu'à sa restauration par Grégoire XIII (1578)', *Mélanges d'Archéologie et d'Histoire*, lxxv (1963), pp. 179–240, 467–559.

L. D. Ettlinger, 'Pollaiuolo's Tomb of Pope Sixtus IV', *Journal of the Warburg and Courtauld Institutes*, xvi (1953), pp. 239–74.

Giuseppe Fabiani, *Ascoli nel Quattrocento*, 2 vols (Ascoli Piceno, 1950).

Angelo Fabroni, *Laurentii Medicis Magnifici Vita*, 2 vols (Pisa, 1784).

Vittorio Fanelli, *Ricerche su Angelo Colocci e sulla Roma Cinquecentesca, Studi e Testi*, 283 (Vatican City, 1979).

Henri Forgeot, *Jean Balue, Cardinal d'Angers (1421–1491)* (Paris, 1895).

Umberto Foschi, 'La Bolla di Giulio II alla Comunità di Cervia (1511)', *Studi Romagnoli*, xxii (1971), pp. 71–87.

Lodovico Frati, 'Il Card. Francesco Alidosi e Francesco Maria della Rovere', *Archivio Storico Italiano*, series V, xlvii (1911), pp. 144–58.

Cristoph Luitpold Frommel, 'Die Peterskirche unter Papst Julius II.', *Römische Jahrbuch für Kunstgeschichte*, xvi (1976), pp. 57–136.

—— '"Capella Iulia": Die Grabkapelle Papst Julius' II in Neu-St. Peter', *Zeitschrift für Kunstgeschichte*, xl (1977), pp. 26–62.

—— 'Papal Policy: The Planning of Rome during the Renaissance', in Robert I. Rotberg and Theodore K. Rabb (eds), *Art and History: Images and their Meaning* (Cambridge, 1988).

A. P. Frutaz, *La Basilica di S. Pietro in Vincoli, Roma* (Rome, 1981).

Romeo Galli, 'Imola tra la Signoria e la Chiesa (1503–1505)', *Atti e Memorie della R. Deputazione di Storia Patria per le Romagne*, series IV, xvii (1927), pp. 358–443.

Clara Gennaro, 'La "Pax Romana" del 1511', *Archivio della Società Romana di Storia Patria*, xc (1967), pp. 17–60.

Felix Gilbert, *The Pope, His Banker and Venice* (Cambridge, Massachusetts, 1980).

Giovanni Gozzadini, 'Di alcuni avvenimenti in Bologna e nell'Emilia dal 1506 al 1511 e dei Cardinali Legati A. Ferrerio e F. Alidosi', *Atti e*

Memorie della R. Deputazione di Storia Patria per le Provincie di Romagna, series III, iv (1886), pp. 67–176, vii (1889), pp. 161–267.

Carlo Grillantini, *Storia di Osimo*, vol. I, *Dagli Inizi al 1800* (Pinerolo, 1957).

J. R. Hale, 'The Early Development of the Bastion: An Italian Chronology *c*.1450–*c*.1534', in J. R. Hale, J. R. L. Highfield and B. Smalley (eds), *Europe in the Late Middle Ages* (London, 1965).

Howard Hibberd, *Michelangelo* (London, 1978).

R. Honig, *Bologna e Giulio II, 1511–1513* (Bologna, 1904).

Charles Hope, 'Artists, Patrons and Advisers in the Italian Renaissance', in G. Fitch Lytle and S. Orgel (eds), *Patronage in the Renaissance* (Princeton, 1981), pp. 293–343.

Itinerari Rovereschi: Savona nei Secoli XV e XVI (Savona, 1985).

Julian Klaczko, *Jules II* (Paris, 1898).

L.-H. Labande, *Avignon au XVe Siècle: Légation de Charles de Bourbon et du Cardinal Julien de la Rovère* (Monaco, 1920).

Alessandro Luzio, 'Federico Gonzaga ostaggio alla Corte di Giulio II', *Archivio della Società Romana di Storia Patria*, ix (1886), pp. 509–82.

—— 'Isabella d'Este e Giulio II (1503–1505)', *Rivista d'Italia*, xii (1909), pp. 837–86.

—— 'La reggenza d'Isabella d'Este durante la prigionia del marito (1509–1510)', *Archivio Storico Lombardo*, series IV, xiv (1910), pp. 5–104.

—— *Isabella d'Este di fronte a Giulio II negli ultimi tre anni del suo pontificato* (Milano, 1912).

Torgil Magnuson, *Studies in Roman Quattrocento Architecture* (Stockholm, 1958).

Giuseppe Manchini, *Giuliano da Sangallo* (Florence, 1942).

Sigismondo Marchesi, *Supplemento Istorico dell'Antica Città di Forlì in cui Si Descrive La Provincia di Romagna* (Forlì, 1678; reprinted Bologna, 1968).

Giovanni Mercati, *Per la Cronologia della Vita e degli Scritti di Niccolò Perotti, Arcivescovo di Siponto, Studi e Testi*, xliv (1925).

Michele Michaeli, *Memorie Storiche della Città di Rieti e dei Paesi Circostanti, dall'Origine all'Anno 1560*, vol. IV (Rieti, 1899).

Nelson H. Minnich, 'The Healing of the Pisan Schism (1511–13)', *Annuarium Historiae Conciliorum*, xvi (1984), pp. 59–192.

Stanislaus von Moos, 'The Palace as a Fortress: Rome and Bologna under Julius II', in Henry A. Millon and Linda Nochlin (eds), *Art and Architecture in the Service of Politics* (London, 1978), pp. 46–79.

Paolo Negri, 'Le missioni di Pandolfo Collenuccio a Papa Alessandro VI (1494–1498)', *Archivio Storico della Società Romana di Storia Patria*, xxxiii (1910), pp. 333–439.

—— 'Milano, Ferrara e Impero durante l'impresa di Carlo VIII in Italia', *Archivio Storico Lombardo*, series V, xliv (1917), pp. 423–571.

—— 'Studi sulla crisi italiana alla fine del secolo XV', *Archivio Storico Lombardo*, series V, l (1923), pp. 1–135, li (1924), pp. 75–144.

E. Nunziante, 'Il Concistoro d'Innocenzo VIII per la chiamata di Renato, Duca di Lorena, contro il Regno (Marzo 1486)', *Archivio Storico per le Provincie Napoletane*, xi (1886), pp. 751–66.

John W. O'Malley, *Giles of Viterbo on Church and Reform: A Study in Renaissance Thought* (Leiden, 1968).

Cesare d'Onofrio, *Castel S. Angelo e Borgo tra Roma e Papato* (Rome, 1978).

Paul Ourliac, 'Le Concordat de 1472. Étude sur les rapports de Louis XI et de Sixte IV', *Revue Historique de Droit Français et Étranger*, series IV, xx (1941), pp. 174–223, xxi (1942), pp. 117–54.

Peter Partner, *The Pope's Men: The Papal Civil Service in the Renaissance* (Oxford, 1990).

Loren Partridge and Randolph Starn, *A Renaissance Likeness: Art and Culture in Raphael's Julius II* (Berkeley, 1980).

L. Pastor, *The History of the Popes from the Close of the Middle Ages*, ed. F. I. Antrobus and R. F. Kerr, vols IV–VI (London, 1894–8).

R. Patrizi Sacchetti, 'La caduta dei Bentivoglio e il ritorno di Bologna al dominio della Chiesa', *Atti e Memorie della Deputazione di Storia Patria per le Provincie di Romagna*, n.s., ii (1950–51), pp. 109–56.

L.-G. Pélissier, 'Sopra alcuni documenti relativi all'alleanza tra Alessandro VI e Luigi XII (1498–1499)', *Archivio della Società Romana di Storia Patria*, xvii (1894), pp. 303–73, xviii (1895), pp. 99–215.

—— *Louis XII et Ludovic Sforza (8 avril 1498–23 juillet 1500)*, 2 vols (Paris, 1896) (*Bibliothèque des Écoles Françaises d'Athènes et de Rome*, vol. 75).

G. B. Picotti, 'Per le relazioni fra Alessandro VI e Piero de' Medici: Un duplice trattato di matrimonio per Laura Orsini', *Archivio Storico Italiano*, lxxiii (1915), pp. 37–100.

—— 'Giovanni de' Medici nel conclave per l'elezione di Alessandro VI', *Archivio della Società Romana di Storia Patria*, xliv (1921), pp. 87–168.

Cesare Pinzi, *Storia della Città di Viterbo lungo il Medioevo*, vol. IV (Viterbo, 1913).

E. Pontieri, *Ferrante d'Aragona, Re di Napoli* (Naples, 1969).

—— 'Il Comune dell'Aquila nella Congiura dei Baroni Napoletani contro Ferrante I d'Aragona (1485–1486)', *Atti dell'Accademia di Scienze Morali e Politiche*, lxxxi (1970), pp. 181–235.

Daniel Reichel, 'Matthieu Schiner (v. 1465–1522): Cardinal et homme de guerre', *Atti e Memorie della Società Savonese di Storia Patria*, n.s., xxv (1989), pp. 251–68.

Bartolomeo Righi, *Annali della Città di Faenza*, vol. III (Faenza, 1841).

Caterina Santoro, *Gli Sforza* (Milan, 1968).

Vinzenz Schweizer, 'Zur Wahl Alexanders VI', *Historisches Jahrbuch*, xxx (1909), pp. 809–14.

Federico Seneca, *Venezia e Papa Giulio II* (Padua, 1962).

Christine Shaw, 'The Political Role of the Orsini Family in the Papal States *c*.1480–1534' (Oxford D.Phil. thesis, 1983; unpublished).

—— 'A Pope and his *Nipote*: Sixtus IV and Giuliano della Rovere', *Atti e Memorie della Società Savonese di Storia Patria*, n.s., xxiv (1989), pp. 233–50.

J. Soward, 'The Two Lost Years of Erasmus: Summary, Review and Speculation', *Studies in the Renaissance*, pp. 161–86.

Sigfrido Sozzi, *Breve Storia della Città di Cesena* (Cesena, 1972).

Charles L. Stinger, 'Roma Triumphans: Triumphs in the Thought and Ceremonies of Renaissance Rome', *Medievalia et Humanistica*, n.s., x (1981), pp. 189–201.

—— *The Renaissance in Rome* (Bloomington, 1985).

Giulio Cesare Tonduzzi, *Historie di Faenza* (1675; reprinted Bologna, 1967).

Baron de Terrateig, *Politica en Italia del Rey Catolico 1507–1516: Correspondencia Inedita con el Embajador Vich*, 2 vols (Madrid, 1963).

Walter Ullmann, 'Julius II and the Schismatic Cardinals', *Studies in Church History*, ix (1972).

P. Verdier, 'La Rocca d'Ostia dans l'architecture militaire du Quattrocento', *Mélanges d'Archéologie et d'Histoire*, lvi (1939), pp. 280–331.

Roberto Weiss, 'The Medals of Pope Julius II (1503–1513)', *Journal of the Warburg and Courtauld Institutes*, xxviii (1965), pp. 163–82.

Hermann Wiesflecker, *Kaiser Maximilian I: Das Reich, Österreich und Europa an der Wende zur Neuzeit*, 5 vols (Munich, 1971–86).

Index

Acciaiuoli, Roberto, 230
Accolti, Pietro, Cardinal (1511), 178, 237, 238
Acquasparta, 146
Admiral of France – see de Bourbon, Louis; d'Amboise, Charles
Adorno family, of Genoa, 253
Adrian VI, Pope (1522–3), 163
Agnadello, Battle of, 235, 308
d'Aguerre, Gratien, 105; Menaud, 43–4, 105
Albert, Pierre, 101
Albi, county of, 52
d'Albret, Amanieu, Cardinal (1500), 282, 292
Alby, Cardinal – see d'Amboise, Louis
Alessandro di Gabbioneta, 172
Alexander VI, Pope (1492–1503), 7, 25–6, 27, 40, 50, 54, 55–6, 57, 58–9, 68–9, 79, 81–2, 84, 85–94, 95, 96, 97, 98, 99–100, 101, 102, 104, 106, 107–110, 111–13, 114–15, 117, 124, 132, 139, 141, 150, 163, 168, 176, 177, 178, 179, 182, 193, 196, 206, 255, 260, 290, 313, 314
Alfonso V, King of Portugal, 36
Alfonso d'Aragona, Duke of Calabria, King Alfonso II of Naples (1494–5), 63–4, 65, 67, 71, 75, 92, 96, 98
Alidosi family, of Imola and Castel del Rio, 134; Francesco, Cardinal (1505), 106, 112, 134, 135, 137–8, 139, 150, 160, 166, 168, 170, 173,
174, 178, 181, 184, 185, 187–8, 210, 227, 235, 236, 246–9, 250, 251, 252, 260, 261, 262, 263, 264, 265, 270, 271, 275–6, 277–8, 287, 314
Altamura, Prince of – see Federico d'Aragona
d'Alviano, Bartolomeo, 141, 143–4, 145, 228, 235
d'Amboise, Charles, seigneur de Chaumont, 161, 175, 216, 248, 249, 263, 264, 265, 267, 282; Georges, Archbishop of Rouen, Cardinal (1498), 111, 118–19, 120, 121, 130, 136, 175, 180, 213, 214–15, 218, 230, 231, 232, 247, 248, 249, 250, 251, 261, 263, 264, 279–80, 282; Louis, Bishop of Alby, Cardinal (1506), 175, 212, 248, 249, 250, 279–80, 282
Amelia, 143
Ancona, 73, 74, 77, 140, 238, 239, 262, 282
Anguillara, 87, 88, 89, 90, 191
Anjou, house of, 27; Duke René, 28, 35, 43
Anne, daughter of Louis XI, 29
Anne of Brittany, Queen of France, 101, 111, 183
Apostolic Chamber, 49, 57, 60, 147, 153, 163, 165, 173
Aquila, 69
Aragon, King of – see Ferdinand II, King of Aragon; Juan II, King of Aragon

Note – Dates given for cardinals are dates of election.

Printed in the United Kingdom by
Lightning Source UK Ltd., Milton Keynes
138168UK00001B/181/P